EUROPEAN CIVIL LIBERTIES AND THE
EUROPEAN CONVENTION ON HUMAN RIGHTS

International Studies in Human Rights

VOLUME 48

The titles published in this series are listed at the end of this volume.

EUROPEAN CIVIL LIBERTIES AND THE EUROPEAN CONVENTION ON HUMAN RIGHTS

A Comparative Study

edited by

C. A. GEARTY

*Professor of Law and
Director of the Civil Liberties Research Unit,
King's College,
London, United Kingdom*

MARTINUS NIJHOFF PUBLISHERS
THE HAGUE / BOSTON / LONDON

A C.I.P. Catalogue record for this book is available from the Library of Congress.

ISBN 90-411-0253-1

Published by Kluwer Law International,
P.O. Box 85889, 2508 CN The Hague, The Netherlands.

Sold and distributed in the U.S.A. and Canada
by Kluwer Law International,
675 Massachusetts Avenue, Cambridge, MA 02139, U.S.A.

In all other countries, sold and distributed
by Kluwer Law International, Distribution Centre,
P.O. Box 322, 3300 AH Dordrecht, The Netherlands.

Printed on acid-free paper

Printed in the Netherlands

TABLE OF CONTENTS

ACKNOWLEDGEMENT

This book is the culmination of a project which has been conducted under the auspices of the Civil Liberties Research Unit at King's College London. The project would not have been possible without a grant from the College's Research Strategy Fund, for which support the editor and contributors are delighted to express their gratitude.

LIST OF CONTRIBUTORS

Iain Cameron, Reader in Public International Law, University of Uppsala

Leo Flynn, Lecturer in Law, King's College London

Conor A. Gearty, Professor of Law and Director of the Civil Liberties Research Unit, King's College London

Eric Janse de Jonge, Lecturer in Constitutional Law, University of Tilburg

Yvonne Klerk, Lecturer in International Law, University of Utrecht

Danilo A. Leonardi, PhD graduate from the University of Edinburgh

Ingrid Persaud, Associate Professor, Fletcher School of International Law and Diplomacy

Eva Steiner, Lecturer in French Law, King's College London

Adam Tomkins, Lecturer in Law, King's College London

Eileen Voss, formerly Lecturer in German Law, King's College London

INTRODUCTION

Conor Gearty

This book is a comparative study of the impact of the European Convention on Human Rights, both generally and in relation to eight selected jurisdictions within Europe. The Convention can legitimately claim to be more central to Europe's sense of unity and of democratic identity than the treaties that underpin any other supra-national European organisation. The European Union, for example, remains restricted in its geographic reach and continues, despite recent dramatic changes, to display traces of its relatively narrow, market-oriented, origins. The Convention, in contrast, has emerged from the Council of Europe, an institutional environment which has always been entirely focused on the preservation of democracy and human rights. Its success in the post-Cold War world has been such that its reach now extends beyond the narrow confines of western Europe to embrace countries scattered across the Continent. As the newly re-emerging and sometimes entirely new nations of central and eastern Europe join their western neighbours in subscribing both to the Convention and to the investigative and judicial dimensions that make it work, so it becomes increasingly credible to view this already venerable document, with its many Protocols, as a potential bill of rights for Europe as a whole.

This resurgence of the Convention has led to an explosion of litigation, with the European Commission and the European Court of Human Rights at Strasbourg, both seeing a dramatic increase in the number of applications being filed by individuals alleging violation of their human rights by member states. It is well known that this state of affairs, sometimes described as a crisis of success, has produced proposals for institutional reform which have materialised in the form of a Protocol which has, however, yet to come into force. It has also given rise to a plethora of cases on most of the Convention's provisions, so much so that it is now meaningful to discuss not only the jurisprudence of the Court in general, but also its approach to this or that Article or paragraph. Even as recently as ten years ago, such an exercise would have been built on self-defeatingly flimsy data, but now there are many rich veins in the case-law into which it is possible to tap.

This book is not directly concerned either with that case-law or with the mechanics of taking a case to Strasbourg. Both subjects are already dealt with extensively in the literature. Our concentration is instead on the civil liberties aspects of the Convention and its application within selected member states. In our first chapter, Adam Tomkins provides a critical survey of the protection of civil liberties afforded by the Council of Europe. His brief takes him into an appraisal not only of the Commission and the Court but also of the much less well known work done in this field by the Committee of Ministers. Tomkins draws out not only the tension in the distinction between the protection of civil liberties and the affirmation of human rights, but also in the double-edged nature of the Convention's juristic personality, perpetually caught between its judicial id and its political super-ego. The latter is to be detected not only in the qualifying sub-clauses and the potential for derogation that are to be found in the document and its Protocols, but also in the way in which the Commission reports and Court judgments are overseen by the states' own representatives on the Committee of Ministers rather than by the Convention organs themselves.

Whereas Tomkins' focus is directly on the Convention, the rest of the book (with the exception of Persaud's essay on the role of the Convention in the emerging European Union) is concerned with national law. It is frequently said of the Convention that it applies within the national legal order of the majority of the member states of the Council of Europe. Indeed, in one country in our volume where this is indubitably not the case, the United Kingdom, the argument for such domestic incorporation is frequently underpinned by assertions that Britain is Europe's "odd one out" in not having already taken this step. Though this is of course a powerful debating point in the context of an ongoing debate about constitutional reform in Britain, the general assertion that the Convention is part of a member state's national law begs more questions than it answers. What status does the Convention enjoy in such states? Can it override national constitutional or municipal law? What is the Convention's relationship with the state's indigenous bill of rights if such a document exists? Why should cases continue to reach Strasbourg, and be decided in favour of applicants, if the country from which they are emerging is one within which the Convention is stated to have full force and effect?

These are among the questions that the seven essays on different European countries in this volume attempt to answer. Each of these chapters provides first a general introduction to the constitutional system of the country under discussion, before going on to address the precise role, if any, of the Convention within its legal system. Where it exists, that role is invariably deeply rooted in and defined by the constitutional order which it is the purpose of part one of each of these chapters to describe. A third section in each of these chapters is then devoted to discussion of the ways in which judgments adverse to the state under discussion have been (or have not been) implemented within the jurisdiction. This latter survey embraces efforts by some nations to implement decisions not directed against themselves and addresses an area of concern that has not perhaps received the attention it deserves, namely the consequences that flow from European Court verdicts adverse to a defendant state. The information thrown up by each of our authors in this section deepens the critical perspective on the Convention's institutions laid out by Tomkins in Chapter One, and aims to give us a more profound understanding of the operation of the Convention, both generally and in respect of its impact on our selected member states.

The book is a modest attempt at comparative scholarship in a field in which the seductive universality of the Convention has sometimes tempted those interested in its application to gloss over the often deep differences of legal culture and of language that are to be found across the Europe in which its writ supposedly runs. Our modesty manifests itself not only in the limited nature of the goals we have set ourselves but also in the fact that we have restricted our analysis to a small number of states. There is no magic formula that underpinned our choice of the seven that feature in this volume. All our jurisdictions belonging culturally and historically to the western European family, and all are now also members of the European Union. Each has had extensive experience in the sometimes very difficult task of implementing adverse Strasbourg judgments. More recent adherents of the Convention from other parts of Europe in contrast do not yet have sufficient track record in its application to make meaningful the kind of study in which this book is engaged, though we would not expect this observation to be sustainable for long. Of the countries that we have selected, two (the United Kingdom and Ireland) have not incorporated the Convention into their domestic legal regimes, while in the remaining five the Convention does enjoy the force of law, though as we shall see, the way in which this is true varies widely from nation to nation. Each state apart from the United Kingdom operates on the basis of a written constitution, though as we shall see this formula also contrives to hide more than it reveals, with many of our chapters revealing very different frameworks of government behind apparently common facades. The same is true of the operation of domestic bills of rights, another area in which Britain's uniqueness (in not having such a document) is once again much in evidence.

It is for the reader to judge whether there are any overarching lessons to emerge from this book. Its purpose is not analytical in the sense of seeking to provide an overall evaluative judgment or to deliver a series of conclusions confidently rooted in interconnecting insights derived from close comparative study. Such intellectual ambition has taken second place to the twin challenges of information retrieval and descriptive clarity. Those judgments that have been hazarded have tended to be country-specific and even then to be couched in hesitant, even diffident, terms. Three observations of a very general nature may be offered at this preliminary stage. First, it is clear that there is no set pattern to the impact of the Convention in our chosen states. Each of our seven countries connect with the Convention in a way that is peculiar to its own historical, political and legal context. Secondly, one general theme that does however shine through many of the chapters is the extent to which the power of courts to oversee the actions of a democratic legislature is a predominantly post-second world war phenomenon. This is true not only of the Convention jurisdiction itself of course, but also of the indigenous constitutional arrangements to be found in our selected states. It is a remarkable fact that among our countries, it is only in the United Kingdom that the elected body remains truly sovereign, a state of affairs that has already been transformed by membership of the European Union and one that is likely to be further affected if the opposition Labour Party win the next general election in that country, since the Party has committed itself to incorporation of the Convention into domestic law. This explosion of judicial power, which would have been startling to political theorists from earlier generations, deserves wider academic notice than it currently receives, not least from political scientists and historians.

Thirdly, the breadth of the European Convention's reach is a common feature of many of our country-specific contributions. The focus of our book is on civil liberties, and this connotes a concentration on what the Convention has to say about our political liberties, such as those guaranteeing personal liberty and the freedoms of expression, assembly and association. It is well-known that the Convention extends far beyond this civil libertarian remit, however, and this is evidenced in the large number of cases discussed in this book on such issues as criminal justice, administrative and planning law and on such pure human rights topics as transsexuality and homosexual law reform. Our chapters combine to provide an insight into the sheer variety of, and sometimes the awkward consequences that flow from, Strasbourg-inspired interventions in our chosen domestic legal systems. If litigated to the full, the Convention has the potential to be a far more intrusive instrument, in a great many areas of public policy, than it has been heretofore.

There can be little doubt that the European Convention, its Protocols and its institutions are likely to play a central part in the new European order that is fast emerging. The challenge for this new order, represented not only in the Convention but also in other supra-national bodies such as the European Union institutions and a reformed NATO, is to get the balance right between local interests and transfrontier priorities. In the context of the EU, the concept of subsidiarity is the means through which this delicate balancing act is sought to be achieved. In the European Convention, it has been the doctrine of a "margin of appreciation" that has been developed. None of these ideas, or others like them, will work sensitively without a deep understanding of the local environments in which they are operating and without an awareness of the need for transparency, accountability and democratic legitimacy. On such sensitivity will the moral acceptability of the new European order ultimately depend.

1. CIVIL LIBERTIES IN THE COUNCIL OF EUROPE: A CRITICAL SURVEY

Adam Tomkins

Introduction

The purpose of this chapter is to tell Strasbourg's story. By describing and discussing the Council of Europe's human rights institutions and by outlining and analysing the main stages in the processes by which applications to those institutions are examined, the aim is to give a critical public lawyer's overview of more than forty years of human rights history. The focus will be on the Council of Europe's centrepiece, the European Convention on Human Rights, and on the Convention's two creations, the European Commission of Human Rights and the European Court of Human Rights. While the substantive law of the Commission and Court will not be considered in any detail,[1] an understanding of the structure and functions of the Strasbourg authorities is essential if we are to understand exactly what it is that the Convention does and if we are properly to evaluate the central question of how effective the Convention is and has been in protecting European civil liberties. While parts of this story may already be reasonably well known, it remains the case that there are surprisingly large and significant gaps in the knowledge of the average European public lawyer. This is especially true of the third institution examined at length in this chapter, the Committee of Ministers of the Council of Europe.

The story of this chapter will be dramatically affected by the prospective reforms to the Commission and Court contained in the recently concluded Protocol No. 11 to the Convention. These reforms, which are discussed towards the end of this essay, are unlikely to come into force for many years (as they require the prior ratification of every high contracting party) and indeed they may never see the light of day. The existing institutions will, therefore, continue in their current mode for some time to come—and even

---

[1] On this, see C. A. Gearty, "The European Court of Human Rights and the Protection of Civil Liberties: An Overview" (1993) 52 *Cambridge Law Journal* 89.

1

C. A. Gearty (ed.), *European Civil Liberties and the European Convention on Human Rights*, 1–51.

if Protocol 11 does come into effect the changes it will bring about will not meet all the concerns and criticisms identified in this essay.

The central issue here is not so much the question whether bills of rights work, or whether bills of rights *in abstracto* are the most appropriate way of protecting civil liberties. Rather, our concern is with how *this* bill of rights works in practice. How effective has *this* bill of rights been in the past 45 years in promoting the cause of liberty in Europe? In examining the institutions and functions of the Strasbourg authorities, this chapter will identify a number of themes which inevitably affect any answer to these questions. The first theme is undoubtedly one of at least surface success. Despite all the shortcomings and limitations that we will presently consider, the European Commission and Court of Human Rights are unquestionably the world's most powerful international human rights bodies—to such an extent that the President of the Court Rolv Ryssdal was recently able to describe the Convention as "the basic law of Europe".[2] This is and should be recognised as a considerable and positive achievement. Further themes explored in the article take this level of success for granted and probe more deeply into the workings of the Convention. They include: the pervasive dilemma of statism, in terms of appointments, finance and access, which immediately leads to the suspicion of government-friendliness; issues of personnel; the immense logistical problems of overwork, delay and backlog; and all of this against a background of budgetary constraints and general uncertainty as to the future of the Council of Europe.

Part I: The Council of Europe

The Council of Europe is a product of the hope and idealism of the immediate post-war years. It was founded in 1949 and initially had 10[3] member states. It now has 38.[4] It is an international organisation of European states whose work covers all the major areas of European life, culture and government except defence.[5] Any European state may become a member pro-

---

[2]   In a speech delivered on the occasion of the Court's first session of the year: 27 January 1994.

[3]   Denmark, Sweden, the United Kingdom, Norway, Ireland, Italy, Luxembourg, France, the Netherlands and Belgium.

[4]   As of January 1996.

[5]   National defence is expressly excluded from the activities of the Council of Europe by Article 1(d) of the Council's Statute.

vided that it is "willing and able"[6] to accept the principle of the rule of law and to guarantee to everyone under its jurisdiction the enjoyment of human rights and fundamental freedoms. The Council of Europe is the only international body which makes respect for democracy a precondition of entry. No similar requirement is set by the United Nations or the Commonwealth. The Preamble of the Council of Europe's Statute declares that the organisation is dedicated to the "pursuit of peace based upon justice and international co-operation". Article 1 of the Statute provides that "the aim of the Council of Europe is to achieve a greater unity between its members" for the purpose of safeguarding and realising common ideals and principles. These common ideals are identified in the Preamble as "individual freedom", "political liberty", "the rule of law" and "genuine democracy". The Council can thus be seen to have three main aims: first, to protect and strengthen pluralist democracy and human rights; second to seek solutions to the problems facing society and third to promote the emergence of a genuine European cultural identity. Within the overall framework of these three broad aims, the Council carries out work in such diverse areas of European life as the media, legal co-operation, social and economic affairs, health, education, youth, sport, heritage, local and regional government, the environment and, of course, human rights.

The Council of Europe is funded by the national governments of its member states. The 1992 budget amounted to approximately £97 million, which is shared between the nine main directorates which between them carry out most of the Council's work. Much of this work goes largely unnoticed. The Council does not generally enjoy the same high profile as the European Community, for example. The conventions and agreements that it secures do not share the same directness of effect and applicability as does much of the law of the European Community. Even international legal and political scholars are often unaware of much of what the Council of Europe does day by day. How many of us are able to cite any activity of the Territorial Authorities Transfrontier Cooperation and Regional Planning Division, for example? Or of the Drugs Section's Partial Agreement of the Pompidou Group? Or of the Scientific Cooperation Division's Open Partial Agreement on the Prevention of, Protection Against and Organisation of Relief in Natural and Technological Disasters? Importance is no guarantee of notoriety. The one major exception to this, however, is the work done by the Council of Europe in the field of human rights. The Council's many activities and

---

[6]   Statute of the Council of Europe, Ch. II, Article 4.

achievements concerned with human rights do take place much more in the public eye.

Given the ever-changing context of European politics and the growing importance of the European Community, it may be difficult to see a continuing role for the Council of Europe. Indeed in recent years there have been some people, both observers of and employees within the Council, who have suggested that within the next decade or so the only remaining part of the Council will be its Human Rights Directorate and its starchild, the European Convention on Human Rights. However, morale in Strasbourg is widely reported to be far more optimistic now than it was in the mid-1980s. This is probably due to the dramatic changes in 1989 which have led to the renaissance of the Council of Europe. No country joined the Council in the ten years following 1978. But since 1988, San Marino, Finland, Hungary, Poland, Bulgaria, Estonia, Lithuania, Slovenia, the Czech Republic, Slovakia,[7] Romania, Andorra, Latvia, Albania, Moldova, Ukraine and Macedonia have become full members, while Belarus, Croatia, and Russia have applied for full membership.[8] Thus the Council is currently engaged in what might (perhaps a little unkindly) be seen as a form of international imperialism— trying to encourage various parts of eastern Europe (and, depending on your geographical definitions, Western Asia[9]) to turn westwards and to embrace Strasbourg and European democracy, rather than the perceived tyrannies of fundamentalist Islam to the south or Chinese communism to the east.[10] How long this renaissance will persist and how successful it will be remain to be seen. There is a sense in which the broader a church the Council becomes, the more diluted its commitment to democracy, human rights and the rule of law may have to become.

---

[7] The former Czechoslovakia had been a member of the Council of Europe from 1991–1992.

[8] As from January 1994 Armenia, Azerbaijan, Bosnia-Herzegovina and Georgia have requested special guest status.

[9] Rolv Ryssdal, the President of the Court, recently described the former Yugoslavia as being "in the centre of our continent". The occasion was a speech delivered on the opening of the Court's first session of the year, on 27 January 1994.

[10] The Council has set up what is known as the Demosthenes Programme to assist the countries of central and eastern Europe to carry out the constitutional and political reforms necessary before full membership of the Council may be attained. In 1993 50 million French francs were voted from the Council's budget to support this programme.

Part II: Civil Liberties and the Council of Europe: The European Convention on Human Rights

The showpiece of the Council of Europe's achievements over the last 45 years is without doubt the European Convention on Human Rights, and the institutions established in Strasbourg responsible for implementing and enforcing it—the European Commission of Human Rights, the European Court of Human Rights and the Committee of Ministers. The Convention was a very early creation of the newly formed Council. Indeed, the initial impetus had come even before the Council formally came into existence. In May 1948 the International Committee of the Movements for European Unity organised a Congress of Europe at The Hague. A resolution was adopted at this Congress which recommended that European nations should undertake to respect a charter of human rights. The Congress also resolved that a commission should be established to draft such a charter.[11] Once it was formally established, the first meeting of the Council of Europe's Consultative Assembly discussed these recommendations, with the result that the Assembly's Committee on Legal and Administrative Questions[12] was charged with the responsibility of considering the matter in more detail. From that point on, the Convention was drafted and agreed upon in remarkably short time. The Council of Europe Convention for the Protection of Human Rights and Fundamental Freedoms, to give it its full title, was signed in Rome in November 1950. In its 66 Articles and the 11 Protocols that have been subsequently added, it sets out what is the most comprehensive international legal order for the protection of human rights the world has yet seen. Neither the United Nations Covenants nor the Inter-American Convention nor the African Charter can compare with the European Convention in terms either of the vast number of applications that have been made or the relative strength of the implementation and enforcement mechanisms available to it. As of January 1996, 33 of the Council of Europe's 38 member states had ratified the Convention. All had signed it. The five which have yet to ratify are: Albania, Moldova, Macedonia, Ukraine and Estonia.

By Article 1 of the European Convention on Human Rights, national governments which have ratified the Convention (known as high contracting

---

[11] See P. van Dijk and G. van Hoof, *Theory and Practice of the European Convention on Human Rights*, 2nd ed. (Deventer, 1991), p. 1.

[12] Then chaired by the United Kingdom's foreign secretary, Ernest Bevin. On the views of and divisions within the UK government at the time, see A. Lester, "Fundamental Rights: The United Kingdom Isolated?" [1984] *Public Law* 46.

parties) "shall secure to everyone within their jurisdiction the rights and freedoms" the Convention describes. In outline, these include: the right to life (Article 2); freedom from torture, inhuman and degrading treatment (Article 3); freedom from slavery (Article 4); the right to liberty and security of the person (Article 5); the right to a fair trial (Article 6); freedom from retrospective criminal law (Article 7); the right to respect for private and family life (Article 8); freedom of thought, conscience and religion (Article 9); freedom of expression (Article 10); freedom of peaceful assembly and association (Article 11) and the right to marry (Article 12). By Article 13 of the Convention there is a right to an effective remedy in a national court in the event of a violation of any of the rights defined in Articles 2 to 12. Article 14 provides that the enjoyment of the rights set out in Articles 2–12 shall be secured "without discrimination on any ground". Most of the rest of the text of the Convention deals with the establishment of the European Commission and Court of Human Rights (Articles 20–37 and 38–56 respectively).

Further rights and liberties have been provided for in the several Protocols which have been added to the Convention since 1950. The First Protocol, signed in Paris in 1952, includes: the right to the peaceful enjoyment of possessions (Article 1); the right to education (Article 2); and an obligation on High Contracting Parties to hold free elections at reasonable intervals by secret ballot (Article 3). The Fourth Protocol, signed in Strasbourg in 1963, provides for: the right not to suffer deprivation of liberty simply on the ground of an inability to fulfil a contractual obligation (Article 1); freedom of movement (Article 2); the right not to be expelled from a country of which you are a national (Article 3); and a prohibition on the collective expulsion of aliens (Article 4). The Sixth Protocol, signed in Strasbourg in 1983, provides for the abolition of the death penalty. Under international law, states are not bound by any of the provisions in these (and the other) Protocols unless and until they have expressly signed and ratified them. Ratification of the main Convention text does not automatically lead to such states also ratifying the Protocols.

Thus it will be seen that the Convention seeks to protect civil and political rights and liberties, rather than economic, social or cultural rights. The protection that the Council of Europe affords to economic, social and cultural rights finds its focus in a quite separate treaty, the European Social Charter. This was signed in Turin in 1961 and came into force in 1965. As of January 1996, 20 countries had ratified it.[13] Among the rights which the

---

[13] A further six had signed it.

European Social Charter seeks to protect are: the rights to work and to just, safe and healthy conditions of work; the right to fair remuneration; the rights to organise and to bargain collectively; the right of children and young persons to protection; the right of employed women to protection; the rights to vocational guidance and training; the right to the protection of health and the rights to social security and to medical assistance.[14] Articles 20–29 of the Charter deal with enforcement. States which are contracting parties to the Charter must submit reports to the Secretary-General of the Council of Europe every two years explaining how the Charter's obligations are applied within their jurisdictions. These reports are then considered by a Committee of Experts appointed by the Committee of Ministers. The International Labour Organisation also has an input, as does the Council's Governmental Social Committee.

This inexact[15] division between civil and political liberties on the one hand, and economic and social rights on the other, is a key feature of the Council of Europe's systems of protecting human rights. The narrow scope in terms of the content of the European Convention on Human Rights can be seen as one of its central limitations: it would more accurately be called the European Convention on Civil Liberties—or even the European Convention on Some Civil Liberties.[16] But this drawback, significant though it is, is far from being the only limitation arising out of the Convention's structure. Of great practical importance are the two related matters of derogation and limitation. Under Article 15 of the Convention, "in time of war or other public emergency threatening the life of the nation" High Contracting Parties may take measures derogating from their obligations under the Convention. Most, but not quite all, of the provisions in Articles 2–12 are derogable. The exceptions are: Article 2 (the right to life, except in respect of

---

[14] These and other rights and freedoms are set out as general principles in Part I of the Charter and again in more detailed form as concrete obligations in Articles 1–19 of Part II.

[15] There is some degree of overlap between the Convention and the Social Charter: Article 11 of the former (dealing with freedom of assembly and association) and Article 5 of the latter (dealing with the right to organise) for example.

[16] There are a number of civil and political liberties which are not included in the Convention. Among those which are excluded from the European Convention but included in the United Nations International Covenant on Civil and Political Rights are the right of accused persons to be kept separately from convicted persons (ICCPR Article 10); the prohibition of war propaganda (ICCPR Article 20); certain childrens' rights (ICCPR Article 24); rights as to political participation (ICCPR, Article 25); and protection of minorities (ICCPR Articles 26 and 27).

deaths resulting from lawful acts of war); Article 3 (freedom from torture, inhuman and degrading treatment); Article 4.1 (freedom from slavery and servitude) and Article 7 (freedom from retrospective criminal laws). Article 15 effectively means that whenever there is a public emergency threatening the life of the nation, the Convention's supposed protection of such central civil liberties as the right to liberty and freedom of expression is significantly reduced. Yet times of public emergency (or times during which the state perceives there to be a public emergency) are exactly those periods when civil liberties are themselves most threatened. Thus when it is needed most, in situations such as in Northern Ireland[17] and during the colonels' rule in Greece, much of the Convention is simply unavailable and unusable.[18] This reflects one of the major weaknesses of the Convention—namely, its statism, that is, its general deference to the position of governments and its overall tendency to allow the balance between the interests of the individual and the state to be weighted in favour of the state. This is a theme which we will return to later and is one which should be constantly borne in mind when considering this Convention and the protection of civil liberties within the Council of Europe generally.

Apart from derogation, the second important drawback with the way the Convention is framed lies in the number of limitations placed on many of the rights and liberties within it. Not all the substantive provisions of the Convention are drafted in this way—the non-derogable rights in Articles 3 and 4.1 (above) for example are specifically designed to be interpreted and applied without limitation. But this form of drafting is the exception rather than the general rule. Articles 8, 9, 10 and 11, dealing with the four classic liberties of privacy, thought, expression and assembly respectively are all worded in such a way that the first paragraph of the Article grants the right, only for the second paragraph then heavily to qualify it. Article 10, for example, states:

---

[17] The Court's decision in *Ireland* v. *UK* Series A, No. 25 (1978) 2 E.H.R.R. 25 was rightly seen as an important breakthrough for individual liberty, but this was an unusual case in that it was an inter-state application. More recent cases concerning Northern Ireland have not been met by such a progressive Court: see especially *Brogan* v. *UK* Series A, No. 145–B (1988) 11 E.H.R.R. 117 and *Brannigan and McBride* v. *UK* Series A, No. 258–B (1993) 17 E.H.R.R. 539. See generally Gearty, below, pp. 85, 87.

[18] In *Denmark, Norway and Sweden* v. *Greece*, the Commission disagreed with the Greek government's view that there was a public emergency within the meaning of Article 15 but the Greek government simply ignored Strasbourg's ruling: see (1969) 12 *Yearbook of the European Convention on Human Rights* 1, at paras. 157–165.

"1. Everyone has the right to freedom of expression. This right shall include freedom to hold opinions and to receive and impart information and ideas without interference by public authority and regardless of frontiers. This article shall not prevent States from requiring the licensing of broadcasting, television or cinema enterprises.
2. The exercise of these freedoms, since it carries with it duties and responsibilities, may be subject to such formalities, conditions, restrictions or penalties as are prescribed by law and are necessary in a democratic society, in the interests of national security, territorial integrity or public safety, for the prevention or detection of disorder or crime, for the protection of health or morals, for the protection of the reputation or rights of others, for preventing the disclosure of information received in confidence, or for maintaining the authority and impartiality of the judiciary."

It can be seen from this Article that governments may lawfully limit the Convention's protection of freedom of expression provided for in Article 10.1 in an apparently wide variety of situations. As long as the limitation is prescribed by law, and is necessary in a democratic society, there are no fewer than eight sets of circumstances in which expression may be legitimately infringed—eight situations where the *prima facie* right to freedom of expression may quite properly be violated. Thus the degree to which these interests will be genuinely protected under the Convention will in practice depend on how widely the first paragraph of Article 10 and how narrowly the second paragraph are interpreted. As with the issues of derogation and statism, judicial interpretation of the key phrase "necessary in a democratic society" will often be a central question on which to focus when examining the Convention's effectiveness as a tool for protecting freedom. When will interference with expression be seen as "necessary" for the sake of protecting, say, national security? What criteria will the judges draw up in order to adjudicate properly on this point? What evidence will judges see (or hear) in order to enable them to make such determinations properly? Is it wise to leave the judiciary such a degree of discretion? Is the form of words used in Articles 8, 9, 10 and 11 a strength or a limitation of the protection the Convention accords to civil liberties?

Part III: The European Commission of Human Rights

The European Commission of Human Rights is established under Article 19 of the Convention, "to ensure the observance of the engagements undertaken by the High Contracting Parties in the...Convention". Section III of the Convention (Articles 20–37) deals with the main features of the Commission's structure, functions, composition and responsibilities. Article 20[19] provides that the number of members of the Commission shall be equal to that of the high contracting parties, and that no two members of the Commission may be nationals of the same state. According to Article 21, the members of the Commission are elected by the Committee of Ministers from a list of names drawn up by the Parliamentary Assembly of the Council of Europe, but in practice the first choice of the national government concerned is almost always elected.[20] Members are elected for a renewable term of six years.

But who exactly are these members of the Commission? Who becomes a member? What sort of people do this job? Very brief biographical data are published on all new members of the Commission every year in the Convention's Yearbook.[21] The table below sets out the new appointments that were made to the Commission in the 13 year period, 1980–92.

---

[19] As amended by the Eighth Protocol, which entered into force on 1 January 1990.

[20] Under Article 23 of the Convention, the members of the Commission sit in their individual capacity. During their term of office they may not hold any position which is incompatible with their independence and impartiality.

[21] Published annually, although the most recent *Yearbook*, published in 1995, was that in respect of 1992. Thus there is at present a three-year delay. The information in Table A was drawn from the information provided in the *Yearbooks.*

Name	Member State	Sex	Age on Appoint- ment	Background
Loukis Loucaides	Cyprus	Male	52	Government Lawyer
Christos Rozakis	Greece	Male	46	Academic Lawyer
Jane Liddy	Ireland	Female	38	Government Lawyer
Luis Ruiz	Spain	Male	66	Judge
Basil Hall	UK	Male	67	Government Lawyer
Jorge Campinos	Portugal	Male	47	Former Judge, Government Minister and Member of Parliament
Gro Thune	Norway	Female	41	Government Lawyer & Deputy Member of Parliament
Hugo Vandenburghe	Belgium	Male	42	Academic Lawyer & Adviser to Prime Minister
Hans Danelius	Sweden	Male	49	Government Lawyer & Diplomat
Gerald Batliner	Liechtenstein	Male	55	Former Head of Government & Minister of Justice
Seref Gözübüyük	Turkey	Male	57	Academic Lawyer
Jean-Claude Soyer	France	Male	52	Academic Lawyer
Albert Weitzel	Luxembourg	Male	53	Supreme Court Judge
Henry Schermers	Netherlands	Male	53	Academic & Government Lawyer
Jean-Claude Geus	Belgium	Male	44	Government Lawyer and Conseiller d'Etat
Angelo Ribeiro	Portugal	Male	69	Ombudsman
Matti Pellonpaa	Finland	Male	40	Academic Lawyer
Benedict Marxer	Liechtenstein	Male	36	Judge

From this table it can be seen that in this period 18 new appointments were made to the Commission, of whom 16 were men, and two women. The average age upon appointment was 50 years. The youngest was 36, the oldest 69—and note that these were the ages upon appointment, not upon leaving the Commission. All of the appointees were lawyers; 11 had previously worked in or for their national governments, three were former judges and four were academic lawyers.[22] Hardly representative of the people of Europe, either in age or in gender, and hardly likely to calm fears of statism—of deference to the views of governments rather than to those of complaining individuals. There are no civil liberties lawyers, no former advisers to pressure groups to balance the large number of former government lawyers. Some of the younger appointees to the Commission stay an astonishingly long time. The current[23] President, Carl Norgaard of Denmark, was first appointed at the age of 49 in 1973. He had formerly been an academic lawyer. Felix Ermacora is currently the longest serving member of the Commission: he was appointed in 1960 at the age of 37.

Under Article 24 any high contracting party may refer to the Commission, through the Secretary General of the Council of Europe, any alleged breach of the Convention's provisions by another high contracting party. Under Article 25 the Commission may also receive petitions addressed to the Secretary General from "any person, non-governmental organisation or group of individuals claiming to be the victim of a violation of one of the High Contracting Parties of the rights set forth in [the] Convention," if, and only if, the high contracting party against which the complaint has been lodged has declared that it recognises the competence of the Commission to receive such petitions. Thus, the right of states bound by the Convention to make petitions to the Commission is automatic, whereas the right of individuals to complain to the Commission is not.[24] For an individual's complaint to be recognised, the relevant state must first have made a voluntary declaration allowing this to be done. Such declarations may be made for specific periods. Another example of the general theme of statism identified above, perhaps? All states which have ratified the Convention have made this optional declaration under Article 25. This is, however, a recent development. The Convention entered into force in respect of Cyprus in 1962, for example, yet the Cypriot government did not make the optional declaration

---

[22] Some governments tend always to nominate the same kinds of people. The UK government, for example, usually nominates former civil servant government lawyers (Sir Basil Hall in the Commission, Sir John Freeland in the Court, for example). Usually, but not always: when Sir Basil Hall retired in 1993, Nicolas Bratza QC was nominated (and appointed) as his successor—Bratza is a practising barrister, was 48 years old upon appointment and is a Vice-Chair of the British Institute of Human Rights (based at King's College London). There is, however, some government connection: Bratza was Junior Counsel to the Crown from 1979–1988.

[23] As of July 1995.

[24] As there have only ever been 12 inter-state applications, this chapter will concentrate on individual applications.

under Article 25 until as late as 1989. Similar was Turkey, for which the respective dates were 1954 and 1987.[25]

Each year the Commission holds eight or nine sessions, usually of about twelve days each. The Commission may sit either in plenary session or in chambers of at least seven members (Article 20.2). Petitions are now generally examined by chambers unless they raise new points of Convention law and cannot be resolved straightforwardly by reference to the Court's case law. Under Article 20.2 the member of the Commission appointed in respect of the high contracting party against which a petition is lodged always has the right to sit on the chamber to which the petition has been referred. Both plenary sessions and meetings of chambers are always held *in camera* (Article 33). Once a recognised petition has been made, the Commission acts in a mixed judicial and administrative way. Its first task is one of fact-finding. This will usually be carried out by correspondence, but occasionally visits either by members of the Commission themselves or more usually by members of the Commission's secretariat may be made. Once sufficient facts are found and the petition is formally registered, the Commission meets and decides whether or not it is admissible, within the meaning of Articles 26 and 27. Article 26 provides that, according to the generally recognised rules of international law, a petition may only be dealt with after all domestic remedies have been exhausted, and that the petition must have been made within a period of six months from the date on which the final domestic decision was taken. These admissibility requirements apply to both inter-state and individual applications. There are, however, further requirements which apply only to individual applications. Thus Article 27 lays down that the petition must not be anonymous. Neither may such a petition be substantially on a matter which has already been examined either by the Commission or by any other procedure of international investigation or settlement. The Commission is also directed to find inadmissible any petition which it considers "incompatible with the…Convention, manifestly ill-founded, or an abuse of the right of petition".

The admissibility aspect of the Commission's work is not as mundane as the dry words of these Articles might suggest. The statistics reveal that the overwhelming majority of petitions never progress beyond even this preliminary stage. There is no appeal against a finding of inadmissibility. Such a finding puts an end to the matter, and has the practical effect of barring the

---

[25] Other states have been much more prompt in making the relevant declarations: Belgium, for example ratified the Convention and made the declarations under both Articles 25 and 46 in 1955.

Court from hearing the case. As of December 1994, 26,058 petitions have been formally registered since the inception of the Commission's work in 1955,[26] and yet only 2,027 (8 per cent.) have been declared admissible. In 1992 the Commission delivered 1,704 decisions concerning individual petitions, of which 1,505 (88 per cent.) were declared inadmissible or struck off the list with only 189 (11 per cent.) being declared admissible. In 1993 the figures were broadly similar: the Commission delivered 1,765 such decisions, of which 1,547 (88 per cent.) were declared inadmissible or struck off the list and 218 (12 per cent.) were declared admissible. In 1994, however, there were significant changes. In that year the Commission delivered 2,372 decisions concerning individual petitions, of which 1,790 (75 per cent.) were declared inadmissible or struck off the list and 582 (25 per cent.) were declared admissible.[27] This is not only a considerably higher number of decisions, but interestingly is also a significantly greater proportion of petitions being declared admissible. It may be that this reflects the rapidly growing number of new high contracting parties in respect of whom petitions are now being made for the first time.

The decision on admissibility is not a matter of bland administrative work. Deciding what an effective domestic remedy is under Article 26, for example, is not always as straightforward a matter as might at first be thought. Moreover, the wide discretionary powers conferred upon the Commission under Article 27.2 have in practice proven to be immensely important. The meanings of the phrases "manifestly ill-founded" and "incompatible with the Convention" are far from clear. These have also turned out to be somewhat controversial matters. In its case-law the Commission has taken "incompatible with the Convention" to mean three different things:[28] either that the application falls outside of the scope of the Convention *ratione personae, ratione materiae,*[29] *ratione loci* or *ratione temporis*; or that the individual applicant does not fall within the definition

---

[26] Over 56,000 others never even made it this far, often because they were not pursued beyond the initial correspondence once the applicant (or his or her lawyers) realised that the petition would not be likely to succeed. Up to the end of 1994 a total of 82,356 provisional files had been opened.

[27] These are the published statistics taken from the Commission's annual Surveys of Activities and Statistics.

[28] See van Dijk and van Hoof, *op. cit.*, note 11, p. 75.

[29] Examples of this include applications which have in the Commission's view concerned a right to divorce, to a passport, to a driving licence, to a university qualification, to a pension or to start a business, and so on. Further examples are given in van Dijk and van Hoof, *ibid*, p. 79.

of a victim under Article 25.1; or that the application is contrary to Article 17 in that it is interpreted as designed to achieve the destruction of one of the rights or freedoms guaranteed in the Convention. Among the better known examples of an application being found inadmissible on this particular ground is the application of the German Communist Party (KPD), members of which sought to challenge the decision of the German Constitutional Court to dissolve and prohibit it. The Commission held that as the aim of the KPD was to establish a communist state by means of revolution and the "dictatorship of the proletariat" their principles could be construed as being aimed at the destruction of the rights and freedoms provided for in the Convention and the application was therefore held to be inadmissible.[30]

The Commission has more than once found extremely politically sensitive petitions to be inadmissible when many observers and lawyers have been of the opinion that there has been (at the very least) an arguable point about which there should have been a clear judgment, preferably (for reasons both of legal certainty and of publicity) from the Court. The so-called GCHQ case from the United Kingdom is a classic example. Amid much political controversy Mrs Thatcher in 1983 declared that trade unions would be banned from Government Communications Headquarters, a part of the security and intelligence services. The trade unions challenged this decision in the domestic courts, but the House of Lords unanimously held for the government, on the ground that the public interest of national security justified the decision even though in other circumstances it might have been open to challenge. After this ruling, the unions petitioned the Commission, but despite the fact that the case clearly raised an important matter related to the freedom of association guarantee under Article 11 of the Convention,[31] the Commission declared the petition to be inadmissible on the ground of it being manifestly ill-founded.[32] "Manifestly ill-founded" is generally taken to mean that "there is not even a *prima facie* case against the respondent state".[33] Yet cases such as the GCHQ case sit very uncomfortably with the position as expressed by the Commission in *Klass* v. *Germany* that applications which raise complex questions of law or which are of general interest

---

[30] Application 250/57, (1955–57) 1 *Yearbook of the European Convention on Human Rights*, p. 222.

[31] That is to say, the extent to which there was a pressing social need justifying this restriction on the freedom of association guaranteed in Article 11.1.

[32] Application no. 11603/85 v. U.K., 50 D. & R. 228 (1988) 10 E.H.R.R. 269.

[33] *Boyle and Rice* v. *United Kingdom* Series A, No. 131 (1988) 10 E.H.R.R. 425, paras. 53–54.

should not be regarded as manifestly ill-founded. As Harris, O'Boyle and Warbrick argue, "how can a case be rejected as *manifestly* ill-founded after extensive legal argument, often involving an oral argument and a *lengthy* fully reasoned opinion of the Commission with which not all members agree?"[34]

In the recent report of the Committee of Experts for the improvement of procedures for protecting human rights[35] it was suggested that the rules of admissibility should be tightened up, so as to include, perhaps, a requirement that an application must be demonstrated to have a "realistic prospect of success" before it could be declared admissible. This is possibly already an aspect of the manifestly ill-founded criterion.[36] Whether or not such a *de minimis* rule is appropriate in a human rights context is highly dubious. Apart from concern over these relatively prominent decisions, there is also a more functional worry. Consideration of the "manifestly ill-founded" aspect of admissibility is different in character from the other admissibility criteria, in that it leads to the Commission pronouncing on and in effect giving a *prima facie* judgment as to the merits of the application, and not just as to its procedural admissibility. Again, whether this often unappealable process, which is always held in private and which therefore does not enjoy the same degree of publicity as does a judgment of the Court, and in respect of which only the most cursory of reasons are generally given, is entirely appropriate in the human rights field is questionable.

Once a petition has been accepted by the Commission as admissible, the next stage is the examination. This will begin by trying to establish the full facts. Under Article 28 this will be carried out with the assistance of the parties' representatives. During the examination stage the Commission is under a duty to take positive steps to encourage the parties to reach a friendly settlement. The Commission may also strike the petition out during this stage if, on further investigation, the petition should after all have been declared inadmissible; or if the applicant does not intend to pursue the complaint; or if the matter has been resolved; or if "for any other reason established by the Commission, it is no longer justified to continue the examination of the petition" (Article 30.1(c)). Under Article 31, if no friendly settlement is reached, and if the petition has not been struck out, the Com-

---

[34] D. J. Harris, M. O'Boyle and C. Warbrick, *Law of the European Convention on Human Rights* (London, 1995), at p. 628.

[35] This report is discussed in more detail, below, text at note 142.

[36] There is no way of finding this out, as all Commission hearings, at both admissibility and merits stages are held *in camera*, a rule which is strictly enforced.

mission will draw up a report on the merits of the complaint. The report will relate the facts as found, and will state the Commission's opinion as to whether (and if so, the extent to which) the provisions of the Convention have been breached. Minority and dissenting opinions of individual members of the Commission may also be included. Recommendations as to necessary changes in the law or in practice if a breach of the Convention has been found may also be made in the report. The report will be transmitted to the state(s) concerned and also to the Committee of Ministers. The report will not be published at this stage: publication only takes place after the Committee of Ministers has completed its consideration of the case and may even then be delayed further.[37]

Part IV: The European Court of Human Rights

As with the Commission, the European Court of Human Rights is established by Article 19 of the Convention "to ensure the observance of the engagements undertaken by the High Contracting Parties in the...Convention". Section IV (Articles 38–56) deals with the main features of the Court's role under the Convention. Article 38 provides that the Court is to consist of a number of judges equal to that of the members of the Council of Europe. No two judges may be nationals of the same state. Thus there is a subtle difference between the Court and Commission on this point—to have a member on the Commission a state must have ratified the Convention, whereas any member state of the Council of Europe may have a judge on the Court irrespective of whether or not that state has ratified. The rationale behind this apparent contradiction is unclear. It should be noted that there does not have to be one member of the Commission, or one judge on the Court, from each relevant country: it is simply the rule that there must not be more than one judge from any one state. Thus the judge presently elected in respect of Liechtenstein, for example, is in fact Canadian (Judge MacDonald).

Judges are elected by the Parliamentary Assembly from a list drawn up by the Committee of Ministers. This procedure, too, is subtly different from that used to elect members of the Commission,[38] but the net result is generally the same: that is to say, the first choice of the national government concerned is more often than not elected. As with the members of the Commission brief biographical data are published on new members of the Court in

---

[37] See generally, below, text at note 68 ff.

[38] Compare Article 21.1 considered above with Article 39.1.

the Convention's Yearbook. The table below sets out the new appointments that were made to the Court in the 13 year period, 1980–92.

Name	Member State	Sex	Age on Appointment	Background
Raimo Pekkanen	Finland	Male	62	Academic Lawyer; Judge 1969–82; Senior Government Lawyer since 1982
S K Martens	Netherlands	Male	58	Judge; Vice President of Supreme Court Since 1978
Elisabeth Palm	Sweden	Female	52	Judge; Former Government Lawyer
Isi Foighel	Denmark	Male	61	Academic & Government Lawyer
Jan de Meyer	Belgium	Male	65	Academic & Government Lawyer
Juan Antonio Carrillo Salcedo	Spain	Male	52	Judge; Academic & Government Lawyer & Member of European Commission of Human Rights, 1979–1986
Nicolaos Valticos	Greece	Male	68	Academic Lawyer
Jorgen Gersing	Sweden	Male	55	Judge; Senior Government Lawyer
Carlo Russo	Italy	Male	61	Government Lawyer & Member of Parliament
Rudolf Bernhardt	Germany	Male	56	Academic Lawyer
Louis-Edmond Pettiti	France	Male	64	Academic & Practising Lawyer
Brian Walsh	Ireland	Male	62	Judge
Max Sørensen	Denmark	Male	67	Academic Lawyer; Former Member of European Commission of Human Rights & Judge of ECJ
Vincent Evans	United Kingdom	Male	65	Government Lawyer
Ronald MacDonald	Liechtenstein	Male	52	Academic & Practising Lawyer
Andreas Loizou	Cyprus	Male	64	Judge
Jose Morinella	Spain	Male	64	Judge
Federico Bigi	San Marino	Male	71	Lawyer and former Government minister and Judge
John Freeland	United Kingdom	Male	64	Government Lawyer

Name	Member State	Sex	Age on Appoint-ment	Background
Andras Baka	Hungary	Male	39	Academic Lawyer
Manuel Rocha	Portugal	Male	60	Former Judge and Attorney-General
Luzius Wildhaber	Switzerland	Male	54	Judge
Giuseppi Bonnici	Malta	Male	62	Judge
Bohumil Repik	Czechoslovakia	Male	64	Judge
Jerzy Makarczyk	Poland	Male	54	Lawyer and Government Minister
Dimitar Gotchev	Bulgaria	Male	56	Judge

From this table it can be seen that in this period 26 new appointments were made to the Court, of whom 25 were men. The average age upon appointment was 60 years. The youngest was 39, the oldest 71. All the appointees were lawyers; 12 had previously worked in or for their national governments, 12 were former judges and five were academic or practising lawyers. As with the Commission, this is hardly a representative group of Europeans. Again, as with the Commission, there are some judges who have remained on the Court for a long time. The current President, Rolv Ryssdal of Norway, was first appointed at the age of 59 in 1973 and was made President of the Court in 1985. He had formerly been a government lawyer and then a Supreme Court Judge.

Bringing a case to the Court is even harder than it is in respect of the Commission. Before the Court may hear a case the High Contracting Party concerned must have granted its consent. This may be done in two ways: either on an *ad hoc* case by case basis, or more formally through the granting of a declaration under Article 46 of the Convention. This Article provides that any High Contracting Party may at any time declare that it recognises the jurisdiction of the Court as compulsory *ipso facto*. As with the declarations regarding the right of individual petition under Article 25 (considered above) all High Contracting Parties have made Article 46 declarations. But again, as with Article 25, this has only very recently been achieved. In Malta, for example, the Convention came into force in 1967, yet that state made a declaration under Article 46 only in 1987; and in Turkey the Convention came into force in 1954 whereas that country's Article

46 declaration was made as recently as 1990. Until very recently the position was that even after a declaration has been made under Article 46, the Court could only hear a case once it had been referred to it either by a high contracting party or by the Commission. A right of individual petition to the Court was added only from October 1994 when Protocol No. 9 came into force in respect of those high contracting parties that had ratified it.[39]

Once a case has been properly referred to the Court, then if the Court has jurisdiction to hear the matter,[40] written submissions will be made by the parties and also by the Commission. There will then be a public oral hearing, which will be followed by private deliberations. The public hearing will normally last only for about half a day—by far the more important submissions are those in writing. The procedure at the public hearing is usually that a delegate from the Commission speaks first, introducing the Court to the Commission's report on the merits of the case, and seeking to defend the Commission's reasoning in support of the report. Then there are speeches from advocates representing the parties. The order of speeches varies and appears to be a matter to be agreed by the President of the Court (or chamber) with the advocates concerned. There is a brief right of reply and judges do have the opportunity to ask questions. Very few are in practice asked. The public hearing is hardly, then, the most central element of the Court's decision-making process, yet very few people would argue that it should be dispensed with. The applicant's "day in court" is important, not only to the applicant, but also for the sake of publicising the Court's work. The greater the awareness of the Court and the Convention becomes, the greater the potential for the effective protection of liberty.

It is usually about six months after the public hearing that the judgment of the Court is delivered. The judgment has to be reasoned, but does not have to be unanimous. Dissenting and minority opinions are printed alongside the majority judgment and are available to the public. Unlike the reports of the Commission, the judgment of the Court is final (Article 52), and High Contracting Parties undertake to abide by the decisions of the Court in any case to which they are a party (Article 53). Thus, judgments of the Court do not have to be confirmed by the Committee of Ministers in the same way as reports of the Commission are—the Court's judgments are binding without further ado. The Committee of Ministers is, however, responsible for super-

---

[39] As of June 1995 Protocol No. 9 was in force in respect of 18 High Contracting Parties.

[40] Under Article 49, in the event of any dispute as to whether the Court has jurisdiction, the matter falls to be decided by the Court.

vising the execution and implementation of the Court's judgments.[41] The Court also has jurisdiction under Article 50 of the Convention to award costs and, if necessary, just satisfaction to an injured party. As with the Commission, due both to the volume of cases and to the size of the Court, cases are usually now dealt with by chambers of nine judges, although "where a case raises serious questions affecting the interpretation of the Convention the Chamber may relinquish jurisdiction in favour of a Grand Chamber of 19 judges".[42] The judge elected in respect of the respondent state in a case is entitled as of right to sit in the chamber which hears the case (Article 43).

Relations between the Court and the Commission are said generally to be reasonably good. However, there are notable exceptions to this. It has been said that there have in the past been periods when the members of the Commission and the Court have been hardly on speaking terms, because of differences of deeply held beliefs as to aspects of their work. Such a time was said to be the early 1970s.[43] Nowadays, relations are nothing like this bad, but there are important points of contention between the members of, and the lawyers working for, the Court and Commission. These points of contention may be broken down into three different kinds of divergences. First, there are the differences in the interpretation of substantive provisions of the Convention. Articles 13 and 6.1 are the most frequently cited examples of this.[44] The Court, it is said, takes a comparatively wide view of the breadth of Article 6.1 (that is, of the number of determinations of civil rights and obligations covered by Article 6.1) but a relatively narrow view of the depth and strength of the substantive protection guaranteed by Article 6 once an applicant has surmounted this first hurdle. An example of this is the case of

---

[41] See generally, below, text at note 100 ff.

[42] Rules of the Court, rule 51. The Grand Chamber may exceptionally, "when the issues raised are particularly serious or involve a significant change of existing case-law" relinquish jurisdiction in favour of the full court (rule 51).

[43] The disagreements from this period centred on the number and variety of cases being referred by the Commission to the Court. There was a view in the Commission that because the Court was composed primarily of national judges, the Court could only properly deal with alleged violations of Articles 5 and 6, because judges were only really expert in these matters and knew comparatively little of generally held European standards concerning more overtly political matters such as free speech and privacy. After certain key members of the Commission retired in the mid-1970s, and more cases began to be referred to the Court, this area of disagreement was apparently cleared up.

[44] On Article 13, compare, for example, the Court in *Klass v. Germany* Series A, No. 28 (1978) 2 E.H.R.R. 214 with the Commission in *Kaplan v. United Kingdom*, 17 July 1980, (1981) 21 D. & R. 5, at p. 35.

Moreira de Azevedo v. *Portugal.*[45] Here, the applicant was the victim of a shooting in 1977. His assailant was convicted in 1985, but the conviction was then overturned by a higher court on grounds of delay. The applicant then complained that this delay was to his detriment also, as it was relevant to his claim of compensation. After putting this argument in the domestic courts, the applicant alleged in Strasbourg that his rights under Article 6.1 of the Convention had been breached. The Commission held that Article 6.1 did not apply, and that therefore an examination of the merits of the case was not possible. The Court took a different view, holding that Article 6.1 was applicable, and had indeed been violated.[46]

Secondly there have been differences of opinion concerning procedural matters arising under the Convention. The Court has taken the view in a number of cases, most notably in *Cardot* v. *France*,[47] that questions of admissibility may be reopened in the Court. The Commission has taken the view that this practice is not only irrational, but also, having regard to the terms of the Convention, wrong.[48] It is worth considering what the Court is doing in these cases, because this feeds back into our earlier argument about the statism of the Strasbourg machinery in a quite alarming way. If the Commission decides that an application is inadmissible (because, for example, it is outside of the six month time limit) then, as we have seen, the applicant has no right of appeal. But if the Commission decides that an application is admissible and is therefore within the prescribed time limit, the respondent state may object in proceedings before the Commission. If the case should eventually go on to be decided by the Court, and the Court's presently held view of the reopening of admissibility criteria is correct, then the state may raise its arguments yet again, in the form of preliminary objections, before the Court goes on to decide the substance of the case. Thus the state has two bites at the cherry, whereas the applicant has none. There are two examples from the court's case law where this policy has actively operated to the applicant's detriment: in *Cardot* itself the Commission had decided that Articles 6.1 and 6.3 had been violated, whereas the Court held

---

[45]   Series A, No. 189 (1991) 13 E.H.R.R. 721.

[46]   So this case is a rare example of the Court being more progressive than the Commission.

[47]   Series A, No. 200 (1991). Other instances where questions of admissibility have been reopened by the Court include *Van Oosterwijck* v. *Belgium,* Series A, No. 40 (1981) 3 E.H.R.R. 557; *De Wilde, Ooms and Versijp* v. *Belgium* Series A, No. 12 (1971) 1 E.H.R.R. 438; and *Brozicek* v. *Italy* Series A, No. 167 (1989) 12 E.H.R.R. 373.

[48]   Some members of the Court are also vehemently opposed to the majority's view that questions of admissibility may be reopened: see for example the lengthy and powerful dissenting judgment of Judge Martens in the *Brozicek* case, *ibid.*

that it was unable to take cognisance of the merits of the applicant's case because it decided that the applicant had not exhausted local remedies. The Court took a similar line in *Van Oosterwijck*[49] where the Commission had decided that Articles 8 and 12 had been violated.

The third type of divergence between the Commission and the Court is more general and thematic. This is that the Court is more conservative and more "government-friendly" than the Commission. If all the cases where the Court and Commission have come to different conclusions as to whether or not there has been a violation of the Convention are listed, up to the end of 1990 that list would contain 52 cases. In only 12 of these 52 cases did the Court find a violation where the Commission did not,[50] and in the remaining 40 the Court found no violation whereas the Commission did. This shows that, statistically at least, the Court is frequently more conservative than the Commission, and perhaps demonstrates the concerns of some of those who are rather more progressive in their views of the protection of liberty under the Convention.[51] A second aspect of the Court's present conservatism is the paucity of its reasoning. In what are sometimes called the formative years in the development of Strasbourg human rights jurisprudence, that is to say the series of central decisions in the late 1970s, the Court made a number of broad, sweeping statements designed to be of general application throughout the legal understanding of the Convention. The development and use in the

---

[49] *Van Oosterwijck* v. *Belgium, op. cit.*, note 47.

[50] These 12 cases are *Engel* v. *Netherlands* Series A, No. 22 (1976) 1 E.H.R.R. 647 (concerning Articles 5 and 6); *Sporrong and Lonnroth* v. *Sweden* Series A, No. 52 (1982) 5 E.H.R.R. 35 (concerning Article 6 and the First Protocol, Article 1); *Benthem* v. *Netherlands* Series A, No. 97 (1985) 8 E.H.R.R. 1 (concerning Article 6); *Feldbrugge* v. *Netherlands* Series A, No. 99 (1986) 8 E.H.R.R. 425 (concerning Article 6); *Deumeland* v. *Germany* Series A, No. 100 (1986) 8 E.H.R.R. 448 (concerning Article 6); *Unterpertinger* v. *Austria* Series A, No. 110 (concerning Article 6); *Brogan* v. *United Kingdom, op. cit.*, note 17, (concerning Article 5); *Hauschildt* v. *Denmark* Series A, No. 154 (1989) 12 E.H.R.R. 226 (concerning Article 6); *Soering* v. *United Kingdom* Series A, No. 161 (1989) 11 E.H.R.R. 439 (concerning Article 3); *Weber* v. *Switzerland* Series A, No. 177 (1990) 12 E.H.R.R. 508 (concerning Article 6); *Darby* v. *Sweden* Series A, No. 187 (1990) 13 E.H.R.R. 774 (concerning Article 14); and *Moreira de Azevedo* v. *Portugal* Series A, No. 189 (1990) 13 E.H.R.R. 721 (concerning Article 6).

[51] One recent and very controversial exception to this general trend was *McCann* v. *United Kingdom* Series A, No. 324 (1995) 21 E.H.R.R. 97 where a Grand Chamber of the Court, disagreeing with the Commission, held by ten votes to nine that Article 2 had been violated. The four most senior judges to hear the case all dissented and six of the seven most recent recruits to the Court were in the majority, a point the UK government was not slow to make! Only time will tell if the newer members of the Court will become more conservative the longer they stay.

Sunday Times case[52] of the "pressing social need" idea to explain what was meant in the Convention by "necessary in a democratic society" in the limitation paragraphs of Articles 8, 9, 10 and 11 is a good example. The Court now seems reluctant to engage in the same sort of reasoning. Even groundbreaking cases like *Tomasi* v. *France*[53] contain only very limited reasoning. Perhaps this is because there is no longer any need for broad and sweeping statements, or for fuller explanation of the Court's reasoning, as the statements have already been made, and the explanations have already been given, in earlier case-law. Certainly this argument would justify the Court's present conservative reasoning in many run-of-the-mill cases (such as many of the Italian Article 6 cases, many of which largely repeat one another)[54] but surely it does not apply to the (now admittedly fewer) cases where the Court is confronted with a new issue.

In *Tomasi*, the applicant had been arrested and detained in connection with a criminal investigation relating to a terrorist attack in Corsica. After spending 48 hours in police custody he proceeded to spend a further five years and seven months on remand before a specially convened court (without a jury) acquitted him in October 1988. During his detention Tomasi had made twenty applications for release, but had been unsuccessful every time on the ground that the charges he faced were very serious and that if released he might abscond and attempt to intimidate witnesses. This was despite the fact that, as the *Cour de Cassation* in France itself admitted, there was no evidence that any witnesses had been intimidated after the escape from detention of a Mr Pieri (Tomasi's fellow suspect) and also despite the fact that only "weak and insufficient evidence had been collected over the five and a half year period"[55]. On these and other grounds both the European Commission and Court of Human Rights found that there had been a violation of Articles 5.3 (which concerns being brought promptly before a judge) and 6.1 (the entitlement to a fair trial within a reasonable time).The Court also held that Article 3 had been breached, basing this finding on a combination of a reversed burden of proof with an assumed, rather than proven, causal connection.[56]

---

[52] *Sunday Times* v. *United Kingdom* Series A, No. 30 (1979) 2 E.H.R.R. 245.

[53] Series A, No. 241 (1992) 15 E.H.R.R. 1.

[54] See for example *Pizzetti, De Micheli, Salesi, Trevisan and Billi* v. *Italy* (Judgments of 26 February 1993) concerning length of proceedings and Article 6.1. See Leonardi, below, pp. 325 ff.

[55] *Op. cit.*, note 53, at para. 41 of the Court's judgment.

[56] *Ibid.*, at paras. 108–110.

Yet, important though these steps forward were, the Court could have been much more forthright in its approach. The Court, could, for example, have broken with its recent habit of not making more general statements and updated and strengthened its earlier *dicta* from the *Ireland* v. *United Kingdom* case where it had held that:

> In order to satisfy itself as to the existence or not in Northern Ireland of practices contrary to Article 3, the Court will not rely on the concept that the burden of proof is borne by one or other of the two Governments concerned....[T]he Court examines all the material before it...[and] to assess this evidence, the Court adopts the standard of proof 'beyond all reasonable doubt' but adds that such proof may follow from the coexistence of sufficiently strong, clear and concordant inferences or of similar unrebutted presumptions of fact.[57]

Being based on an evaluation of the Court's reasoning, this is perhaps an easier breed of conservatism to demonstrate than our earlier, statistically-based, evidence. Certainly, present members of the Commission find on occasions that the Court's reasoning is not as helpful as it might have been. In its report on *Tomasi*, for example,[58] the Commission had been more forthright, and more progressive than the Court eventually proved itself to be.

A third aspect of the Court's conservative personality relates to its composition. As observed above, there are generally three different categories of candidates who become elected to the Court: national judges, government lawyers or civil servants, and academic lawyers. In some cases the differences of training and hence of outlook between these three groups may be crucial to the way cases are decided. Among the most frequently cited examples is *Cruz Varas* v. *Sweden*.[59] This case concerned the deportation of a Chilean national from Sweden. Acting under Rule 36 of its Rules of Procedure, the Commission requested the Swedish government not to deport the applicant until after the merits of the case had been decided in Strasbourg. The applicant was deported nonetheless. When the case reached the Court, the applicant argued that Articles 3, 8 and 25 were breached. The Court held by 18 votes to one that Article 3 was violated and unanimously that Article 8 had not been infringed. The more interesting point of the case, however, lay in the Court's treatment of the Article 25 argument. As we have already noted, Article 25 provides for a right of individual petition to the Commission. The Court held by ten votes to eight that Article 25.1 was not violated

---

[57] *Op. cit.*, note 17, paras. 160–161.

[58] Application no. 12850/87; report of 11 December 1990.

[59] Series A, No. 201 (1991) 14 E.H.R.R. 1.

by Sweden's actions in this case. The majority ruled that the Convention does not provide the Court or the Commission with a specific power to order interim measures to protect the rights of parties in pending proceedings, and that such a power could not be inferred from either Article 25.1 or Rule 36 of the Commission's rules of procedure.[60] Rule 36, according to the majority, constituted simply a request, not a binding obligation on states. Significantly, however, there were eight dissenters on this point, most of whom were former national court judges.[61] Thus the argument is that this decision is an example of how judges' backgrounds can affect their decisions. Only practising lawyers and judges, the argument runs, fully understand and are wholly familiar with the crucial importance of the availability of interim measures, whereas former members of governments or former civil servants and academics will generally have less appreciation of the significance of such measures.

Part V: The Committee of Ministers[62]

The Committee of Ministers is a political body of the Council of Europe. Unlike the Commission and Court, the Committee of Ministers is not a creature solely of the Convention; while it has a number of roles to play under the Convention, it also exists independently of it. The Committee of Ministers was established in 1949 under the Statute of the Council of Europe. In theory the Committee's membership is made up of ministers from

---

[60]   Rule 36 provides that the Commission "may indicate to the parties any interim measure the adoption of which seems desirable in the interest of the parties or the proper conduct of the proceedings...".

[61]   The dissenters were Judges Cremona, Thor Vilhjalmsson, Walsh, MacDonald, Bernhardt, DeMeyer, Foighel and Morinella. The majority of judges who shared in the opinion of the Court were not former national court judges. They included Judges Bindschedler-Robert, Golcuklu, Matscher, Pettiti, Evans, and Russo. The joint dissenting opinion stated that

"it is, in our view, implicit in the Convention that in cases such as the present the Convention organs have the power to require the parties to abstain from a measure which might...give rise to serious harm....[Although] the Convention does not contain any express provision as to the indication of provisional measures...it is of the essence that the Convention organs should be able to secure the effectiveness of the protection they are called on to ensure" (paras 4–5).

[62]   An earlier version of parts of this section was published in the *European Human Rights Law Review*: see A. Tomkins, "The Committee of Ministers: Its Roles under the European Convention on Human Rights" (1995) 1 *European Human Rights Law Review* 49–62.

the foreign affairs departments of the governments of member states[63] but in practice ministers are usually represented by a deputy such as the member state's permanent representative to the Council. The Committee of Ministers is the executive organ of the Council of Europe, Article 13 of the Statute describing it as "the organ which acts on behalf of the Council of Europe". Its role is to determine the action which should be taken by the Council in furtherance of its aims. Such determination may be on the Committee's own initiative, or in response to recommendations from the Council's Parliamentary Assembly.

The primary mechanism used by the Committee in carrying out its function is the passing of Resolutions and Recommendations.[64] Such Resolutions and Recommendations are not binding on member states; they are merely expressions of good or desirable practice. They have the status of policy statements or proposals for action. They may vary in character as much as the governmental papers of any nation state. They cover all the areas of the Council's activities, from youth to sport to culture to human rights. A Recommendation may be addressed to one member state in particular or may be more general in scope. The Council's various directorates periodically publish collections of the Committee's Resolutions and Recommendations which concern their particular field. The Directorate of Human Rights, for example, published in 1989 a 214 page collection of Resolutions and Recommendations dating from 1949–1987 concerned with various aspects of human rights. The collection contains Resolutions on topics as diverse as the teaching of human rights and the award of the European Human Rights prize and Recommendations on areas such as the regulation of data protection, copyright, film distribution, assistance to victims of crime, foster families, prison rules and medical care.

Our main interest, however, lies in the functions assigned to the Committee of Ministers under the European Convention on Human Rights. These can be grouped under three heads: first, various administrative functions; secondly, duties in relation to the European Commission of Human Rights (arising under Article 32 of the Convention) and thirdly, duties in relation to the European Court of Human Rights, arising out of Article 54.

---

[63] See Article 14 of the Statute.

[64] Initially all were called resolutions, but a distinction between resolutions and recommendations was created in 1979. Resolutions relate to the work or functions of the Council, such as an agreement to construct a new human rights building, whereas recommendations relate to action which it is proposed should be taken by national governments of member states.

1. ADMINISTRATIVE FUNCTIONS

The Committee of Ministers has three main types of administrative function concerned with the Convention. The first concerns the membership of the Commission and Court. Under Article 21 of the Convention the Committee of Ministers elects the members of the Commission by an absolute majority from a list drawn up by the Parliamentary Assembly. Article 39 of the Convention provides that the Court's judges are to be elected by the Parliamentary Assembly "from a list of persons nominated by the members of the Council of Europe". While Article 39 does not expressly mention the Committee of Ministers, it is in practice in the Committee of Ministers where this list is drawn up. Secondly, the Council's statute[65] provides that the Secretary-General of the Council of Europe is responsible to the Committee of Ministers and is under a duty to submit budgetary requirements to the Committee. The Committee will decide on the amount to be paid to the Commission and the Court, and will thus indirectly determine the size both of the Commission's Secretariat and the Court's Registry.

Thirdly, the Committee of Ministers acts as a forum for discussion on various general or specific aspects of the content and operation of the Convention. It was the Committee of Ministers, for example, which determined in 1956 that when the Secretary-General of the Council of Europe was informed under Article 15.3 of measures taken by a High Contracting Party which constituted a derogation from its obligations under the Convention, it was appropriate for him or her to communicate such information to other contracting parties and to the Commission.[66] The Committee of Ministers also plays a role in negotiations concerning the drafting and adoption of Protocols to the Convention. The Committee formally adopts the final text of any Protocol before it is opened for signature by the states.

2. THE COMMITTEE OF MINISTERS AND THE COMMISSION: ARTICLE 32

Of far greater significance than these administrative functions are the roles played by the Committee of Ministers under Articles 32 and 54 of the Convention. Article 32 governs the relationship between the Committee of Ministers and the Commission, and Article 54 provides for the supervisory responsibility of the Committee of Ministers over the execution of the

---

[65] Articles 37 and 38.
[66] See generally A. H. Robertson and J. Merrills, *Human Rights in Europe*, 3rd ed. (Manchester, 1993).

Court's judgments. It is to the first of these central tasks that we now turn our attention.

Where the Commission has drawn up a report on the merits of an application under Article 31 of the Convention, one of two things may then happen. As already discussed, the first possibility is that the report is referred to the Court for a final and binding judgment. Article 47 provides for a time limit of three months for this to occur. The second possibility occurs if no reference is made within this prescribed period. Article 32 provides that in such a case, the Commission's report is required to be transmitted to the Committee of Ministers. Once there "the Committee of Ministers shall decide by a majority of two-thirds of the members entitled to sit on the Committee whether there has been a violation of the Convention." By Article 32.4, High Contracting Parties are bound by such decisions of the Committee of Ministers. Thus, no report of the Commission is binding on the respondent state unless and until it has been confirmed by the Committee of Ministers. Under Article 32.2, where the Committee of Ministers has found there to have been a breach of the Convention, it then prescribes a period during which the respondent state is to take such measures as are required by the decision. If these measures are not satisfactorily taken by the member state, the Committee may, again by two-thirds majority, decide what effect shall be given to its original decision and shall then publish the Commission's report.[67] Rule 9 *ter* of the rules adopted by the Committee of Ministers for the application of Article 32 provides that the Commission's report will usually be published automatically once the Committee of Ministers has completed its consideration of the case. The rule goes on to state that by way of exception the Committee of Ministers may "decide not to publish a report of the Commission or a part thereof upon a reasoned request of a contracting party or the Commission".

Considering the significant number of cases which are not referred to the Court, it is astonishing how little is known, and how little has been written about the Committee of Ministers' powers under Article 32.[68] Collections of resolutions made under Article 32 are published by the Council of Europe's Human Rights Directorate. Altogether, 147 resolutions made by the Committee of Ministers under Article 32 have been published in these collec-

---

[67] Article 32(3).

[68] Robertson and Merrills, *op. cit.*, note 66, devote nine pages (pp. 329–339) to Article 32, and van Dijk and van Hoof, *op. cit.*, note 11, 16 pages (pp 191–206). For a short but useful summary of some aspects of the Committee's work, see C. Tomuschat, "Quo Vadis, Argentoratum?" (1992) 13 *Human Rights Law Journal* 401.

tions, covering the period from the Convention's beginnings until the end of 1992. The number of cases that the Committee of Ministers has had to consider has mushroomed in recent years in the same way as have the numbers of applications to the Commission and cases heard by (and pending before) the Court. In 1992 for example 89 new Article 32 cases were brought before the Committee, and at the end of 1992, 93 Article 32 cases were pending before it. The analysis offered in this part of this article is based on a detailed study of these 147 resolutions. This study reveals a number of highly significant, and quite well kept secrets concerning the effectiveness of the operation of the Convention in Strasbourg. There are four points, in particular, which will be focused on in this section: first, what is the position of the applicant; secondly, what happens when the Committee of Ministers is unable to agree with the Commission; thirdly, how long the Committee of Ministers takes in dealing with reports from the Commission, and fourthly, what remedies are available, both in theory and in practice, in respect of the Committee of Ministers' resolutions.

A.   The position of the applicant

Even though the greater part of the work of the Commission and the Court is carried out in written form, individual applicants[69] and their lawyers or other representatives may appear before both bodies during the course of their oral hearings. In respect of the Commission this applies both to admissibility hearings and to hearings on the merits. Individual applicants, in contrast, are not party to proceedings before the Committee of Ministers under Article 32. The Committee of Ministers has published the rules it has adopted for the application of this Article. These rules were initially adopted in 1959 but have been variously amended, most recently in 1991. Paragraph 3 of the appendix to these rules deals with the position of the individual applicant. It provides:

> 3.(a) The Committee of Ministers decided not to establish a procedure permitting the communication to an applicant of the report of the Commission on his application, or the communication to the Committee of Ministers of the applicant's observations on the report.

---

[69]   The significance of the distinction established in Articles 24 and 25 of the Convention between individual applications and inter-state applications has already been discussed: see, above, text at note 24 ff.

(b) The communication to an individual applicant of the complete text or extracts from the report of the Commission should take place only as an exceptional measure (for example, where the Committee of Ministers wishes to obtain the observations of the applicant), only on a strictly confidential basis, and only with the consent of the state against which the application was lodged.

(c) Since the individual applicant is not a party to the proceedings before the Committee of Ministers under Article 32 of the Convention, he has no right to be heard by the Committee of Ministers or to have any written communication considered by the Committee. This should be explained by the Secretary General to the applicant....

The appendix goes on to explain that "an individual applicant ought *normally* to be informed of the outcome of the examination of his case before the Committee of Ministers. It would be for the Committee of Ministers to decide in each particular case on the information to be communicated and on the procedure to be followed."[70] Compare this to rule 2, which governs the position of states: "the representative of any member state on the Committee of Ministers shall be fully qualified to take part in exercising the functions and powers set forth in Article 32 of the Convention, even if that state has not yet ratified the Convention". Rule 3 provides that each representative of the Committee of Ministers has an intrinsic right to make submissions and deposit documents. Consequently even a government which is not a party to the proceedings before the Commission may play a full part in the proceedings before the Committee of Ministers.

Other commentators have observed that the delays and backlog presently facing the Court may constitute a violation of the provision in Article 6.1 of the Convention that "everyone is entitled to a...hearing within a reasonable time". But it may be that the more widespread and more significant threat to the spirit of Article 6.1 emanates from these rules of the Committee of Ministers. Article 6.1 provides that "in the determination of his civil rights...everyone is entitled to a fair and public hearing...by an independent and impartial tribunal". What is fair about a procedure by which when you allege that a state has violated your fundamental freedoms your complaint is determined in the absence of either you or your lawyers, in private, with no guarantee that you will even be informed of the result, by a group of government representatives? The pervasive dilemma of statism may well rear its ugly head in the Commission and the Court, but it is nowhere more over-

---

[70] Emphasis added.

whelming, and yet nowhere more inappropriate, than in the Committee of Ministers.[71]

B. Where the Commission and the Committee of Ministers differ

In the vast majority of cases the Committee of Ministers will agree with the recommendations and opinions contained in the Commission's report. In 53 of the 147 resolutions adopted under Article 32 from the inception of the Convention until the end of 1992 the Committee of Ministers agreed with the Commission that there had been no violation of the Convention. In 83 cases the Committee of Ministers agreed with the Commission that the Convention had been violated. In none of the 147 resolutions did the Committee of Ministers find that there had been a breach of the Convention where the Commission had concluded in its report that there had been no violation. In the remaining cases the Committee of Ministers was unable (or unwilling) to make a determination either way as to whether there had or had not been a violation, and it is to these rare, but revealing instances that we now turn. They fall into two categories: cases involving individual applicants and inter-state applications.

As regards the first, in a small number of these cases there was no apparent reason explaining the Committee of Ministers' failure to make a final determination. In *Inhabitants of Les Fourons* v. *Belgium*,[72] the Committee of Ministers simply "took note" of the Commission's finding that there had been a breach of Article 2 of the First Protocol taken together with Article 14 without expressly agreeing or disagreeing with this finding. The Committee of Ministers concluded that no further action was required as Belgium had already addressed the language/schools problem through legislative and constitutional amendment. A similar instance is *Eggs* v. *Switzerland*[73] where the Commission found Article 5.1 to have been violated and the Committee of Ministers simply "took note" of this. Swiss law was later changed so as to bring it into compliance with the requirements of the

---

[71] An illustration of the differences in standing before the Committee of Ministers between individuals and states is resolution DH (82) 1 (*McVeigh, O'Neill and Evans* v. *UK*) where the Committee of Ministers' resolution contains a paragraph outlining the UK government's continued disagreement with the Commission's (and Committee of Ministers') view that Article 8 had been breached. While it is admittedly a rare occurrence for resolutions to include such statements, this is a reminder at least that states will always have the opportunity of making such statements even at this late stage, whereas the individual applicant never has such a chance.

[72] Resolution DH (74) 1; application 2209/64.

[73] Resolution DH (79) 7; application 9731/76.

Convention. Such cases are rare, and the behaviour of the Committee of Ministers, though unusual, does not appear to have significantly weakened the effectiveness of the Convention's protection of freedom.[74]

Aside from these exceptional cases, the main reason which may explain why the Committee of Ministers does not feel able to reach a final determination in these individual applications relates to the requirement that the Committee's decision as to whether there has or has not been a violation of the Convention must be reached by a two-thirds majority. If no such majority can be found among the Committee's membership, then no determination can be made. The rules adopted by the Committee of Ministers for the application of Article 32 prohibit the Committee from repeatedly delaying the determination of a case by reason of its failure to reach the required majority. Rule 9 *bis* states that "when a vote is taken in accordance with Article 32.1 and the majority required...has not been attained, a second and final vote shall be taken at one of the three following meetings of the Committee of Ministers". Failure to reach a two-thirds majority occurred in *Huber* v. *Austria*,[75] *Dores Silveira* v. *Portugal*,[76] *Dobbertin* v. *France*[77] and *Warwick* v. *UK*.[78] In all of these cases the Commission had found there to be a breach of the Convention. Presumably the Commission did not refer these cases to the Court because they were not regarded to be sufficiently difficult or controversial.[79] The Commission's general policy of not referring cases to the Court unless they are particularly controversial or call for the determination of issues which have not already been considered in the Court's jurisprudence is surely a sensible way of limiting the serious backlog facing the Court,[80] yet these cases show that where the Commission does not refer a

---

[74] There are two similar cases concerning Austria in each of which the Commission had found a violation of Article 6.1 but by the time the cases reached the Committee of Ministers the parties had reached friendly settlements and the Committee of Ministers therefore did not formally pronounce on whether it agreed with the Commission's finding of a violation: *P* v. *Austria* (resolution DH (91) 33, application 13017/87) and *Garzarolli* v. *Austria* (resolution DH (91) 34, application 12100/86).

[75] Resolution DH (75) 2, concerning Article 6.1.

[76] Resolution DH (85) 7, concerning Article 6.1.

[77] Resolution DH (88) 12, concerning Article 5.3.

[78] Resolution DH (89) 5, concerning Article 3.

[79] In all of these cases there were big majorities in favour of the findings of violations: eight to two in *Huber*, unanimous in *Dores Silveira*, ten with 1 abstention in *Dobbertin* and 12 to five in *Warwick*.

[80] Although it should be noted that such a policy does have the significant negative implication of denying an applicant his or her day in Court, and also results in considerably less

case to the Court, it cannot be sure that the Committee of Ministers will support the Commission's findings. It is a serious indictment of the mechanisms employed by the Strasbourg authorities to monitor compliance with the protections supposedly guaranteed by the Convention that even after an ostensibly judicial body finds that there has been a violation of the Convention, an overtly political body can then step in and effectively overturn this decision.

This is an embarrassment which the Council of Europe has endeavoured to remedy. There is now a Tenth Protocol to the Convention which when (or if) it comes into force will amend Article 32.1 by abolishing the requirement of a two-thirds majority. After the coming into force of this Protocol a straight majority (*i.e.* half of the members entitled to sit) will be sufficient. While there is no guarantee that even a straight majority will always be found, this amendment will hopefully reduce the number of occasions where the Committee of Ministers is able to thwart the will of the Commission. The amendment provided for in Article One of Protocol 10 was first mooted in 1982 in a meeting of the intergovernmental Committee of Experts for the Improvement of Procedures for the Protection of Human Rights. It took ten years for the Protocol to be adopted by the Committee of Ministers and opened for signature. The Protocol will not come into force until ratified by all the Convention's contracting states.[81]

Turning now to inter-state applications in which the Committee of Ministers has been unable or unwilling to make a final determination, we should note first that Article 32 makes no distinction between these and individual applications. As of the end of 1994 there had only been 12 inter-state applications. Of these 12, one was referred to the Court (*Ireland* v. *UK*), one ended in a friendly settlement (*Denmark, France, the Netherlands, Norway and Sweden* v. *Turkey*, an application introduced in 1982 and resolved in 1985), one was struck off the list (*Ireland* v. *UK (No 2)*, dating from 1972) and one has yet (as of December 1994) to be declared admissible by the Commission.[82] The remaining eight were dealt with by the Committee of Ministers under Article 32. These eight cases were *Greece* v. *UK (Nos. 1 and 2); Austria* v. *Italy; Denmark, Norway, Sweden and the Netherlands* v. *Greece (Nos. 1 and 2)* and *Cyprus* v. *Turkey (Nos. 1, 2 and 3)*. As with the cases where the Committee of Ministers failed to establish a two-thirds ma-

---

publicity surrounding any eventual finding of a violation.

[81] Article 3 of the Protocol.

[82] *Ireland* v. *United Kingdom* is at *op. cit.*, note 17. The case being considered for admissibility is Application No. 25781/94.

jority, these inter-state applications also showed the significant limitations of this aspect of the protection of freedom provided for in the Convention.

In the *Greece* v. *UK* cases, both of which concerned disputes over the British government's involvement in Cyprus, the Committee of Ministers did not adopt a resolution until after what it called the "final (*sic*) settlement of the Cyprus question", thus rendering Greece's application somewhat out of date. The Committee did not look into the allegations which had been made by the Greek government; nor did it examine the substance of the Commission's report. It simply stated that "no further action [was] called for", without making a final determination either way as to whether there had been a violation of the Convention.[83] The next inter-state application, *Austria* v. *Italy*, concerning Article 6, was not so controversial, as the Committee of Ministers merely agreed with the Commission, which had concluded in its report that Austria's application disclosed no breach of the Convention.[84] In what has become known as *The Greek case*,[85] four states brought applications in 1967 against Greece where it was alleged that Articles 5, 6, 8, 9, 10, 11, 13 and 14 of the Convention had been violated, and that these violations were not excused by any purported derogation under Article 15. Denmark, Norway and Sweden later extended their allegations to violations of Articles 3 and 7, and Articles 1 and 3 of the First Protocol. In its report, the Commission found that Greece had violated Articles 3, 5, 6, 8, 9, 10, 11, 13 and 14 of the Convention and Article 3 of the First Protocol and further that the measures Greece had taken were not justified under Article 15.

This case can be seen, therefore, as one of the most serious ever to have come to the attention of the Strasbourg authorities, with the Convention being comprehensively ignored by the Greek government. What then was the reaction of the Committee of Ministers? In 1970 the Committee of Ministers agreed with the opinion of the Commission as to the violations of the Convention and the First Protocol, but was impotent to do anything about it. The Greek government, declaring that it considered the Commission's report "null and void" refused to take part in the Committee of Ministers' discussions of the report, and expressed the view that such participation would be "inconsistent with Greece's formal denunciation of…the European Convention." It might have been thought that such a flagrant breach of Greece's in-

---

[83] Resolutions DH 59(12) (application 176/65) and DH 59(32) (application 299/57).

[84] Resolution DH 63(3) (application 778/60).

[85] *Denmark, Norway, Sweden and the Netherlands* v. *Greece* Resolutions DH 70 (1) and 74 (2).

ternational treaty obligations arising under the Convention would have resulted in significant action by the Committee of Ministers, but all it felt able to do was meekly to conclude that the circumstances of the case were "not precisely those envisaged in the Convention" and that there was therefore no basis for further action other than to make public the Commission's report, to urge Greece to restore human rights without delay and to follow developments in Greece. Four years later in 1974, after a change in government in Greece, the new government having applied for readmission to the Council, the Committee dropped the case. Perhaps as a question of international law or real politics there was very little that the Committee of Ministers could have done in the face of Greece's open hostility towards and contempt for the Convention, but the Committee of Ministers' response was nevertheless disappointing. There was no impassioned condemnation of what Greece had done; there was no departure from the Committee's customary diplomatic language—even when a member had left the club, the words remained polite and the cosy gathering of states never appeared too perturbed or shaken.

Finally, and perhaps most tellingly, in 1983 in *Cyprus* v. *Turkey (Nos. 1 and 2)* the Committee of Ministers agreed with the Commission that the Convention had been violated by the Turkish government in Cyprus, but instead of going on as it usually does to examine what the respondent state had already done, or proposed in the future to do about the violations, the Committee of Ministers then simply urged the parties to resume intercommunal talks under the auspices of the Secretary-General of the United Nations. This action (*i.e.* urging the parties to talk to each other) was considered by the Committee of Ministers to satisfy the requirements of Article 32. As Tomuschat has rightly observed,[86] the spirit of political mediation in which the Committee of Ministers dealt with these cases is wholly alien to the legal task entrusted to it under Article 32. It is also wholly alien to the spirit in which the Committee usually deals with complaints made by individual applicants. Talking diplomatically about talks, and taking note of human rights violations but doing nothing about them does not obviously accord with the Committee of Ministers' legal duties under Article 32.[87]

C. Delays—how long does it all take?

The serious problems of delay and backlogs facing the Commission and the Court have already been highlighted. The Committee of Ministers is also

---

[86] C. Tomuschat, *op. cit.*, note 68, at p. 402.

[87] Only in 1992 did the Committee of Ministers finally agree to order the Commission's report to be published: resolution DH (92) 12.

affected by these difficulties. Of the 147 resolutions made under Article 32 of the Convention between 1970 and 1992, 102 were made within two years of the date on which the Commission's report was transmitted to the Committee of Ministers. The norm is for the Committee of Ministers to have finished its consideration of a case between six and eighteen months after the Commission has transmitted its report. There are some cases where this period is considerably extended: in *Biondo* v. *Italy*,[88] for example, the Commission transmitted its report (in which it expressed the view that Article 6.3 of the Convention had been violated) in April 1984, yet the Italian government did not satisfy the Committee of Ministers that the necessary legislative amendments had been introduced until November 1989, some five and a half years later. Biondo's application had originally been made in 1979, so this case took a total of ten years to wind its way through the Strasbourg machinery.[89] Occasionally delays occur because the Committee of Ministers takes a particularly strong line on a case, as happened with a string of Italian cases concerning Article 6.1 in 1991–92. Here, the Committee of Ministers decided that the Italian government should pay the applicants as just satisfaction, but the Italian government refused. The Committee of Ministers decided to resume consideration of the cases at each forthcoming meeting until the applicants were properly paid, which they eventually were.[90]

D.   Remedies

Taking all 147 resolutions adopted by the Committee of Ministers under Article 32 of the Convention up until the end of 1992, the Convention was found to have been breached in 83 of these cases. In 36 of these cases some form of legislative change followed the Commission's and Committee of Ministers' findings.[91] In two cases the position was resolved by subsequent judicial decisions which meant that there was no perceived need for legisla-

---

[88]   Resolution DH (89) 30; application 8821/79.

[89]   Other instances of more than two years' delay between the Commission's report and the Committee of Ministers' final resolution include *Inhabitants of Les Fourons* v. *Belgium* (resolution DH (74) 1); *East African Asians* v. *UK* (resolution DH (77) 2); *T* v. *UK* (resolution DH (86) 12); *Savoldi* v. *Italy* (resolution DH (90) 11); *D* v. *Belgium* (resolution DH (91) 6); and *Azzi and others* v. *Italy* (resolutions DH (92) 45–50).

[90]   These cases are: *Azzi, Lo Giacco, Savoldi, Van Eesbeeck, Sallustio and Minniti* v. *Italy*, resolutions DH (91) 12, 13, 21, 22, 23, 24; (92) 2–7 and (92) 45–50.

[91]   In the term 'legislative change' I include regulatory and administrative amendment, as well as constitutional amendment and changes in primary legislation.

tive change.[92] In 36 cases financial compensation was awarded to the victims of the violation.

It is extremely difficult to analyse the effectiveness of the remedies which were awarded in these cases, as detailed knowledge of the background to and facts of the cases is required, as is some degree of expertise in the legal system of the country involved. This is just as true in cases where a legislative amendment ensues as it is where the victim is financially compensated. Is the new legislation in force? Does it effectively and fully cover all the points raised by the case? Is it in force in the entire country? Is there any guarantee that it will not be repealed? Is the compensation sufficient or will lawyers' fees and other associated costs swallow up the entire sum? Has the money been paid? Reading the texts of the Committee of Ministers' resolutions allows the researcher to answer few of these questions adequately. It all has to be taken on trust, which might lead the cynic to suspect that perhaps the Committee of Ministers itself takes these issues on trust from the governments concerned. There is little evidence to suggest that this does happen, but equally there is a stark absence of effective mechanisms to ensure that it cannot happen.

Certainly there are cases where suspicions might be raised, even on the scant information which the texts of the resolutions provide. Three examples should illustrate the kinds of ways in which some cases are perhaps less than satisfactorily resolved. In *Marijnissen* v. *The Netherlands*,[93] for example, the Commission and the Committee of Ministers found that Article 6.1 had been violated. The remedy provided for was that the sentence passed against the applicant during the defective judicial proceedings would not be executed. But there was no financial compensation here, and no apparent guarantee that it would not happen again. In *Neubeck* v. *Germany*,[94] which again concerned a breach of Article 6, the German government undertook to do no more than merely to inform the appropriate local authority (*Land*) that their action had given rise to a breach of the Convention. In *Grace* v. *UK*,[95] which concerned the violation of a prisoner's rights under Article 8 of the Conven-

---

[92] *Farrant and Five others* v. *UK* (resolution DH (87) 3) where the breach of Article 13 was met by the UK courts' decision in *Raymond* v. *Honey* [1983] 1 A.C. 1 and *Byrne and Four others* v. *UK* (resolution DH (87) 7) where the breach of Articles 6.1 and 8 were met in part by revised prison standing orders and in part by the decision in *R* v. *Secretary of State for the Home Department, ex parte Anderson* [1984] 1 All E.R. 920 (Q.B.D.).

[93] Resolution DH 85 (4), application 9193/80.

[94] Resolution DH 85 (8), application 9132/80.

[95] Resolution DH (89) 21, application 11523/85.

tion, the UK government explained to the Committee of Ministers how the violation had occurred due to a misapplication of the existing prison rules, and that "the necessary measures had been taken to ensure that the rules were correctly applied in the future". We are not, however, told what these measures are, and nor are we told whether the Committee of Ministers were told. No financial compensation was awarded, and the rules were not changed.

Financial compensation is provided for in the rules adopted by the Committee of Ministers for the application of Article 32. Rule 9(2) states that where the Committee of Ministers has found a violation, it "may request the Commission to make proposals concerning...the appropriateness, the nature and extent of just satisfaction". Paragraph 2 *bis* of the appendix to the rules provides that in every case where the Committee of Ministers has found a violation it "would consider, taking into account any proposals from the Commission, whether just satisfaction should be awarded to the injured party and, if necessary, indicate measures on this subject to the state concerned". As we have seen, a financial payment is not always awarded and the texts of the resolutions do not disclose the reasoning behind apparently inconsistent decisions in this regard. Why, for example was just satisfaction awarded in *Jesso* v. *Austria*[96] but not in *I and C* v. *Switzerland*[97] both of which concerned breaches of Article 6? Further, the amount of money awarded is not always especially generous: in *Manuel Mendes Godinho e Filhas* v. *Portugal*, for example, the princely sum of a "token" one escudo was awarded![98]

3. THE COMMITTEE OF MINISTERS AND THE COURT: ARTICLE 54

The Committee of Ministers' third function in respect of the Convention arises under Article 54. This Article governs the relationship between the Committee of Ministers and the European Court of Human Rights. Article 54 provides that "the judgment of the Court shall be transmitted to the Committee of Ministers which shall supervise its execution". Unlike the Commission's reports, the Court's judgments are binding on states without their first having to be confirmed by the Committee of Ministers: Article 52 states that "the judgment of the Court shall be final" and Article 53 provides that "High Contracting Parties undertake to abide by the decision of the

---

[96] Resolution DH (87) 4; application 9315/81.
[97] Resolution DH (86) 11; application 10107/82.
[98] Resolution DH (91) 36, application 11724/85.

Court in any case to which they are parties". Thus the role of the Committee of Ministers in relation to Court judgments is significantly different from its role with regard to reports of the Commission. The Committee of Ministers' consideration of the Court's judgments is far less extensive than its examination of cases under Article 32. Under Article 54 the Committee of Ministers does not make a final determination as to whether there has been a violation of the Convention, as the Court's judgment is final. While all Court judgments will be transmitted to the Committee of Ministers, it is only in respect of those judgments in which a violation of the Convention has been found that the Committee of Ministers will play any role.

But even though the role the Committee of Ministers plays under Article 54 is a comparatively limited one, it remains extremely important. The Committee of Ministers' responsibility to supervise the execution of the Court's judgments means that it is the Committee of Ministers which oversees the action taken by governments in response to a finding of a violation, and it is to the Committee of Ministers that such governments are accountable. As with resolutions adopted by the Committee of Ministers in the application of Article 32, Article 54 resolutions are also published from time to time by the Council of Europe's Human Rights Directorate. From the period starting with the inception of the Court's work until the end of 1992, 162 resolutions adopted under Article 54 have been published. As with all the other statistics concerning the work of the Strasbourg authorities under the European Convention on Human Rights, the number of cases considered by the Committee of Ministers under Article 54 has mushroomed in recent years. Nearly half (80) of the 162 resolutions were adopted in just the last three years (1990–92) of the period. In 1992 the Committee of Ministers concluded the examination of 38 cases dealt with under Article 54 and 60 new cases were brought before the Committee. At the end of 1992, 78 Article 54 cases were pending before the Committee.

The role of the Committee of Ministers under Article 54 is not as controversial as are its duties in respect of the Commission. The Committee of Ministers is not in a position to disagree with the judgment of the Court in the same way as it may differ from the opinion of the Commission. Judgments of the Court become binding without first having to be confirmed by the Committee of Ministers. But despite this, a study of the 162 resolutions adopted under Article 54 between 1972 and 1992 nevertheless reveals a number of significant features relating to the effectiveness of the Convention, which, as with the Committee of Ministers' role under Article 32, are not as widely known as perhaps they ought to be.

A. The position of the applicant

The controversial issue of the denial to individual applicants of standing before the Committee of Ministers under the rules adopted for the application of Article 32 was outlined above. This is a central concern in respect of Article 32 as the Committee of Ministers is charged under that provision with the judicial function of coming to a final determination as to whether there has been a violation of the Convention. Under Article 54, however, the Committee of Ministers' only role is to supervise the execution of the Court's judgment. No decision as to the merits of the applicant's allegations is made—as the Court has already done this (and the applicant will, it should be noted, have had the opportunity of making both oral submissions and written representations to the Court). Thus it is hardly surprising that there is no general provision for the individual applicants to have standing before the Committee of Ministers when it is exercising its functions under Article 54. There is no need for applicants to appear before the Committee of Ministers in this context. Paradoxically, however, in some cases an individual applicant may have better access to the Committee of Ministers in Article 54 examinations than he or she would have had with regard to Article 32, as the rules adopted by the Committee of Ministers for the application of Article 54 provide that "the Committee of Ministers is entitled to consider a communication from an individual who claims that he has not received damages in accordance with decision of the Court under Article 50…affording him just satisfaction as an injured party, as well as any further information furnished to it concerning the execution of such a judgment…".[99] There is no similar provision in the rules adopted in respect of Article 32.

B. Remedies

The primary focus of the Committee of Ministers' role under Article 54 is in ensuring that the appropriate remedies are put into effect by the state concerned. This is in practice what supervision of the execution of the Court's judgments means. Precisely what this will involve will vary widely from case to case. The most straightforward (and least controversial) cases are those in which the Court has ruled that the only remedy required is the payment of financial compensation as just satisfaction to the injured party. Here the Committee of Ministers simply has to ensure that the payment has

---

[99] Note to rule 2(a) of the rules adopted by the Committee of Ministers for the application of Article 54. The rules were adopted in 1976.

been made.[100] But very often a financial contribution will not of itself be deemed to be sufficient. Some kind of legislative, constitutional, administrative or regulatory amendment might also be required. Alternatively a simple change in practice might be necessary in order to comply with the Court's judgment. In other cases the circumstances which gave rise to the violation of the Convention in the first place may no longer exist—they may have been overtaken or rendered obsolete by subsequent governmental action or by judicial resolution. In all of these cases the Committee of Ministers will have to exercise considerable discretion in determining whether the measures taken (or promised) by the state concerned genuinely do meet all the requirements which follow from the Court's judgment.

In the 162 resolutions adopted by the Committee of Ministers under Article 54 until the end of 1992, money was paid by way of just satisfaction in 144 instances. In 52 of these instances, a financial payment was the only remedy. In 74 of these cases, the payment of money was accompanied by some kind of legislative or administrative change. In the remaining 18 cases where money was paid, this was accompanied by some additional remedy other than legislative amendment (such as judicial resolution). Some kind of legislative amendment was required in 83 cases. The issues were judicially resolved[101] in a total of 7 cases. As with the measures taken by states after the Committee of Ministers has found a violation of the Convention under Article 32.1, it is difficult to assess the effectiveness of the measures taken in response to judgments of the Court. The same problems arise in both

---

[100] Even this task, however, can on occasion prove to be more difficult than it should be. In the *Ringeisen* case Series A, No. 13 (1971) 1 E.H.R.R. 455, for example, the Austrian government was required to pay just satisfaction to Mr Ringeisen, but there was a problem in that he was a bankrupt. The question therefore arose as to whether the money should be paid to Ringeisen personally, or to his creditors. The Court initially left this question to be determined by the Austrian authorities, and the Committee of Ministers advised Ringeisen to submit an application for the money to the Regional Court in Vienna. Ringeisen refused to do this, however, apparently arguing that the Court intended the money to be paid to him personally. He then asked the European Commission for an interpretation of the Court's judgment (in accordance with the Rules of the Court) which they then provided. A further judgment of the Court then ensued, interpreting their earlier decision in Ringeisen's favour: Series A, No. 16 (1973) 1 E.H.R.R. 513. The Committee of Ministers was then able to dispose of the case when Austria paid the money to Ringeisen. All this took just over two years to be resolved: the original judgment of the Court being delivered in July 1971 and the final resolution of the Committee of Ministers eventually disposing of the case being adopted in October 1973. For details of the saga, see Robertson and Merrills, *Human Rights in Europe, op. cit.*, note 66, pp 341–342.

[101] Judicially resolved here means that the issues were resolved in cases heard by the domestic courts of the state concerned.

situations: the general absence of details in the texts of the resolutions; the difficulty in assessing the effectiveness of any action taken without a thorough understanding of the relevant state's political culture and legal system and the lack of information about the discussions which have taken place between the Committee of Ministers and the government concerned all combine to make any full analysis of this question extremely difficult.[102]

But again, as with the position with regard to Article 32, this does not mean that it is impossible to say anything at all, and some provisional views may be expressed even on the scant information available.[103] There are a number of cases where the Committee of Ministers appears not to have been especially strict with the state concerned, and where it might have been expected that more severe measures would have been deemed appropriate. One such instance is *Ireland* v. *UK*[104] where the Court had found that Article 3 had been violated. In the proceedings before the Committee of Ministers, the UK government's response to this ruling was to promise that the so-called "five techniques" which had given rise to the breaches of the Convention would no longer be used. But the undertaking of the UK government here took the form merely of a political promise[105]—there was no formal legal guarantee that the five techniques could not be re-employed. The Committee of Ministers decided that no further consequential measures needed to be taken in addition to these political promises. *Tyrer* v. *UK* is similar. Here the Court had found that the practice of birching which took place on the Isle of Man was in breach of Article 3. The action of the UK government in re-

---

[102] For an example of how significant these difficulties are, but how they may be overcome by commentators who have some expertise in a particular jurisdiction, see R. Churchill and J. Young, "Compliance with Judgments of the European Court of Human Rights and Decisions of the Committee of Ministers: The UK Experience, 1975–1987" (1991) 62 *British Yearbook of International Law* 283–346.

[103] Examples from the UK of cases where the Convention might be said to have been rather less than effective in its protection of individual liberty would include the *Malone* case (resolution DH (86) 1) which resulted in the Interception of Communications Act 1985 being passed—a piece of legislation which actually extends the circumstances in which the state may tap phones; and the *Abdulaziz* case (resolution DH (86) 2) where the UK decided to end discriminatory practices in the field of immigration not by improving the position of women, but instead by worsening that of men. For a general appraisal, see Gearty, below, Ch. 2.

[104] Resolution DH 78 (35).

[105] The information supplied by the UK government to the Committee of Ministers stated that the then Prime Minister, Edward Heath, had announced that the five techniques "would not be used in the future as an aid to interrogation". This was followed by a "solemn undertaking" by the Attorney-General to the same effect.

sponse to this judgment was simply to inform the Isle of Man authorities that birching was in breach of the Convention, and to ensure that all Isle of Man courts were made aware of this. As with the previous case, however, there was no formal legal guarantee that it would not happen again.[106] Other cases which have seen similar responses, of political promises without legal guarantees, include *Boyle and Rice* v. *UK*[107] and *Berrehab* v. *The Netherlands*.[108]

There are three cases involving Switzerland where a slightly unusual course was taken. These are *Minelli* v. *Switzerland*,[109] which concerned Article 6.2, *Zimmermann and Steiner* v. *Switzerland*,[110] which concerned Article 6.1 and *Schoenenberger* v. *Switzerland*,[111] which concerned Article 8. In these three cases the response of the Swiss government to the Court's findings of violations was not to change the relevant laws by way of legislative or administrative amendment. Instead the Committee of Ministers considered that it would be sufficient for the Swiss government simply to publicise the Court's judgment along with an outline of its reasoning in order that the relevant authorities could take the views of the European Court into account in future similar cases.[112]

Another way in which the actions of the Court and Committee of Ministers leave some cause for concern relates to those cases where it is decided that no remedy at all is required, and that just satisfaction is met simply by the finding of a violation and that no money need be paid the injured party. This occurred in *Deumeland* v. *Germany*,[113] *Benthem* v. *The Netherlands*,[114] *Huvig* v. *France*,[115] *Kruslin* v. *France*[116] and *Ezelin* v. *France*.[117] The respon-

---

[106] Resolution DH 78 (39). There is an even sorrier postscript to this story: after the *Tyrer* case had been finally disposed of, the UK government withdrew the Isle of Man from the jurisdiction of the European Convention. See P. Edge, "Dancing to the Beat of Europe" (1994) 144 *New Law Journal* 770.

[107] Resolution DH (88) 17.

[108] Resolution DH (89) 13. *Koster* v. *Netherlands* (resolution DH (92) 20) is similar. Here the Dutch authorities simply assured the Committee of Ministers that the case was exceptional and was very unlikely to recur.

[109] Resolution DH (83) 10.

[110] Resolution DH (83) 17.

[111] Resolution DH (89) 12.

[112] This also occurred in *Moustaquim* v. *Belgium* (resolution DH (92) 14), *Thorgeirson* v. *Iceland* (resolution DH (92) 59) and *Megyeri* v. *Germany* (resolution DH (92) 62).

[113] Resolution DH (87) 6.

[114] Resolution DH (88) 6.

[115] Resolution DH (92) 40.

sibility for this lies with the Court rather than the Committee of Ministers, but it can nevertheless be seen to represent a further limitation on the effectiveness of the Convention. It also serves as a reminder of the relatively weak position of the Committee of Ministers under Article 54. The Committee of Ministers enjoys no power to disagree with the view of the Court that there is no need for just satisfaction. This is one area where perhaps the inconsistency as between the Committee of Ministers' relations with the Commission on the one hand and the Court on the other could usefully be examined. A similar way in which the supposed role of the Committee of Ministers can be undermined or thwarted is through the controversial use of a state's ability to enter a derogation under Article 15. Among the more notorious examples of this practice is the sequel to the Court's decision in *Brogan* v. *UK*.[118] In this important case the Court found the UK to be in violation of Article 5 of the Convention with regard to the length of time that suspects could be (and were) kept in detention under the Prevention of Terrorism Act. In response to this judgment the UK government simply entered a derogation. The response of the Committee of Ministers was to state that by derogating from Article 5 the UK had effectively removed the case from the Committee of Ministers' jurisdiction under Article 54, as it was for the Court, not for the Committee of Ministers to consider the validity of any such purported derogation.[119]

The final set of cases which illustrate the weaknesses of the Committee of Ministers' function with regard to remedies under Article 54 are perhaps the most significant. In *Öztürk* v. *Germany*[120] and again in *F* v. *Switzerland*[121] the Committee of Ministers adopted interim resolutions which, while not finally disposing of the cases with which they were concerned, held them in abeyance and removed them for a certain time from the Committee's agenda. Rule 2(b) of the rules adopted by the Committee of Ministers for the application of Article 54 states that if in any case a government is unable or unwilling to take the measures necessary to meet the requirements of the Court's judgment, then that case will automatically fall to be reconsidered by the Committee within six months. The effect of this rule is that if a gov-

---

[116] Resolution DH (92) 41.

[117] Resolution DH (92) 41.

[118] *Op. cit.*, note 17.

[119] Resolution DH (90) 23. This derogation was later unsuccessfully challenged in *Brannigan and McBride* v. *UK, op. cit.*, note 17).

[120] Interim resolution DH (89) 8.

[121] Interim resolution DH (89) 9.

ernment fails to act promptly it will face repeated embarrassment before the Committee of Ministers, as the Committee will return to that case at least every six months. In an international environment such as the Council of Europe, where this kind of political embarrassment is often the only sanction available to bring a government into line with its international obligations, such a rule is essential if the work of the Committee of Ministers under Article 54 is to be at all effective. Yet despite this, the action of the Committee of Ministers in the *Öztürk* and *F* cases directly defeated this rule, and thus constituted a significant, self-inflicted, and wholly unnecessary limitation on the Committee's effectiveness in supervising the execution of the Court's judgments.

In *Öztürk*, which concerned a breach of Article 6.3, the German government explained to the Committee of Ministers that provisional legislation, which would come into effect by 1991, would meet the requirements set by the Court's judgment. The Committee of Ministers adopted an interim resolution in 1989[122] agreeing to suspend consideration of the case, but to resume examination of it in 1991, or earlier in the event that the legislation would come into force earlier than the German government then anticipated.[123] In *F*, which concerned a violation of Article 12, the Committee of Ministers allowed the Swiss government to follow a similar course. Here the Swiss government stated to the Committee that their provisional legislation would meet the requirements of the Court's judgment, but that it was not foreseen that this would come into effect until 1995: six years later, and eight years after the Court's judgment. Despite such a long delay, the Committee agreed to the temporary removal of the case from its agenda.

C. Delays and the length of proceedings

It has already been shown that one of the most significant limitations on the effectiveness of the protection of freedom under the Convention is the length of time it can take before a case is fully resolved. The problems of delay and of backlog are just as real with regard to the Committee of Ministers' role under Article 54 as they are for the Commission and the Court. The cases of *Öztürk* v. *Germany* and *F* v. *Switzerland*, considered above, can be criticised for the length of time it took them to be resolved as well as for

---

[122] Interestingly, this case had already been before the Committee of Ministers for five years: the Court had delivered its judgment in 1984. The question of delays and the length of proceedings is considered below, text at note 124 ff.

[123] In the event, the legislation actually came into force later in 1989, and the Committee of Ministers was able finally to dispose of the case: see resolution DH (89) 31. See below, Voss, pp. 161–163.

the Committee of Ministers' use of interim resolutions. The record length of time for a case to remain pending before the Committee of Ministers under Article 54 is just over eight and a half years. The Court's judgment in *Marckx* v. *Belgium* was delivered in June 1979. Belgium waited until March 1987 before it passed the required amending legislation. The Committee of Ministers adopted its final resolution in this case in March 1988.[124] The other cases which have remained before the Committee of Ministers for more than two years include: *Winterwerp* v. *The Netherlands*,[125] *Luedicke, Belkacem and Koc* v. *Germany*,[126] *Deweer* v. *Belgium*,[127] *Le Compte, van Leuven and De Meyere* v. *Belgium*,[128] *Campbell and Cosans* v. *UK*,[129] *Vallon* v. *Italy*,[130] *Can* v. *Austria*,[131] *Benthem* v. *The Netherlands*,[132] *Unterpertinger* v. *Austria*,[133] *X and Y* v. *The Netherlands*,[134] *Inze* v. *Austria*,[135] *Van Droogen-broeck* v. *Belgium*,[136] *Feldbrugge* v. *Netherlands*,[137] and *Ben Yaacoub* v. *Belgium*.[138]

Conclusion: Procedural Reform

Several themes and problems have been identified in the preceding analysis of human rights in the Council of Europe, and while there is no need to re-cite them all here, one in particular does demand further consideration. This is the growing problem of size—which as we have seen is leading to embar-rassing delays. This has become such a colossal problem that there is now a very real threat that the European Convention on Human Rights will become a victim of its own success. Catherine Lalumiere, Secretary-General of the

---

[124] Resolution DH (88) 3.
[125] Resolution DH (82) 2.
[126] Resolution DH (83) 4.
[127] Resolution DH (83) 16.
[128] Resolution DH (85) 13.
[129] Resolution DH (87) 9.
[130] Resolution DH (88) 4.
[131] Resolution DH (88) 5.
[132] Resolution DH (88) 6.
[133] Resolution DH (89) 2.
[134] Resolution DH (89) 3.
[135] Resolution DH (90) 21.
[136] Resolution DH (90) 31.
[137] Resolution DH (92) 8.
[138] Resolution DH (92) 58.

Council of Europe, has talked openly of this threat for some time: she told a conference in London in 1992 that "the machinery established by the European Convention...is in real danger of collapsing under the effect of the additional influx of applications".[139] The numbers continue to mushroom: during the 1970s the number of registered applications was on average 449 per year; during the 1980s this grew to 708 per year but in the first five years of the 1990s the average number per year has shot up to 2,029. Further, as more countries sign up to the Convention process, the size of both the Commission and the Court grows correspondingly (to a total of 32 judges on the Court by July 1995). This is all becoming too large and too unwieldy a process. Surely a less inefficient mechanism can be found, and should be found, before the Commission and Court lose the public esteem that they have so carefully striven to build up over the last decades. And, perhaps most significantly of all, surely the national governments who pay for the Council of Europe will soon realise how expensive this present machinery is becoming and will soon demand reform.

The vast increase in the number of cases coming before the Commission and Court obviously has great propaganda value, but it also increasingly signifies a worryingly long backlog of frustrated applicants and alarming delays. In *Tomasi* v. *France*, for example, a case concerning (among other things) a violation of Article 3, where it might have been thought that particularly speedy proceedings were called for, the Court delivered its judgment in August 1992. Tomasi's application to the Commission is dated March 1987; it was declared admissible in March 1990 and the Commission's report was published in December 1990. The relevant facts of the case commenced with Tomasi's initial arrest in March 1983. This scale of length of proceedings is representative of the current general picture. Yet a period of five and a half years from the registration of an application to the delivery of the Court's judgment can hardly be regarded as speedy. And things are gradually getting even worse! Drzemczewski has written that in 1992 it took an average of five years and six months for a case to be dealt with in Strasbourg, and an average of five years and eight months in 1993.[140]

---

[139] Statement of Catherine Lalumiere: "The Council of Europe in a Radically Changing Europe" at the European Movement's conference, *Europe—Where Does It End?* in London in October 1992. Issues of procedural reform are considered in more detail below. Similarly Andrew Drzemczewski has argued that "the credibility of what is perceived as the greatest ever achievement in the field of the international protection of human rights is at stake" (A. Drzemczewski, "Putting the European House in Order" (1994) 144 *New Law Journal* 644).

[140] Drzemczewski, *Ibid*, at p. 645.

A related problem is the ever growing backlog of cases. As of the end of 1994, for example, the number of cases pending before the Commission stood at 3,096. There are similar problems in respect of the Court: as of December 1993, a total of 447 cases had been referred to the Court, of which 57 were pending before it. Whereas up to 1988 there were never more than 25 cases referred to the Court in one year, 31 were referred in 1989, 61 in 1990 and 93 in 1991.[141]

The authorities in Strasbourg have long been aware of these problems, and high level discussions have been underway for over ten years with a view to reforming, cheapening, speeding up and streamlining the procedures. At least three different ideas have been floated. The first is that the present structure of having two separate bodies should be maintained, but that the secretariat should be beefed up so as to allow for cases to be more rapidly decided. The second idea is what is colloquially but inaccurately known as the merger option. This is that both the Commission and the Court would be abolished and replaced with a single, full-time tribunal. The third idea is that there should continue to be two bodies, but that one should be effectively full-time, with the other having a reduced role, being a Court of Appeal for particularly difficult or new or sensitive cases.

The Commission confirmed its (then) support for a single body as long ago as 1983. A Committee of Experts for the improvement of procedures for the protection of human rights was established, which reported to the Council of Europe's Steering Committee for Human Rights in 1989.[142] The Dutch and Swedish governments responded to the publication of the Committee of Experts' report by submitting their own alternative proposals. These proposals centred upon the suggestion that there should continue to be a two tier system, with a full time Court of First Instance and a part time Court of Appeal, for which leave to appeal would be required and to which only the parties could appeal (*i.e.* the first instance court could not). The views of the Commission, the Court and the Parliamentary Assembly of the Council of Europe were also sought and have now been published.[143] While the recommendation of the Parliamentary Assembly was that the Committee of Ministers should give preference to a single body, about two thirds of the Commission would have preferred a two tier system where members of both tiers

---

[141] This figure has, however, started to come down again (for the time being at any rate)—50 cases were referred to the Court in 1992 and 52 in 1993.

[142] This report, along with relevant accompanying documentation is reprinted at (1993) 15 E.H.R.R. 321–377.

[143] These are also reprinted at (1993) 15 E.H.R.R. 359, 363 and 366 respectively.

remained part time. The minority would have preferred more radical reform with the establishment of a single body. All seemed to agree that the role of the Committee of Ministers should be reduced. Opinions in the Court were split three ways: some would have maintained the status quo but improved working conditions; some would have preferred a two tier system along the lines of Dutch and Swedish proposals; and some felt that there should be a single body.

The debates now appear to be over—at least for the time being. October 1993 saw an unprecedented summit of the Heads of State of the members of the Council of Europe, in Vienna. At this summit it was agreed that the Convention machinery should, as matter of urgency, be reformed. In May 1994 Protocol No. 11 was formally opened for signature and ratification and when (or possibly if) this Protocol comes into effect (*i.e.* when ratified by all the member states of the Council of Europe) it will radically alter the make-up of the Council of Europe's human rights institutions. The new Protocol leaves the rights and freedoms set out in Articles 2–18 of the Convention unchanged, but completely transforms the rest of the Convention's provisions. The existing text of the Convention from Articles 19–56 is repealed and replaced. The present Commission and Court are both abolished and replaced by a new, permanent Court.

The new Court will consist of a number of judges equal to that of the High Contracting Parties. The judges will be appointed by the Parliamentary Assembly from a list of three candidates drawn up by the nominating state. The judicial term (which will be renewable) will be for six years, but there will be a (new) compulsory retirement age of 70 years. The Court will generally sit either as a Grand Chamber of seventeen judges, a Chamber of seven judges or a committee of three. The judge appointed to serve in respect of the state concerned in the case shall continue to be entitled *ex officio* to hear the case. There will continue to be an admissibility stage, and the admissibility criteria will remain unchanged. A committee of three judges may unanimously declare an application to be inadmissible—there will be no appeal against such decisions. If a committee cannot reach unanimity then questions of admissibility will be determined by a Chamber. Even if an application is initially declared to be admissible, it can later be thrown out as inadmissible: the Court may do this "at any stage of the proceedings" (new Article 35.4). Decisions as to the merits of cases deemed admissible will also generally be made by a Chamber. The intention is that only (rare) cases which raise serious questions affecting the interpretation of the Convention will fall to be heard by a Grand Chamber, although there is a provision (new Article 43) to the effect that any party to a case may in exceptional circumstances request that the case be referred to a Grand Chamber. If a request for a referral is made then the request will be reviewed by a panel of five judges.

Under the new arrangements, the role of the Committee of Ministers is to be reduced, but not altogether abolished. Its current role with regard to the Commission under Article 32 is abolished, but under the new regime it will continue to be responsible for supervising the execution of the Court's judgments. A further significant reform is the abolition of the current requirement that states periodically have to declare their recognition of an individual's right of petition (Article 25) and of the Court's jurisdiction (Article 46), both of which will be automatic under Protocol 11.

Thus, when/if the reforms contained in Protocol 11 come into effect it may be the case that they will go some way towards alleviating some of the concerns and criticisms identified in this chapter which at present detract from the effectiveness that might have been expected of the Council of Europe's human rights protection. However, this remains to be seen—and even on the most optimistic reading, such central issues as the pervasive dilemma of statism, the difficulties concerning non-appealable (but crucially important) admissibility decisions and the lack of democratic accountability, in terms both of appointments to and the representativeness of the Court, are set to remain for some time to come.

2. THE UNITED KINGDOM

Conor Gearty

Part I: General Constitutional Background

1. INTRODUCTION

The constitutional structure of the United Kingdom is unique in Europe in that it has been erected without the firm foundation of a written constitution. This is not to say that the nation's framework of government is an imagined construction, contrived on the basis of some ancient oral tradition rather than of law. Its constitution is largely composed of a range of written laws emanating from a variety of diverse sources such as the courts, the crown and the succession of parliaments that have governed the nation in its various constitutional incarnations as England and Scotland, Great Britain (from 1707) and the United Kingdom of first Great Britain and Ireland (from 1801), and latterly (since 1922) of Great Britain and Northern Ireland. Since the United Kingdom's entry into the European Communities in 1973, it has been appropriate also to add the Treaty of Rome to this list of sources, although the constitution in this context is naturally one that is shared with other nations. Far from having no written constitution, therefore, it could be said of Britain with more glibness than inaccuracy that it has a surfeit of written documents making up its constitution; that the uniqueness of its structure lies in too much rather than too little of that "written constitution" that is said so frequently to be absent.

Apart from this plethora of laws that makes up Britain's constitution, important clues to the nation's system of government are also to be found in the constitutional penumbra that lies between, on the one hand, the judicially enforceable requirements of the law, and on the other, the wholly unenforceable and merely transient dictates of political convenience. While it is true to say that no written constitution can remove entirely this penumbra, in which the constitution is guided more by the political morality of its principal actors than by law, it is equally clear that such non-legally enforceable rules of political obligation are far more likely to thrive in the empty spaces around an unwritten framework of government than they are when the whole

C. A. Gearty (ed.), European Civil Liberties and the European Convention on Human Rights, 53–103.

system is laid out in a fresh and ambitiously comprehensive manner, for all to see and for future generations diligently to follow. The United Kingdom's constitution is awash with such constitutional conventions.[1] It is claimed on behalf of these conventions that they are the main means by which Britain's constitution has been able to transcend its origins in the laws of a pre-democratic age, and been capable of continually restructuring itself so as to keep up with the changing wishes of successive generations.

It is the prevalence of these conventions that mainly explains why the constitution is so frequently described as "unwritten." They also provide a clue as to why the British framework of government should have remained uncodified for so long. Conventions are creatures of history, confirmed in their existence only with the passage of time and with an adherence to them that is initially volunteered by, and only much later required of, the nation's governing elite. There is therefore little room for constitutional conventions in a nation enervated by frequent forays into radical institutional change. The brief Cromwellian period apart, such revolutionary drives have not only been infrequent in England and later in Britain; they have barely existed at all. Among the states that are the subject of study in this book, indeed al-most uniquely among the modern nations of the world, the United Kingdom is alone in not having had any turning point in its history, any key moment on which the framework of government has thereafter ever rested. Britain has been neither colonised[2] nor defeated in war like Germany and Italy.[3] Nor has it been the subject of a massive, ideologically driven internal revolt like France.[4] Without the impetus of invasion, defeat or revolution, the nation has at no point in its modern history felt the need to reconstruct itself radi-cally, to build a new constitutional home on fresh institutional foundations. A consequence of this stability as a nation has been the stasis of its consti-tution. To the extent that there has been any radical change in the modern

---

[1]   E. C. S. Wade and A. W. Bradley, *Constitutional and Administrative Law*, 11th ed. by A. W. Bradley and K. D. Ewing (London, 1993), pp. 19–36.

[2]   For Ireland's constitutional framework, see Flynn below, ch. 5. After the Act of Union in 1800, Ireland became part of the Kingdom itself rather than a colony of the UK as a whole. Uniquely among those places settled by Britain therefore, it was (at least from 1801) part of the settler nation rather than a subjugated region governed by it. This did not stop the development in the 19th and 20th centuries of an Irish revolutionary tradition which saw the problem of Ireland in colonial terms as one of British domination.

[3]   For the constitutional structures of which see respectively Voss, below, ch. 4 and Leon-ardi, below, ch. 8.

[4]   See Steiner, below, ch. 7.

era, it has (with the one Cromwellian exception in England[5]) been driven not by a vision of the future but rather by a militant memory of a better past. To the extent that it has existed at all, English constitutional radicalism has been rooted more in nostalgia than in ideology.

2. THE DEVELOPMENT OF THE ENGLISH CONSTITUTION

Exposition of the constitutional structure of the United Kingdom more resembles an archaeological excavation than a learned exegesis on a basic framework of government. Each layer of history has added its own contribution to what has gone before. What appears on the surface today can only be understood by knowing what lies beneath. There is no bottom layer. Even the pre-Norman Anglo-Saxon period has given England many of its county boundaries and the title of one of its still extant local functionaries.[6] In the 150 years that followed the Norman conquest in 1066, England saw the gradual emergence of an executive branch of government, in the form of the crown assisted by the *curia regis*, a body composed of advisers (including the lord chancellor and the chancellor of the exchequer) drawn from the king's tenants in chief. As early as the twelfth century, during the reign of Henry II, the rudiments of an independent judiciary were put in place with the evolution into separate courts of parts of that same *curia regis* and with the inclination of those who heard such cases to articulate a body of law by which later jurists considered themselves to be bound.[7] Under the same monarch, the system whereby the king's justice was administered on a local basis by itinerant justices was put in place, as was the beginning of what was to become known as jury trial; each has survived the centuries to stand today as two of the linchpins of Britain's administration of justice. Equally durable, but more anachronistic, is the title of knight, once descriptive of those prepared to do battle on behalf of the king,[8] but now just another of the

---

[5] Even the movement for electoral reform in the 19th century which was so instrumental in the democratisation of Britain was not consciously revolutionary in its ideology.

[6] The sheriff.

[7] Glanville's *Treatise on the Laws and Customs of the Kingdom of England* dates from this period. For extracts see D. C. Douglas and G. W. Greenaway (eds.), *English Historical Documents, 1042–1189*, 2nd ed. (London, 1981), p. 495 ff.

[8] See the military summons probably dating from about 1072 translated from the original Latin in *ibid.*, p. 960: "William, king of the English, to Aethelwig, abbot of Eversham, greeting. I order you to summon all those who are subject to your administration and jurisdiction that they bring before me at Clarendon on the octave of Pentecost all the knights they owe me duly equipped. You, also, on that day, shall come to me, and bring with you fully equipped those five knights which you owe me in respect of your abbacy.

vast sources of patronage enjoyed by a contemporary British prime minister. Other honorific relics of bygone eras include the lord lieutenancies and high sheriffs of county administration. Under Britain's unwritten constitution, it is not only the useful that survives.

Magna Carta is of crucial importance to the growth of the English constitution not so much because of its precise content as because of its occurrence and the fact (even more important) that it was never forgotten. Only a few of its clauses speak a constitutional language recognisable today. The commitment to "the lawful judgment of [a freeman's] peers" in clause 39 and the ringing assurance in clause 40, that "To no one will we sell, to no one will we deny or delay right or justice", are very much exceptions rather than the rule. But shining through the otherwise generally archaic language of feudal rights and narrow vested interests reluctantly agreed to by King John at Runnymede on 15 June 1215 is the dramatic assertion that henceforth in England no man, not even a monarch, can claim to be above the law. Already clear is the propensity of the English constitution to camouflage the full power of an enunciated principle with practical matters and to present radical change as a commitment to the past rather than as part of a vision for the future. Even if they could have articulated it, those who gathered at Runnymede would have shown no interest in anything so grand as a new constitution. It was not a new king that they wanted, merely adherence to the ways of his predecessors.

It was also pragmatism rather than principle that underpinned the development of parliament in the latter half of the thirteen century. The king having been prevailed upon to summon a gathering of persons drawn on a representative basis from the shires and the boroughs, it was thought appropriate to describe the group in terms which reflected its function as what would in modern terms be called a "talking shop". The French verb *parler*, to speak, provided the basis for the descriptive label that quickly took hold, and parliaments became frequent events towards the end of the thirteenth century. The representative principle was evident from the start, with shires and recognised boroughs all sending their people to reflect their interests. Initially, these gatherings dealt with judicial as well as political matters, though the effectiveness of the law courts meant that it was the latter rather than the former function that quickly became predominant. During the two hundred years of war and civil war that marked the 14th and much of the 15th centuries in England, parliament survived as an institution, meeting occa-

---

Witness Eudo the steward. At Winchester."

sionally, frequently treated as a pawn in this or that side of a dispute, but growing in stature through the respect that gradually came with familiarity.

In the social and political revolution that was the mark of the Tudor period (1485–1603), such strong monarchs as Henry VIII and Elizabeth I achieved their ambitions not in defiance of but rather in partnership with the parliaments that they chose (invariably for tactical reasons) to summon. The first of the monarchs mentioned above pushed through his break with the Roman church via the famous Reformation Parliament (1529–1536), through which were promulgated many of his most important and far reaching reforms such as the Act of Ecclesiastical Appeals, passed in 1532 and the Act of Supremacy, enacted in 1534. Elizabeth also developed her religious policies by means of parliament, principally through the Act of Supremacy and the Act of Uniformity, both passed in 1558, in the first parliament of her reign. By the end of the Tudor period, therefore, England enjoyed what could be described without too much historical crudity as a strong and independent judiciary, a tradition of representative government and a monarch inured to the management of far-reaching executive power in a way which recognised the existence of other centres of power in the state.

This was the constitutional harmony that the Stuart monarchs, successors to the Tudors, quite consciously desired to destroy in the seventeenth century. Already ruler of the separate and independent nation of Scotland when he came into his English inheritance in 1603, James I and afterwards his son Charles I sought to model their new nation's government on a basis that was both more European and more respectful of a monarch's divine right than had previously been the case. This led to a calamitous civil war and a brief period without a monarch (the Cromwellian period, referred to above) before the Stuarts were restored in 1660, only for a later member of the same family, James II (son of the executed Charles I), to be driven from the country in 1688, after his reign had threatened to drift back towards the style of his father and grandfather, a manner that had been carefully avoided during the twenty-five years that his brother, Charles II, had reigned following his return to England at the head of the revived Stuart dynasty twenty-eight years before. The details of the century's struggles are long and complex, but out of it was forged a constitution that both respected its Tudor past and was sufficiently flexible subsequently to be able to evolve without further military turmoil into the United Kingdom constitution of today.

The victory represented by the forced removal of James II in 1688 was unequivocally that of parliament, and it was achieved over two forces, those of the crown and those (jurisprudential in nature) of the courts. As far as the first of these was concerned, the seventeenth century had been a series of thrusts and counter-thrusts between successive Stuart monarchs and their legislative assemblies. In the Petition of Right, addressed to "the King's most excellent majesty" in 1627,[9] parliament inveighed against such perceived abuses as taxation without the consent of parliament, the forcing of soldiers into private homes and the misuse of executive powers in respect of martial law. Quoting from *Magna Carta* and later legislative acts, parliament "most humblie pray[ed] of your most excellent Majestie" that he respect "their rights and liberties according to the lawes and statutes of this realme". Charles I's response was both to accept the petition but shortly afterwards to dissolve parliament, thereby inaugurating an eleven year period during which he contrived to rule on the basis of his royal prerogative alone. As his reign lurched towards civil war, however, he found himself forced again to summon a parliament, only to dissolve it after a mere five weeks when it proved less friendly than he had hoped. This was hardly a decision of strategic value, and inevitably he was forced to make compromises with a later assembly called almost immediately afterwards under duress of circumstances, when the continuing turmoil in the kingdom made essential the kind of financial support that in England only parliament could efficiently provide.

The first few years of this "Long Parliament" (as it came to be called) were a success, with the monarch and his parliament slowly feeling their way towards a consensus. Had the divisive intensities of rival religious tenets not then intervened, it is even possible that the Stuart kings would in the 1640s have accepted (or been forced relatively peacefully to accept) the evolution of the English system of government away from divine right and absolute monarchical sovereignty and back towards the Tudor model, albeit with a stronger parliament and a weaker crown. By 1642, the Long Parliament had abolished the special courts set-up by the crown and the extra-parliamentary taxes devised by it and had established that parliaments should thenceforth be held regularly and should not be dissolved without their consent. But it could not resist also issuing the Grand Remonstrance, a savage attack on papist influences in government. By the time of Charles' answer to another document from parliament, the Nineteen Propositions, which he delivered on 21 June 1642, it was already too late implicitly to reject divine right by accepting that "[i]n this kingdom the laws are jointly made by a king, by a House of Peers, and by a House of Commons, chosen by the people, all having free votes and particular privileges."[10] The theory

---

[9] 3 Car. I, c. 1.

[10] See R. L. Schuyler and C. C. Weston, *Cardinal Documents in British History* (Princeton,

of mixed government expounded in this paper came into its own only with the restoration of the monarchy, but in this latter era it was always implicit that parliament was the dominant partner.

This fact was made brutally clear by the physical expulsion of James II in 1688, an action afterwards justified by the following resolution carried by the "Convention" Parliament which had been "summoned" in pseudo-royal style by parliament's triumphant military commander, William of Orange:

> That King James II, having endeavoured to subvert the constitution of his kingdom by breaking the original contract between the king and people; and by the advise of Jesuits and other wicked persons, having violated the fundamental laws; and having withdrawn himself out of the Kingdom, has abdicated the Government; and that the throne is thereby vacant.[11]

Never has a revolution tried so hard to present itself as little more than a conservative return to the status quo. Despite such rhetoric, it was clear that parliament's position had immeasurably strengthened in the half century between 1640 and 1690. The reality of its new sovereign power was hammered home in the Bill of Rights Act 1688,[12] which despite its apparently modern name is a document largely concerned with establishing conclusively the rights of parliament vis-à-vis the new royal dispensation. Having given the necessary assurances, William of Orange was selected as monarch in partnership with his wife, Mary, whose great virtue from the perspective of these still reluctant revolutionaries was that she was the daughter of the disgraced James. In 1701, however, parliament ignored the Stuart family entirely when it settled the succession to the throne on the family of the Protestant Electress Sophia of Hanover.[13] The last vestiges of the theory of divine right were thereby jettisoned in favour of the new orthodoxy of parliamentary sovereignty.

Parliament's victory over the courts was as conclusive as its triumph over the monarchy, and the results of this second seventeenth century dispute reverberate today with as much force as the battles fought against the crown. Early in the reign of James I, the question of the legality of the king's power to issue proclamations fell to be decided by the chief justice Sir Edward Coke and his colleagues on the bench. In an important statement of principle, Coke declared that the "King by his proclamation cannot create any offence which was not an offence before" and that he had "no prerogative but

---

New Jersey, 1961), p. 80.

[11] See S. B. Chrimes, *English Constitutional History*, 3rd ed. (London, 1965), at p. 162.

[12] 2 Will. and Mary, c. 1.

[13] 12 and 13 Will. III, c. 2.

that which the law of the land allow[ed] him."[14] This clear reaffirmation of the powers of parliament and the courts as against those of the monarch did not fit with the Stuart view as to the exercise of royal power and shortly afterwards Coke was peremptorily dismissed from the bench. This case was exceptional; throughout most of the century, the courts gave their support to royal rather than parliamentary interpretations of the extent of executive power. Three cases may be given by way of example. In the *Case of Impositions*,[15] John Bate refused to pay a duty on an imported product on the basis that the duty was contrary to statute. The Court of Exchequer unanimously found for the crown, holding that the king had a total discretion as to the imposition of duties for the regulation of trade and that the court had no power to scrutinise his statement that this was the purpose of the tax.[16] In the *Case of Ship Money*,[17] the king claimed a prerogative right to raise funds without the authority of parliament to meet a national emergency, the existence and extent of which he claimed to be the sole judge. The Court of Exchequer Chamber found by a majority in his favour.[18] Finally in *Godden* v. *Hales*,[19] a wide power claimed by James II to dispense with certain Acts of Parliament was upheld by the courts, and this precipitated the wholesale suspension of legislation which was the immediate cause of the revolution of 1688. Not surprisingly therefore, the Bill of Rights Act, like much of the legislation of the Long Parliament forty years before, was intent on overturning these judicial legitimisations of royal power.

The parliamentary triumph of these years was therefore achieved in the teeth of judicial as well as of royal objections. A lasting effect of this was a deep mistrust on the part of parliament about the exercise of judicial power, particularly as far as its own sovereignty was concerned. The judges also learned the lesson of 1688; though given security of tenure in the Act of Settlement in 1701, it was to be three hundred years before a court again dared to flout an Act of Parliament, and this occurred only because it could by then be said that parliament had consciously subjugated itself to the will

---

[14]   (1611) 12 *Coke Reports* 74.

[15]   (1606) 2 *State Trials* 371.

[16]   See G. D. G. Hall, "Impositions and the Courts 1554–1606" (1953) 69 *Law Quarterly Review* 200.

[17]   *R.* v. *Hampden* (1637) 3 *State Trials* 825.

[18]   See D. L. Keir, "The Case of Ship-Money" (1936) 52 *Law Quarterly Review* 546.

[19]   (1686) 11 *State Trials* 1165. *Cf. Thomas* v. *Sorrell* (1677) *Vaughan* 330.

of another judicial body entirely, the Court of Justice of the European Communities.[20]

3. THE SLOW DEMOCRATISATION OF THE ENGLISH CONSTITUTION

By the end of the first decade of the 18th century, the legal facade of Britain's contemporary constitution was more or less firmly in place. This was particularly the case after the union between England and Scotland in 1707 had formally created the new nation of Great Britain. Like the parliaments that had existed in England for over four hundred years before it, the first assemblies in this post-revolutionary state were constructed on the representative principle but on the basis of an extremely restricted franchise. This gradually changed in the nineteen and early twentieth centuries, when a series of extensions to the franchise were enacted by successive parliaments. The most famous change occurred in the Great Reform Act in 1832 though Disraeli's later legislation in 1867 was wider in its impact. After the first world war, a uniform franchise based on residence was established for both county and borough constituencies, and the same year saw the extension to women over 30 of the right to vote, with this age limit being reduced to 21 in 1928. By this latter year therefore it was finally right to categorise Britain's constitution as being based on universal mass suffrage.[21] These changes had been achieved without revolution, though political protest, violent subversion and the fear of revolution had all played a part in forcing the old order to yield.

Parliament was also instrumental in protecting that other right so basic to popular movements in a democracy, the freedom to associate. Here, the absence both of a written constitution and of judicial supremacy turned out to be vital. In 1871, the Gladstone administration's Trade Union Act protected unions from the consequences of an earlier court ruling which had "effectively classed trade unions as outlaws, unable to recover funds which had been misappropriated by members."[22] An even more vital later piece of legislation enacted in 1913 reversed an earlier House of Lords' decision

---

[20] See *R. v. Secretary of State for Transport, ex parte Factortame Ltd.* [1990] 2 A.C. 85. On 10 March 1989, the High Court disapplied Part II of the Merchant Shipping Act 1988, pending a ruling from the E.C.J. to which it referred the case under the Article 177 procedure.

[21] Note however that some plural voting lingered on until 1948.

[22] K. D. Ewing, "Freedom of Association" in C. McCrudden and G. Chambers (eds.), *Individual Rights and the Law in Britain* (Oxford, 1994), p. 242, citing *Hornby v. Close* (1867) L.R. 2 Q.B. 153.

which had declared it unlawful for trade unions to use their funds to finance the Labour Party.[23] The combination of electoral reform and the growth of trade unions made possible the emergence in 1924 of a socialist government in a constitutional system designed for the needs of a landed aristocracy a century before the industrial revolution.

Apart from these legislative reforms, the other way in which the British constitution radically changed in the years after 1700 lay in the realm of conventions. At first glance the monarch still appeared to enjoy a plenitude of executive power even after his or her legislative role had been emasculated by the 1689 revolution. The monarch retained the legal power to veto bills which had passed both Commons and Lords. He or she could in law appoint what ministers of the crown he or she desired, and get rid of them whenever it was thought convenient. Each session of parliament was still initiated by a queen's or a king's speech in which the monarch could in legal theory set out his or her intentions for the upcoming parliamentary year. Clearly none of this could be compatible with the modern democratic state which the legislation described above was instrumental in achieving. In fact, none of these legal powers has altered, but the manner of their exercise has come to be governed by constitutional conventions so firm that the fact that they are unwritten has become an irrelevance.

First, there is a conventional rule that the royal assent to bills is granted on the advise of ministers. This means in practice that it is never withheld, regardless of how distasteful the monarch finds the measure that he or she is being asked to enact. The last occasion of such a refusal, and it appears to have been non-controversial, was the Scottish Militia Bill in 1708.[24] Secondly, the monarch will now always appoint a prime minister, and is duty bound by convention to accept his or her advise as to the appointment of other ministers. These ministers must by convention be drawn from one or other of the houses of parliament, a requirement which has developed as a means of ensuring the effective exercise of the convention of ministerial responsibility. The first holder of the office of prime minister is generally considered to have been Sir Robert Walpole, whose long grip on power between 1721 and 1742 more or less invented the post. Walpole was a member of the House of Commons and though there have been prime ministers drawn from the House of Lords (the last such being Lord Salisbury who left office in 1902), it is now the invariable rule that the holder of the office

---

23 *Amalgamated Society of Railway Servants* v. *Osborne* [1910] A.C. 87.
24 For George V's reluctance to sign the Irish home rule bill in 1914, see V. Bogdanor, *The Monarchy and the Constitution* (Oxford, 1995), pp. 122–135.

must be not only a member of parliament (which has always been the case) but also that he or she be a member of the lower house. This is to facilitate a third fundamental conventional rule, which is that the monarch is duty bound to appoint as prime minister the person whose administration will be or is likely to enjoy the confidence of the Commons. As Bogdanor points out, this "can mean either that a government commands the *positive* support of a majority in the Commons; or that there is no majority in the Commons *against* it."[25] With the development of the party system, it has usually been a straightforward question for the monarch as to which leader of which party should after an election, be asked to form an administration. That there will inevitably be uncertainty where no party has an overall majority in the lower house is a problem that has to be resolved by all systems of parliamentary democracy, and is not a peculiarity of Britain's unwritten constitution.

4.   THE PLACE OF HUMAN RIGHTS

The effect of these legislative and conventional developments has been to transform the content if not the apparent structure of the British constitution. Glaringly missing from the framework so far described is any commitment to "human rights". The English revolution of 1688 came too early for any such notion to have been embraced by the designers of this new constitutional order. The victory over the king was to be enjoyed by parliament, not the people. The threat that parliamentary sovereignty obviously posed for freedom and for liberty was to some extent met by the development of a parallel commitment to "the rule of law". The concept is best explained in the work of the influential Victorian jurist A. V. Dicey, for whom it involved three propositions: first, that "no man [was] punishable or [could] be made to suffer in body or goods except for a distinct breach of law established in the ordinary legal manner before the ordinary courts of the land"; secondly, "not only that no man [was] above the law, but (what is a different thing) that here every man, whatever be his rank or condition, [was] subject to the ordinary law of the realm and amenable to the jurisdiction of the ordinary tribunals"; and thirdly, that "the general principles of the constitution (as for example the right to personal liberty, or the right of public meeting) are with us as the result of judicial decisions determining the rights of private persons in particular cases brought before the courts."[26]

---

[25]   *Ibid.*, p. 151. Emphasis in the original.

[26]   A. V. Dicey, *An Introduction to the Study of the Law of the Constitution*, 10th ed. with an introduction by E. C. S. Wade (London, 1959), at pp. 188, 193 and 195.

This has long been the basis on which "human rights", or more accurately civil liberties and fundamental freedoms, are said to have been protected in Britain. Such rights have not been so much guaranteed by statute as allowed to exist merely because no law has prohibited them. It is a negative version of rights, viewing them as residual liberties rather than as positive entitlements. Dicey's confidence in the quality of the constitution he was describing was rooted in his belief that the concentration of British law on remedies protected the nation from the risk of European excess. There was, he wrote, "in the English constitution an absence of those declarations or definitions of rights so dear to foreign constitutionalists", but this meant that "the suspension of the constitution, as far as such a thing can be conceived possible, would mean with us nothing less than a revolution" whereas the "general rights guaranteed by the constitution may be, and in foreign countries constantly are, suspended."[27] There was an obvious complacency in the whole Dicey perspective even when he was completing, in 1885, his first edition of *An Introduction to the Study of the Law of the Constitution*. For example, it was already clear that the cases he cited in support of his thesis that the British constitution permitted freedom of assembly were easily contradicted by repressive decisions from Ireland[28] and the trade unions were hardly likely to have been persuaded by his profoundly narrow, anti-collectivist version of freedom at a time when the judiciary were waging civil war on their whole existence.

In the generations after Dicey, his version of the constitution has become ever more influential while, paradoxically, it has moved further than ever from reality. The first world war saw the enactment of the defence of the realm legislation, with a draconian and anti-libertarian power of regulation being given to the executive for its duration and for some years after its practical conclusion. The social disorder that followed the war was greeted with further repressive law, this time in the form of the Emergency Powers Act, 1920, invoked twice during this period, first in 1920 and secondly during the general strike in 1926. In the 1930s, the disorder that flowed from the depression led not to special emergency legislation but to the normalisation of emergency powers via case law[29] and statute.[30] The second world war followed with, inevitably, further draconian legislation and great diminution

---

[27] *Ibid.*, at pp. 197, 202 and 200.

[28] See in particular *O' Kelly* v. *Harvey* (1883) 15 *Cox Criminal Cases* 435.

[29] See in particular *Elias* v. *Passmore* [1934] 2 K.B. 164; *Thomas* v. *Sawkins* [1935] 2 K.B. 249 and *Duncan* v. *Jones* [1936] 1 K.B. 218.

[30] See in particular the Incitement to Disaffection Act 1934 and the Public Order Act 1936.

of liberty.[31] Meanwhile throughout this period, Northern Ireland was governed under the extraordinarily harsh regime of special powers introduced as almost the first act of the Northern Ireland government established within the United Kingdom by the Government of Ireland Act 1920.[32]

It may be thought surprising, therefore, that the signing of the European Convention on Human Rights at Rome in 1950 provoked no soul-searching on the part of British officials or scholars as to the inadequacy (or even the non-existence) of the United Kingdom's protection of rights. On the contrary, there was a strong sense that the British system had come through a turbulent half century in better shape than almost all its continental partners, and this was of course largely true. While many of the restrictions on freedom described above had been aimed at organised labour and at socialism in general, the United Kingdom was in 1950 being governed by a Labour administration which had already been in power for five years. Universal suffrage seemed to have delivered the sort of administration that some of its members may have felt it had been at least partly the purpose of earlier repressive laws to prevent. Furthermore, Labour was mistrustful of the language of rights, feeling that too close an alignment of domestic law with the European Convention might have hindered its radical agenda by erecting judicial barriers to further progress.[33]

Part II: The Status of the European Convention on Human Rights in UK Law

1. THE LEGAL AND POLITICAL BACKGROUND

Being a dualist state, the ratification of the European Convention by the United Kingdom government did not have the effect of making that Convention part of UK domestic law. Despite being the first state to ratify the treaty, Britain felt under no political pressure to take this extra step, and nor did the Conservative administration that had taken over from Labour by the

---

[31] The most famous decision from the period is *Liversidge* v. *Anderson* [1942] A.C. 206. See generally A.W.B. Simpson, *In the Highest Degree Odious: Detention without Trial in Wartime Britain* (Oxford, 1992).

[32] Civil Authorities (Special Powers) Act 1922 (Northern Ireland) and regulations made thereunder.

[33] For the general background, see G. Marston, "The United Kingdom's Part in the Preparation of the European Convention on Human Rights, 1950" (1993) 42 *International and Comparative Law Quarterly* 796.

time the Convention entered into force in 1953.[34] The ECHR was slow to fire the legal or political imagination. In the fifteen years that followed ratification, only international lawyers gave the Convention much attention, with a conference held under the auspices of the British Institute of International and Comparative Law in London in November 1965 being the highlight of an otherwise relatively barren period.[35] Recognition of the right of individual petition, which took effect on 14 January 1966, produced a flicker of interest in the periodical literature,[36] but little notice was taken of the possible implications for the domestic legal system.[37] This academic neglect of the Convention on the part of domestic constitutional scholars was hardly surprising. The 1960s can be seen in retrospect as the heyday of parliamentary sovereignty, when a series of legislative reforms both by private members[38] and (after 1964) by Mr. Wilson's new Labour administration[39] appeared to confirm the elected chamber as the centre of the political life of the nation. It was during this period that Ungoed-Thomas J. declared in a well-known dicta that "What [a] statute itself enacts cannot be unlawful, because what the statute says and provides is itself the law, and the highest form of law that is known to this country."[40] This was only the most forthright of numerous judicial interventions to the same effect.[41]

A change in the approach to the ECHR began gradually to occur in the late 1960s and continued throughout the 1970s. The new interest came from three sources in particular. First, the scholarly literature on the subject grew in volume and quality, and with it came a new awareness of the domestic legal implications of the Convention and the Convention organs. This trend

---

[34] *Ibid.* See also A. Lester, "Fundamental Rights: the United Kingdom Isolated" [1984] *Public Law* 46.

[35] The conference proceedings were published as an *International and Comparative Law Quarterly* supplementary publication, no. 11, London, 1965.

[36] See K. R. Simmonds, "The United Kingdom and the European Convention on Human Rights" (1966) 15 *International and Comparative Law Quarterly* 539.

[37] A notable exception was R. Beddard, "The Status of the European Convention of Human Rights in Domestic Law" (1967) 16 *International and Comparative Law Quarterly* 206. See also United Kingdom Committee for Human Rights Year, *Human Rights: A Study Guide for the International Year for Human Rights, 1968* (London, 1967).

[38] For example the Abortion Act 1967, sponsored by David Steel, MP.

[39] See in particular the Race Relations Act 1965.

[40] *Cheney* v. *Conn* [1968] 1 All E.R. 779, at p. 782.

[41] The case-law from the period, together with its origins in the nineteenth century decisions, is conveniently gathered in the leading House of Lords' decision of *Pickin* v. *British Railways Board* [1974] A.C. 765.

was already discernible in 1968, with D. R. Gilmour's important article reviewing the compatibility with the ECHR of the Iron and Steel Act 1967,[42] and with Anthony Lester's intensely original and brilliantly argued Fabian tract, *Democracy and Individual Rights*.[43] In submitting the case for a domestic bill of rights in the latter pamphlet, Lester suggested that it "would be a considerable advance even if the Bill did no more than incorporate the provisions of the European Human Rights Convention directly into English law."[44] This was one of the central, albeit still slightly oblique, arguments of the immensely influential twenty-sixth series of Hamlyn lectures delivered in December 1974 by the distinguished High Court judge Sir Leslie Scarman. In the context of analysing the "human rights movement" as part of the "challenge from overseas" that was facing English law, Scarman argued unequivocally for "entrenched or fundamental laws protected by a Bill of Rights—a constitutional law which it [would be] the duty of the courts to protect even against the power of Parliament."[45] With the United Nations Declaration of Human Rights, the European Convention reflected "a rising tide of opinion which, one way or another, [would] have to be accommodated in the English legal system."[46] The publication of Scarman's lectures was followed by a vast increase in the academic literature on the ECHR, much of it by now arguing openly the merits of incorporation.[47]

In his lectures, Scarman had drawn attention to "current newspaper reports of the case now before the court of Mr. Golder who alleges he was denied access to his lawyers while in custody in a British prison".[48] This was to become the celebrated decision of the European Court of Human Rights,

---

[42] D. R. Gilmour, "The Sovereignty of Parliament and the European Commission of Human Rights" [1968] *Public Law* 62.

[43] Fabian tract 390 (London, 1968).

[44] *Ibid.*, p. 14.

[45] Sir Leslie Scarman, *English Law—the New Dimension* (London, 1974), p. 20.

[46] *Ibid.*, at p. 14.

[47] For a taste of the debate that followed Scarman's lectures, see F. Jacobs, *The European Convention on Human Rights* (Oxford, 1975); P. Wallington and J. McBride, *Civil Liberties and a Bill of Rights* (Cobden Trust, London, 1976); J. E. S. Fawcett, "A Bill of Rights for the United Kingdom?" (1976) 1 *Human Rights Review* 57; A. H. Robertson, *Human Rights in Europe* (Manchester, 1977); A. J. M. Milne, "Should we have a Bill of Rights?" (1977) 40 *Modern Law Review* 389; J. Jaconelli, *Enacting a Bill of Rights* (Oxford, 1980); C. Campbell (ed.), *Do we need a Bill of Rights?* (London, 1980). The most durable work to have emerged in the period was M. Zander, *A Bill of Rights* (London, 1975) the third edition of which was published in 1985. (The references that follow are to the third edition.)

[48] Scarman, *op. cit.*, note 45, p. 15n.

Golder v. *United Kingdom*, decided on 21 February 1975 and the first case involving Britain to be resolved by the Court.[49] *Golder* was one of four highly publicised decisions by the Commission and the Court which were the second great generator of interest in the Convention in the 1970s. The other three cases involved *The Sunday Times'* reporting of the thalidomide litigation,[50] the punishment by birching of a convicted criminal in the Isle of Man[51] and the finding of breaches of Article 3 which were made against the authorities in respect of the treatment meted out to certain internees in Northern Ireland in 1971.[52] These decisions had two effects. They popularised the Convention with lawyers, public interest groups and journalists, bringing home to them the extent to which the Convention could be deployed as an avenue of law reform at home. Secondly, and from a quite different perspective, they lead to calls from critics of them for the Convention to be incorporated so as (it was argued) to protect English law from scrutiny by foreign judges.[53] Both reactions served to drive home the new relevance of the Convention to Britain's legal system.

The third source of change in the 1970s lay in the political arena. As early as 23 April 1969, the Conservative peer Lord Lambton had attempted to introduce a bill "to preserve the rights of the individual" and during the same year a Liberal Party pamphlet[54] had provoked a four hour debate in the

---

[49]   Series A, No. 18 (1975) 1 E.H.R.R. 524.

[50]   *The Sunday Times* v. *United Kingdom* Series A, No. 30 (1979) 2 E.H.R.R. 245.

[51]   *Tyrer* v. *United Kingdom* Series A, No. 26 (1978) 2 E.H.R.R. 1.

[52]   *Ireland* v. *United Kingdom* Series A, No. 25 (1978) 2 E.H.R.R. 25.

[53]   A particularly harsh critic of many of the judgments of the European Court of Human Rights during this period was F. A. Mann. See his "Britain's Bill of Rights" (1978) 94 *Law Quarterly Review* 512 where he characterises the decision in *Golder* as "almost grotesque" (at p. 524). In his note on *The Sunday Times* case ("Contempt of Court in the House of Lords and the European Court of Human Rights" (1979) 95 *Law Quarterly Review* 348), he asserts of the decision that "it is probably no exaggeration to say that the gravest blow to the fabric of English law that has ever occurred has been dealt by the majority of eleven judges coming from Cyprus, Denmark, Eire, France, Germany, Greece, Italy, Portugal, Spain, Sweden and Turkey…" (at p. 349). Mann's scepticism lead him to suggest that "the English lawyer will have to ask himself whether it would not be sounder policy to entrust judicial review in the light of a Bill of Rights to a tribunal imbued with the spirit and history of English fundamental law rather than to a tribunal that is predominantly foreign in nationality, training and standards, that includes judges from nineteen countries as diverse as Malta and Iceland, Turkey and Portugal, Cyprus and Luxembourg, and that displays little inclination to seek guidance from comparative material or, in particular, from the wealth of American learning and its English ideological base" ((1978) 94 *Law Quarterly Review* 512, at p. 530).

[54]   J. McDonald, *A Bill of Rights* (London, 1969).

Lords and a further (albeit much shorter) discussion in the Commons.[55] Accession to the European Communities in January 1973 provided an additional political impetus to the case for incorporation, with F. A. Mann being among those drawing attention to the fact that already "since January 1966 Parliament's sovereignty has been much curtailed by this country's acceptance of the right of individual petition under the European Convention."[56] The political climate after the Scarman lectures referred to above[57] was influenced by further debates in the House of Commons and by a highly significant report by a number of influential Labour Party ministers arguing the case for incorporation.[58] This latter initiative was followed in 1976 by a paper on the subject from the Standing Advisory Commission on Human Rights for Northern Ireland[59] and by a Home Office discussion document in the same year, *Legislation on Human Rights*, published under the authority of a secretary of state who was himself becoming increasingly persuaded by the arguments for incorporation, Roy Jenkins.[60] With a favourable report from the Standing Advisory Commission in 1977,[61] new evidence of support from members of the opposition Conservative Party's front bench[62] and a very narrow vote against incorporation by a House of Lords Select Committee,[63] it seemed only a matter of time before incorporation of the ECHR

---

[55] The details are at Zander, *op. cit.*, note 47, at pp. 4–5.

[56] See his note at (1974) 90 *Law Quarterly Review* 295, at p. 296. Mann had been aware earlier than most of the implications of the ECHR for United Kingdom law; see his "The United Kingdom's Bill of Rights" (1972) 122 *New Law Journal* 289.

[57] *Op. cit.*, note 45.

[58] The ministers were Shirley Williams and the two law officers Sam Silkin and Peter Archer. The former Lord Chancellor Lord Gardiner was also a signatory. The paper was published on 15 February 1976. These details are drawn from Zander, *op. cit.*, note 47, pp. 13–14. Silkin went on to set out his views at greater length in the course of giving the second McDermott lecture, held at Queen's University Belfast on 14 April 1976: see S. Silkin, "The Rights of Man and the Rule of Law" (1977) 28 *Northern Ireland Legal Quarterly* 3.

[59] Northern Ireland Standing Advisory Commission on Human Rights, *Bill of Rights* (Belfast, 1976).

[60] *Legislation on Human Rights* (London, 1976). For details of a speech made by Jenkins on 12 February 1975 and which indicated his changing thoughts on the subject, see Zander, *op. cit.*, note 47, pp. 14–15.

[61] Northern Ireland Standing Advisory Commission on Human Rights, *The Protection of Human Rights by Law in Northern Ireland* (Cmnd. 7009, London, 1977).

[62] The details are at Zander, *op. cit.*, note 47, pp. 20–22.

[63] Report of the Select Committee on a Bill of Rights (House of Lords Paper 176, London, 1978).

would be achieved. Even the eleven lords who split six to five against incorporation were unanimous that "if there was to be a Bill of Rights, it should be a Bill based on the European Convention of Human Rights."[64]

In retrospect, it is possible to see the 1977–79 period as the high water mark (so far) of governmental support for incorporation of the Convention. Though strongly articulated, the party-political support for the measure was always thinner than it looked. Almost all the protagonists of the reform on the Labour side (then in government) were shortly to leave the Party to found a new centre-left movement which was later to be absorbed within the stronger centrist tradition of the old Liberal Party.[65] Though they held high office, the support for incorporation evinced by these senior Labour figures was never widely shared across the broader Labour movement which continued throughout the 1970s to maintain its distrust of individual rights and of British judges in about equal measure. What Conservative support there was for incorporation, in contrast, was born out of a pessimism as to the party's electoral prospects combined with an optimism that the Convention if entrenched would be able to stem the tide of a socialist movement that seemed in the mid and late 1970s to be (at least electorally) irresistible. This politically partisan support for the Convention had always been possible; though not itself narrow in this way, Gilmour's piece in 1968 had been about the controversial Iron and Steel Act rather than any obviously anti-civil libertarian measure, and Lord Lambton had explained his 1969 legislative initiative as an attempt to undo the damage he believed had been done to human rights by Labour's policies on such broadly political matters as education, planning and race relations. After Labour's second successive election victory in 1974, a bill of rights was needed, in the words of the influential Conservative Sir Keith Joseph, "to save the law from Parliament and Parliament from itself."[66]

There was always something skin-deep about an argument for change that was rooted in the politically unattractive consequences of electoral defeat, and what little Conservative momentum there was for reform disappeared with Mrs Thatcher's electoral victory in 1979. The approach of reform-minded Tories to incorporation is exemplified in the variety of positions adopted by the party's long serving Lord Chancellor, Lord Hail-

---

[64] *Ibid.*, p. 20.

[65] The result of a series of complicated political manoeuvres during the 1980s is that there is now one mainstream centre party, known as the Liberal Democrats.

[66] Sir Keith Joseph, *Freedom Under Law* (Conservative Political Centre, London, 1975), at p. 13, quoted in Zander, *op. cit.*, note 47, at p. 11.

sham. In opposition in 1969, he argued the need for a human rights bill.[67] A year later, now newly appointed in his first spell as lord chancellor, he felt obliged in the course of a debate in the Lords to set out his many "basic difficulties about accepting a Bill of Rights of any kind".[68] In opposition again after 1974, Hailsham felt able to rediscover his enthusiasm for constitutional change, writing in 1978 of his radical proposals to curb governmental power that "in this armoury of weapons against elective dictatorship, a Bill of Rights, embodying and entrenching the European Convention might well have a valuable, even if subordinate, part to play."[69] A "Bill of Rights would be a blessing" to the extent that it would be able to control "the unlimited power of Parliament".[70] Despite such sentiments, Hailsham's second tenure as lord chancellor, from 1979 to 1987, was as unproductive of constitutional reform as had been his first.

2. THE CASE LAW IN THE 1970s AND EARLY 1980s

This was the scholarly, European and political background against which the European Convention on Human Rights made its first tentative steps into British jurisprudence in the 1970s. The prize for the first judicial mention is claimed by Stephenson L.J. who "unearthed" the ECHR in a case in which it was "not mentioned in argument" before the Court of Appeal.[71] The decision, *Waddington* v. *Miah*,[72] went on appeal to the House of Lords where the ambiguity of the statutory provision under scrutiny allowed reference to the ECHR. The issue before the judges was the potential retrospectiveness of part of the Immigration Act 1971. Having quoted from Article 7 of the ECHR, Lord Reid went on to decide against retrospectiveness, it being "hardly credible that any government department would promote or that Parliament would pass retrospective criminal legislation."[73] The case said nothing new in that it treated the Convention in exactly the same way as any other treaty to which the country was a signatory, namely as a legitimate

---

[67] Q. Hogg, *New Charter* (Conservative Political Centre, No. 430, London, 1969).

[68] House of Lords Parliamentary Debates, vol. 313, col. 243 (26 November 1970), quoted in Zander, *op. cit.*, note 47, at p. 7.

[69] Lord Hailsham, *The Dilemma of Democracy* (London, 1978), at p. 174.

[70] *Ibid.*

[71] The words are those of the judge himself; see his note at (1979) 95 *Law Quarterly Review* 34.

[72] Reported at [1974] 1 W.L.R. 683. Stephenson L.J.'s comments are to be found at pp. 690–691.

[73] *Ibid.*, at p. 694.

source of guidance for the judges where a statutory provision was ambiguous.

In a succession of cases in the mid-1970s, however, two senior members of the judiciary, the head of the civil division of the Court of Appeal Lord Denning M.R. and his judicial colleague Lord Justice Scarman (as he had become on promotion to the Court of Appeal), staked out a further and more ambitious claim for the relevance of the Convention to English law. In one of his first utterances on the subject, Lord Denning went so far as to suggest that the courts should be able to subjugate an Act of Parliament to the Convention even without incorporation,[74] but this was an opinion from which he later resiled.[75] Despite this, he continued for a time to insist on a central role for the Convention, asserting in one case that the courts "should take the Convention into account...whenever interpreting a statute which affects the rights and liberties of the individual."[76] Scarman L.J. was equally robust if more careful and consistent in his commitment to an expanded place for even an unincorporated Convention in English law, suggesting in one judgment that it was "the duty of the courts, so long as they do not defy or disregard clear and unequivocal provision, to construe statutes in a manner which promotes, not endangers" the basic rights to be found in the ECHR.[77] In a later case, Scarman L.J. suggested that the ECHR should be "considered by courts even though no statute expressly or impliedly incorporates it into our law."[78]

Dicta such as these went far beyond the ordinary rule that international treaties such as the ECHR could only be referred to in cases of statutory ambiguity, and they were not generally followed. More typical were decisions in which the Convention played the normal part of an international treaty in English law, doing no more than pointing a route through uncer-

---

[74] *Birdi* v. *Secretary of State for Home Affairs* (1975) 119 *Solicitor's Journal* 322.

[75] *R.* v. *Secretary of State for Home Affairs, ex parte Bhajan Singh* [1975] 3 W.L.R. 225.

[76] *Ibid.*, at p. 231. But see Lord Denning's more conservative position in *R.* v. *Chief Immigration Officer, Heathrow Airport, ex parte Salamat Bibi* [1976] 3 All E.R. 843. The ECHR could also be used to underpin a restriction on an individual's freedom: see Lord Denning M.R.'s judgment in *Ahmad* v. *Inner London Education Authority* [1978] 1 All E.R. 574.

[77] *R.* v. *Secretary of State for Home Affairs, ex parte Phansopkar; R.* v. *Secretary of State for the Home Department, ex parte Begum* [1975] 3 All E.R. 497. at p. 511. See also the same judge's dissenting opinion in *Ahmad* v. *Inner London Education Authority, op. cit.*, note 76.

[78] *Phansopkar and Pan American World Airways Inc.* v. *Department of Trade* [1976] 1 Lloyd's Reports 257, at p. 261.

tainty in a statute.[79] In *Gold Star Limited* v. *Director of Public Prosecutions*,[80] magazines were seized under the Obscene Publications Act 1957, and this was followed by an order for forfeiture issued by the magistrates. The material was bound for export and the question before the House of Lords was as to the power of an English court to make a finding of obscenity in such circumstances. The appellant used Article 10 of the ECHR and the European Court of Human Rights judgment in *Handyside* v. *United Kingdom*[81] to try to build a local margin of appreciation into the definition of obscenity, in the hope that the English judges would then hold that a finding of obscenity on the facts before them pre-empted what was really a matter for the jurisdiction to which the material was to be sent. This ambitious claim foundered on the lack of ambiguity in the statute. Giving the leading judgment, Lord Roskill recognised that these were "powerful" arguments but they "overlook[ed] the fact that the Act of 1959 was concerned amongst other matters to strengthen the law concerning pornography and...[o]n a fair reading of section 3(1) [his lordship was] unable to see why [the appellant] cease[d] so to publish an obscene article for gain because its ultimate destination [was] in Scotland, Northern Ireland or anywhere else in the world."[82]

This was the restricted view of the place of the Convention that had prevailed by the early 1980s, as far as statutory interpretation was concerned. Nowhere is this more evident than in the judgment of Lord Scarman (as he had by now become) in *R.* v. *Barnet London Borough Council, ex parte Shah*, an important case on students grants decided in 1983. Giving the leading judgment in the House of Lords, his lordship considered that the key phrase in the statute before the court, "ordinarily resident", was to be given "in the present context the natural and ordinary meaning recognised and adopted by the House" in an earlier decision.[83] Because of this, the ECHR point raised in argument by Anthony Lester Q.C. did not arise, his lordship considering himself "in duty bound to resist, as unnecessary, the invitation to explore the fascinating vistas of legal speculation which Mr. Lester has

---

[79] The leading authority on the right approach in general is *Salomon* v. *Commissioners of Customs and Excise* [1967] 2 Q.B. 116. On the ECHR, see *Ostreicher* v. *Secretary of State for the Environment* [1978] 1 All E.R. 591; *R.* v. *Secretary of State for the Home Department, ex parte Hosenball* [1977] 1 W.L.R. 766.

[80] [1981] 1 W.L.R. 732.

[81] Series A, No. 24 (1976) 1 E. H.R.R. 737.

[82] *Ibid.*, at p. 742.

[83] [1983] 2 A.C. 309, at p. 350.

skilfully and temptingly opened to our view."[84] This was similar to the more conservative position that had by then already been adopted for a number of years by his fellow proto-revolutionary from earlier days, Lord Denning.[85]

The role of the Convention and its case-law in the development of the common law was also addressed in the 1970s and early 1980s, with even more modest results than those that resulted from scrutiny of its relevance to the interpretation of statutes. As early as 1976, the distinguished law lord Lord Wilberforce had indicated his reluctance to allow the content of public policy for common law purposes to be infused with a meaning drawn from the Convention.[86] The courts were equally careful not to be drawn into the making of declaratory judgments or orders which were rooted solely in obligations incurred by the state in international law.[87] The Convention did not even seem to be helpful as a source of new common law rights. The leading case from the period on this point is *Malone* v. *Metropolitan Police Commissioner*, which concerned the lawfulness of telephone tapping by the police, a practice that was then unregulated by law.[88] Counsel for the victim of the tapping treated this gap in the law as an opportunity to argue that the Convention as interpreted in the *Klass* case[89] "conferred a direct right on all citizens of the United Kingdom" or that at least "it aided the courts of this country" by guiding them "in interpreting and applying English law so as to make it accord as far as possible with the Convention" and in providing "a guide in cases of ambiguity or a lack of clarity in English law".[90] The submission was comprehensively rejected by the then Vice-Chancellor, Sir Robert Megarry: "The Convention is plainly not of itself law in this country, however much it may fall to be considered as indicating what the law of this country should be, or should be construed as being."[91] Moreover, if "authority on a point is lacking, neither equity nor common law is incapable

---

[84] *Ibid.*

[85] See *R.* v. *Chief Immigration Officer, Heathrow Airport, ex parte Salamat Bibi, op. cit.,* note 76.

[86] *Blathwayt* v. *Baron Crawley* [1976] A.C. 397. *Cf. Cheall* v. *Association of Professional Executive Clerical and Computer Staff* [1983] 2 A.C. 180.

[87] *Uppal* v. *Home Office*, unreported decision by Megarry J., 20 October 1978, referred to by the same judge in *Malone* v. *Metropolitan Police Commissioner* [1979] Ch. 344, at p. 353, where the decision is followed on this point, *ibid.*, at p. 354.

[88] [1979] Ch. 344. For the European and domestic legislative sequels, see below text at note 215 ff.

[89] *Klass* v. *Federal Republic of Germany* Series A, No. 28 (1978) 2 E.H.R.R. 214.

[90] [1979] Ch. 344, at p. 356.

[91] *Ibid.*, at p. 366.

of filling the gap in a proper case."[92] However, any "regulation of so complex a matter as telephone tapping [was] essentially a matter for Parliament not the courts."[93]

The most that could be said for the Convention was that while it could not underpin a new common law right as such, it could nevertheless still influence the development of the common law in a situation of uncertainty of a type in which it was appropriate for the courts to become involved. Thus in *Attorney-General* v. *BBC*,[94] the House of Lords unanimously held that a local valuation court was not subject to the law of contempt of court and two of their lordships mentioned the ECHR in the course of their judgments. Lord Fraser thought the Convention and the decisions of the European Court to be matters to which the courts "should have regard...in cases...where our domestic law is not firmly settled."[95] In a predictably more assertive vein, Lord Scarman thought that "[i]f the issue should ultimately be, as I think in this case it is, a question of legal policy, we must have regard to the country's international obligation to observe the Convention as interpreted by the Court of Human Rights."[96] In refusing to extend the contempt laws, his lordship considered that it had "not been demonstrated...that there is 'a pressing social need' for this is what the ECHR declares necessary in our democratic society to mean."[97] Significantly however the three remaining judges in the case thought the common law robust enough to develop in the same way without the assistance of the Convention, Lord Salmon, for example, describing "freedom of speech and freedom of the press" as "two of the pillars of liberty" without making any reference to the ECHR.[98] These opinions and the occasional further dicta from Lords Scarman[99] and Denning[100] apart, the common law case-law of the period showed a far greater inclination on the part of the courts to develop the law

---

[92] *Ibid.*, at p. 356.

[93] *Ibid.*, at p. 380.

[94] [1981] A.C. 303.

[95] *Ibid.*, p. 352.

[96] *Ibid.*, p. 354.

[97] *Ibid.*, p. 362.

[98] *Ibid.*, p. 342.

[99] *United Kingdom Association of Professional Engineers* v. *Advisory, Conciliation and Arbitration Service* [1981] A.C. 424, at p. 445. See also *R.* v. *Lemon and Gay News Limited* [1979] 1 All E.R. 898.

[100] *United Kingdom Association of Professional Engineers* v. *Advisory, Conciliation and Arbitration Service* [1979] 2 All E.R. 478, at pp. 485–486.

independently of the Convention,[101] and to refer to the Convention (if at all) more to demonstrate the compatibility of the English law with it than to reveal any need for domestic law to be altered to take it into account.[102]

The position at the end of this period was well summed up in a House of Lords decision in 1983, *Harman* v. *Secretary of State for the Home Department*.[103] The case arose out of the disclosure to a journalist by a solicitor of documents that had been made available to her by way of discovery in a civil action. Three of their lordships held that the solicitor's action amounted to the breach of an implied undertaking to the court and that this constituted a contempt of court, despite the fact that the documents had been read aloud in court. Speaking for the majority, Lord Diplock considered the case to be about "an aspect of the law of discovery of documents in civil actions in the High Court" and not to be concerned with "freedom of speech, freedom of the press, openness of justice or documents coming into 'the public domain'." As a result the case did not call for "consideration of any of those human rights and fundamental freedoms which in the European Convention on Human Rights are contained in separate articles."[104] In their joint dissenting opinion, Lords Scarman and Simon argued that there being no "pre-existing rule which answers the question", they were inevitably "concerned with policy and principle" and in "framing a new rule" account should be taken of "the important constitutional right to freedom of communication" which was similar to the "perhaps slightly narrower" concept of freedom of expression in Article 10 of the ECHR."[105] While Lords Scarman and Simon were of the view that the new rule proposed by the majority "might well be inconsistent with the requirements of the European Convention",[106] they saw the Convention as one source of inspiration together with

---

[101] As in three of the judgments in *Attorney-General* v. *BBC*, *op. cit.*, note 94; Lord Diplock's judgment in *R.* v. *Lemon and Gay News Limited*, *op. cit.*, note 99.

[102] *Science Research Council* v. *Nassé* [1980] A.C. 1028, at p. 1068 *per* Lord Wilberforce; *Cheall* v. *APEX*, *op. cit.*, note 86, at p. 190–191, *per* Lord Diplock; *Raymond* v. *Honey* [1983] 1 A.C. 1, at p. 10 *per* Lord Wilberforce.

[103] [1983] 1 A.C. 280.

[104] *Ibid.*, at p. 299. Compare the same judge's opinion in *Gleaves* v. *Deakin* [1980] A.C. 477 in which Article 10 formed the centrepiece of his argument in favour of the modification of the criminal libel laws. Compare also his subtle interpretation of the Contempt of Court Act 1981 the effect of which might well have been to pre-empt an application to Strasbourg in the case before him: *Attorney-General* v. *English* [1983] 1 A.C. 116.

[105] [1983] 1 A.C. 280, at p. 311.

[106] *Ibid.*, at p. 317.

others (such as the "common law achieved in America"[107]) for the development of the common law. As had become the situation with the case law on statutory interpretation by 1983, deployment of the ECHR as a means of developing the common law was clearly a minority legal tradition and it was not one in which even its protagonists any longer believed the Convention had an exclusive role.

3. CONSERVATIVE HEGEMONY AND THE PUSH FOR INCORPORATION

The Conservative Party has enjoyed a continuous term in government in the United Kingdom since 1979, with the next general election not being required as a matter of law before the late Spring of 1997. These years of effective one Party rule have been marked by greatly increased support for incorporation of the ECHR on the part of all the opposition parties and many judges at all levels in the British judiciary. Writing as early as 1984, Anthony Lester identified two former Lord Chancellors, two former Home Secretaries and two former Attorney-Generals as "[r]anged on the side of incorporation."[108] In November 1992, the serving Lord Chief Justice Lord Taylor used a prestigious televised public lecture to inform his audience that "[w]e should have the courage of our treaty obligations and incorporate the convention."[109] The incumbent Master of the Rolls, Sir Thomas Bingham, voiced the same opinion the following year when he argued in the course of his Denning Lecture that incorporation "would over time stifle the insidious and damaging belief that it is necessary to go abroad to obtain justice."[110] The opposition Labour Party has joined with the Liberal Democrats in officially committing itself to incorporation[111] and two important public interest groups have done much to publicise what they see as the need for a bill of

---

[107] *Ibid.*, at p. 316.

[108] A. Lester, "Fundamental Rights: The United Kingdom Isolated?", *op. cit.*, note 34, at p. 63.

[109] Lord Taylor, "The Judiciary in the Nineties", Richard Dimbleby Lecture, BBC 1, 30 November 1992. The lecture is discussed in J. Rozenberg, *The Search for Justice* (London, 1994), at p. 213.

[110] Sir Thomas Bingham, Denning Lecture, Bar Association for Commerce, Finance and Industry, 2 March 1993.

[111] See Lord Irvine of Lairg, "Judges and Decision-Makers: The Theory and Practice of *Wednesbury* Review" [1996] *Public Law* 59, at p. 77. See also the speech by the Labour spokesman Lord Williams of Mostyn in the House of Lords debate on Lord Lester's Human Rights Bill: House of Lords Parliamentary Debates, vol. 560, cols. 1161–1163 (25 January 1995).

rights for Britain.[112] In March 1993, the Law Society's council unanimously supported incorporation of the Convention. As the years of Conservative rule have rolled by, and the cases in Strasbourg adverse to the United Kingdom have multiplied, the government has seemed more isolated than ever in its view that "our present arrangements, both in principle and in practice, provide properly and effectively...for the securing of rights and freedom, including but not exclusively, those in the European Convention on Human Rights."[113]

This movement in domestic politics, in which many judges have played a part,[114] has not been matched by any increase in the justiciability of the Convention in United Kingdom law.[115] If anything the trend in the case-law has been in the opposite direction. The broader the push for incorporation has become, the more reluctant the judges have been to contrive the same end result through what they now almost without exception see as the backdoor of illicit judicial activism. Thus we have the paradoxical situation that while references to the Convention in the case-law have multiplied enormously in recent years, the way in which the Convention has been regarded in these cases has been reflective of a judicial conservativism that has been at least as traditional in outlook as that which characterised the earlier pre-Thatcherite era. The courts have denied to themselves the opportunity to

---

[112] Charter 88, *New Statesman and Society*, 2 December 1988; Liberty, *A People's Charter* (London, 1991).

[113] The words are those of Baroness Blatch, setting out the government's case against incorporation in a House of Lords debate initiated by Lord Lester of Herne Hill. The debate is at House of Lords Parliamentary Debates, vol. 560, cols. 1136–1174 (25 January 1995). Baroness Blatch's quoted remarks are at col. 1163. The literature on the subject is well surveyed in D. Oliver, *Government in the United Kingdom: The Search for Accountability, Effectiveness and Citizenship* (Milton Keynes, 1991), ch. 9. For the case against incorporation from a non-governmental perspective, see K. D. Ewing and C. A. Gearty, *Freedom under Thatcher: Civil Liberties in Modern Britain* (Oxford, 1990), ch. 8, and more recently C. A. Gearty, "After Gibraltar" *London Review of Books*, 16 November 1995.

[114] In the debate in the House of Lords referred to in the preceding note, the serving law lords Lord Browne-Wilkinson (*ibid.*, cols. 1148–1150) and Lord Lloyd of Berwick (*ibid.*, cols. 1152–1154) spoke in favour of incorporation.

[115] In what follows, reference is made exclusively to English cases. The position in the rest of the United Kingdom is broadly similar. Wales has no separate legal system and therefore the English case-law applies within it. For a recent Northern Ireland case following the English authorities see *In the matter of applications by John William Alexander Stewart*, Decision of Carswell J., High Court of Justice in Northern Ireland, reported in the *Irish Times*, 15 April 1996. For the position in Scotland, see *Kaur* v. *Lord Advocate* [1980] 3 C.M.L.R. 79; *Moore* v. *Secretary of State for Scotland* 1985 S.L.T. 38.

subjugate the exercise of discretionary power to the constraints of the ECHR[116] and they have been likewise reluctant to extend their reach over the prerogative power on the same basis.[117] The law on the relevance of the ECHR to statutory interpretation has likewise remained largely unchanged. *R. v. Radio Authority, ex parte Bull*[118] may be mentioned as a recent example of the latter point.

The issue before the court was whether a certain provision in the Broadcasting Act 1990 could rightly be interpreted so as to prevent Amnesty International from advertising on radio. The relevant section prohibited *inter alia* "any advertisement which is inserted by or on behalf of any body whose objects are wholly or mainly of a political nature...'.[119] In upholding the authority's decision to ban Amnesty advertising on this basis, the Divisional Court naturally encountered the argument that the provision should be read subject to Article 10 of the ECHR with its guarantee of freedom of expression. Kennedy L.J. considered Article 10 in detail, pointing out that the action of the Authority before him was "part of a licensing system for which art 10 specifically provides, and that therefore art 10 is unlikely to have any significant part to play in its construction...".[120] His conclusion in the case in favour of the Authority was arrived at entirely through the application of the principles of English public law. In coming to the same result as his colleague, McCullough J. pointedly referred to the "difficulty with any submission based on the convention [which was] that it presuppose[d] that there [was] ambiguity in the statute; otherwise the convention has no part to play in the interpretation of a statutory provision."[121] The judge went on to say of the statutory provision before him that in his "belief, it [was] not ambigu-

---

[116] *R. v. Secretary of State for the Home Department, ex parte Brind* [1991] 1 A.C. 696. *Cf. R. v. Secretary of State for the Home Department, ex parte McQuillan* [1995] 4 All E.R. 400, at pp. 422–423 *per* Sedley J. See also *R. v. Khan, The Times*, 5 July 1996, discussed in S. Nash and M. Furse, 'The Role of the Convention in Domestic Cases' (1996) 146 *New Law Journal* 1363

[117] *R. v. Ministry of Defence, ex parte Smith* [1996] 1 All E.R. 257: "The relevance of the convention in the present context is as background to the complaint of irrationality. The fact that a decision-maker failed to take account of convention obligations when exercising an administrative discretion is not of itself a ground for impugning that exercise of discretion" at pp. 266–267, *per* Sir Thomas Bingham M.R.

[118] [1995] 4 All E.R. 481.

[119] Broadcasting Act 1990, s. 92.

[120] [1995] 4 All E.R. 481, at pp. 494–5.

[121] *Ibid.*, at p. 500.

ous."[122] The point has been echoed in a recent decision in the highest domestic tribunal the House of Lords, with Lord Lowry declaring in the course of giving the only substantive judgment of their lordships in a case arising out of the Contempt of Court Act 1981 that if the "enactment is clear, compliance with the Convention for the Protection of Human Rights and Fundamental Freedoms...is not immediately in issue."[123]

This traditional approach to statutory interpretation has been tested in a couple of recent cases in which what has been before the judges has been legislation enacted by parliament in the light of earlier rulings by the European Court of Human Rights. In *R. v. Canons Park Mental Health Review Tribunal, ex parte A*,[124] Sedley J. thought the problem posed by the wording of the statutory provision before him to be one of "straightforward construction"[125] and therefore to be capable of being dealt with in the ordinary way. He also recognised that the interpretation of the relevant provision which he rejected would have "put the legislation into conflict with the convention." Noting that it was "accepted on both sides" that after a Strasbourg court decision on the very issue before it,[126] "Parliament [was] to be taken to have sought by its legislation to conform with the decision of the European Court of Human Rights",[127] Sedley J. considered this interpretive route to be blocked "on policy grounds"[128] as well as for the ordinary reasons of construction which he had earlier outlined. To similar effect is *R. v. Secretary of State for the Home Department, ex parte T*.[129] In the course of finding against the Secretary of State in a case involving the treatment of prisoners, Kennedy L.J. identified the purpose of the key provision before him as being "to meet the criticism voiced in *Thynne* v. *United Kingdom*" in the European Court of Human Rights[130] and the judge went on to observe that if he

---

[122] *Ibid.* McCullough J. thought that in any event the margin of appreciation would probably apply; see *ibid.*, at p. 501.

[123] *Attorney-General* v. *Associated Newspapers Ltd.* [1994] 1 All E.R. 556, at p. 564.

[124] [1994] 1 All E.R. 481. Mann L.J. delivered a short concurring judgment.

[125] *Ibid.*, at p. 492.

[126] *X.* v. *United Kingdom* Series A, No. 46 (1981) 4 E.H.R.R. 188.

[127] [1994] 1 All E.R. 481 at p. 493.

[128] *Ibid.*, at p. 492.

[129] [1994] 1 All E.R. 794. See further *R. v. Secretary of State for the Home Department, ex parte Hickey (No. 1)* [1995] 1 All E.R. 479 where the case was decided by the Court of Appeal on grounds different from those that had determined the approach of the Divisional Court.

[130] *Thynne, Wilson and Gunnell* v. *United Kingdom* Series A, No. 190 (1990) 13 E.H.R.R. 666.

adopted the interpretive route suggested to him by the Secretary of State, these "criticisms [would] not be met".[131] Clearly the more legislation that there is on the statute book seeking to implement rulings of the European Court of Human Rights, the more likely it is that judges will be asked to adjudicate on the meaning of statutes which are charged with this sort of explicit European dimension. The possibility for conflict is slight, not only because straightforward construction will usually lead to the same result but also because if there is any ambiguity it will be proper in the ordinary way both to have regard to the Convention and its case-law and also to consider the purpose behind the enactment, if necessary by having regard to the relevant ministerial statements in parliament.[132]

Turning now to the contemporary position of the ECHR in the English common law, it is clear that the Convention continues to enjoy little more than the minor role assigned to it by the prevailing jurisprudence of the mid 1970s and early 1980s. The dicta of Lords Scarman and Fraser in *Attorney-General* v. *BBC*[133] remain a high water mark rather than the start of a trend. The leading case is now the decision in *Derbyshire County Council* v. *Times Newspapers Limited*.[134] The issue before the House of Lords was whether or not a local authority could sue for libel. Faced with two conflicting High Court decisions on the point,[135] the Court of Appeal had found against the local authority by relying explicitly on Article 10 of the ECHR. Balcome L.J. thought that where the common law was uncertain the Convention should be taken into account, and Butler-Sloss L.J. had likewise seen the court in such circumstances as "obliged to consider the implications of Article 10." Their Lordships came to the same conclusion on the legal point but "without finding any need to rely upon the European Convention".[136] Giving the only substantive judgment, Lord Keith drew upon case-law from North America and South Africa as well as from domestic and Privy Council decisions closer to home. It was "appropriate"[137] in the circumstances for the lower court to have had regard to the Convention but Lord Keith's careful

---

[131] [1994] 1 All E.R. 794, at p. 800. Pill J. concurred in Kennedy L.J.'s judgment.

[132] *Pepper (Inspector of Taxes)* v. *Hart* [1993] A.C. 593.

[133] *Op. cit.*, note 94.

[134] [1993] 2 W.L.R. 449.

[135] *Manchester Corporation* v. *Williams* [1891] 1 Q.B. 94; *Bognor Regis Urban District Council* v. *Campion* [1972] 2 Q.B. 169.

[136] [1993] 2 W.L.R. 449, at p. 460, *per* Lord Keith of Kinkel.

[137] *Ibid.*

written opinion provided overwhelming evidence that it was by no means obligatory.

In a similar vein is the more recent decision of *John* v. *MGN Limited*,[138] in which the Court of Appeal laid down new guidelines on the award of damages in libel actions. Significantly, the case fell to be decided shortly after the decision of the European Court of Human Rights in *Tolstoy Miloslavsky* v. *United Kingdom*,[139] in which an award of £1.5 million compensatory damages against the applicant was held in the circumstances of the case to have amounted to an infringement of his right to freedom of expression under Article 10. Though the Court of Appeal referred to the decision and developed the common law in a way that made further applications to Strasbourg of a similar nature much less likely, it was emphatic that what it was engaged in was the development of the common law rather than merely the application of Convention principles in the domestic arena. Giving the judgment of the Court, Sir Thomas Bingham M.R. observed that,

> The European Convention on Human Rights is not a free-standing source of law in the United Kingdom. But there is…no conflict or discrepancy between art 10 and the common law. We regard art 10 as reinforcing and buttressing the conclusions we have reached and set out above. We reach those conclusions independently of the convention, however, and would reach them even if the convention did not exist.[140]

Sir Thomas's assertion of the absence of conflict between the common law and the ECHR, particularly Article 10, is a recurring feature of the case-law of the post-Thatcher period, just as it was in the 1970s. The dicta are too numerous to mention in their entirety. In the course of the controversial *Spycatcher* litigation that dogged the final years of Mrs Thatcher's tenure at 10, Downing Street, Lord Denning's successor as Master of the Rolls Sir John Donaldson could "detect no inconsistency between our domestic law and the

---

[138] [1996] 2 All E.R. 35. *Cf. Rantzen* v. *Mirror Group Newspapers* [1993] 4 All E.R. 975, in which a somewhat more robust and engaged role was accorded the ECHR in the evolution of the law in precisely the same area. In *Re H-S (minors: protection of identity)* [1994] 3 All E.R. 390, Articles 8 and 10 were a relevant backdrop against which the balancing of public interests took place in the context of balancing the freedom of the press with the need to protect children from unwarranted exposure.

[139] Series A, No. 323 (1995) 20 E.H.R.R. 442.

[140] [1996] 2 All E.R. 35, at p. 58. *Cf.* the same judge's comments in *Attorney-General* v. *Observer Ltd.; Attorney-General* v. *Times Newspapers Ltd.* [1990] 1 A.C. 109, at pp. 219–220, where he appeared to follow the line suggested by Lords Scarman and Fraser in *Attorney-General* v. *BBC, op. cit.*, note 94.

Convention"[141] and in the House of Lords in the same case Lord Goff equally could "see no inconsistency between English law on this subject [of confidentiality] and article 10 of the European Convention on Human Rights."[142] This was "scarcely surprising, since we may pride ourselves on the fact that freedom of speech has existed in this country perhaps as long as, if not longer than, it has existed in any other country in the world."[143] Judicial pride in the common law may or may not be justifiable but it has meant that the courts have been loathe to allow themselves to be forced into recognising a conflict between its precepts and a document which so potently describes itself as a "human rights charter". The judges have either developed the law so as to increase individual freedom, thereby incidentally rendering a conflict with Europe less likely, or they have persuaded themselves that apparently illiberal decisions under the common law would be decided identically under the Convention. The *John* and *Derbyshire* decisions referred to above are examples of the former. As regards the latter, we may note that when upholding the temporary injunctions in the *Spycatcher* case, Lord Templeman consciously echoed Article 10(2) in declaring them to be "necessary in a democratic society in the interests of national security, for protecting the reputation or rights of others, for preventing the disclosure of information received in confidence or for maintaining the authority and impartiality of the judiciary...".[144] In upholding a court order requiring a journalist to disclose a source in a later case, the same judge thought the order necessary under local law but also "necessary in the sense in which that word has been interpreted by the European Court of Human Rights".[145] (The European Court of Human Rights was subsequently to take a different view of the Convention from Lord Templeman in both cases.[146])

---

[141] *Attorney-General* v. *Observer Ltd.; Attorney-General* v. *Times Newspapers Ltd, op. cit.,* note 140, at p. 178.

[142] *Ibid.*, at p. 283.

[143] *Ibid.*

[144] *Attorney-General* v. *Guardian Newspapers* [1987] 1 W.L.R. 1248, at p. 1297. Lord Ackner agreed, at p. 1307. See also *Attorney-General* v. *Observer, re an application by Derbyshire County Council* [1988] 1 All E.R. 385.

[145] *X Ltd.* v. *Morgan-Grampian Ltd.* [1991] 1 A.C. 1, at p. 49. See also *In re an Inquiry under the Company Securities (Insider Dealing) Act 1985* [1988] A.C. 660, at p. 706 *per* Lord Griffiths.

[146] *Observer and Guardian* v. *United Kingdom* Series A, No. 216 (1991) 14 E.H.R.R. 153; *Goodwin* v. *United Kingdom*, (1996) 22 E.H.R.R. 123.

Part III: The Decisions of the European Court of Human Rights Involving The United Kingdom[147]

1. GENERAL

In the period from the acceptance of the right of individual petition in 1966 to the end of 1995, the United Kingdom found itself before the European Court of Human Rights on no fewer than 60 occasions.[148] In 37 of these cases the Court found a breach of one or more of the provisions of the Convention or its protocols, with a combined total of 49 violations being recorded against the UK in these 37 cases. Sixteen of these violations were of Article 8; thirteen were of Article 6; five were of Article 5; four were of Article 10; three were of Article 13; and three were of Article 3. The remaining (one-off) violations were of Articles 2, 7, 11, 14 (in conjunction with Article 8) and the Second Protocol. It is frequently said of Britain that it is the worst offender in Strasbourg, but (though once true in terms of the volume of cases decided against the country) this is a claim that is now out-of-date. At the end of March 1995, when the figure against the UK stood at 35, Italy had been held to have infringed the Convention on no fewer than 82 occasions, and France (29), Austria (27) and the Netherlands (23) had also clocked up a substantial number of adverse judgments.[149] It is not necessary to share the UK government's scepticism about incorporating the Convention to recognise the relevance of factors such as population and the date of acceptance of the right of individual petition to a fair evaluation of any nation's true place in a European league table for human rights.[150]

Even making allowance for such factors, however, any such table is bound to be arbitrary insofar as it relies for data solely on adverse judgments of the Court. Important Commission opinions which never reach the Court

---

[147] See the excellent surveys by F. J. Hampson, "The United Kingdom Before the European Court of Human Rights" [1990] *Yearbook of European Law* 121 and A. W. Bradley, "The United Kingdom before the Strasbourg Court 1975–1990 in W. Finnie, C. Himsworth and N. Walker (eds.), *Edinburgh Essays in Public Law* (Edinburgh, 1991), p. 185.

[148] One of these cases was the inter-state application, *Ireland* v. *United Kingdom*, *op. cit.*, note 52. The total of 60 mentioned in the text excludes a further sixteen cases which were concerned only with the issue of just satisfaction under Article 50. Also excluded are four cases which the Court formally struck out after friendly settlements had been achieved: for details, see note 152, below.

[149] See House of Lords Parliamentary Debates, vol. 563, col. 43 (written answer) (18 April 1995) (Baroness Chalker).

[150] See the debate at House of Lords Parliamentary Debates, vol. 560, cols. 1136–1174 (25 January 1995) and in particular the speech by Baroness Blatch at cols. 1164–1170. On the government's assessment, the UK is 15th overall: see col. 1166.

do not figure in the statistics quoted above, and neither do decisions which have fallen to be decided by the Committee of Ministers under Article 32.[151] Governments can keep their negative ratings low by settling cases in advance of defeat in the European Court, and there is some recent evidence that the United Kingdom has on occasion engaged in such tactical manoeuvring.[152] Just as important is the assumption behind any such league table that the European Court of Human Rights is necessarily always right in its assessment of the requirements of human rights, and that the Convention is a perfect document with which to execute this moral task. In fact, many of the cases in which the United Kingdom has been exonerated from any infringement of the Convention have been as important as those in which she has been held to account. Controversial decisions such as those on asylum,[153] on the UK's derogation in respect of Article 5,[154] and on the breadth of army and police powers in Northern Ireland[155] do not figure in the statistics above because the Court upheld the government's submission of no infringement in each case, but this does not mean that all three subjects do not continue to figure in critical assessments of the UK's record on human rights and civil liberties. The jurisprudence of the European Court of Human Rights is not an exclusive yardstick as far as the protection of human rights and civil liberties is concerned.

As we shall see, the United Kingdom's record of dealing with ECHR judgments adverse to it with relative efficiency is a good one. As Baroness Blatch pointed out on behalf of the government in January 1995, "of the 89 cases that [were] currently on the books of the Council of Ministers as awaiting substantive resolution under Article 54, only three [arose] from the United Kingdom, of which two relate[d] to judgments given as recently as October 1994."[156] Controversy in Britain surrounds not so much the fact of

---

[151] See generally Tomkins, above, Chapter 1.

[152] Note the cases of *Y* Series A, No. 247–A (1992) 17 E.H.R.R. 238; *Lamguindaz* Series A, No. 258–C (1993) 17 E.H.R.R. 213; *Colman* Series A, No. 258–D (1993) 18 E.H.R.R. 119; and *Boyle* Series A, No. 282–B (1994) 19 E.H.R.R. 179, all of which were struck out by the Court after late friendly settlements had been achieved.

[153] *Vilvarajah* v. *United Kingdom* Series A, No. 215 (1991) 14 E.H.R.R. 248.

[154] *Brannigan and McBride* v. *United Kingdom* Series A, No. 258–B (1993) 17 E.H.R.R. 539.

[155] *Murray* v. *United Kingdom* Series A, No. 300–A (1994) 19 E.H.R.R. 193.

[156] House of Lords Parliamentary Debates, vol. 560, col. 1165 (25 January 1995). The three cases Baroness Blatch had in mind probably were *Gaskin* v. *United Kingdom* Series A, No. 160 (1989) 12 E.H.R.R. 36; *Boner* v. *United Kingdom*, below, note 170; and *Maxwell* v. *United Kingdom* below, note 170.

executive action as the extent to which the government's responses to the decisions have accorded with their spirit and sometimes even with their text. Few judgments of the Court are as straightforward as *Boyle and Rice*,[157] *McCallum*[158] or *Fox, Campbell and Hartley*,[159] in each of which legislative reform had pre-empted the need for any further response. Nor was *Gillow* typical, in which case a breach of the applicants' right to respect for their home was found, not because the system of licensing operated by the Guernsey Housing Authority was flawed in itself but because it had been wrongly applied in the applicants's case so as to deprive them of a license that they should have received.[160] Here compliance entailed nothing more than the payment of the compensation assessed by the Court under Article 50 as amounting to £10,000.[161] In what follows, we shall concentrate on cases that required some more robust executive response than in either of these situations, and we shall attempt to assess not only its occurrence but also its efficacy. (In what follows I am happy gratefully to acknowledge the help I have received from the exhaustive survey conducted by Churchill and Young.[162])

In assessing the implementation of the decisions of the Court, it is obvious that it is necessary to categorise the cases in some way, just as it is equally obvious that any system of categorisation is bound to be somewhat arbitrary. The method adopted here will be based on a threefold division of the case-law into first, those decisions concerned with technical due process; secondly, those that deal with the protection of domestic minorities; and thirdly those decisions that are concerned with the protection of civil liberties.[163] A fourth group of cases, covering decisions dealing with substantive rights under the Convention and its Protocols, is considered by way of conclusion to this part.

---

[157] Series A, No. 131 (1988) 10 E.H.R.R. 425.

[158] Series A, No. 183 (1990) 13 E.H.R.R. 596.

[159] Series A, No. 182 (1990) 13 E.H.R.R. 157.

[160] Series A, No. 109 (1986) 11 E.H.R.R. 335.

[161] For these consequential proceedings, see Series A, No. 124 (1987) 13 E.H.R.R. 593.

[162] R. R. Churchill and J. R. Young, "Compliance with Judgments of the European Court of Human Rights and Decisions of the Committee of Ministers: The Experience of the United Kingdom 1975–1987" [1991] *British Yearbook of International Law* 283.

[163] See C. A. Gearty, "The European Court of Human Rights and the Protection of Civil Liberties: An Overview" (1993) 52 *Cambridge Law Journal* 89.

2. TECHNICAL DUE PROCESS

What we are concerned with here are those cases in which the Court has found in Article 5, 6 or 7 a mandate for the imposition of better procedural safeguards for the individual in the arenas of criminal, civil, or administrative law.[164] A good example is *Fox, Campbell and Hartley*,[165] in which the applicants were detained in Northern Ireland for periods ranging between 30 and 44 hours under section 1 of the Northern Ireland (Emergency Provisions) Act 1978, which allowed the arrest without warrant of "any person suspected of being a terrorist". The Court found by a narrow majority (four votes to three) that this provision infringed Article 5.1(c) under which a "reasonable suspicion" was required before such an arrest. As we have noted, the legislation had already changed before the judgment of the Court, so no issue of compliance arose.[166] More serious from the government's point of view was the earlier due process decision of *Brogan*,[167] in which the Court by a majority of 12 votes to seven held that the detention of four men under the Prevention of Terrorism Act, for periods ranging from four days and six hours to six days and 16 and a half hours, infringed the requirement in Article 5.3 that "[e]veryone arrested or detained in accordance with the provisions of paragraph 1.c of this Article shall be brought promptly before a judge or other officer authorised by law to exercise judicial power." The government's response was to derogate from the requirements of the provision insofar as this was warranted by the "public emergency threatening the life of the nation" which was how the crisis in Northern Ireland was described, this being the formula that is required under Article 15. This derogation was subsequently upheld by the Court in an important decision in May 1993.[168]

Another decision on due process whose implementation could hardly be described as unequivocal was *Granger*,[169] in which the Court held that a refusal of legal aid by the relevant state authorities should have been reviewed during the appeal proceedings in the case by which time it had become apparent that the case was more complex than it had earlier appeared. By the

---

[164] See *ibid.*, at pp. 99–108.

[165] *Op. cit.*, note 159.

[166] (1990) 13 E.H.R.R. 157, at para. 22. For a critique of other aspects of this decision, see C. A. Gearty, "The Cost of Human Rights: English Judges and the Northern Irish Troubles" (1994) 47 *Current Legal Problems* 19, at pp. 29–31.

[167] Series A, No. 145 (1988) 11 E.H.R.R. 117.

[168] *Brannigan and McBride* v. *United Kingdom*, *op. cit.*, note 154.

[169] Series A, No. 174 (1990) 12 E.H.R.R. 469.

time this judgment emerged from Strasbourg, the whole system for the administration of legal aid had been reformed for Scotland by the Legal Aid (Scotland) Act 1986, which had come into effect on 1 April 1987. According to a practice note circulated by the Lord Justice General to all appeal courts after *Granger*, the Scottish appeal courts are now invited to make a recommendation to the Legal Aid Board that an earlier decision to refuse legal aid should be reviewed where it is considered that "prima facie an appellant may have substantial grounds for taking the appeal and it is in the interests of justice that the appellant should have legal representation in arguing his grounds". It is arguable that *Granger* required a more robust implementation than a judicial circular of this sort. After the note had been issued, two appeals against two separate and serious convictions took place in Edinburgh in January and in March 1991, in both of which the appellants were not legally represented because they had been refused legal aid to pursue their appeals. These cases also eventually ended up in Strasbourg, where the European Court found the circumstances of each to amount to a violation of Article 6.3(c), notwithstanding the "undoubtedly...positive development" of a "new practice more favourable to the unrepresented appellant" in the aftermath of the *Granger* decision.[170] In the course of its submissions to the Court in both these later cases, the government had warned that an adverse ruling might "have as its consequence the ending of the automatic right of appeal"[171] presently enjoyed by such accuseds, but the Court twice answered the point by declaring it not to be its "function to indicate the measures to be taken by national authorities to ensure that their appeals system satisfies the requirements of Article 6.[172] By the end of 1995, there had been no Committee of Ministers' resolution under Article 54 in either case.

A final criminal case, also as yet unimplemented, which may be briefly mentioned at this juncture, is *Welch*.[173] In this case the retrospective imposition of a confiscation order following a conviction in respect of drugs offences was unanimously held to infringe Article 7's prohibition of retrospective penalties. In later Article 50 proceedings, the Court denied the applicant any monetary compensation for this breach of his rights, holding that the decision in his favour on the point of principle was sufficient just

---

[170] *Boner* v. *United Kingdom* Series A, No. 300–B (1994) 19 E.H.R.R. 246, at para. 41; *Maxwell* v. *United Kingdom*, Series A, No. 300–C (1994) 19 E.H.R.R. 97, at para. 38.

[171] *Boner, ibid.*, at para. 42; *Maxwell, ibid.*, at para. 39.

[172] *Boner, ibid.*, at para. 43; *Maxwell, ibid.*, at para. 40.

[173] Series A, No. 307–A (1995) 20 E.H.R.R. 247.

satisfaction for him.[174] This ruling does not of course end the United Kingdom's obligations in respect of the original judgment, however.

The requirements of due process under the European Convention extend beyond the criminal law, a fact that may be seen from *McMichael*, in which the Court found violations of Articles 6 and 8 in a case in which the applicants were not given sight of certain documents submitted in legal proceedings which were to determine the custody and access arrangements in regard to their son who had been taken into care by the local authority.[175] Decided in February 1995, the case has yet to be the subject of an Article 54 resolution. The implications for the law in England and Wales of an earlier set of cases, on the procedures followed and remedies available with regard to decisions as to parents' access to their children placed in the care of a local authority,[176] were addressed in the Children Act 1989, which came into force in October 1991. *Darnell*, finally, was also a decision in which the procedural remit of the ECHR was seen to extend beyond the criminal law.[177] The case concerned the unjustifiable length of proceedings relating to the termination of the applicant's employment by Trent Regional Health Authority, and the Committee of Ministers accepted that the payment of the sum awarded the applicant by the Court was all that was required of the UK by way of implementation.

3. THE PROTECTION OF DOMESTIC MINORITIES

The protection provided by the Court in this category of cases is to groups within member states that are in a comparatively weak political position, the fragility of which leaves them vulnerable to being oppressed by insensitive majorities.[178] The means of protection accorded these groups by the Court has once again been mainly procedural rather than substantive in character. By far the largest number of these cases emanating from the United Kingdom have been to do with prisoners' rights. No fewer than eight such deci-

---

[174] *Welch* v. *United Kingdom (Article 50)* Judgment of the European Court of Human Rights, 26 February 1996.

[175] Series A, No. 308 (1995) 20 E.H.R.R. 205.

[176] *O* v. *United Kingdom* Series A, No. 120 (1987) 10 E.H.R.R. 82; *H* v. *United Kingdom* Series A, No. 120 (1987) 10 E.H.R.R. 95; *W* v. *United Kingdom* Series A, No. 121 (1987) 10 E.H.R.R. 29; *B* v. *United Kingdom* Series A, No. 121 (1987) 10 E.H.R.R. 87; *R* v. *United Kingdom* Series A, No. 121 (1987) 10 E.H.R.R. 74.

[177] Series A, No. 272 (1993) 18 E.H.R.R. 205.

[178] See C. A. Gearty, *op. cit.*, note 163, at p. 108. See generally *ibid.*, at pp. 108–115.

sions (more than one-fifth the total of all the adverse decisions) involve prisoners and fall to be considered under this head.

The most important of these was the first, *Golder*.[179] While the applicant had been an inmate in a British jail he had desired to sue a prison officer for libel, as a result of an incident that had taken place during his incarceration. At the time the authorities refused him permission to consult a solicitor with a view to instituting these proceedings. After his release, Golder took his case to Strasbourg, where the Court unanimously held that the prison authorities' action had infringed Article 8.1's guarantee of respect for the applicant's correspondence, and moreover that none of the exceptions to this right set out in Article 8.2 applied. The Court also held (albeit by nine votes to three) that the applicant's right of access to the courts, assured by Article 6.1, had been infringed. The government's response was to amend the prison rules so as to allow a prisoner "to correspond with a solicitor for the purpose of obtaining legal advise concerning any cause of action in relation to which the prisoner may become a party to civil proceedings or for the purpose of instructing the solicitor to issue such proceedings."[180] However further directions qualified this rule by requiring that the prison complaints procedure first be exhausted in cases arising out of or in connection with a prisoner's incarceration.

This "prior ventilation" rule was subsequently declared to be an infringement of Article 6.1 in *Campbell and Fell*,[181] by which time, however, it had already been altered after earlier Strasbourg proceedings which had not reached the Court.[182] *Campbell and Fell* also impugned another aspect of the British prison system—regarding consultations between prisoners and their legal advisers—which had been altered before the Court reached its judgment, but the alteration was not formalised in an amendment to the Prison Rules until 1989, five years after the judgment.[183] This issue came before the European Court yet again in 1992 in *Campbell*.[184] The applicant prisoner's

---

[179] *Op. cit.*, note 49.

[180] Rule 37A(4), introduced by S.I. 1976, No. 503. The rule change was preceded by a circular instruction to prison governors to the same effect.

[181] Series A, No. 80 (1984) 7 E.H.R.R. 165. The full story is at Churchill and Young, *op. cit.*, note 162 above, at pp. 300–303.

[182] The simultaneous ventilation rule that replaced the prior ventilation rule was itself struck down as *ultra vires* in the English High Court insofar as it restricted access to the courts: *R. v. Secretary of State for the Home Department, ex parte Anderson* [1984] Q.B. 778.

[183] S.I. 1989, No. 30.

[184] Series A, No. 233–A (1992) 15 E.H.R.R. 137.

correspondence with his lawyer and his mail from the European Commission of Human Rights was being regularly opened and read by the authorities in accordance with the Prison Rules and Standing Orders then in place. The Court, by a majority of eight to one, found both practices to be an infringement of Article 8. Following the decision, an administrative circular[185] was promulgated with a view to amending the standing orders applying to the correspondence of all categories of prisoners, and this circular was followed by a change in the standing orders themselves on 18 November 1992. The general question of prisoners' correspondence was the subject of *Silver*,[186] under which various restrictions on a convicted prisoner's right to send and receive letters were found to infringe Article 8. However, action that the government had taken after the Commission's Report in 1981 meant that, as regards England and Wales, no changes were required in the aftermath of the Court's decision, and these reforms were eventually extended to Scotland in 1983 and to Northern Ireland in 1985. This meant that, as regards Scotland, two subsequent adverse Court decisions which were based on the rules before 1983 were found not to require further implementation.[187]

Three cases taken to Strasbourg by prisoners remain to be considered. The first of these has already been mentioned in other contexts though its main importance lies in its effect on the prison disciplinary system. As a result of the ruling in *Campbell and Fell*[188], the government wrote to the chairpersons of the relevant disciplinary tribunals around the country advising them (in the interests of the open justice the Court confirmed was required by Article 6) to inform the local press of the details of any especially grave disciplinary charge that was brought against any inmate. The government also implemented another part of the judgment by advising the same chairpersons of the fact that legal representation should be permitted in all cases involving especially grave offences.[189] Arrangements were also made for the

---

[185] No. 50A 6/92. See DH (93) 5 for the resolution of the Committee of Ministers under Article 54.

[186] Series A, No. 61 (1983) 5 E.H.R.R. 347. Infringements of Articles 6 and 13 were also found.

[187] *Boyle and Rice* v. *United Kingdom, op. cit.*, note 157. The letter sent by the applicant in this case was stopped by the governor "as a result of an erroneous application of the Prison Rules. The necessary measures have been taken to ensure that the rules are correctly applied in future" see DH (88) 17 [1988] *Yearbook of the European Convention on Human Rights 1988* (Dordrecht, 1993), at pp. 209–210; *McCallum* v. *United Kingdom, op. cit.* note 158.

[188] *Op. cit.*, note 181.

[189] The issue was at this point also covered by English public law: see *R.* v. *Secretary of State*

provision of legal aid.[190] The decision of *Weeks*[191] concerned the plight of prisoners facing indeterminate life sentences. The applicant had been given such a sentence after a robbery involving a starting pistol and a blank cartridge had yielded a "take" of 35 pence. The sentencing court accepted evidence of the defendant's aggressive and unstable nature which led it to the view that he was a danger to the public. After conviction and in accordance with the then applicable law, Weeks' continuing incarceration became a matter for the Home Secretary. In the following twenty years, he was three times released on license, with his license being revoked on each occasion by the Home Office.

When the *Weeks* case finally came before it, the Court held that the revocation of the license in such circumstances could be compatible with Article 5.1(a)[192] if it were for the same reasons as had led to the decision to impose a life sentence in the first place. On the facts, taking due account of the margin of appreciation, this was found to be the case as far as Weeks was concerned. However, the Court went on to hold that there had been an infringement of Article 5.4, under which everyone "who is deprived of his liberty...shall be entitled to take proceedings by which the lawfulness of his detention shall be decided speedily by a court...". Weeks had not had the chance to apply to a court for an assessment of the lawfulness of his imprisonment on the occasion of any recall and at reasonable intervals during his imprisonment. The Court found that the parole board did not fulfil the function of a court in this instance because its power was generally advisory rather than adjudicative and in any event its procedural guarantees were somewhat deficient.

Weeks was an important decision with far reaching implications for the management of Britain's life prisoners. Many such inmates are persons whose sentences have been imposed so as to protect the public from their mental instability. For such prisoners, there is bound to be a time in their sentence when they are no longer being detained for punishment but are being held only because it is judged that they continue to represent a threat to the public. Such inmates would seem to fall full square within *Weeks*. The

---

    for the Home Department, ex parte Tarrant [1985] Q.B. 251.

[190] See Churchill and Young, *op. cit.*, note 162, at pp. 311–313 for the full details of this case and its aftermath.

[191] Series A, No. 114 (1987) 10 E.H.R.R. 293.

[192] "No one shall be deprived of his liberty save in the following cases and in accordance with a procedure prescribed by law:

    (a) the lawful detention of a person after conviction by a competent court...".

government's immediate reaction to the case was, however, to declare its implications to be "very limited".[193] Weeks' life sentence was remitted and he was paid the £8,000 that he had been awarded by the European Court for loss of opportunity and for feelings of frustration and helplessness caused him by the infringement of his Convention rights.[194] There matters appeared to have rested until *Thynne, Wilson and Gunnell*,[195] decided over three years later in which *Weeks* was applied in the context of three sex offenders who had been sentenced to life imprisonment. This decision finally produced a legislative response in the form of section 34 of the Criminal Justice Act 1991, under which a court sentencing a discretionary life prisoner could specify that part of the sentence which reflected the severity of the offence. After this part of the sentence had been served, the section went on to provide a procedure whereby his or her sentence would then be automatically reviewed at regular intervals by an autonomous Parole Board, thereby complying with the requirements of Article 5.4.[196]

The three other domestic minorities that have been protected by the European Court of Human Rights may be dealt with more briefly since none has attracted more than a single case. First in *X. v. United Kingdom*,[197] the applicant was ordered to be detained for an indefinite period in a mental hospital, after he had been convicted of a serious criminal office. After some time his mental health improved and he was conditionally discharged, only to be recalled following complaints from his wife. Like Weeks some years later, X complained that there was no procedure in place which would allow him to have the lawfulness of his compulsory return to hospital speedily decided by a court, as was (he claimed) required by Article 5.4. The Court agreed that the procedures infringed the Convention guarantee and that they were not saved by the possibility of *habeas corpus* or by recourse to a mental health tribunal since neither option had the engagement with both the law and the merits that Article 5.4 was held to require. The judgment was implemented by enlarging the jurisdiction of the mental health tribunals through enactment of the Mental Health (Amendment) Act 1982 which

---

[193] House of Commons Parliamentary Debates, vol. 115, col. 152 (written answer) (29 April 1987).

[194] The full story is at Churchill and Young, *op. cit.*, note 162, at pp. 313–315.

[195] *Op. cit.*, note 130.

[196] For the interrelationship between section 34 and the ECHR, see *R. v. Canons Park Mental Health Review Tribunal, ex parte A, op. cit.*, note 124; *R. v. Secretary of State for the Home Department, ex parte T., op. cit.*, note 129.

[197] *Op. cit.*, note 126.

came into force on 30 September 1983.[198] Secondly there is the well known case of *Dudgeon*,[199] under which the laws criminalising certain homosexual acts in Northern Ireland were held to infringe Article 8 of the Convention. Like *X*, this case provoked a legislative response, albeit in the form of secondary rather than primary legislation.[200] Though the government acted quickly and in the face of strong objections from many in Northern Ireland, it did not take the opportunity offered by the Court to extend the effect of the judgment to the two other jurisdictions under its aegis which had at the time of the judgment similar bans on homosexual behaviour firmly in place.[201]

Our final example of the Court's role in relation to the protection of minorities provoked a very controversial response from the government. In *Abdulaziz, Cabales and Balkandali* v. *United Kingdom*,[202] the Court unanimously found a breach of Article 8 taken in conjunction with Article 14 in immigration rules which allowed the wives of immigrants to join them in Britain but at the same time denied the same right to the husbands of women permanently settled in the United Kingdom. Three months after the judgment, the government amended the rules so as to remove from wives (and fiancées) the privilege of entry that had previously been accorded them.[203] The assimilation of their position to that of the men meant that no Article 14 issue could now arise. The apparent triumph for the immigrant minority in the Court turned out in fact to be a defeat, and a worse defeat than if the case had found in favour of the UK authorities.

4. THE PROTECTION OF CIVIL LIBERTIES

Here we are concerned with cases which deal with the traditional civil liberties of expression (Article 10) and association (Article 11), together with a couple of decisions which have deployed the right to privacy in Article 8 as a means through which to improve the democratic accountability of state authorities or to force such organs to be more open. Interestingly, there has been no case from the United Kingdom which has raised an issue of free-

---

[198] See further the Mental Health Act 1983 and generally Churchill and Young, *op. cit.*, note 162, at pp. 298–300.

[199] Series A, No. 45 (1981) 4 E.H.R.R. 149.

[200] Homosexual Offences (Northern Ireland) Order, S.I. 1982, No. 1536, which came into force on 9 December 1982.

[201] The two places were the Isle of Man and Jersey.

[202] Series A, No. 94 (1985) 7 E.H.R.R. 471.

[203] See H.C. 503 (1984–85), amending HC 169 (1982–83).

dom of assembly under Article 11, notwithstanding the draconian changes in this area of the law over the past ten years.[204] The controversial decision on freedom of association under that Article did not require any implementation as the new Conservative administration that was in place when the judgment emerged was more than happy to go along with its ECHR-based objections to the "closed shop" in the workplace.[205] Of the four Article 10 cases, the first and most important is *The Sunday Times* v. *United Kingdom (No. 1)*,[206] in which a unanimous House of Lords ruling on the common law of contempt was held by the Court by the narrowest of margins (eleven to nine) to have infringed Article 10. The government's response to the judgment was the Contempt of Court Act 1981, which put the law in this area on a largely statutory basis and which gave a greater priority to freedom of expression than had previously been the case. Though it has been doubted whether the Act complies entirely with the requirements of the Convention, no case challenging its strict liability contempt provisions has as yet reached the European Court.[207]

Two of the remaining three Article 10 cases which have resulted in defeat for the United Kingdom grew out of the *Spycatcher* litigation that was such a dominant feature of British politics in the late 1980s, when the government tried all manner of legal means to prevent the publication of the memoirs of the former member of the British security service, Peter Wright.[208] In both *Observer and Guardian* v. *United Kingdom*[209] and *The Sunday Times* v. *United Kingdom (No. 2)*,[210] the Court was unanimously of the view that it was inappropriate and a breach of Article 10 for the English courts to have kept in place temporary injunctions of a wide-ranging nature

---

[204] See in particular the Public Order Act 1986 and the Criminal Justice and Public Order Act 1994.

[205] *Young, James and Webster* v. *United Kingdom* Series A, No. 44 (1981) 4 E.H.R.R. 38. See the Employment Act 1982, s. 2.

[206] *Op. cit.*, note 50. For evidence of the adverse reaction the decision provoked from some quarters in the United Kingdom, see note 53, above.

[207] This may be at least partly because of the ECHR-sensitive way in which the legislation was interpreted by the House of Lords in *Attorney-General* v. *English, op. cit.,* note 104. For a recent judgment, adverse to the United Kingdom, on the question of the disclosure of journalists' sources (a matter covered by s. 10 of the Contempt of Court Act 1981), see *Goodwin* v. *United Kingdom, op. cit.*, note 146.

[208] See the text at notes 141–146, above.

[209] *Op. cit.*, note 146.

[210] Series A, No. 217 (1991) 14 E.H.R.R. 229.

in respect of the book after it had been published in the United States.[211] The government was ordered by the Court to pay each applicant a sum of money to reflect the cost and expense of embarking on the litigation, and the Committee of Ministers in due course held that the payment of these sums was sufficient implementation of the judgments for the purposes of Article 54. The two cases therefore managed not to raise the difficult question of how, short of legislative action, a judgment of the Court which finds fault in the judge-made or common law of the United Kingdom can be properly implemented, short of legislation. Had the public body involved not been a court, it is surely the case that a direction from the government requiring regard for the Convention in future similar situations would have been the very least that would have been expected As we have seen, this issue has arisen once again in the light of the judgment of the Court in *Tolstoy Miloslavsky* v. *United Kingdom*,[212] in which a jury award of £1.5 million damages in a libel action was held to have infringed Article 10's guarantee of freedom of expression. It is, however, probable that common law developments since that decision, culminating in the very recently decided *John* v. *MGN*,[213] mean that the law is presently in line with the spirit as well as the letter of *Tolstoy Miloslavsky*. (We should recall that the judgment in *John* v. *MGN* was explicitly stated to have been arrived at independently of the Convention and its case-law.[214])

Finally in this section, we turn to the two Article 8 cases, in which the Court has sought to impose procedural controls on the exercise of power by the state. The first of these decisions was *Malone* v. *United Kingdom*,[215] which was the Strasbourg case that followed the ruling on telephone tapping by the Vice-Chancellor Sir Robert Megarry. (This was the case which we earlier considered in the context of analysing the relative lack of influence of the ECHR in the evolution of the common law.[216]) The telephone tapping engaged in by the authorities was not controlled or structured by any law, and this fact was sufficient in itself for the European Court unanimously to rule that the interference with the applicant's right to privacy that was necessarily involved in the tapping was not "in accordance with the law" under

---

[211] The Court upheld (by 14 votes to 10) the validity of the injunctions in the period before publication in the United States.

[212] *Op. cit.*, note 139.

[213] *Op. cit.*, note 138.

[214] Text at note 138, above.

[215] Series A, No. 82 (1984) 7 E.H.R.R. 14.

[216] See above text at note 88.

Article 8.2. The UK government was therefore held to be in breach of Article 8, without any consideration of the extent to which such tapping, if it were prescribed by law, would be "necessary in a democratic society". The legislation that followed the ruling put the interception of communication on a statutory basis but it is not clear as to the extent to which it complied with the requirements of the ECHR, particularly if the earlier and fuller case of *Klass* v. *Federal Republic of Germany*[217] is also taken into account.[218]

In the second Article 8 case, *Gaskin* v. *United Kingdom*,[219] the applicant had been refused disclosure of confidential records relating to the time when he had been in care as a child. The Court ruled that this amounted to a breach of Article 8 because there was no independent body in place to make a fair and balanced judgment as to what should be disclosed. The Court found an infringement of the Convention in the fact that the public authority involved was both a party to the dispute and the body with responsibility for adjudicating upon it. This case was decided early in 1988, despite which it has yet to be the subject of a determination by the Committee of Ministers under Article 54. The reluctance to implement the decision may be because of its cost implications or it may be on account of a governmental hostility to any kind of freedom of information initiative. However, on 17 December 1993, the minister at the Home Office Mr Douglas Hogg assured parliament that "legislation [was] to be introduced".[220]

5. SUBSTANTIVE RIGHTS

Even *Gaskin* is not so much a freedom of information decision as one rooted in the requirement of procedural fairness. Though it is primarily with various types of such fairness that the Court has been concerned, both generally and specifically in relation to the United Kingdom, there are a couple of Convention Articles which are more substantive in nature. The first of these is the right to life guaranteed in Article 2, and this has been the subject of the notable decision of *McCann* v. *United Kingdom*, in which the Court held by a ten to 9 majority that the killing of three IRA members by a state undercover team breached the victims' Article 2 rights on account of the fact (as the majority found) that the planning of the operation was so inefficient as to make their deaths its likely (but nevertheless properly avoidable) out-

---

[217] *Op. cit.*, note 89.

[218] See K. D. Ewing and C. A. Gearty, *op. cit.*, note 113, ch. 3; Churchill and Young, *op. cit.*, note 162, at pp. 321–326.

[219] *Op. cit.*, note 156.

[220] House of Commons Parliamentary Debates, vol. 234, col. 960 (written answer).

come.[221] In view of the fact-specific basis for the finding of a violation, it remains to be seen whether more than the payment of the applicants' costs will be required to satisfy the Committee of Ministers. An even more controversial decision to emerge out of the Northern Ireland troubles was the earlier *Ireland* v. *United Kingdom*,[222] the only inter-state application so far to have reached the Court. The case mainly concerned allegations of systematic ill-treatment against suspects held by the authorities under the regime of internment that was introduced in the Province in August 1971. The Court found that the five techniques involved in the practice of "interrogation in depth" (wall-standing; hooding; continuous noise; deprivation of food; and deprivation of sleep) amounted to "inhuman and degrading treatment" contrary to Article 3.[223] By the time of the Court hearing, the UK government had already given parliament an assurance that the techniques were no longer in use and would not once again be resorted to.[224] This undertaking was then buttressed by directives to the police and army and by other initiatives in the realm of police accountability.[225] These reforms were enough to allow the Committee of Ministers to satisfy itself that the UK had complied with the Court's judgment.[226]

As Churchill and Young have remarked of *Ireland* v. *United Kingdom*, "the difficulty in evaluating compliance…was that a change in the law was not necessary, since the powers conferred on the security forces by law did not require amendment. What required amendment was official tolerance of, or complicity in, behaviour that was already unlawful under the law of Northern Ireland and was in breach of existing disciplinary regulations."[227] The same point can be made about *McCann*. The Convention mechanisms are unfortunately singularly ill-equipped to deal with an alleged culture of state lawlessness. These Article 3 cases may be contrasted with *Campbell and Cosans* v. *United Kingdom*,[228] in which the claim that corporal punishment in Scottish state schools was "inhuman and degrading treatment" was

---

[221] Series A, No. 324 (1995) 21 E.H.R.R. 97.

[222] *Op. cit.*, note 52.

[223] The Commission's earlier finding of "torture" under the same Article was therefore departed from.

[224] House of Commons Parliamentary Debates, vol. 832, col. 744 (2 March 1972) (Mr Edward Heath).

[225] The details are at Churchill and Young, *op. cit.*, note 162, at pp. 293–296.

[226] Resolution DH (78) 35.

[227] Churchill and Young, *op. cit.*, note 162, at pp. 295–296.

[228] Series A, No. 48 (1982) 4 E.H.R.R. 293.

avoided by the Court in favour of a finding that such a punishment regime wrongly inhibited the right of the parents involved to have their sons' education conducted in conformity with "their own...philosophical convictions."[229] The breach of the Convention was undenied but the necessary mode of implementing the judgment—legislation—proved difficult to achieve. The government's first suggestion was that parents be allowed to exempt their children from corporal punishment, but the Bill that sought to enact this fairly narrow form of compliance was withdrawn after an amendment which would effectively have banned all corporal punishment was carried in the House of Lords. A further education bill the following year contained no mention of the issue when it was published by the government, but a Lords amendment once again added outright abolition to its clauses. Such a change needed the sanction of the Commons, where it was supported by the narrowest of margins, 231 votes to 230, despite a degree of governmental hostility. The Education (No. 2) Act 1986, which among other provisions abolished corporal punishment in all British state schools, eventually came into force on 15 August 1987,[230] five-and-a-half years after the original judgment.

The final two judgments to be discussed in this section are both Article 3 cases. In the first, *Tyrer* v. *United Kingdom*,[231] the Court's condemnation of judicial corporal punishment in the Isle of Man as "degrading treatment" was considered by the government to be difficult to implement via Westminster legislation. This was because the island had its own legislature, the Tynwald, to which Westminster by convention deferred on matters relating to the internal affairs of the island. At this time, this assembly was certain to be opposed to any reform in this area. Accordingly, implementation was effected by the markedly indirect route of a circular from the senior member of the judiciary on the island to all his judicial colleagues legally entitled to pass such sentences, drawing their attention to the judgment. When such a sentence was subsequently imposed, the Isle of Man's High Court quashed it on appeal, holding that its imposition was contrary to the island's international obligations. In 1976, the right of individual petition from the Isle of Man was allowed to lapse, though the issues that might have precipitated an

---

[229] Article 2 of Protocol No. 1.

[230] Ss. 47 and 48. For the position in Northern Ireland, see Education (Corporal Punishment) (Northern Ireland) Order 1987, SI 1987, No. 461. Compare the position in private schools: *Costello-Roberts* v. *United Kingdom*, Series A, No. 247-C (1993) 19 E.H.R.R. 112 (corporal punishment in such schools not in violation of Article 3).

[231] *Op. cit.*, note 51.

application to Strasbourg, homosexual law reform and judicial corporal punishment, have both been the subject of reforming legislation in the Tynwald in recent years.

Our final decision, *Soering* v. *United Kingdom*,[232] also involved a curious mode of implementation. The case was unusual and important in that the complaint that the Court upheld was that, if extradited from the UK to the United States to stand trial on two counts of murder, Soering would if convicted run the risk of being placed on "death row", and that this would amount to treatment of him in breach of his Article 3 rights. The Court held that to send a person involuntarily to a country where he or she was likely to be subjected to treatment in violation of Article 3 was in itself a breach of that Article. After the judgment, the UK government informed the US authorities by means of a diplomatic note that the extradition of the applicant on charges the penalty for which might include the imposition of the death penalty would be refused. The government agreed to extradite Soering on the basis only that he would be proceeded against for first degree rather than capital murder. The US authorities confirmed that, in the light of the applicable provisions of the relevant extradition treaty between the two nations, United States law would prohibit the applicant's prosecution on other than the two first-degree murder charges that were outstanding against him. With this assurance that the death penalty could not be available, Soering was extradited to the US.

Conclusion

We can be fairly confident that each of the thirty-seven victories secured against the United Kingdom in the European Court (up to the end of 1995) has been of importance to the applicant or applicants involved. To what extent have the cases mattered more than this? At the end of 1995, 30 of these 37 decisions had been the subject of resolutions of the Committee of Ministers under Article 54. In eight of these cases, it had been decided that no changes in UK law were required, either because the issue had already been dealt with by the legislature,[233] or because on the facts all that was required was an assurance that no violation would occur,[234] or because it was consid-

---

[232] Series A, No. 161 (1989) 11 E.H.R.R. 439.

[233] *Fox, Campbell and Hartley* v. *United Kingdom*, *op. cit.* note 159; *McCallum* v. *United Kingdom, op. cit.*, note 158.

[234] *Boyle and Rice* v. *United Kingdom*, *op. cit.*, note 157; *Soering* v. *United Kingdom*, *op. cit.*, note 232.

ered that the payment of compensation in accordance with the Court's ruling was a sufficient compliance with it.[235] In one case, an assurance that an unlawful administrative practice had been brought to an end was accepted[236] and in another a derogation resulted from the finding of an infringement.[237] The remaining twenty cases all led to substantive change. In three decisions involving the exercise of judicial or quasi-judicial discretion, a circular or practice note was sent to the relevant decision-making authorities.[238] In five cases, the required change was effected via subordinate legislation or alteration to the relevant standing orders or both.[239] No fewer than fifteen of the cases have resulted in primary legislation,[240] with statutes such as the Contempt of Court Act 1981, the Interception of Communications Act 1985, together with sections of the Mental Health Act 1983, the Criminal Justice Act 1991 and the Education (No. 2) Act 1986, being the direct result of Strasbourg rulings. The European Court of Human Rights can point to substantial liberalisations in the legal regimes governing prisoners, the mentally ill, schoolchildren and (in Northern Ireland) homosexual practices that would probably not have occurred had it not been for the intervention of the Court.[241]

The Court's success in stimulating such change has depended on the willingness of successive United Kingdom governments to implement its

---

[235] *Gillow* v. *United Kingdom, op. cit.,* note 160; *Observer and Guardian* v. *United Kingdom, op. cit.,* note 146; *The Sunday Times* v. *United Kingdom (No. 2), op. cit.,* note 210; *Darnell* v. *United Kingdom, op. cit.,* note 177.

[236] *Ireland* v. *United Kingdom, op. cit.,* note 52.

[237] *Brogan* v. *United Kingdom, op. cit.,* note 167.

[238] *Campbell and Fell* v. *United Kingdom, op. cit.,* note 181; *Granger* v. *United Kingdom, op. cit.,* note 169; *Tyrer* v. *United Kingdom, op. cit.,* note 51.

[239] *Golder* v. *United Kingdom, op. cit.,* note 49; *Dudgeon* v. *United Kingdom, op. cit.,* 199; *Silver* v. *United Kingdom, op. cit.,* note 186; *Abdulaziz et al* v. *United Kingdom, op. cit.,* note 202; *Campbell* v. *United Kingdom, op. cit.,* note 184.

[240] *The Sunday Times* v. *United Kingdom (No. 1), op. cit.,* note 49; *Young, James and Webster* v. *United Kingdom, op. cit.,* note 205; *X.* v. *United Kingdom, op. cit.,* note 126; *Malone* v. *United Kingdom, op. cit.,* note 215; *Weeks* v. *United Kingdom, op. cit.,* note 191; *O, W, B, R and H* v. *United Kingdom, op. cit.,* note 176; *Thynne, Wilson and Gunnell* v. *United Kingdom, op. cit.,* note 130; *Campbell and Cosans* v. *United Kingdom, op. cit.,* note 228.

[241] It is more probable that the laws on contempt, on telephone-tapping and on the "closed shop" in employment would eventually have been reformed even if there had been no Strasbourg proceedings in any of these cases, though clearly the fact of such proceedings was an important factor in the timing of each piece of legislation and in the decision as to its content.

decisions. As was earlier suggested and as the record above indicates, the overall picture is not a bad one, with the government having generally fulfilled its Treaty obligations to the satisfaction of the Committee of Ministers. Implementation has been easiest of all when the Court ruling has been pushing at an open legislative door, as in *Young, James and Webster*. It has also been more likely to occur and more likely to be more effective when the Court ruling has been just one of a number of pressures for reform that has been brought to bear on government on a particular issue. This was the case with both *Malone* and *The Sunday Times (No. 1)* cases, and also with the more recent decisions on mentally unwell life sentence prisoners.[242] In the same way, the European Court decisions on prisoners have been all the more effective for the powerful domestic judgments that have accompanied them, at least during the 1980s.[243] In contrast, *Campbell and Cosans* was difficult to implement because the ruling offended the commitment to corporal punishment felt by many in the governing Conservative Party. It was nevertheless, and after a delay, achieved, just as was the decriminalisation of certain homosexual practices in Northern Ireland and an effective end to judicial corporal punishment in the Isle of Man, despite doubts as to the mode of implementation that have been quite rightly voiced by Churchill and Young about the latter.[244] The mean-spirited implementation of *Abdulaziz et al.* and the derogation after *Brogan* apart, it is hard to see how, in the real as supposed to an ideal political world, the record could be very much better. The doubts that there undoubtedly are about the implementation of *The Sunday Times (No. 1)* and *Malone* may flow as much from weaknesses in the Convention instrument and the Court's interpretation of it as they do from a malevolent conservatism on the part of the authorities. The one serious blot on the UK copybook at the end of 1995 was the continuing failure to bring *Gaskin* to an end through a satisfactory Article 54 resolution.

The United Kingdom's record of compliance should not be taken as evidence that the role of the European Court of Human Rights has not been controversial. As we have seen, the Court has been subject to criticism from the moment of its first intervention in UK domestic law in 1975.[245] The long running *Ireland* v. *United Kingdom* case was extremely contentious, though

---

[242] *Weeks* v. *United Kingdom, op. cit.* note 191; *Thynne, Wilson and Gunnell* v. *United Kingdom, op. cit.*, note 130.

[243] See generally C A Gearty, "Prisons and the Courts" in J. Muncie and R. Sparks (eds.), *Imprisonment: European Perspectives* (Milton Keynes, 1991), pp. 219–242.

[244] See Churchill and Young, *op. cit.*, note 162, at pp. 345–346.

[245] *Golder* v. *United Kingdom, op. cit.* note 49. For the criticisms, see note 53 above.

the eventual Court ruling that there had been no torture on the facts diluted the savagery of the criticism that had previously been directed at the Commission, which had found the opposite. It has been the Irish cases which have been the most difficult for successive British governments to accept. As we have seen, its response to *Brogan* was to derogate from Article 5, and the *McCann* decision in September 1995 on the IRA killings in Gibraltar provoked an absolutely furious reaction from the authorities. Despite this, the legal costs of the applicants in the case were paid in the way required by the Court and the right of individual application to Strasbourg was quietly renewed for a further five years in January 1996.[246] By this time, however, the European Court of Human Rights had become embroiled in a bigger debate about the role of Europe in British society in general and in British law in particular. Decisions in the European Court of Justice adverse to the government's perception of Britain's national interest were receiving wide and not necessarily sympathetic coverage in the popular as well as in the broadsheet press. Three decisions adverse to the UK from the European Court of Human Rights in the first few months of 1996, on the imprisonment of juvenile offenders,[247] the right of access to a lawyer for terrorist suspects[248] and the right of a journalist to refuse to disclose his or her sources,[249] meant that it was inevitable that the Strasbourg Court would also be drawn into further public controversy, particularly with memories of the *McCann* decision still fresh in the minds of ministers and Conservative backbench members of the House of Commons. Taken with the 1995 cases on which there has yet to be action, these early 1996 decisions will test to the full the government's commitment to implementing all the judgments of the Court adverse to it.

---

[246] House of Lords Parliamentary Debates, vol. 567, col. 117 (written answer) (Baroness Chalker) (14 December 1995).

[247] *Hussain* v. *United Kingdom*, (1996) 22 E.H.R.R. 1.

[248] *Murray (John)* v. *United Kingdom*, (1996) 22 E.H.R.R. 29.

[249] *Goodwin* v. *United Kingdom*, *op. cit.* note 146.

3. THE NETHERLANDS

Yvonne Klerk and *Eric Janse de Jonge*

Introduction

When the European Movement in July 1949 presented a draft for a European Convention on Human Rights, the Netherlands were not enthusiastic. The Ministry of Foreign Affairs at that time was afraid that it would be impossible to remove the issue from the agenda. However, it was thought important to minimise the effects of the decisions to be taken: the Convention should preferably not include a supervisory mechanism, or, if that proved to be impossible, only very limited powers should be granted to the planned Commission and Court. One of the considerations that played a role in this negative attitude was the fear that a new court might damage the prestige of the International Court of Justice, and thus of The Hague.

This negative outlook persisted throughout the drafting process. However, the Dutch government felt that it was inevitable that it would subscribe to the Convention, both from a national and an international point of view, and in the end the Netherlands voted in favour of the proposal. The ratification, though, was delayed for almost four years. When submitting the proposal for ratification to parliament the government acted in a rather complacent way. The Convention was something for other countries; for the Netherlands it was unnecessary. However, the Netherlands, "as a champion of the development of international law", could not refrain from ratifying the Convention.[1]

When ratification finally took place on 31 August 1954, the Netherlands did not recognise the individual complaints procedure. Prime Minister Drees in particular, a Social Democrat, had been a particularly fervent opponent of the right of individuals to lodge a complaint with the European Commission of Human Rights. In his opinion, a procedure in a place as far away as

---

[1] This was the answer given by the government to the advisory report of the Council of State regarding the ratification of the ECHR, 4 June 1953 (source: archives of the Ministry of Foreign Affairs, 321.20, Council of Europe, Convention on Human Rights, IV, 1953–1954).

C. A. Gearty (ed.), European Civil Liberties and the European Convention on Human Rights, 105–141.
© 1997 *Kluwer Law International. Printed in the Netherlands.*

Strasbourg, in a foreign language, would be cumbersome and expensive. Besides, he was afraid of unfounded complaints being lodged by querulous persons, particularly Communists. The government also stressed the fact that after ratification the Convention could be invoked before the Dutch courts and that this in its view offered a sufficient guarantee of adequate human rights protection. Through the 1950s, both the Council of Europe and the Dutch parliament put pressure on the Dutch government to make a declaration under Article 25.1 of the Convention. Studies by some public servants proved that the European Commission had been very cautious in its admissibility policy.[2] A decision by the European Commission to declare a complaint of some German Communists inadmissible was welcomed by the authorities. This latter case turned the scale. Eventually, on 28 June 1960 the Netherlands recognised the competence of the Commission to receive complaints against the Netherlands.

It may have been thought at that time that the European Convention would not have any influence on the Dutch legal order. The reality has proved to be quite different. On the contrary, as will be shown in this article, the influence has been great, so great in fact that it is now impossible to imagine the Dutch legal order today without the European Convention.

Part I: The Constitution and Charter of the Netherlands

1. INTRODUCTION[3]

The Netherlands gradually emerged as a united and centralised state at the end of the 16th century. In 1579 the seven Dutch provinces agreed on the establishment of a confederation of independent provinces. The basic rules for this confederation were laid down in a charter, called the Union of Utrecht. This charter laid the basis for a Republic (1581–1795). In the 17th century (known as the "Golden Age"), the Dutch Republic became a major colonial power. Parliament, the states general, was composed of the representatives of the provinces who had to vote in accordance with their instructions and the government was responsible for external relations, defence,

---

[2] See in particular: the paper by T. Koopmans to the Minister of Justice, 20 March 1957; the paper from the Minister for Foreign Affairs to the Minister of Justice, 9 July 1957; the paper by P. Eyssen to the Minister of Justice, 9 August 1957 (source: archives of the Ministry of Justice).

[3] For a general introduction to Dutch constitutional law, see J. Chorus, P.-H. Gerver, E. Hondius, A. Koekkoek (eds.), *Introduction to Dutch Law for Foreign Lawyers* (Deventer/Boston, 2nd revised ed., 1993).

overseas trading and finance. The powerful provinces were often dominated by a relatively open class of respectable bourgeois families. These families mostly owed their wealth and influence to commerce and trade. During the Republic these powerful families exercised a liberal rule displaying tolerance with respect to each other's religion and accepting freedom of the press. However, fundamental rights and rules for international relations were not to be found in the charter of 1579.

After the French occupation, the Netherlands regained their independence in 1813. The leaders of those days decided not to return to a Republic, but to introduce a monarchy under the House of Orange. The son of the last *stadhouder*, William of Orange, was welcomed as the "Sovereign" and it was decided that he should become King after fifteen months. He accepted sovereignty under the condition of "a thoughtful Constitution". This first written Constitution entered into force in 1814 but it was soon replaced by the Constitution of 1815 in order to include Belgium (added to the Netherlands by the decision of the Congress of Vienna in 1815). After 1815 the Constitution was amended and revised several times. A memorable revision took place in 1848. On this occasion the parliamentary system was introduced and this brought about a gradual shift in governmental power away from the king and towards the Dutch legislature (government in co-operation with both houses of parliament). After the revision of 1848 the Dutch constitutional system based on a written Constitution gradually developed from a rather unstable into a very stable and smoothly working system. The following 140 years were roughly dominated by two major political issues: the loss of the colonies and internationalisation. These two issues forced the legislature to change the Constitution and to introduce a charter for the former colonies.

2. THE CHARTER FOR THE KINGDOM OF THE NETHERLANDS

The Netherlands were a major colonial power for a long time. The country had territories in the East Indies (nowadays Indonesia), present-day Surinam and a number of islands in the Caribbean Sea. This situation changed drastically after the second world war when Indonesia became independent in 1949, followed by Surinam in 1975.

In 1954 the relationship between the Netherlands and its overseas territories, Surinam and the Dutch Antilles, was transformed into a quasi-federal structure. The basis for this structure can be found in the Charter of the Kingdom of the Netherlands. This Charter was revised after the independence of Surinam and forms nowadays, together with the Dutch Constitution, the constitutional basis of the Kingdom of the Netherlands (which includes the Netherlands, the Dutch Antilles and Aruba). According to Article 5, paragraph 2, the Charter is superior to the Constitution. However, a number of federal matters are referred to the Constitution for further regulation. In general terms the Charter is concerned with matters such as foreign relations, defence, nationality and the general policy concerning aliens. These issues are "matters of the Kingdom" and are handled by special organs, usually the regular Dutch organs extended with representatives from the overseas territories. The parliamentary bodies of the overseas islands inform the Dutch Parliament about their opinion with respect to bills on kingdom affairs. The king and the kingdom's government are represented in the islands by governors. Finally, the Netherlands Supreme Court also acts as a court of cassation with respect to the overseas islands. The Court has no special judges from the islands. The Netherlands have made a declaration under Article 63 of the European Convention and have extended the European Convention to the Dutch Antilles and Aruba.

3. FUNDAMENTAL RIGHTS IN THE CONSTITUTION

Despite many changes, and a complete revision in 1983, the Dutch constitution has retained the basic structure of its first edition of 1814. As to the procedure for changing it, the constitution may be considered to be a rigid one. The procedure is more ponderous than that for an ordinary Act of Parliament. In terms of its content, however, the Dutch constitution tends towards a more flexible constitution. In many cases the constitution leaves the setting of standards to the legislature or to the administrative authorities. Elsewhere it contains concepts which are open to various interpretations.

The most important renewal as a consequence of the revision of 1983 concerned the constitution's chapter on fundamental rights. In this first chapter the traditional rights are brought together with new classical and social rights. This articulation of fundamental rights is preceded by a statement of the principle of equality and non-discrimination.[4] This principle is further detailed in the General Equal Treatment Act of 1994. As for the formulation and effects of fundamental rights, three characteristics may be given. First, the principal formulation of each fundamental right can be found in section 1 of each Article. The necessary limitation of such a fun-

---

[4] Article 1: "All persons in the Netherlands shall be treated equally in equal circumstances. Discrimination on the grounds of religion, belief, political opinion, race or sex or on any other grounds whatsoever shall not be permitted".

damental right can be found—in most cases—in section 2 of each Article. An illustration of this "system" is Article 6 which reads as follows:

> 1. Everyone shall have the right to manifest freely his religion or belief, either individually or in community with others, without prejudice to his responsibility established by Act of Parliament.
> 2. Rules concerning the exercise of this right other than in buildings and enclosed places may be laid down by Act of Parliament for the protection of health, in the interest of traffic and to combat or prevent disorder.

A second feature of fundamental rights in the Dutch constitution is that it is generally held that (some) fundamental rights can also apply to relations between private persons and organisations (third party applicability). Although there has been a great deal of confusion and debate about this aspect of fundamental rights since the revision of 1983, it is clear from several recent judgments of the Supreme Court that fundamental rights play an important role in solving fundamental controversies between citizens.[5] However, the above-mentioned system of limitations which applies in the so-called vertical relationship, has no place in these horizontal relationships. A third feature is that fundamental rights equally apply to individuals with a special status such as civil servants, military personnel and prisoners. The exercise of fundamental rights by these specific categories of individuals is however somewhat restricted. These limitations should be in accordance with their explicit provisos.

The second category of fundamental rights in the constitution are social rights, for the first time introduced by the revision of 1983. Social rights have an entirely different structure and meaning as compared to the classical fundamental rights. In the first place social rights are formulated in very general terms.[6] Secondly, these rights rarely involve personal rights which can be legally enforced by a judge, though some provisions in these rights are enforceable by law. Thirdly, social rights are not intended to have any (enforceable) effect in the relations between private persons and organisations. Individuals are not responsible for creating sufficient employment, distributing wealth or promoting public health. Finally, the constitution does not recognise any hierarchy between classical and social fundamental rights.

---

[5] Supreme Court 9 January 1987, NJ [Dutch Case Law] 1987, No. 928; Supreme Court 15 April 1994, NJ 1994, No. 608.

[6] See for example Article 21: "It shall be the concern of the authorities to keep the country habitable and to protect and improve the environment."

Case law shows, however, that the government has to take classical fundamental rights into consideration when implementing social rights.[7]

4. THE RELATIONSHIP BETWEEN NATIONAL AND INTERNATIONAL LAW

Apart from the constitution itself, another important source of Dutch constitutional law is primary EC law, parts of secondary EC law, certain treaties and supra- and international jurisprudence. With regard to EC law, the Dutch constitutional system is simple and clear; Article 92 reads as follows:

> Legislative, executive and judicial powers may be conferred on international institutions by or pursuant to a treaty, subject, where necessary, to the provisions of Article 91, paragraph 3.

This provision has been the basis for conferring part of Dutch sovereignty to the EC.

Treaty law is implemented by a monistic system in the Netherlands. This means that no further national order is required for the direct operation of international law in the Dutch legal system. Of course, parliament has to approve a treaty. Most important in this respect are three paragraphs in the constitution. Article 91 defines the role of parliament in general (approving each treaty by Act of Parliament[8]) and states in paragraph 3:

> Any provisions of a treaty that conflict with the Constitution or which lead to conflicts with it can be approved by the Chambers of the States General only if at least two-thirds of the votes cast are in favour.[9]

Article 93 reads as follows:

> Provisions of treaties and of decisions by international organisations which, according to their contents, may be binding on all persons, shall have binding effect after they have been published.

Article 94 reads as follows:

> Statutory regulations in force within the Kingdom shall not be applied if such application is in conflict with provisions of treaties or of decisions by international organisations that are binding to all persons.

---

[7] See for further details C. Kortmann and P. Bovend'eert, *The Kingdom of the Netherlands. An Introduction to Dutch Constitutional Law* (Deventer/Boston, 1993), pp. 129–142.

[8] For more detail, see P. van Dijk and B. G. Tahzib, "Parliamentary Participation in the Treaty-Making Process of the Netherlands" (1992) 67 *Chicago-Kent Law Review* 413–436.

[9] On only two occasions has this Article been applied, namely the Act approving the European Defence Community (Statute Book 1954, No. 25) and the Act approving the treaty with the Indonesian Republic about Western New Guinea (Statute Book 1962, No. 363).

These provisions make it clear that international law automatically forms a part of the Dutch legal order. Certain treaties and international orders amount to constitutional law, which means that they limit or extend the powers of the Dutch authorities and grant citizens fundamental rights. The most important treaties in this respect are the European Convention on Human Rights and the International Covenant on Civil and Political Rights.

An important question is whether or not a treaty provision is self-executing, *i.e.* whether or not a provision can be invoked before the court by an individual. Neither the constitution, nor any other Act of Parliament, has specified who is competent to decide whether a treaty provision is self-executing. In the Dutch constitutional system it is up to the courts themselves to decide whether a treaty provision is to function in this way. In addition, Article 94 of the constitution covers the situation where the application of a provision in a national statute conflicts with a self-executing treaty provision. If this is the case, the court has the duty not to apply the national provision. Article 94 imposes upon the judge both an order to review and, implicitly, an order not to review. The judge is not allowed to review the application of national statutory provisions under any other provisions apart from self-executing treaty provisions. Nor is the judge allowed to review them under unwritten (customary) international law.[10]

5.   JUDICIAL REVIEW

The constitution prohibits judicial review in Article 120:

> The constitutionality of Acts of Parliament and treaties shall not be reviewed by the courts.

All Dutch courts are allowed to review lower statutory provisions under higher ones and to declare the former to be incompatible with the latter. In addition to this instruction all courts are competent and obliged to review all national statutory provisions under EC law. As mentioned above, the constitution also obliges the courts to review all domestic legislation, including Acts of Parliament and the constitution itself, under self-executing provisions of treaties to which the Kingdom of the Netherlands is a party and of binding decisions of international organisations. However, review by the courts of Acts of Parliament and provisions of treaties under the constitution is not allowed. The consequence of both sets of provisions (Articles 120 and 93–94) is that international fundamental rights, especially human rights,

---

[10]   See for further details: H.H.M. Sondaal, "Some Features of Dutch Treaty Practice" [1988] *Netherlands Yearbook of International Law* 179–257.

prevail over Acts of Parliament and even over the constitution. However, as is made clear above, the national judge is not allowed to review Acts of Parliament under national fundamental rights as laid down in the constitution. This prohibition against judicial review of Acts of Parliament was broadly interpreted by a widely and intensively discussed judgment of the Supreme Court in 1989.[11] The Court held that not only may Acts of Parliament not be examined for compatibility with the constitution, but they may also not be reviewed under the Charter (see above) or under any general legal principle either. This judgment resulted in increased criticism of the Article 120 prohibition. At the time of writing, a discussion is taking place as to whether judicial review should be introduced and, if so, as to what form it should take. However, it is not clear whether proposals for introducing judicial review for the courts can get the required two-thirds majority in both chambers of parliament, which as we have seen is necessary for changing the constitution. Part of this discussion concerns whether this review should be granted to a single judicial body such as the Supreme Court, or whether all courts should have the proposed power of judicial review.

6.   THE ORGANISATION OF THE ADMINISTRATION OF JUSTICE

The constitution of the Kingdom of the Netherlands is rather simple and clear in respect of the organisation of the judicial branch. Chapter six deals with the judiciary and states that there is a single type of judicial office which is competent to decide all kinds of disputes (except administrative disputes) and to impose penalties. The Judicial Organisation Act of 1827, as amended, is decisive for the organisation of the so-called ordinary courts. The ordinary courts are competent in civil and criminal matters and are hierarchically organised: the Supreme Court; five courts of appeal; 19 regional courts and 62 district courts. The district courts are competent with respect to claims concerning debts of less than 5,000 guilders and any claims about contract on hire, lease or employment. Against their decisions appeal can be lodged with the Regional Court and subsequently on cassation with the Supreme Court. The regional courts are competent on all matters concerning civil and criminal law. Their decisions are subject to appeal to the Court of Appeal and subsequently to the Supreme Court. As a result, the Supreme Court acts as a cassation court and is only competent on matters concerning questions of law. On fiscal disputes, the Court of Appeal is competent and the Supreme Court acts as a court of cassation.

---

[11]   Supreme Court 14 April 1989, NJ 1989, No. 469.

Members of the Supreme Court, like members of other institutions which are part of the judiciary, are appointed for life by the crown. In practice they hold office until they reach the age of seventy. It is noteworthy that members of the Supreme Court themselves recommend candidates for the membership of the Court; the Supreme Court submits a list of three persons to the second chamber of the states general. It is common practice that the first person is nominated by the second chamber and appointed by the crown. Nominees for the Supreme Court are recruited from lower courts, the Bar and from the universities.

Regarding administrative jurisdiction, the organisation has drastically changed since the introduction of the General Administrative Law Act of 1994. This Act came into force on 1 January 1994.[12] If a citizen or organisation is affected by an administrative decision, the administrative authority (local, regional or central) which is competent to take the decision is forced by the provisions of the General Administrative Law Act to reconsider the challenged decision. From this reconsidered decision of the administrative authority appeal is possible to the regional court. In 1994 the regional courts were all extended by the addition of an administrative division. From the decision of the regional court appeal lies to the Administrative Law Division of the Council of State. This Law Division is responsible for the Council's judicial functions. This Division thus reviews the legality of decisions of administrative authorities and the judgments of the administrative divisions of the regional courts. The decision of the Administrative Law Division of the Council of State is decisive.

A second source of administrative decisions can be found in the Civil Servants Act of 1929.[13] Disputes concerning the position, status and salary of civil servants and concerning social benefits, allowances and pensions (social security) are subject to a different procedure. After an administrative decision by the competent public authority, appeal lies with one of the regional courts (see above). From a judgment of this court appeal is only possible to the Central Board of Appeal. The decision of this tribunal is decisive. A third administrative court which may be briefly mentioned is the Industrial Appeals Tribunal. This court has jurisdiction over disputes arising from decisions as mentioned in several Acts in the social and economic field. This court hears cases in first and last instance, mainly based on a procedure laid down in the Industrial Organisation Act.

---

[12] Statute Book 1994, No. 1.
[13] Statute Book 1995, No. 250 (as amended).

This brief oversight of the system of administrative jurisdiction reveals a diversity of courts, which are organised along different lines. Before the introduction of the General Administrative Law Act of 1994, the system of administrative justice was even more of a hotchpotch. At this moment a full-scale reorganisation of the judiciary is at hand. The most important proposals are concerned with the merging of the district and regional courts and the judicial position of the Council of State. The latter issue is in full discussion. The central question is whether the Supreme Court's jurisdiction will also be extended to include cassation in administrative decisions by the lower courts. Strong (political) forces within the Council of State try to continue the sovereign position of its Administrative Law Division. As will be shown below, the European Court of Human Rights has had an influence on the organisation of the administration of justice in the Netherlands.

Part II: The Judiciary and the ECHR

1. INTRODUCTION

During the first twenty-five years of its existence the European Convention had no noticeable effect on the Dutch legal order. A famous anecdote tells the story of a judge before whom the Convention had been invoked. He took the view that he could not apply the Convention because he had not been able to find it in his library. In another anecdote a lawyer said that it was not recommendable to invoke the Convention before the court since such an argument would make the court believe that one had a bad case.

The standing of the Convention was not everywhere as low as this. Thus, the Supreme Court did apply the Convention on several occasions but it hardly ever found a violation of it. The reason was not that the Supreme Court took the view that the provisions in the European Convention were not self-executing. On the contrary, almost all the provisions in the European Convention were and are considered to be self-executing, the only exceptions being Article 13 and Article 6, and the latter Article only insofar as it provides for a right of access to court in situations where national law has not granted any jurisdiction to a national court.[14] The reasons given for not finding a violation were invariably that the Supreme Court was of the opinion that the Convention provision was not applicable or that the interference with the Convention right invoked was justified. Two well-known cases

---

[14] Supreme Court 18 February 1986, NJ 1987, No. 62.

from the 1960s, both concerning Article 9 of the ECHR in which the right to freedom of thought, conscience and religion is laid down, may illustrate this.

In the first case a clergyman did not want to pay his contribution under the General Old Age Pensions Act because in his opinion, which was derived from the Bible and the rules governing church life, the church had to support him after his retirement. The General Old Age Pensions Act could not apply to him therefore, and such an application would be a violation of the Convention. The Supreme Court, however, stated that Article 9 did not imply that everybody had the right to review laws to ensure their compatibility with his or her religious beliefs or conscience. It came down to a narrow interpretation of the term "practice" in Article 9.1: compliance with ecclesiastical rules in the practice of life would not come within the ambit of the term "practice", which includes only acts that naturally, in one form or another, were expressions of a religion or belief. Thus, the regulation laid down in the General Old Age Pensions Act did not come within the ambit of Article 9 and there was therefore no need to examine the case under paragraph 2 of Article 9.[15] In favour of the Supreme Court it must be admitted that the European Commission in a similar case had earlier found an application under Article 9 of the ECHR to be manifestly ill-founded.[16]

In the second case the Supreme Court considered Article 9 to be applicable, but this time the case failed under paragraph 2. In the constitution as it was at that time, 1962, a prohibition on processions—dating from 1848—was embodied in all those places where processions had not been permitted in 1848. When the Dutch government had considered whether the Netherlands should become a party to the Convention and should accept the individual complaints procedure, it had been submitted on several occasions that in this respect Dutch law might be in conflict with the Convention. However, the Supreme Court did not share this view. It considered the protection of public order as the legitimate aim of the prohibition; the restriction was meant to prevent tension and turmoil. When the Supreme Court came to consider whether the prohibition was necessary in a democratic society, it pointed to the fact that there existed various religious convictions among the Dutch population. If a religion were manifested in public, other people would be inevitably involved against their will. Therefore, according to the Supreme Court, a law that would limit such manifestations of religious be-

---

[15] Supreme Court 13 April 1960, ARB [Administrative and Judicial Decisions] 1960, No. 567.

[16] No. 1497/62, 14 December 1962, (1962) 5 *Yearbook of the European Convention on Human Rights* 286 (298).

lief, could be considered as a necessary means for the protection of public order. The Supreme Court continued by stating that it did not want to review the concrete situation under Article 9 but only the law. The legislator had to weigh the interest in the freedom to manifest a religion in public against the necessity to protect public order. The result of this weighing process, according to the Supreme Court, would in general not be subject to judicial review; it would be the responsibility of the national legislator. A judge could only find a violation of Article 9 if it were to be considered totally unthinkable that a legislator, confronted with the necessity to make regulations for the protection of public order, could in reasonableness make this regulation. Consequently, there was a wide margin of appreciation for the legislator. In the case of the injunction to hold a procession, the Supreme Court thought it not inconceivable that a reasonable legislator would have made the same choice that the Dutch constitutional legislator had made.[17]

The turning point as far as the European Convention is concerned came in the late 1970s and at the beginning of the 1980s. It is now quite common for the Convention to be invoked before the Dutch courts and it is just as normal for a violation of it to be found. Thus, in 1994 for example, the ECHR was cited in 173 judgments given by the Dutch courts.[18] What are the reasons for this change in attitude on the part of the Dutch judiciary? Without pretending to be complete—a study from the point of view of the sociology of law would be needed for that—we would like to point to three circumstances. In the first place the fact that in 1976 the European Court of Human Rights for the first time found a violation of the Convention by the Netherlands, a decision followed in 1979 by a second judgment against the Netherlands, might have raised the awareness that the Convention could have relevance for the Netherlands as well as for other countries.[19] In the second place at the universities, more and more attention was being paid to the Convention in the curriculum of law studies. Thus, a new generation of lawyers with at least some knowledge of the Convention arose. In the third place in 1974 the Dutch section of the International Commission of Jurists was established. Two years later this section started to publish a magazine on human rights. In this bulletin important articles on human rights, including on the Convention, appeared. Moreover, this bulletin has paid (and is

---

[17] Supreme Court 19 January 1962, NJ 1962, No. 107.

[18] This figure is drawn from a survey of Dutch case law concerning the international law on human rights in: *NJCM-Bulletin* 20–8 (1995), at pp. 1023–1069.

[19] The decisions are discussed below, text at notes 46 and 52.

still paying) a great deal of attention to case law, both national and international, on human rights.

It is impossible to give a complete overview of the relevance of the European Convention on Human Rights for Dutch case law. Suffice it to say that this influence has been great, especially in the field of criminal law, family law, tax law (in particular in relation to Article 6.1 of the ECHR) and in respect of the law on aliens. In this section a number of more general issues will be discussed: the review of Acts of Parliament under the Convention (although it must be realised that in most cases the conformity of an Act of Parliament with the Convention is not at stake); the relevance of the European Court's judgments for Dutch case law; third party applicability; and the possible conflict between the European Convention and other international treaties.

2. REVIEW OF ACTS OF PARLIAMENT UNDER THE CONVENTION

As can be concluded from Part I, section 4, above, under the Dutch Constitution, Acts of Parliament should be not applied when they are in violation of the European Convention. Dutch case law indeed reveals several examples in which a provision in an Act of Parliament has been considered to be in violation of one of the rights embodied in the European Convention; with the result that such a provision could not therefore be applied. One of these examples is a case in which the Supreme Court considered a provision in the Civil Code to be in violation of Article 12 of the ECHR.[20] The Civil Code provided that, if one of the parents refused to give permission for the marriage of his or her minor legal child of whom he or she has legal guardianship, then legal permission by the judge could not replace it. According to the Supreme Court this provision was not in conformity with Article 12 (in which the right to marry is embodied) in the case of an unmotivated, or not reasonably motivated refusal by a parent to give his or her child of marriageable age permission to get married. After this judgment the legislature repealed the provision concerned.

It is not always necessary to take such a drastic measure as not applying a provision in an Act of Parliament because it is considered to be in violation of the European Convention. Often the courts try to interpret such a provision in conformity with the Convention. In other cases, when a gap in the legislation is identified, the legislation is supplemented in such a way that

---

[20] Supreme Court 4 June 1982, NJ 1983, No. 32.

conformity with the Convention is ensured. An example may be the fact that Dutch law did not include a provision under which judges in tax cases could be challenged. The Supreme Court, however, referring *inter alia* to Article 6.1 of the ECHR and the *Hauschildt* judgment of the European Court,[21] has added such a rule to Dutch law.[22] Subsequently, the Dutch legislator enacted a provision dealing with the challenge of a judge in such cases.

An unusual line of cases are those in which the Supreme Court has found that it could not apply Article 94 of the Constitution and refrain from applying a provision of national law, because to do so would require the making of choices which the judges felt should be left to the legislative power. In some of these cases the Supreme Court first found a conflict between the European Convention and national law; in others it left undecided whether such a conflict existed. An example is a case which ultimately led to a judgment by the European Court of Human Rights, *Kroon and Others*. The facts of this case were as follows. Mrs Kroon had a stable relationship with Mr Zerrouk. Their son Samir was born while Mrs Kroon was still married to Mr M'Hallem-Driss, whose whereabouts had been unknown since before Samir's birth. Under Dutch law the ordinary instrument for creating family ties between Mr Zerrouk and Samir was recognition. However, since Samir was the "legitimate" child of Mr M'Hallem-Driss, Mr Zerrouk would only be in a position to recognise Samir after Mr M'Hallem-Driss's paternity had been successfully denied. This could only be done by Mr M'Hallem-Driss himself, who, however, was untraceable. Under Dutch Civil Code also a mother may deny the paternity of her husband, but only in respect of a child born within 306 days of the dissolution of the marriage. Since Samir was born during the marriage between Mrs Kroon and Mr M'Hallem-Driss, this possibility was not open in the present case.

The issue came before the Supreme Court.[23] That court did not however rule on the question whether the relevant provision of the Dutch Civil Code violated Article 8 of the ECHR, or Article 14 taken together with Article 8. It considered that it was not necessary to do so, because it took the view that, even if there had been such a violation, solving the problem of what should replace the relevant provision in the Civil Code would go beyond the limits of the judiciary's powers to develop the law. If a possibility were to be created for the mother to deny her husband's paternity of a child born during marriage, the question would immediately arise as to what other limitations

---

[21] *Hauschildt* v. *Denmark* Series A, No. 154 (1989) 12 E.H.R.R. 266.

[22] Supreme Court 20 February 1991, BNB [Decisions in Tax Cases] 1991/134.

[23] Supreme Court 16 November 1990, NJ 1991, No. 475.

should apply in order not to jeopardise the child's interest in certainty regarding its descent from its legitimate parents. Many variations would be conceivable. To choose from all the options would be a task for the legislative power, not for the courts. By thus refraining from answering the question whether or not the Convention had been violated, the Supreme Court could not safeguard the Netherlands from the later finding of a violation of the Convention by the European Court.[24] The sole issue, of course, that is before the European Court is the state's responsibility;[25] it does not need to go into the question of whether the legislative power or the judiciary should bring a violation to an end.

3. THE INFLUENCE OF THE EUROPEAN COURT'S CASE LAW

Two lines of thinking are possible when we consider the question of the role of the judgments of the European Court in Dutch case law. In the first line of thinking these judgments are considered to be decisions of international organisations. As stated in Part I, section 3, above, these decisions are adopted as such in the Dutch legal order. However, these decisions should be binding; in the words of the Supreme Court, they should be based on a power to take binding decisions in respect of the Netherlands granted by or pursuant to a treaty.[26] In this respect no problem arises in relation to judgments against the Netherlands. It is more difficult to argue that judgments against other state parties are binding on the Netherlands, particularly in view of Article 53 of the ECHR, which provides that the High Contracting Parties undertake to abide by the decision of the Court *in any case to which they are parties* [emphasis added]. In the second line of reasoning it is suggested that the Dutch courts should apply the European Convention *as interpreted by the European Court*. The judgments of the European Court should be considered to be incorporated in the European Convention. It seems that in this approach the above-mentioned problem would be avoided.

References in Dutch judgments to judgments of the European Court are frequent. Not only have judgments directed against the Netherlands been referred to by Dutch courts, but judgments against other state parties have also figured. We have already mentioned the example of the *Hauschildt* judgment, a case against Denmark. The *Marckx* v. *Belgium* judgment has

---

[24] *Kroon and others* v. *The Netherlands* Series A, No. 297–C (1994) 19 E.H.R.R. 263.

[25] See for *e.g.* the comments of the Court in *Lingens* v. *Austria* Series A, No. 103 (1986), 8 E.H.R.R. 103 at para. 46.

[26] Supreme Court 23 November 1984, NJ 1985, No. 604.

also been repeatedly referred to.[27] The *Brogan* case is another example of a judgment directed against another state party, in this case the United Kingdom, which nevertheless has had a great influence on the Dutch legal order.[28] In this judgment the European Court held that a person who had spent four days and six hours in police custody without appearance before a judge or other judicial officer, had not been brought "promptly" before a judge or other officer authorised by law to exercise judicial power in the sense of Article 5.3 of the ECHR. Under Dutch law as it was at that time it could take four days and fifteen hours before a suspect would be brought before a judge; the police could detain him or her for a maximum of fifteen hours and thereafter a public prosecutor could order detention for a maximum of four days. Because the European Court in *Brogan* had explicitly stated that the context of terrorism in Northern Ireland had the effect of prolonging the period during which the authorities might keep a person suspected of serious terrorist offences in custody before bringing him or her before a judge or other judicial officer, without violating Article 5.3, it seemed probable that the maximum period in the Netherlands for non-terrorist crimes was too long. Dutch judges reacted to this in very different ways. To name but a few examples: one judge concluded that, in a case in which it had taken 93 hours before a suspect had been brought before a judge, the period was acceptable; another found 87.5 hours too long; and yet another judge was of the opinion that the public prosecutor could be considered as an "other officer authorised by law to exercise judicial power" within the meaning of Article 5.3. This confusion led to action first by the executive power and ultimately by the legislative power (see below, Part III, section 3).

In some cases Dutch courts have found themselves compelled to depart from earlier case law, because of judgments by the European Court. Thus, in a line of early cases, the Supreme Court had established that between the biological father and his child there existed a "family life" within the meaning of Article 8.1 of the ECHR.[29] However, the Supreme Court felt compelled to re-consider its case law as a consequence of the *Berrehab* judgment.[30] Since this judgment by the European Court, the Supreme Court now considers the sole fact that the father has procreated the child not to be

---

[27] *Marckx* v. *Belgium* Series A, No. 31 (1979) 2 E.H.R.R. 330.

[28] *Brogan and others* v. *United Kingdom* Series A, No. 145–B (1988) 11 E.H.R.R. 117.

[29] See, *inter alia*, Supreme Court 22 February 1985, NJ 1986, No. 3.

[30] *Berrehab* v. *The Netherlands* Series A, No. 138 (1988) 11 E.H.R.R. 322. For the Dutch decision, see Supreme Court 10 November 1989, Rechtspraak van de Week [Weekly Case Law] 1989, No. 248.

sufficient to establish "family life"; more is now needed for this.[31] In consequence of the European Court's judgment in the *Kostovski* case,[32] the Supreme Court agreed that stricter standards should be set for the use of anonymous witnesses than it had so far adopted.[33] Taking the European Court's *Lala*[34] and *Pelladoah*[35] judgments into consideration, the Supreme Court also took the view that it should take a different position from that which it had earlier adopted in another area of the law.[36] Under Dutch law an accused is, as a rule, not under an obligation to attend his or her trial. Under the case law of the Supreme Court a defendant who has been declared in default is not entitled to have his or her defence conducted by counsel unless there appear to be compelling reasons for his or her absence. The European Court, however, was of the opinion that the fact that the defendant, in spite of having been properly summoned, does not appear, cannot—even in the absence of an excuse—justify depriving him or her of his or her right under Article 6.3 of the ECHR to be defended by counsel. In its judgment of 3 January 1995 the Supreme Court stated that, if not the accused but his or her counsel had attended the trial, then the judge under Article 6.1 and Article 6.3 (c) of the ECHR should allow the counsel to defend the accused.

A somewhat peculiar judgment is that of the Supreme Court in a case similar to the *Kroon* case (on which see above, Part II, section 2), pronounced one week after the judgment of the European Court in *Kroon*. In this judgment of 4 November 1994 the Supreme Court repeated its view, which it had earlier expressed in *Kroon*, that it did not have to rule on the question whether the relevant provision of the Dutch Civil Code violated Article 8 of the ECHR, or Article 14 taken together with Article 8, because

---

[31]   In the *Berrehab* judgment, *ibid.*, the European Court held that a child born of a lawful and genuine marriage, by the very fact of his or her birth, has a "family life" with his or her parents. However, subsequent events may break that tie. That was not so in the *Berrehab* case itself, since Mr Berrehab saw his daughter four times a week during several hours, which proved that he greatly valued the meetings with his daughter: see *ibid.*, at para. 21.

[32]   *Kostovski* v. *The Netherlands* Series A, No. 166 (1989) 12 E.H.R.R. 434. In this judgment the European Court found a violation of Article 6.3 (d) taken together with Article 6.1 since the applicant's conviction for armed robbery had been based to a decisive extent on reports of statements by two anonymous witnesses heard, in the absence of the accused and his counsel, by the police and, in one case, by the examining magistrate but not by the trial courts.

[33]   Supreme Court 2 July 1990, NJ 1990, No. 692.

[34]   *Lala* v. *The Netherlands* Series A, No. 297–A (1994) 18 E.H.R.R. 586.

[35]   *Pelladoah* v. *The Netherlands* Series A, No. 297–B (1994) 19 E.H.R.R.81.

[36]   Supreme Court 3 January 1995, *NJCM-Bulletin* 20–2 (1995), p. 154.

even if there had been such a violation, solving the problem of what should replace the relevant provision in the Civil Code would go beyond the limits of the judiciary's powers to develop the law. This is a peculiar judgment because of the fact that one week earlier the European Court had found a violation in the *Kroon* case. Why then did the Supreme Court leave undecided whether a violation in a similar case had occurred? One gets the impression that the Supreme Court was still uninformed about the European Court's judgment. In another similar case the Court of Appeal of The Hague, on 12 May 1995, referring to the European Court's *Kroon* judgment, and explicitly deviating from the Supreme Court's judgment of 4 November 1994, did find a violation of Article 8 of the ECHR. The Court of Appeal ordered the registrar of births to register the recognition of the paternity by the child's real father.

4.   THIRD PARTY APPLICABILITY

A complaint against another private person will be declared incompatible *ratione personae* by the European Commission and for that reason will be inadmissible. This does not mean that any third party applicability of the European Convention is completely excluded, although it can only exist in an indirect way, via the responsibility of the State Party.

For national legal orders the third party applicability of the European Convention is to a certain extent easier to realise. Indeed, Dutch courts have used the European Convention in deciding conflicts between private individuals. Often, Article 8 of the ECHR, which includes, *inter alia*, the right to respect for private life, has been involved in such cases.[37] A case in which Article 10 of the ECHR, the right to freedom of expression, was involved concerned a newspaper that had published three articles in which it had been suggested that a certain Mr V. had murdered for predatory reasons a Jewish person living in hiding during the second world war. However, a District Court had acquitted V. of the murder in 1944, and in 1946 he had been rehabilitated when it was established that he had been acting in the interests of the resistance movement. The Supreme Court in this case weighed the right of V. to be left in peace—without explicitly referring to Article 8 of the ECHR—against the right laid down in Article 10 of the ECHR. It found that

---

[37]   See, *inter alia*, Supreme Court 9 January 1987, NJ 1987, No. 928 (concerning a woman on social security watched by her neighbour to check whether she had a relationship with a man which would make her ineligible for a benefit); Supreme Court 1 July 1988, NJ 1988, No. 1000 (concerning the publication of a picture of a woman embracing her fiancé in a public park).

the interference with the newspaper's right to freedom of expression was justified under Article 10.2. The interference was prescribed by law, namely the provision in the Civil Code concerning defamation. Moreover, the interference was necessary in a democratic society for the protection of the reputation and rights of others. Making an accusation of this nature after such a long time and giving to this accusation wide publicity could, if ever, only be justified in special circumstances in which such information would serve a justifiable public interest. Therefore, to justify publication in such a case, compelling reasons relating to the public interest had to exist, and it was legitimate to require that the accusation be based on extremely meticulous research.[38]

5.   A CONFLICT BETWEEN THE ECHR AND OTHER TREATIES

The European Court's only task is to interpret and apply the European Convention. If a potential conflict arises between the European Convention and another international treaty the European Court will only pronounce judgment on the question whether or not the European Convention has been violated. It will not pass judgment on the question whether the other treaty has been violated, let alone the question of which international obligation has to take precedence in cases of conflict.

This may be different for a national court. Thus, in a case that was before the Dutch Supreme Court shortly after the European Court had pronounced its judgment in the *Soering* case,[39] the Supreme Court had to decide on a conflict between the Sixth Protocol to the European Convention on the one hand and the NATO Status Treaty on the other.[40] The facts were as follows. An American soldier quartered in the Netherlands had killed his wife. Under

---

[38]   Supreme Court 6 January 1995, *NJCM-Bulletin* 20–7 (1995), p. 903. Another example of a case between private individuals in which Article 10 of the ECHR was involved was a case in which a women's organisation brought an action against a magazine which had published a photo-reportage which was hostile to women (Supreme Court 21 October 1994, *NJCM-Bulletin* 20–4 (1995), p. 416).

[39]   *Soering* v. *United Kingdom* Series A, No. 161 (1989) 11 E.H.R.R. 439. In this judgment the Court found that the Secretary of State's decision to extradite the applicant to the United States would, if implemented, give rise to a breach of Article 3 of the ECHR which provides that no one shall be subjected to torture or to inhuman or degrading treatment or punishment. The Court stated that the applicant ran a real risk of a death sentence and hence of exposure to the "death row phenomenon". In the Court's view, having regard to all the circumstances in this case, the applicant's extradition to the United States would expose him to a real risk of treatment going beyond the threshold set by Article 3. For the UK's response to the judgment, see C. Gearty, above, p. 100.

[40]   Supreme Court 30 March 1990, NJ 1991, No. 249.

the NATO Status Treaty the military authorities of the USA had the primary right to exercise jurisdiction over him and under the American Uniform Code of Military Justice the soldier could be sentenced to death. The Supreme Court had no difficulty in finding that the soldier was within the jurisdiction of the Netherlands, as stated in Article 1 of the ECHR. The soldier found himself in the Netherlands and the Netherlands had factual power over him since they could decide whether or not to hand over the soldier to the USA. The Supreme Court was of the opinion that Article 1 of the ECHR should be broadly interpreted; the state parties were bound to secure the Convention rights to everyone within their jurisdiction, not only within their territories but even outside. It pointed out that the Strasbourg organs themselves had interpreted this provision in a broad way; it referred to the *Soering* judgment and to several decisions of the European Commission.

The Supreme Court went on to argue that, as far as the Netherlands were concerned, the fact that it was a party to the Sixth Protocol to the ECHR—which provides that the death penalty shall be abolished and that no one shall be condemned to such a penalty or executed—meant that the final words of Article 2, paragraph 1, second sentence ("No one shall be deprived of his life intentionally *save in the execution of a sentence of a court following his conviction of a crime for which this penalty is provided by law* [emphasis added]") no longer applied. Therefore, the Netherlands, under the ECHR, were bound to refrain from acts which might lead to someone within its jurisdiction being subjected to the death penalty, even if this sentence would be imposed or executed in another state. Again, the Supreme Court referred to the *Soering* case: it argued that the reasoning of the European Court in respect of Article 3 of the ECHR should be applied here in respect of Article 2 of the ECHR and the Sixth Protocol. This was the basis on which the Supreme Court concluded that there was indeed a conflict between the ECHR and the NATO Status Treaty.

This finding led inevitably to the question of which of the two treaties was to prevail. In addressing this issue, the Supreme Court weighed the interest of the soldier to have his right under the ECHR and the Sixth Protocol thereto not to be subjected to the death penalty respected against the interest of the Netherlands in observing its obligations under the NATO Status Treaty towards the USA and the international interest in general that the NATO Status Treaty be respected. The conclusion of the Supreme Court was clear: in view of the great importance that should be attached to the right not to be subjected to the death penalty, the soldier's interest should be given priority. Accordingly, the Supreme Court forbade the Netherlands to extradite the soldier to the USA if and to the extent that there was a risk that the soldier would be executed. The final result of this judgment was the same as in *Soering*: The American authorities assured the Dutch that the soldier would be prosecuted for a crime which was not punishable by death and shortly thereafter the soldier was extradited.

From a legal point of view, the approach of the Supreme Court seems to be purer than the approach of the European Court in *Soering*. The latter, when dealing with the applicant's complaint that the United Kingdom would infringe Article 6 of the ECHR because on his return to the United States he would not be able to secure his legal representation as required by Article 6.3 (c), had ruled:

> ...that an issue might exceptionally be raised under Article 6 by an extradition decision in circumstances where the fugitive has suffered or risks suffering a flagrant denial of a fair trial in the requesting country.[41]

The question arises of what would amount to "a flagrant denial". It seems that the European Court implicitly weighs the interest of the applicant against the interest of the state, when deciding on the question of whether the Convention has been violated. It appears that in the view of the Supreme Court, on the other hand, in extradition cases any violation of the Convention in the requesting country would amount to a violation of the Convention by the extraditing country. After having established this violation the Supreme Court weighs the interest of the person to be extradited in having his Convention right to be respected against the interest of the state. However, this purer approach cannot be followed by the European Court since it can only deal with the question of whether the European Convention has been violated and cannot make the second step that is made by the Supreme Court in the Dutch context.

Part III: The Legislative and the Executive Powers and the ECHR

1.   INTRODUCTION

As we have seen, when ratifying the European Convention the Dutch government did not think it necessary to amend any Dutch law or to make a reservation to the Convention: Dutch legislation was considered to be in conformity with the Convention. For years the Netherlands could believe that it was right in this rather complacent attitude. It was not until 1976 that the European Court for the first time found a violation of the Convention in re-

---

[41] *Op. cit.*, note 39, at para. 113.

spect of the Netherlands. So far the Court has delivered 23 judgments with respect to the Netherlands in which it has found one or more violations. In seven judgments directed against the Netherlands no violation has been found by the Court.[42] In Part III, section 2 below, the judgments in which one or more violations were found will be considered and the follow-up to them on the part of the legislative and executive powers will be reviewed.

It should be noted that the European Court holds the opinion that it is not empowered under the Convention to oblige a state to take certain concrete measures, other than paying just satisfaction under Article 50 of the ECHR. In particular, the Court cannot annul a national judgment or oblige a state to re-open national procedures.[43] Nevertheless, several state parties have national legislation which expressly provides for the possibility of judicial review following a finding of a Convention violation by the Court or even by the Committee of Ministers of the Council of Europe. In other states no explicit provision exists but review procedures may take place on the basis, for instance, that the findings of the Strasbourg organs will be considered as "fresh information" or as "new facts" warranting a re-opening of a case. In some states these possibilities are only available in criminal proceedings, in others they are also available in civil and/or administrative proceedings.[44] However, such possibilities do not exist under Dutch law; no explicit provision exists and it is established in the case law of the Supreme Court that a change in jurisprudence cannot be considered as "fresh information" warranting a re-opening of a case. However, the crown has a discretionary power to grant a pardon, which it could use, *e.g.*, in the case of a violation having been found by the European Court or the Committee of Ministers.

An interesting possibility seems to have been opened up by the Supreme Court in legal proceedings started by an accomplice of Kostovski. This ac-

---

[42] *Van Marle and others* v. *The Netherlands* Series A, No. 101 (1986) 8 E.H.R.R. 483; *Keus* v. *The Netherlands* Series A, No. 185–C (1990) 13 E.H.R.R 700; *Oerlemans* v. *The Netherlands* Series A, No. 219 (1991) 15 E.H.R.R. 561; *Nortier* v. *The Netherlands* Series A, No. 267 (1993) 17 E.H.R.R. 273; *Gasus Dosier und Firdertechnik GmbH* v. *The Netherlands* Series A, No. 306–B (1995); *Masson and Van Zon* v. *The Netherlands* Series A, No. 327–A (1995); *British-American Tobacco Company Ltd.* v. *The Netherlands* Series A, No. 331 (1995) 21 E.H.R.R. 409.

[43] See, *inter alia*, *Pakelli* v. *Germany* Series A, No. 64 (1983) 6 E.H.R.R. 1, at paras. 43, 45 and 47; *Brozicek* v. *Italy* Series A, No. 167 (1989) 12 E.H.R.R. 371.

[44] See the study of the DH-PR Committee, "The European Convention on Human Rights: Institution of Review Proceedings at the National Level to Facilitate Compliance with Strasbourg Decisions" (1992) 13 *Human Rights Law Journal* 71–78. For the position in Germany see below, Voss, at pp. 166–168.

complice had not invoked Article 6.1 before the Dutch courts. When Kostovski's case was pending before the European Court, however, the accomplice demanded that the execution of his prison sentence be suspended until the European Court had pronounced judgment in the *Kostovski* case. The claim was dismissed because Kostovski's case was still pending before the European Court but the Supreme Court added that a convict could turn to the court for an injunction, interruption or limitation of the execution of a sentence, if a later judgment by the European Court would necessarily lead to the conclusion that the decision of the criminal judge had come about in such a way that it could not be said that a fair trial in the sense of Article 6.1 of the ECHR had taken place.[45] In other words, after the judgment of the European Court in Kostovski's case, his accomplice could have claimed before a judge that the execution of his punishment should be forbidden, suspended or limited, even though he himself had not lodged a complaint with the European Commission. The judge would have to sustain the claim if it had been beyond reasonable doubt that the judgment of the European Court would inevitably have led to the conclusion that Article 6.1 had also been violated by the criminal court in respect of the accomplice. It would seem that this judgment of the Supreme Court is also relevant for the person who has received a favourable judgment from the European Court.

Not only judgments directed against the Netherlands have compelled the Dutch legislative and executive powers to take certain action. They have also felt obliged to take action in consequence of judgments by the European Court directed against other state parties. Various examples of this will be given in Part III, section 3.3. But first we consider judgments against the Netherlands.

2. JUDGMENTS AGAINST THE NETHERLANDS

The first judgment in which the Court found a violation of the Convention by the Netherlands was in the case of *Engel and others*.[46] This was also the first of several cases concerning soldiers. The company commander of soldier Engel had imposed a penalty of three days' strict arrest for having disregarded his two previous punishments. The European Court thought this penalty not to be in conformity with Article 5.1 of the ECHR. In particular, the arrest had not been effected for the purpose of bringing Engel before the competent legal authority. Nor did the European Court think the punishment

---

[45] Supreme Court 1 February 1991, in: *NJCM-Bulletin* 16–4 (1991), pp. 325–334.
[46] Series A, No. 22 (1976) 1 E.H.R.R. 647.

"lawful" because it had exceeded the maximum period of twenty-four hours as laid down in the Dutch Military Discipline Act. The European Court also found a breach of Article 6.1 of the ECHR in respect of Engel and the other applicants because the hearings in the presence of the parties had taken place *in camera* in accordance with the then established practice of the Supreme Military Court in disciplinary proceedings.

Even before the judgment of the European Court the Dutch law was amended. Since 1 November 1974 Dutch military disciplinary law has no longer any provision for penalties which, according to the criteria indicated by the European Court, could be considered as constituting a deprivation of liberty within the meaning of Article 5, or for any other penalties such that the procedure under which they would be imposed could be regarded as criminal proceedings according to the European Court's interpretation of this term. Provisional arrest, strict arrest and committal to a disciplinary unit were abolished by this amendment. Besides, in a letter to all the ministers of the government, the Minister of Justice drew his colleagues' attention to the terms of the Court's judgment and urged them to take it into account when elaborating on any new regulations on matters of discipline.

In 1984 the European Court pronounced three further judgments concerning soldiers, namely in the cases of *De Jong, Baljet and Van den Brink*,[47] *Van der Sluijs, Zuiderveld and Klappe*[48] and *Duinhof and Duijf*.[49] All the cases concerned the detention on remand of conscripts accused of military criminal offences. In each case, the European Court found violations of Article 5.3 of the ECHR. The soldiers' hearings before the Military Court did not occur "promptly" after their arrest and the persons involved in the procedure prior to the hearing could not be considered to be "officers authorised by law to exercise judicial power". In the first case the European Court also found a violation of Article 5.4 because the applicants had been deprived of their entitlement to a "speedy" judicial review of their detention.

More than a year before these judgments of the European Court, on 21 March 1983, a directive was issued that provided, *inter alia*, that, where a serviceman was placed in custody, care must be taken to ensure that, within four days of his arrest, his case is brought before the Military Court for confirmation or extension of the detention. The *Koster* judgment, however, proved that this directive was no guarantee against new problems.[50] In that

---

[47] Series A, No. 77 (1984) 8 E.H.R.R 20.
[48] Series A, No. 78 (1984)13 E.H.R.R. 461.
[49] Series A, No. 79 (1984) 13 E.H.R.R. 478.
[50] *Koster* v. *The Netherlands* Series A, No. 221 (1991) 14 E.H.R.R. 396.

case the applicant had been brought before the military court after five days. The government explained that the lapse of time in question had occurred because of the week-end and the two-yearly major manoeuvres, in which the military members of the court had been participating at the time. Nevertheless, they conceded that there had been a failure to comply with the directive of 21 March 1983, which was based on Article 5.3 of the ECHR. In the circumstances, the European Court had no difficulty in finding a violation of Article 5.3.

In consequence of the three 1984 judgments the Dutch government informed the Committee of Ministers of the Council of Europe that bills for the revision of the administration of military justice were currently under consideration by parliament.[51] Again, it took quite a long time before these bills entered into force: not until 1 January 1991. Since this date a strict division has existed between infringements of military disciplinary law and breaches of the criminal law committed by soldiers. In principle, ordinary criminal law now applies to the latter.

The *Winterwerp* judgment[52] concerned an applicant who was committed to a psychiatric hospital. Under the Lunacy Act in force at the time, neither the district court, which had ordered Mr Winterwerp's confinement, nor the regional court, which had renewed this order from year to year, was obliged to hear an individual whose detention was being sought. In fact, Mr Winterwerp was never involved, either personally or through a representative, in the proceedings leading to the various detention orders which were made against him; he was never notified of the proceedings or of their outcome; neither was he heard by the courts or given any opportunity to argue his case. The European Court held on these facts that Article 5.4 of the ECHR had been infringed. Moreover, the Court found a violation of Article 6.1. Under the Lunacy Act as it was at that time any person of full age who was actually confined in a psychiatric hospital automatically lost the capacity to administer his or her property. The European Court was of the opinion that the total absence of the right to a court in the determination of civil rights as embodied in Article 6.1 was a breach of this provision.

Even before this European Court judgment, the Lunacy Act had been amended on a number of points. While the case before the European Court was proceeding, a bill was brought before the Dutch parliament providing for a complete reform of the system with the aim of improving the position

---

[51]   See, *inter alia*, Van der Sluijs, Zuiderveld and Klappe Case, Res. DH (85) 11, 31 May 1985.

[52]   *Winterwerp* v. *The Netherlands* Series A, No. 33 (1979) 2 E.H.R.R. 387.

of the psychiatric patient. During the examination of the *Winterwerp* case by the Committee of Ministers, the government of the Netherlands informed the committee that it had introduced a revised bill into parliament. Provisions had been included to the effect that in all cases of involuntary admission to psychiatric hospitals, prolongation of the admission or requests for dismissal, the patient would have the right to be heard by a court. Besides, the provision which provided for the automatic loss of the patient's right to administer his or her property as a result of his or her involuntary admission to a psychiatric hospital was deleted. After having taken note of this information the Committee, on 24 June 1982, declared that it had exercised its function under Article 54 of the ECHR to supervise the execution of the judgments of the European Court.[53] One may wonder whether the Committee of Ministers was not too hasty in adopting its Article 54 resolution in this case: the Bill entered into force more than eleven years later, on 17 January 1994!

In anticipation of the entry into force of the new legislation, the Minister for Justice sent a circular letter to the public prosecutors instructing them to request the courts to hear a patient in all cases of involuntary admission to psychiatric hospitals, prolongation of the admission or requests for dismissal. The Minister of Justice also sent a circular letter to the public prosecutors instructing them to request a court's decision on whether or not such a patient loses the administration of his or her property. Accordingly, the provision under which a patient would lose the capacity to administer his or her property upon being placed in a mental hospital was no longer applied. This did not however exclude any further problems. Twice the European Court found new violations of the European Convention in cases concerning mentally ill persons, namely in the *Van der Leer* case and the *Wassink* case.[54] In both cases national judges had failed to comply with national law. Accordingly, the European Court found breaches of Article 5.1 of the ECHR. In the former case the European Court also found breaches of paragraphs 2 and 4 of the same Article, since the applicant was not informed of the order authorising her confinement and since the requirement of "speediness" had not been fulfilled. These two judgments, however, do not offer a complete picture; more complaints concerning mentally ill persons have reached Strasbourg, as is shown by the case of, *e.g.*, *H.* v. *The Netherlands*.[55] This

---

[53] Winterwerp Case, Res. DH (82) 2, 24 June 1982.

[54] *Van der Leer* v. *The Netherlands* Series A, No. 170 (1990) 12 E.H.R.R 567; *Wassink* v. *The Netherlands* Series A, No. 185–A (1990).

[55] *H.* v. *The Netherlands*, Commission Report 4 July 1991.

case—as have others—ended in a friendly settlement. It is to be hoped that the new Psychiatric Hospitals (Special Admissions) Act will ensure that these kind of violations will not occur again.

In *X. and Y.* v. *The Netherlands* a gap in Dutch law came to light.[56] Ms Y, a sixteen-year-old mentally handicapped woman, had been the victim of sexual abuse. The Dutch criminal code at that time required a complaint by the actual victim before criminal proceedings could be instituted against the perpetrator. In the case of an individual like Ms Y the legal representative could not act on the victim's behalf for this purpose. On the other hand, she was not capable of filing a complaint herself. Thus, there existed a procedural obstacle in the Dutch legal system which, as the European Court noted, the Netherlands legislature had apparently not foreseen. The Court found a violation of Article 8 of the ECHR. At the hearing of the case, counsel for the Dutch government had informed the Court that the Ministry of Justice had prepared a bill modifying the provision of the criminal code that dealt with sexual offences. By an Act of 27 February 1985, which entered into force on 1 April 1985, the provisions of the Dutch criminal code concerning the lodging of a complaint in respect of criminal offences, the prosecution of which requires a complaint, were amended. Since then a complaint may be lodged by the victim's legal representative in civil matters if the victim is mentally handicapped to such an extent as to be incapable of deciding for him or herself whether it is in his or her interest to lodge a complaint. Thus, the shortcoming in Dutch legislation identified in this case has been remedied.

One of the most disturbing judgments of the European Court for the Dutch legal order has been the decision in *Benthem*.[57] Mr Benthem, a garage owner, applied for a licence to bring into operation an installation for the delivery of liquid petroleum gas to motor vehicles. The licence was granted but the regional health inspector lodged an appeal with the crown. Under this procedure as it was at that time, the crown (*i.e.* the king together with the minister or ministers) issued rulings in administrative litigation which was brought before it on appeal. In carrying out this function, the crown did not take a decision until the Administrative Litigation Division of the Council of State had investigated the matter and had prepared a draft decision. The inspector's appeal was successful; after having received a draft decision from the Administrative Litigation Division in which the licence had been

---

[56] Series A, No. 91 (1985) 8 E.H.R.R 235.
[57] *Benthem* v. *The Netherlands* Series A, No. 97 (1985) 8 E.H.R.R. 1.

refused, the crown quashed the municipal authorities' decision by a Decree in the same terms as the draft.

Mr Benthem then proceeded to lodge a complaint with the European Commission, submitting that his case had not been heard by an independent and impartial tribunal, contrary to Article 6.1 of the ECHR. Eventually, the case came before the European Court. An important part of the judgment of the Court was dedicated to the question of whether a dispute over civil rights and obligations was involved. This question was answered in the affirmative by the European Court. The Court went on to conclude that neither the Administrative Litigation Division—because it could only give advice— nor the crown—because it was an executive body—could be considered a "tribunal" within the meaning of Article 6.1 of the ECHR.

The consequences of this judgment were great. To meet the Court's judgment as quickly as possible a "Provisional Act on disputes before the Crown" was adopted on 18 June 1987; it came into force on 1 January 1988. This Act gave a power of decision to the Administrative Litigation Division of the Council of State. Therefore, from that moment on, the Administrative Litigation Division has acted as a tribunal in the sense of Article 6.1 in matters of litigation in which, before *Benthem*, only the crown had been competent. The Act was only of a provisional nature and the government of the Netherlands informed the Committee of Ministers of the Council of Europe that definitive legislation was to be expected within five years.[58] Indeed, although it took somewhat longer, on 1 January 1994 the General Administrative Law Act came into force, laying down new uniform rules of administrative law procedure. One of the consequences of this law was the abolition of the Administrative Litigation Division of the Council of State.

A more or less similar problem arose in the *Van de Hurk* case.[59] Under Dutch law as it was at the relevant time the crown (in the person of the Minister of Agriculture, Nature Management and Fisheries) was empowered, if it was of the opinion that a judgment of the Industrial Appeals Tribunal was contrary to the general interest, to decide that the judgment should not be followed or should not be followed in its entirety. Although this provision in the 1954 Industrial Appeals Act had never been used, the European Court, holding that the power to give a binding decision which may not be altered by a non-judicial authority to the detriment of an individual party is inherent in the very notion of a "tribunal", concluded that there had been a violation of Article 6.1 in that the applicant's civil rights and ob-

---

[58] Benthem Case, Res. DH (88) 6, 26 April 1988.

[59] *Van de Hurk* v. *The Netherlands* Series A, No. 288 (1994) 18 E.H.R.R. 481.

ligations had not been determined by a tribunal. However, this judgment had no relevance for the future because since 1 January 1994, the General Administrative Law Act has also governed the procedure of the Industrial Appeals Tribunal. No executive authority is therefore any longer empowered to interfere with the binding force of a judgment.

Article 6.1 of the ECHR was also at stake in the *Feldbrugge* case.[60] The applicant, Mrs Feldbrugge, claimed that in the determination of her right to health insurance allowances, she had not received a fair trial before the President of the Appeals Board. The crucial question again was whether Article 6.1 was applicable. After ample consideration the Court concluded that it was. Subsequently, the Court concluded that the (simplified) proceedings conducted before the President of the Appeals Board were not in conformity with Article 6.1. Firstly, Mrs Feldbrugge had not been heard by the President; nor had she been asked to file written pleadings. Secondly, the President had not given her or her representative the opportunity to consult the evidence in the case file. The shortcomings which were proved to exist in respect of this procedure were not capable of being remedied at a later stage. An appeal against the President's decision lay to the full Appeals Board, but solely on one or more of four grounds specifically listed. The appeal brought by Mrs Feldbrugge, however, was not based on one of these grounds and therefore it was declared inadmissible by the Appeals Board.

The response to this judgment was an amendment of the Appeals Act which entered into force on 1 October 1991. The Appeals Act no longer mentioned the four conditions for the admissibility of an appeal. Besides, the parties would now at their request have the opportunity of consulting the case file before expiry of the 30 days' time limit set for lodging the appeal. Furthermore, the Appeals Board might still declare the appeal inadmissible but it had to give the applicant the opportunity to be heard at a public hearing.

In the *Berrehab* case the applicants were Mr Berrehab, a Moroccan citizen, and his daughter, who had Dutch nationality. They complained of the refusal by the Dutch authorities to grant Mr Berrehab a new residence permit after his divorce from his wife, a Netherlands citizen, and of his resulting deportation from the Netherlands. The European Court found a violation of Article 8 of the ECHR: there had been an interference with the right to respect for family life, without there being a justification under Article 8.2. The information on general measures (apart from the information that the

---

[60] *Feldbrugge* v. *The Netherlands* Series A, No. 99 (1986) 8 E.H.R.R. 425.

just satisfaction provided for in the Court's judgment under Article 50 ECHR had been paid to the applicants) which was provided by the Dutch government for the Committee of Ministers was very brief: "The Netherlands Government has formally taken note of the Court's judgment of 21 June 1988. Dutch immigration policy shall henceforth be applied in such a manner as to avoid violations of the convention of the kind found in the *Berrehab* case."[61] The Ministry of Justice has laid down its policy on aliens in the so-called "Circular on Aliens", a body of directives which is in the public domain. The *Berrehab* judgment has led to an amendment of this circular.

In consequence of the *Kostovski* judgment,[62] already referred to in Part II, section 3, above, a number of modifications of the code of criminal procedure were introduced by Act of 11 November 1993, which entered into force on 1 February 1994. The amendments provided new regulations as to who might testify without having to reveal his or her identity and as to the methods to be used in order to safeguard the rights of the accused in case such testimony would have to be used in criminal proceedings.

The applicant in the *Koendjbiharie* case was sentenced to imprisonment, to be followed by two years' detention under a hospital order because he was suffering from a mental deficiency.[63] Under the Dutch Criminal Code the court which makes the initial order may extend the confinement, on each occasion for one or two years, on an application by the crown prosecutor. The court is to give its decision within two months following the lodging of the application. According to the Supreme Court this time limit is merely of an exhortatory nature; even if the court exceeds the two-month time limit the person concerned continues to be detained under a hospital order until the court has ruled on the extension. In Mr Koendjbiharie's case the court had taken its decision after a lapse of more than four months. The European Court considered this a failure to comply with the requirement of "speediness" laid down in Article 5.4 of the ECHR. Unfortunately the European Court thought it unnecessary to consider whether there had also been a breach of Article 5.1 on account of the failure to comply with the two-month period prescribed in the Dutch criminal code. This could have led to some interesting observations as regards the case law of the Supreme Court on the subject.

---

[61] Berrehab Case, Res. DH (89) 13, 27 April 1989.

[62] *Kostovski* v. *The Netherlands op. cit.* note 32.

[63] *Koendjbiharie* v. *The Netherlands* Series A, No. 185–B (1990) 13 E.H.R.R. 820.

On 1 September 1988, even before the judgment of the European Court, the relevant provisions in the Dutch criminal code were repealed. The code of criminal procedure now provides that the person detained under a hospital order has henceforth the possibility of lodging an appeal against the extension decision with the Court of Appeal of Arnhem, except if the extension was granted for the first time and for one year only. In the information which the government provided to the Committee of Ministers it was stated that it was the government's opinion that the existence of this option of appeal would ensure compliance with the time limits since the Arnhem Court of Appeal would have to determine the consequences to be drawn from any non-compliance with the time limits, taking into account, *inter alia*, the judgment that the European Court had delivered in the *Koendjbiharie* case.[64]

The judgments of the European Court in the cases of *Abdoella*[65] and *Bunkate*[66] both concerned the length of criminal proceedings. The Court found violations of Article 6.1 of the ECHR, in particular because after the applicants had filed appeals on points of law to the Supreme Court, in the case of Mr Abdoella it took more than ten months and (in the case of his second appeal) eleven and a half months before the Supreme Court received the case file from the Court of Appeal; in the case of Mr Bunkate it took as long as fifteen and a half months. The European Court could not accept such long periods of inactivity. These judgments did not lead to any active response from the Dutch legislative or executive powers. The information provided by the Dutch government to the Committee of Ministers read:

> The Supreme Court and the courts of appeal have seriously studied the judgments of the European Court of Human Rights in the *Abdoella* and *Bunkate* cases. As a result of this examination, the presidents of the courts of appeal have henceforth instituted regular meetings to examine the organisation of the appeal procedure in order to avoid the kind of problem which arose in these two cases. Considering the small number of cases pending before the Convention organs with regard to the length of criminal proceedings in the Netherlands, the government finds that these measures have been sufficient to remedy the problems pinpointed by the Court.[67]

---

[64] Koendjbiharie Case, Res. DH (92) 25, 15 June 1992.

[65] *Abdoella* v. *The Netherlands* Series A, No. 248–A (1992) 20 E.H.R.R. 585.

[66] *Bunkate* v. *The Netherlands* Series A, No. 248–B (1993) 19 E.H.R.R. 477.

[67] Abdoella Case, Res. DH (95) 91, 7 June 1995; Bunkate Case, Res. DH (95) 92, 7 June 1995.

A length of procedure problem, but this time in social security proceedings, also arose in the cases of *Schouten* and *Meldrum*.[68] At the material time an interested party who wished to contest a decision of an occupational association concerning contributions had to request formal confirmation in writing. In the case of the applicants it took four years and three months, and three years and three months respectively before these formal confirmations were received. However, the General Administrative Law Act already referred to above, which entered into force on 1 January 1994, was relevant here as well. Under this law it is at present no longer necessary to request formal confirmation of a decision of an occupational association.

At the time the European Court pronounced judgment in the case of *Dombo Beheer B.V.*, the relevant law had already been substantially changed.[69] In civil proceedings between Dombo Beheer B.V., a limited liability company, and a bank, the former managing director of Dombo was not allowed to give evidence that an oral agreement existed between Dombo and the bank, because of the principle that a person who is formally or substantively a party to litigation cannot be heard as a witness in his or her own case. However, the branch manager of the bank, who was apart from the former managing director of Dombo the only person present at the meeting at which the agreement had allegedly been reached, had been allowed to testify. The European Court found a breach of Article 6.1 of the ECHR. However, on 1 April 1988, before the Court decision, a law entered into force that now allows parties to give evidence as witnesses in their own case, although differences continue to exist between a witness who is a party to the proceedings in question and a witness who is not.

As stated in Part II, section 3, above, the judgments of the European Court in the cases of *Lala* and *Pelladoah* have already influenced Dutch case law. In consequence of these judgments, however, the legislator is also taking action: a Bill has been introduced to amend the code of criminal procedure, to bring it into conformity with the European Court's judgments in both cases. In Part II, section 3 it also has been shown that the European Court's judgment in the *Kroon* case has already influenced Dutch case law. It is far from certain that the Dutch legislator will soon adopt an Act on this topic. Since 1981 work has been going on in an attempt to revise the law of descent. Two bills have been withdrawn. At present a new bill is in preparation.

---

[68] *Schouten and Meldrum* v. *The Netherlands* Series A, No. 304 (1994) 19 E.H.R.R. 432.
[69] *Dombo Beheer B.V.* v. *The Netherlands* Series A, No. 274 (1993) 18 E.H.R.R. 213.

Finally, we should note that the judgment of the European Court in the case of *Vereniging Weekblad Bluf!* will probably not lead to any legislative action.[70] A newspaper was seized and withdrawn from circulation because it contained information whose secrecy was considered necessary in the interest of the state. However, because the information in question was made accessible to a large number of people by the publishers by reprinting the newspaper after its seizure and because the events were commented on by the media, the European Court considered the measure of withdrawal no longer to be necessary in a democratic society. For this reason, there had been a breach of Article 10 of the ECHR. It may be expected that as a result of this decision in the future Dutch courts will be more careful when deciding on the seizure and subsequent withdrawal from circulation of publications.

3. JUDGMENTS AGAINST OTHER STATE PARTIES

As we have earlier noted, it has not only been judgments directed against the Netherlands which have induced the legislative and executive powers to amend certain laws or practices; judgments against other state parties have also had the same effect. A case in point is the judgment in the *Marckx* case, a judgment against Belgium.[71] In this judgment the European Court considered certain differences between illegitimate and legitimate children in the field of, *inter alia*, patrimonial rights not to be justified. In view of this judgment the Dutch legislative power found it necessary to eliminate the distinction between legitimate and illegitimate children in the law of succession as embodied in the Dutch civil code.[72]

Another example of a judgment against another state party which led to action by the Dutch legislative and executive powers, is the *Brogan* judgment against the United Kingdom, already referred to in Part II of this chapter. As was shown there, this case led to a diversity of case law responses by Dutch courts. The Procurators General found it desirable to issue a uniform code of conduct on detention for the Public Prosecution, pending new legislation. This new legislation has now entered into force. Under the new law a suspect will be brought before a judge within three days and fifteen hours at most. In this respect it should be noted that the European Commission, on 30 March 1992, considered a complaint against the Neth-

---

[70] *Vereniging Weekblad Bluf!* v. *The Netherlands* Series A, No. 306–A (1995) 20 E.H.R.R. 189.

[71] *Op. cit.*, note 27.

[72] Act of 27 October 1982, Statute Book 608.

erlands manifestly ill-founded in which it was submitted that a period of 91 hours between the applicant's arrest and the moment when he was brought before a judge was not "promptly" within the meaning of Article 5.3 ECHR.[73] The Dutch legislative power could therefore rest assured that a period of three days and fifteen hours would be within the limits of Article 5.3.

At present a discussion is going on as to whether the *Procola* judgment, directed against Luxembourg, will have to lead to a reform of the Dutch Council of State.[74] In that judgment the European Court noted that four members of Luxembourg's "Conseil d'Etat" had carried out both advisory and judicial functions in the same case. According to the Court, in the context of an institution such as the Conseil d'Etat, the mere fact that certain persons successively performed these two types of function in respect of the same decision was capable of casting doubt on the institution's structural impartiality. The Court held that there had been a breach of Article 6.1 of the ECHR. It seems that the same problem could occur in the Dutch Council of State. This body likewise carries out both advisory and judicial functions. Among Dutch legal writers, opinions differ as to whether the *Procola* judgment should have any implications for the legal system in the Netherlands. The Ministers of Internal Affairs and of Justice, in consultation with the Council of State, are currently considering the possible consequences of the judgment.

Final Remarks

After the second world war the Netherlands left its traditional isolationist position. More and more it has become a fervent supporter of an international legal order. This enthusiasm was reflected, *inter alia*, in the constitution. In 1953 the constitutional legislature opted for a monistic system as regards the relationship between international treaties and national law. Under the constitution as it has read since then Dutch courts have the duty not to apply a national provision if that would conflict with a self-executing treaty provision. Thus, to a certain extent the Dutch judge can be considered as a detached post of the international legal order.

Since 1983 the constitution has embodied a chapter on fundamental rights, both classical and social rights. However, not all fundamental rights

---

[73] No. 19139/91, 30 March 1992. For the UK response to Brogan, which was rather different, see Gearty, above, p. 87.

[74] *Procola* v. *Luxembourg* Series A, No. 326 (1995) 22 E.H.R.R 193.

that are embodied in the European Convention on Human Rights are laid down in the constitution. This is one explanation of why the ECHR has such an important role in the Dutch legal order. The second explanation is the fact that the constitution prohibits the judiciary to review the constitutionality of Acts of Parliament. Therefore, Dutch courts are not allowed to review Acts of Parliament for consistency with national fundamental rights as they are laid down in the constitution. However—and this seems to be a paradox— they are allowed, and even obliged, to review Acts of Parliament under fundamental rights laid down in, *e.g.*, the European Convention.

Although in theory the position of the European Convention is a strong one (as is that of other international treaties), this does not necessarily mean that its role is important in practice. If, for example, the courts were often to say that the provisions in international treaties are not self-executing, or that there is no conflict between these provisions and national law, then the role of such treaties would be minimal. It appears that this was the situation as regards the European Convention in the first years after the ratification. However, since the end of the 1970s and the beginning of the 1980s the situation has changed and it appears now that the European Convention is part and parcel of the Dutch legal order, not only in theory, but also in practice. However, a nuance should be made to this statement. When dealing with the impact of the European Convention on the Dutch legal order, our attention is inevitably focused on, in particular, the higher judges. However, it may well be the case that lower judges are less accustomed to applying the Convention. Although it is certainly not true to say that lower judges are ignoring the Convention, it is probably true to state that they are not familiar with the "ins" and "outs" of the Convention and the case law of the Strasbourg organs. This may be part of the answer to the question of how it is possible that the European Court of Human Rights has found violations of the Convention when the Convention can be applied by Dutch courts. For example, the Lunacy Act in many cases excludes the possibility of appeal. Thus, possible violations of the judge in first instance cannot be corrected at the Dutch appellate level.

However, other answers can also be given to the question of why not all violations of the Convention are sieved out by Dutch courts. Of course, simply a difference of opinion may exist between, *e.g.*, the Supreme Court and the European Court of Human Rights. Thus, in the case of *Bunkate*, the Supreme Court held that the lapse of time between the filing of the appeal on points of law and the hearing of the Supreme Court was undesirably long but not unreasonably so for the purpose of Article 6.1 ECHR. The European

Court, on the other hand, found a violation of this provision. This does not necessarily mean that the Supreme Court is less willing to find a violation of the Convention. After all, differences of opinion also exist between the European Commission and the European Court. Moreover, there may be cases in which a violation was found by a Dutch court but where one may have one's doubts whether the European Court would have found a violation as well, had the case been referred to it. An example may be the case which was referred to in Part II, section 2 of this chapter. A Dutch constitutional and human rights expert, Alkema, wondered whether the Supreme Court did not go too far in its judgment concerning the not reasonably motivated refusal by a parent to give his or her minor legal child permission to get married.[75]

Another factor is that Dutch judges have sometimes had to decide on cases in which no case law of the European Court has been available. Thus, for a long time the European Court's interpretation of the phrase '[i]n he determination of his civil rights and obligations' in Article 6.1 of the ECHR has been unclear and it is probably not a bold proposition that the Court's interpretation has turned out to be wider than many had expected. In this context it should be noted that the European Court is very much inclined to confine itself to the concrete case before it and to refrain as much as possible from doing general pronouncements. This approach, though understandable from the Court's point of view, does not afford national courts the guidance that they may need.

Finally, we recall the *Kroon* case, referred to in Part II, section 2, above. The reason that the European Court could find a violation of the Convention in this case was that the Supreme Court had refrained from answering the question of whether or not the Convention had been violated. The Supreme Court had argued that, even if there had been such a violation, solving the problem of what should replace the relevant provision in the national law would go beyond the limits of the judiciary's powers to develop the law; as we have seen, the court therefore concluded that the problem should be left to the legislative power. One may wonder whether the Supreme Court did not ignore its constitutional task to review Acts of Parliament under self-executing provisions of treaties and its duty to refuse to apply the national provision in a case of conflict.

The execution of judgments of the European Court in which a violation of the Convention by the Netherlands had been found does not raise any

---

[75] For the case, see the discussion in the text at note 20, above. For the observations of Alkema, see E. A. Alkema, *Een meerkeuzetoets* (Zwolle, 1985), at p. 12.

major problems, although in some cases the legislative and the executive powers took their time. Also judgments directed against other state parties have induced these powers to take action. This does not mean that nothing is left to be desired. In particular, one would wish that the legislative and executive powers would more systematically and more explicitly check whether their intended measures are in conformity with the Convention. However, the same problem as was referred to above, arises here; it is not always clear which obligations derive from the Convention.

In conclusion we would submit that the European Convention is nowadays firmly entrenched in the Dutch legal order. It is inconceivable that the Netherlands would denounce the Convention or recognise no longer the individual complaints procedure or decide to accept the jurisdiction of the Court.[76] Whereas the Dutch government in the 1950s had had the idea that the Convention would hardly have any meaning for the Netherlands, at the end of this century we can without hesitation say that the Convention has had a favourable impact on the protection of human rights in the Netherlands.

---

[76] Although we realise that one should be cautious in making such remarks. Indeed, when the Human Rights Committee, functioning under the UN International Covenant on Civil and Political Rights, found a violation by the Netherlands of Article 26 ICCPR, the non-discrimination principle, for a while the Dutch Government flirted with the idea of denouncing the Covenant. Fortunately, this idea was not put into practice.

4. GERMANY

Eileen Voss

Part I: The Constitutional Structure of the Federal Republic of Germany

1.   INTRODUCTION

In order to explain the protection of human rights in the Federal Republic of Germany (FRG), it is essential first to give a brief outline of Germany's constitutional structure. The German constitution or basic law (*Grundgesetz*) dates from 23 May 1949. Its provisions fall into two groups, the first containing the "basic rights" regulating the relationship between the citizen and the state, the second dealing with the governmental institutions of the Federal Republic of Germany and their functions.

Dealing with the latter group first, it is important to note that Germany is a federal republic consisting of 16 states or *Länder*. The states have their own territories, constitutions, sovereign rights and governmental powers, including the power to legislate within the limits provided for by the constitution.[1] At the same time, the states are integrated into the federal state, their territory being simultaneously federal territory. The federal legislature is made up of two houses, the *Bundesrat* and the *Bundestag*. The *Bundesrat* is composed of members of the governments of the states and thus represents the states in the federation.[2] Depending on the number of inhabitants, the states can send to the *Bundesrat* between three (minimum) and six (if the state has more than seven million inhabitants) representatives.[3] The most important function of the *Bundesrat* is its power to enact federal statutes.[4] Legislation requires the cooperation of another and even more important

---

[1]   See Article 70 *et seq*. of the *Grundgesetz*.

[2]   See Articles 50 and 51 of the *Grundgesetz*.

[3]   Article 51.II of the *Grundgesetz*.

[4]   Federal statutes can only be enacted on matters which the constitution allocates to the legislative competence of the federation (and not to that of the states); *cf*. Article 70 *et seq*. of the *Grundgesetz*.

C. A. Gearty (ed.), *European Civil Liberties and the European Convention on Human Rights*, 143–175.

governmental institution, the *Bundestag*. In the process of passing a statute, the question whether the *Bundestag* can overrule the *Bundesrat* depends on the nature of the statute to be passed. Statutes can be separated into first those that change the constitution, secondly those that require the consent of the *Bundesrat* and thirdly those proposed measures that do not require such consent. Amendments of the constitution require a two-thirds majority in the *Bundestag* as well as in the *Bundesrat*.[5] Whether or not a statute requires the consent of the *Bundesrat* is a matter that is regulated by the constitution.[6] The *Bundesrat* can effectively prevent such statutes from being enacted. From 1949 to the end of December 1995, this has happened in 112 cases.[7] With all other statutes, and under the constitutional framework they constitute the majority of measures, the *Bundesrat* may only object to them.[8] Such an objection can eventually be overruled by the *Bundestag*.[9] The constitution does, however, require a two-thirds majority in the *Bundestag* (including at least half of the statutory votes) to overrule an objection adopted by a two-thirds majority in the *Bundesrat*.[10]

The *Bundestag* represents the German people. Its members are elected for a term of four years.[11] Elections must be "general, direct, free, equal and secret", with further details being left to be determined by federal statute.[12] The system of election is that of a slightly modified form of proportional representation.[13] Apart from its power to legislate, the *Bundestag* also functions as the forum of political discussion and controversy between the political parties represented in it. This function is not explicitly mentioned in the constitution.

---

[5] Article 79.II of the *Grundgesetz*.

[6] See Articles 74a, 87b.II, 87c, 87d.II, 104a.V, 107.1, 108.IV and 109.III. The subject matters have in common that any of these statutes would strongly interfere with the interests of the states.

[7] Fax sent by Bundesrat/Dokumentation on 12 March 1996. An example of a statute not enacted because the *Bundesrat* refused its consent was the 1981 *Volkszählungsgesetz* (statute on the census). The reason for the *Bundesrat* refusing to agree with the statute was reportedly the cost of the census, see *Chronik des Deutschen Bundestages: 8th election period 1976–80* (Bonn, 1981), p. 65.

[8] Article 77.III of the *Grundgesetz*.

[9] Article 77.IV of the *Grundgesetz*.

[10] Articles 77.IV and 121 of the *Grundgesetz*.

[11] Article 39.I of the *Grundgesetz*.

[12] Article 38.I and III of the *Grundgesetz*.

[13] § 1, 5, 6 *Bundeswahlgesetz*.

2. THE *BUNDESVERFASSUNGSGERICHT* (FEDERAL CONSTITUTIONAL COURT)

The ninth chapter of the German constitution provides for the *Bundesverfassungsgericht* (Federal Constitutional Court).[14] The court is empowered to decide only constitutional questions and a limited set of other public law controversies.[15] Half of the members of the *Bundesverfassungsgericht* are elected by the *Bundestag*, the other half by the *Bundesrat*.[16] Appointing the judges of the *Bundesverfassungsgericht* by election in this way is exceptional since the rest of the judiciary of about 16,000 judges are all career judges. The requirement of an election indicates very clearly the political aspect of the work of the *Bundesverfassungsgericht*.

A. Historical Development of the Bundesverfassungsgericht

As a court deciding on the interpretation and application of the constitution, the *Bundesverfassungsgericht* does not have a true predecessor in German legal history.[17] When it was established, constitutional review—in the sense of a court controlling the constitutionality of statutes[18] or allowing individual citizens to take constitutional actions—was new to judicial theory in Germany[19] as under the traditional doctrine of separation of powers a judge's only duty had been to enforce the law as written.[20] However, already in the 1920s, the *Reichsgericht* (Imperial Court) had decided that "in principle courts of law are authorised to examine the formal and material validity of laws and ordinances".[21] When after the end of the second world war a new

---

[14] Article 92 *et seq.* of the *Grundgesetz*.

[15] D. Kommers, *Judicial Politics in West Germany. A Study of the Federal Constitutional Court* (Beverley Hills, California, 1976), p. 3; Article 93 of the *Grundgesetz*.

[16] For details, see below pp. 147–149.

[17] *Law on the Federal Constitutional Court: Documents on Politics and Society in the Federal Republic of Germany* (Bonn, 1982), p. 7.

[18] See Article 93. I, no. 2 and Article 100 of the *Grundgesetz*.

[19] Kommers, *op. cit.*, note 15, p. 6. The *Paulskirchenverfassung* (1849) did allow the complaint of a state against a statute allegedly violating the constitution as well as complaints by ordinary citizens claiming a governmental invasion of their fundamental rights, Kommers, *ibid.*, p. 7, but this never had any practical relevance, see *Das Parlament*, no. 36, 30 August 1991, p. 1; Kommers, *ibid.*, p. 5.

[20] Kommers, *op. cit.*, note 15, p. 6.

[21] *Reichsgericht*, collection of decisions, vol. 102, p. 161 at p. 164 and vol. 107, p. 377 at p. 379. See also *Das Parlament*, *op. cit.*, note 19, p. 10. In a decision of 1900, the *Reichsgericht* struck down the effects of an ordinance only between the parties. The ordinance in question was about the slaughtering of animals and regulated who had the rights in the carcass in the case of infected animals (*Reichsgericht*, collection of decisions, vol. 45, p.

constitution was framed, the influence of the United States' constitutional order was evidenced in the establishment of a separate tribunal with exclusive jurisdiction over all constitutional disputes and with the authority to review the constitutionality of laws.[22] Although this new constitution provided for a constitutional court as early as 1949, the *Bundesverfassungsgericht* did not open its doors for business until 28 September 1951.[23] The reason for this delay was that in spite of general agreement on many aspects of the constitutional court, such as the election of its judges, some areas have been left open in the constitution and had to be decided by a statute.[24] Following detailed discussion, the *Bundesverfassungsgerichtsgesetz* (*BVerfGG*; Federal Constitutional Court Act) was passed in 1951 laying down, *inter alia*, the qualification of the court's members;[25] the procedure for judicial selection;[26] provision for a "twin court", comprising two panels or senates;[27] the allocation to each senate of the subject matter to be dealt with;[28] the specification of the rules of access under the different categories of jurisdiction[29] and the conditions for the removal and retirement of the court's members.[30]

Still unsettled at that time was, however, the status of the *Bundesverfassungsgericht* as opposed to other governmental institutions, a matter on which neither the constitution nor the *Bundesverfassungsgerichtsgesetz* contained any clarification. Whereas the court had first been placed under the authority of the ministry of justice, in 1952 the court drafted a memorandum calling for more independence. Since the 1960s, the court has had budgetary autonomy and full control over its own administration and it is now regarded as a governmental institution of the same rank as the *Bundesrat* and *Bundestag*.[31]

---

267 at p. 275).

22 See Article 93 of the *Grundgesetz*.

23 Kommers, *op. cit.*, note 15, p. 17. According to *Das Parlament, op. cit.*, note 19, p. 1, the *Bundesverfassungsgericht* [afterwards *BVerfG*] started work on 7 September 1951.

24 Article 94.II.1 of the *Grundgesetz*: "The constitution and the procedure of the Federal Constitutional Court shall be regulated by a federal statute...."

25 § 3, *Bundesverfassungsgerichtsgesetz* [afterwards *BVerfGG*].

26 §§ 5–11, *BVerfGG*.

27 § 2.I, *BVerfGG*.

28 § 14, *BVerfGG*.

29 §§ 17 and 21 *et seq.*, *BVerfGG*.

30 §§ 4, 18, 19, *BVerfGG*.

31 Kommers, *op. cit.*, note 15 p. 18. In the United Kingdom, it has been said of the *BVerfG* that it has been "toying with the possibility of causing political chaos" and that it has

B. Panels and their Composition

The *Bundesverfassungsgericht* consists of two senates with eight judges each. A candidate must have reached the age of 40,[32] be eligible for election to the *Bundestag* and must be prepared to accept an appointment to become a member of the *Bundesverfassungsgericht*.[33] Candidates have to be lawyers in the sense that they must be qualified to exercise the function of judges according to the Law on German Judges.[34] Judges at the *Bundesverfassungsgericht* are mostly about 50 years of age by the time they are elected.[35] Three judges from each panel have to be elected from among the judges of the highest federal courts of justice where at the time of election they must have worked for at least three years.[36]

As we have already seen, half of the judges on each panel are elected by the *Bundestag*, the other half by the *Bundesrat*. The *Bundesrat* elects the judges directly, whilst the *Bundestag* has a 12 person electoral committee whose composition depends on the strength of parties in the *Bundestag* (proportional representation). Elections by the *Bundesrat* as well as by the electoral committee of the *Bundestag* require a two-thirds majority.[37] Of those judges to be selected from among the highest courts of justice, one is elected by one of the electoral organs and two by the other. Of the remaining five judges, three are elected by one electoral organ and two by the other.[38] The *Bundesverfassungsgerichtsgesetz* does not specify which electoral organ elects which judges (apart from, of course, half being elected by each of them). Judges must retire after 12 years or at the age of 68, whichever is the earlier.[39] Judges can be debarred from exercising their functions if they are for some reason or other involved in a case before them[40] or if there are reasons to suspect that they are biased.[41] Both happen rarely, so that until 1986,

---

"paralysed the politics of the country" (*Independent*, 30 June 1993, p. 9). In Germany, in contrast, the court is seen as the protector of the German constitution against chaos.

[32] See § 3.I, *BVerfGG*.

[33] *Ibid.*

[34] § 3.II, *BVerfGG*.

[35] See W. Geck, *Wahl und Amtsrecht der Bundesverfassungsrichter* (Baden-Baden, 1986), p. 50, note 90.

[36] § 2.III, *BVerfGG*.

[37] §§ 6.II, 6.V, and 7, *BVerfGG*.

[38] § 5.I, *BVerfGG*.

[39] § 4.I, III, *BVerfGG*.

[40] § 18, *BVerfGG*.

[41] § 19, *BVerfGG*.

there have been only nine cases of the former and until 1987, only three cases of the latter. Judges at the *Bundesverfassungsgericht* can only be dismissed for the following reasons: permanent unfitness for service; dishonourable acts; over six months' imprisonment; and gross breach of duty. Dismissal of a judge requires a majority of two-thirds of the *Bundesverfassungsgericht*.[42]

The federal minister of justice keeps a list of all eligible federal judges.[43] In addition to that, the minister keeps another list of all candidates that have been proposed by the federal government, the government of a state or a parliamentary group amounting to at least five per cent.[44] of the *Bundestag*.[45] The *Bundestag* and *Bundesrat* are not however restricted to these lists.[46] The appointments are rarely discussed in public and rarely become a matter of controversy.[47] It has to be kept in mind that the election of judges is in the end a political question as the leading political party and the opposition both try to gain as much control over the *Bundesverfassungsgericht* as possible.[48] However, party members have often enough disappointed their parties.[49] Both panels presently include two judges (out of eight) who are not members of any political party. In the first Senate the judges who are not members of any political party are Otto Seidl and Dieter Grimm; in the second they are Karin Graßhoff (her election having been proposed by the SPD) and Paul Kirchhof (proposed by the CDU). Of the remaining judges, in the first senate there are three members of the SPD, two of the CDU/CSU and one

---

[42] § 105.IV, *BVerfGG*.

[43] §§ 8.I, 3.I, II, *BVerfGG*.

[44] See § 10 I, *Geschäftsordnung des Bundestages*.

[45] § 8.II, *BVerfGG*.

[46] Geck, *op. cit.*, note 35, p. 22. Candidates can for example also be proposed by the *BVerfG* according to § 7a, *BVerfGG*.

[47] See also C. Fischer, "Die Bestellung der Verfassungsrichter" in B. Großfeld (ed.), *Verfassungsrichter—Rechtsfindung am US Supreme Court und am Bundesverfassungsgericht* (Münster, 1995), 71, at p. 88. Exceptions prove the rule: in 1993, for example, the state of discussion about Judge Mahrenholz's succession could have been read in almost every daily newspaper. The judge that the left-wing SPD had planned to propose for election, Herta Däubler-Gmelin, had—even before an election had taken place—been rejected by the right-wing CDU/CSU. Ms. Däubler-Gmelin is known as a politician, but had worked only a very short time as a judge or in the legal profession.

[48] See Geck, *op. cit.*, note 35, p. 36, note 64.

[49] *Ibid.*

FDP. In the second senate, three judges are members of the SPD and three of the CDU/CSU.[50]

As the election of a judge requires a two-thirds majority in the election committee[51] which consists of members of the *Bundestag* with the same proportionate representation as in the *Bundestag* itself, the opposition party can always veto the election of a judge. A compromise is thus necessary[52] and as shown by judges who are not member of any political party, some of the candidates proposed have political views which are acceptable to both major parties and there is therefore room to take into account their legal qualifications.[53]

Both senates or panels act as the *Bundesverfassungsgericht* and have separate competencies. Each judge is elected to one panel only. As a rule, each panel takes decisions with a simple majority of the judges present (at least six have to be present, however). If the votes are equal, the presiding judge does not have the casting vote. In this case the application is not successful, because a contravention of the constitution cannot be established in such circumstances.[54] The *Bundesverfassungsgericht* is the only German court that allows judges to publish dissenting opinions.[55] According to § 31.I, II *Bundesverfassungsgerichtsgesetz*, the decisions of the *Bundesverfassungsgericht* have an impact going beyond the individual case in question: contrary to all other court decisions, the principles regarding the interpretation of the constitution which derive from a decision by this court and the reasons for it are binding upon constitutional institutions, authorities and courts.[56] Likewise, decisions in which a statutory provision is ruled to be compatible or incompatible with the constitution have the force of law. This also applies if the *Bundesverfassungsgericht* decides that a statutory provision is only compatible with the constitution if interpreted in a specific manner. The *Bundesverfassungsgericht* is not bound by its own previous decisions.[57]

---

[50] Information taken from *Die Zeit*, no. 50 (4 December 1992) and *Das Parlament, op. cit.,* note 19, pp. 6–7.

[51] And, as already mentioned, in the *Bundesrat*.

[52] See Kommers, *op. cit.,* note 15, pp. 25–26.

[53] See Geck, *op. cit.,* note 35, p. 32.

[54] § 15.II, fourth sentence, *BVerfGG.*

[55] § 30.II, *BVerfGG.* (This section was added in 1970.)

[56] N. Foster, *German Law and Legal System* (London, 1993), pp. 55–56.

[57] See the Decisions of the *BVerfG* [afterwards *BVerfGE*] vol. 4, p. 31, at p. 38 and vol. 20, p. 56, at p. 86.

C. Jurisdiction

There is no overall clause authorising the *Bundesverfassungsgericht* to make decisions in all disputes regarding constitutional law. Rather, the *Bundesverfassungsgericht* may only decide in those cases enumerated in the constitution and in the *Bundesverfassungsgerichtsgesetz*.[58] Even then, the *Bundesverfassungsgericht* may not act on its own initiative but only in pursuance of external applications. The right to apply to the *Bundesverfassungsgericht* depends on the type of action taken and is regulated in the *BVerfGG*. Let us take three examples. First, in the case of a dispute between governmental organs, (Article 93.I no. 1 of the *Grundgesetz*), applicants may only be the federal president, the *Bundestag*, the *Bundesrat*, committees envisaged by Article 45 of the *Grundgesetz*, the federal government and sections of these organs that have been vested with their own rights (§ 63, *BVerfGG*). Furthermore all such applicants have to assert that one or other of the rights or duties assigned to them by the *Grundgesetz* have been violated (§ 64.I, *BVerfGG*). Secondly, and in contrast to our first example, constitutional review of a statute (Article 93.I no. 2 *Grundgesetz*) may be requested by the federal government, a state government or by one-third of the members of the *Bundestag* (§ 76 *BVerfGG*).

In the context of human rights, the most important type of application is our third example, the individual constitutional complaint (*Verfassungsbeschwerde*).[59] This complaint may be lodged by any person who claims that one of his or her basic rights[60] has been violated by a public authority. Such constitutional complaints must be lodged within a certain time,[61] identify the offending action or omission and the authority responsible and specify the constitutional right that is alleged to have been violated.[62] The basic rights embodied in the constitution in Articles 1–19, *e.g.* equal rights for men and women, freedom of religion, expression, assembly and association are thus

---

[58] The jurisdiction of the *BVerfG* includes control over legislative bodies to determine whether legislation has been enacted in conformity with the constitution; control over public authorities and courts to determine whether their measures and decisions are compatible with the constitution; decisions on disputes between governmental institutions under constitutional law; decisions on the lawfulness of *Bundestag* elections; decisions on the prohibition of political parties; and decisions on the forfeiture of basic rights (see Article 93.I of the *Grundgesetz* and § 13, *BVerfGG*).

[59] § 13, no. 8a, *BVerfGG*; Article 93.I, no. 4a, of the *Grundgesetz*.

[60] Or of a certain number of similar rights, as *e.g.* the right to be heard by a court. The cases where the *BVerfG* can decide are specified in § 13, *BVerfGG*.

[61] One year against a statute, in all other cases one month, *cf.* § 93.I, II, *BVerfGG*.

[62] See § 92, *BVerfGG*.

directly enforceable law binding the legislature, the executive and the judiciary. The individual thus has a unique legal remedy for the maintenance and enforcement of his or her basic rights.

It is easy to imagine, therefore, that the main workload of the *Bundesverfassungsgericht* consists of individual constitutional complaints. About 96 per cent. of all applications are individual constitutional complaints,[63] but of the approximately 78,000 individual constitutional complaints lodged between September 1951 and the end of 1990, only 2.3 per cent. were successful.[64] There are three main barriers which have kept the success rate so low. First, there must be a violation of basic rights,[65] which is not always the case as when *e.g.* a decision is wrong in terms of ordinary law. Secondly, all remedies within the relevant branch of jurisdiction must first be exhausted before recourse may be had to the *Bundesverfassungsgericht*.[66] Thirdly, and most importantly, in order to ensure that the *Bundesverfassungsgericht* can work effectively, there is an acceptance procedure. In a summary preliminary examination, a committee consisting of three judges who are members of a senate, can decide whether to accept for hearing a complaint made. About 97 per cent. of all complaints are held inadmissible at this early stage.[67] In stating the reasons for an order by which acceptance of a complaint is refused, it is sufficient for the committee to refer to the legal aspect determining the refusal, such as a lack of prospect of success.[68] The committee can, and sometimes does, give a full explanation for not accepting an individual constitutional complaint and these are generally published in legal journals.[69] Furthermore, against decisions of such committees no appeal to the *Bundesverfassungsgericht* is permitted. The committee may impose a fee on the complainant in cases of abuse, especially if the complainant should have realised that the complaint was inadmissible or that it had no prospect of success.[70] A further development occurred in 1985 when the

---

[63] See Kommers, *op. cit.*, note 15, p. 16.

[64] See *Das Parlament, op. cit.*, note 19, p.8.

[65] § 90.I, *BVerfGG*.

[66] § 90.II, *BVerfGG*. An exception can be made if the case is of general relevance or is so urgent that recourse to other courts first would entail a serious disadvantage for the complainant: § 90.II, second sentence, *BVerfGG*.

[67] *Cf.* K. Schlaich, *Das Bundesverfassungsgericht* 2nd ed. (München, 1991), p. 154, note 488.

[68] See § 93b, *BVerfGG*.

[69] See Schlaich, *op. cit.*, note 67, p. 154.

[70] § 34.V, *BVerfGG*; § 93a, *BVerfGG*. The maximum fee chargeable for deliberate misuse of

Bundesverfassungsgerichtsgesetz was amended so as to give these committees even more power whereby they may now uphold a complaint of unconstitutionality by unanimous decision if it is clearly justified because the *Bundesverfassungsgericht* has already decided on the relevant question of constitutional law. This decision is equivalent to one taken by a senate. This power does not extend, however, to a decision whether a statute is unconstitutional or void for other reasons.[71]

3. BASIC RIGHTS IN GERMAN CONSTITUTIONAL LAW

Before turning to the basic rights set out in the constitution, there are two other aspects of the formal protection of such rights which should be briefly mentioned. First, the German constitution contains, in Article 79.III, a so-called perpetuity clause which bars (among others) any amendment to the basic principle laid down in Article 1. This provision proclaims that the "dignity of man is inviolable". Any change to the constitution, including the basic rights contained therein, must not violate the dignity of man. Secondly, Article 19.IV[72] of the German constitution gives a general guarantee that any person whose rights are violated by public authority shall have recourse to a court. In cases where no jurisdiction has been established, recourse is to the courts of ordinary jurisdiction (civil and criminal courts). This provision can hardly be overestimated.[73] An example of its application is the rule of due process[74] and it has in this respect been compared to Article 6 of the European Convention on Human Rights.[75] Another comparison that has been made is to Article 13 of the Convention.[76]

Turning now to the basic rights in the German constitution (*Grundgesetz*), these are very similar to those to be found in the European Convention on Human Rights. To name their (unofficial) titles:

Article 1: Protection of Human Dignity.

Article 2: Rights of Liberty (Life, Physical Integrity).

---

the individual constitutional complaint is DM 5000 (about £2000).

[71] § 93b, *BVerfGG*.

[72] Which reads: "Should any person's rights be violated by public authority, recourse to the court shall be open to him. Insofar as no other jurisdiction has been established, recourse shall be to the courts of ordinary jurisdiction...".

[73] See *BVerfGE* vol. 40, p. 237, at p. 251. *Cf.* S. Hendrichs in I. von Münch, *Grundgesetz Kommentar* 3rd ed. (Munich, 1985), vol. 1, article 19, no. 40.

[74] See *BVerfGE* vol. 60, p. 253, at p. 269 and vol. 55, p. 349, at p. 369.

[75] Hendrichs in von Münch, *op. cit.*, note 73, vol. 1, article 19, no. 53.

[76] *Ibid.*, vol. 1, article 19, no. 57.

Article 3: Equality before the Law.

Article 4: Freedom of faith, of conscience and of creed.

Article 5: Freedom of expression.

Article 6: Marriage and family, illegitimate children.

Article 7: Education.

Article 8: Freedom of assembly.

Article 9: Freedom of association.

Article 10: Privacy of letters, posts and telecommunication.

Article 11: Freedom of movement.

Article 12: Right to choose an occupation, prohibition of forced labour.

Article 12a: Liability for military and other services.

Article 13: Inviolability of the home.

Article 14: Property, right of inheritance, taking of property (expropriation).

Article 15: Socialisation.

Article 16: Deprivation of citizenship, extradition.

Article 16a: Right of asylum.

Article 17: Right of petition.

Article 17a: Restriction of individual basic rights through legislation enacted for defence purposes and concerning substitute service.

Article 18: Forfeiture of basic rights.

Article 19: Restriction of basic rights.

Part II: The Relationship between the Internal Law of the Federal Republic of   Germany and the European Convention on Human Rights

The European Convention on Human Rights was signed by the Federal Republic of Germany on 4 November 1950. The ECHR was ratified on 5 December 1952 and has been in force since 3 September 1953.[77] On 5 July 1955, the jurisdiction of the European Court of Human Rights was accepted and on the same date the right of individual complaint according to Article 25 of the ECHR was acknowledged.[78] Germany has only given a declaration recognising the competence of the Commission to receive such petitions according to Article 25.2 of the ECHR for a specific period, which has usually been five years[79] and which has been regularly renewed.[80]

Within the legal system of the FRG, the ECHR ranks below the constitution and on the same level as other federal statutes.[81] As this was felt to be somewhat unsatisfactory in view of the importance of the ECHR, two different attempts have been made to raise the ECHR above the level of ordinary statutes. Firstly, it has been suggested that as Article 1.II of the German constitution proclaims the German people to be endowed with inviolable and inalienable human rights, the ECHR could be seen as a further explanation of this principle and therefore as of the same importance as the constitution itself.[82] Secondly, reference has been made to Article 25 of the German constitution, which declares that "the general rules of public international law shall be an integral part of federal law. They shall take precedence over statutes and shall directly create rights and duties for the inhabitants of the federal territory." It has been suggested that the ECHR is a

---

[77]   See *Bundesgesetzblatt* 1952 vol. II, p. 685; *Bundesgesetzblatt* 1954 vol. II, p. 14; M. Roš, *Die Unmittelbare Anwendbarkeit der Europäischen Menschenrechtskonvention* (Schweizer Studien zum internationalen Recht, Band 38, Zurich, 1984), p. 117.

[78]   See generally Roš, *ibid.*

[79]   *Cf.* H. Miehsler and H. Petzold (eds.), *European Convention on Human Rights, Convention Européenne des Droits de l'Homme, Europäische Menschenrechtskonvention, Texts and Documents* (Köln, 1982), vol. I, p. 54.

[80]   H. Guradze, *Die Europäische Menschenrechtskonvention* (Berlin, 1968), p. 213.

[81]   See generally Roš, *op. cit.*, note 77; R. Herzog, "Hierarchie der Verfassungsnormen und ihre Funktion beim Schutz der Grundrechte" [1990] *Europäische Grundrechte Zeitung* 483, at p. 486; I. von Münch, *op. cit.*, note 73, no. 80; T. Kleinknecht and K. Meyer, *Strafprozeßordnung, Gerichtsverfassungsgesetz, Nebengesetze und ergänzende Bestimmungen*, bearb. von Th. Kleinknecht, K. Meyer, fortgeführt von L. Meyer-Goßner, 40th ed. (München, 1991), A 4, *Menschenrechtskonvention*, p. 1762; G. Ress, "*Die Europäische Menschenrechtskonvention und die Vertragsstaaten*" in I. Maier (ed.), *Europäischer Menschenrechtsschutz, Schranken und Wirkungen. Verhandlungen des Fünften Internationalen Kolloquiums über die Europäische Menschenrechtskonvention in Frankfurt (Main)* (Heidelberg 1982), 227, at p. 273; *BVerfGE* vol. 10, p. 271, at p. 274 and vol. 74, p. 358, at p. 370.

[82]   R. Echterhölter, "Die Europäische Menschenrechtskonvention im Rahmen der verfassungsmäßigen Ordnung" [1955] *Juristen-Zeitung* 689, at pp. 689 and 692.

general rule of public international law and that, by virtue of Article 25, it must therefore rank above federal statutes.[83]

Both arguments have failed to convince the *Bundesverfassungsgericht*.[84] This is particularly important as recourse to the *Bundesverfassungsgericht*, and therefore also the individual constitutional complaint, is (as we have seen) only possible in the case of the violation of basic, *i.e.* constitutional, rights.[85] There is no recourse to the *Bundesverfassungsgericht* to protect a right protected only by the ECHR and not protected under the German constitution.[86] On the other hand, if a right safeguarded by the ECHR is also covered by the German constitution, a complaint has to be filed with the *Bundesverfassungsgericht* before any application to Strasbourg will be accepted because of the requirement for the exhaustion of legal remedies.[87] Exceptions are only made if the right in question is not protected by the German constitution. This may, however, also be the case if the *Bundesverfassungsgericht* has already dismissed an individual constitutional complaint on a similar matter.[88]

As the ECHR ranks below the German constitution, it is susceptible of being overruled by more recent[89] federal statutes,[90] though it does prevail

---

[83] *E.g.*, see Guradze, *op. cit.*, note 80, at pp. 13 and 17; H. Guradze, "Anmerkung zum Beschluß des *BVerfG* v.14.1.1969 2 BvR 243/60" [1960] *Neue Juristische Wochenschrift* 1243 (case note on *BVerfG Beschluß* of 14 January 1960).

[84] See Kleinknecht and Meyer, *op. cit.*, note 81.

[85] See above, pp. 152–153.

[86] See Roš, *op. cit.*, note 77, p. 118; Foster, *op. cit.*, note 56, p. 63; *BVerfGE* vol. 10, p. 271, at p. 274; Kleinknecht and Meyer, *op. cit.*, note 81, p. 1780.

[87] *Cf.* Article 26 of the European Convention on Human Rights; Roš, *op. cit.*, note 77, p. 118, note 11; Decision of the European Commission of Human Rights on 8 December 1981, 9324/81 [1983] *Europäische Grundrechte Zeitung* 218, No. 132; E. Riedel, "Assertion and Protection of Human Rights in International Treaties and their Impact in the Basic Law" in C. Starck (ed.), *Rights, Institutions and Impact of International Law according to the German Basic Law* (Baden-Baden, 1987), 197, at p. 207.

[88] Decision of the European Commission of Human Rights on 31 May 1956, 27/1955 [1956] *Neue Juristische Wochenschrift* 1376; see also W. Beyer's comment about the decision, "Anmerkung zur Entscheidung der Europäischen Kommission für Menschenrechte Nr. 27/55 vom 31. Mai 1956" at the same point in the journal; Kleinknecht and Meyer, *op. cit.*, note 81, p. 1783.

[89] *I.e.* after 3 September 1953.

[90] Ress in Maier (ed.), *op. cit.*, note 81, p. 274, sees the possibility of the ECHR being overruled as a reason for giving it a systematical status near the constitution and thus allowing it to prevail over federal statutes.

over *Länder* statutes.[91] The danger of systematic contravention of the ECHR has been largely avoided by the very liberal approach that has been adopted when interpreting conflicting statutes.[92] This view has been recently confirmed by the *Bundesverfassungsgericht*.[93] The court ruled that when interpreting a statutory provision which could violate the ECHR, it had to be taken into account that the Federal Republic of Germany would not want to break an international treaty. In addition to taking into account the ECHR, the *Bundesverfassungsgericht* referred to the case-law on the ECHR. Decisions of the European Court are expressly seen by the *Bundesverfassungsgericht* as providing a guideline for interpreting Germany's basic rights.[94] This would not however be allowed to reduce the scope of protection already given by the basic rights of the German constitution, as the ECHR may not be used to curtail human rights granted by the member states.[95] Thus, only statutory provisions expressly stating that they contradict the ECHR are deemed to overrule the ECHR as more recent federal legislation. The impact of this decision has yet to be seen.[96]

An example of the direct applicability of the ECHR by superseding previous law is Article 5.5 of the Convention,[97] declaring that in a case of wrongful detention, the person whose rights are violated may claim compensation.[98] Although German law provided for such a claim as early as 1904,[99]

---

[91] This follows from Article 31 of the *Grundgesetz*. See also Foster, *op. cit.*, note 56, pp. 62 and 63; Roš, *op. cit.*, note 77, p. 118; M. Hilf, "General Problems of Relations between Constitutional Law and International Law" in Starck (ed.), *op. cit.*, note 87, 177 at p. 188; H. H. Kühne, "Ausschluß der Öffentlichkeit im Strafverfahren" [1971] *Neue Juristische Wochenschrift* 224, at p. 226.

[92] See T. Vogler, "Das Recht auf unentgeltliche Zuziehung eines Dolmetschers [1979] *Europäische Grundrechte Zeitung* 640 at p. 642; Roš, *op. cit.*, note 77, p. 118, note 15; Kleinknecht and Meyer, *op. cit.*, note 81, p. 1762.

[93] *BVerfGE* vol. 74, p. 358, at p. 370 (*obiter dicta*). Also worth mentioning is the decision of the *BVerfG* of 23 June 1981, *BVerfGE* vol. 58, p. 1 at p. 34 (Eurocontrol), where the court stressed its responsibility to prevent the violation of international treaties.

[94] See J. A. Frowein, "The Federal Republic of Germany" in M. Delmas-Marty and C. Chodkiewitz (eds.), *The European Convention for the Protection of Human Rights: International Protection Versus National Restrictions* (Dordrecht, 1992), p. 122.

[95] *Cf.* Article 60 of the European Convention on Human Rights.

[96] See also Frowein in Delmas-Marty and Chodkiewitz (eds.), *op. cit.*, note 94.

[97] *Cf.* K. Kühl, "Der Einfluß der Europäischen Menschenrechtskonvention auf das Strafrecht und auf das Strafverfahrensrecht der Bundesrepublik Deutschland: Teil II" (1988) 100 *Zeitschrift für die gesamte Strafrechtswissenschaft* 601, at p. 632.

[98] See *Bundesgerichtshof*, 10 January 1966 III ZR 70/64 [1966] *Neue Juristische Wochenschrift* 726; J. A. Frowein, "Die europäische Menschenrechtskonvention in der neueren

foreign nationals were only granted this right if their own country allowed a similar claim on a basis of reciprocity. The requirement of reciprocity has now become superfluous so far as such claims are concerned,[100] because although the text of the 1904 *Untersuchungshaftentschädigungsgesetz* has not changed, the statute has now been applied in a way that renders it compatible with Article 5.5. In addition to this, the same ECHR provision is applicable insofar as compensation in cases of wrongful detention is not covered by the *Gesetz für die Entschädigung von Strafverfolgungsmaßnahmen* [statute on compensation for criminal prosecution]. As the ECHR does not state whether the right to demand compensation is subject to any limitation as to time, the German courts found themselves forced to fit the—directly applicable—Article of the Convention into their national system when deciding on a claim to compensation for wrongful detention. Holding that no statutory provision was necessary to implement Article 5.5 of the ECHR, the *Bundesgerichtshof* (Federal Supreme Court) found the right to demand compensation under this Article to be subject to a three year limitation period.[101] Although the decision to opt for the rather short period of three years can be criticised,[102] it has to be taken into account that the Court also expressly held that the decision for a longer period of prescription would not be impossible under different circumstances and that the matter should be approached on a case by case basis. Finally, this decision shows that the direct applicability of the ECHR does to a large extent depend on the willingness of the courts (as shown here) to fill gaps that otherwise might prevent the applicability of the ECHR by analogy to similar regulations. The court could well have refused to make use of Article 5.5 ECHR until the enactment of an implementing statute.[103]

Praxis der Europäischen Kommission und des Europäischen Gerichtshofes für Menschenrechte" [1980] *Europäische Grundrechte Zeitung* 231: compensation under Article 5.5 offers better protection that the otherwise comprehensive German rules.

[99] *Untersuchungshaftentschädigungsgesetz, Reichsgesetzblatt* 1904, p. 321 (14 July 1904).

[100] See Roš, *op. cit.*, note 77, pp. 125–126; K. Zörb, "Untersuchungshaftentschädigung für Ausländer nach UHaftEntschG oder Europäischer Menschenrechtskonvention" [1956] *Neue Juristische Wochenschrift* 2146 at p. 2147 sees the whole of the *Untersuchungshaft-Entschädigungsgesetz* as superseded.

[101] *Bundesgerichtshof*, 31 January 1966, III ZR 118/64 [1966] *Neue Juristische Wochenschrift* 1021, at p. 1025; see also Kleinknecht and Meyer, *op. cit.*, note 81, p. 1770.

[102] See for example Roš, *op. cit.*, note 77, at p. 124.

[103] *Ibid.*, at p. 125.

Part III: The Impact of the Judgments of the European Court of Human Rights on German Domestic Law

1. INTRODUCTION

The impact of the ECHR on German law is generally felt to be low because of the high level of protection of human rights afforded by the German constitution.[104] This view was recently confirmed by the German ministry of justice[105] and is, for example, stressed in connection with the rules on criminal procedure.[106] Having said that, the number of cases where the European Court of Human Rights has decided that Germany has been in breach of the ECHR, although small, shows that there are indeed some areas of German law where the German constitution's protection of rights has been found wanting.

Despite Germany's self-assessment, she has been found to be in breach of the ECHR. In most of these cases the committee of three judges at the *Bundesverfassungsgericht* had, in deciding whether to accept the case for discussion in full court, rejected the complaints of unconstitutionality[107] on the grounds that they did not offer sufficient prospect of success. Up to the end of 1995, there have been 12 cases in which the European Court of Human Rights has decided that Germany has been in breach of the Convention. The majority of these cases have involved Article 6.[108] Five further cases

---

[104] R. Herzog, "Hierarchie der Verfassungsnormen und ihre Funktion beim Schutz der Grundrechte" [1990] *Europäische Grundrechte Zeitung* 486; see also Riedel in Starck (ed.), *op. cit.*, note 87, p. 207; Frowein, *op. cit.*, note 98, p. 231. See also R. Uerpmann, *Die Europäische Menschenrechtskonvention und die deutsche Rechtssprechung* (Berlin, 1993), at p. 170.

[105] In its answer to my letter to the *Justizministerium*. The letter was written by Dr. Meyer-Ladewig, 22 January 1993, IV M–9470/2–42 0073 /93. Dr. Meyer-Ladewig frequently appears before the European Court of Human Rights as the agent of the Federal Republic of Germany.

[106] Schäfer in Löwe Rosenberg, *Die Strafprozeßordnung und das Gerichtsverfassungsgesetz (Großkommentar)* 23rd ed. bearb. von H. Dünnebier, W. Gollwitzer, K. Meyer u.a., Erster Band (Einleitung, §§ 1 bis 111 n) (Berlin 1976), Einl. Kap. 1 No. 4.

[107] Under § 93 a (3), *BVerfGG*.

[108] Seven in total: *Bock* v. *Germany* Series A, No. 150 (1989) 12 E.H.R.R. 247; *Deumeland* v. *Germany* Series A, No. 100 (1986) 8 E.H.R.R. 448; *Eckle* v. *Germany* Series A, No. 51 (1982) 5 E.H.R.R. 1; *König* v. *Germany* Series A, No. 27 (1978) 2 E.H.R.R. 170; *Pakelli* v. *Germany* Series A, No. 64 (1983) 6 E.H.R.R. 1; *Öztürk* v. *Germany* Series A, No. 73 (1984) 6 E.H.R.R. 409; and *Luedicke et al.* v. *Germany* Series A, No. 29 (1978) 2 E.H.R.R. 149.

have raised issues under Art. 5.III,[109] 8,[110] 10 and of 4 together with Article 14[111] of the ECHR. Apart from these, there are 15 cases concerning Germany where the Commission has found her in breach of the Convention or at least ruled the complaint to be admissible. Statistics here do not look much different from the court's decisions: the majority of the cases have involved Article 6,[112] followed by four cases involving possible breaches of Article 10,[113] Article 5,[114] Article 3 and Article 8.[115] These cases were either not brought before the court or the court decided that Germany had not infringed the ECHR.[116]

There are few provisions to be found in the ECHR dealing with the influence of decisions by the Strasbourg court on the contracting states. According to Article 46, the jurisdiction of the European Court of Human Rights is accepted. All its decisions are final under Article 52. The contracting parties (including Germany) undertake to follow the decisions of the Court which affect them (Article 53). It remains unclear what exactly is meant by "following" the decisions of the court.[117] Article 50 does not offer much of an explanation: the court can rule that the country in breach of the Convention has to pay damages to the applicant in cases where the internal law of

---

[109] *Megyeri* v. *Germany* Series A, No. 237–A (1992) 15 E.H.R.R. 584.

[110] *Niemietz* v. *Germany* Series A, No. 251–B (1992) 16 E.H.R.R. 97.

[111] *Barthold* v. *Germany* Series A, No. 90 (1985) 7 E.H.R.R. 383; *Vogt* v. *Germany* Series A, No. 323 (1995) 21 E.H.R.R. 205; *Karl Heinz Schmidt* v. *Germany* Series A, No. 291–B (1994) 18 E.H.R.R. 513.

[112] See *e.g. Croissant* v. *Germany* Series A, No. 237–B (1992) 16 E.H.R.R. 135; *Buchholz* v. *Germany* Series A, No. 42 (1981) 3 E.H.R.R. 597; *Colak* v. *Germany* Series A, No. 147 (1988) 11 E.H.R.R. 513; *Englert* v. *Germany* Series A, No. 123 (1987) 10 E.H.R.R. 45; *Nölkenbockhoff* v. *Germany* Series A, No. 123 (1987) 10 E.H.R.R. 163; *Lutz* v. *Germany* Series A, No. 123 (1987) 10 E.H.R.R. 182; and *Hennings* v. *Germany* Series A, No. 237–A (1992) 16 E.H.R.R. 83.

[113] *Glasenapp* v. *Germany* Series A, No. 104 (1986) 9 E.H.R.R. 25; *Kosiek* v. *Germany* Series A, No. 105 (1986) 9 E.H.R.R. 328; *Markt Intern* v. *Germany* Series A, No. 165 (1989) 11 E.H.R.R. 212; *Jacubowski* v. *Germany* Series A, No. 291 (1994) 19 E.H.R.R. 64.

[114] *Stocke* v. *Germany* Series A, No. 199 (1991) 11 E.H.R.R. 46 and *Wemhoff* v. *Germany* Series A, No. 6 (1968) 1 E.H.R.R. 55.

[115] *Klass* v. *Germany* Series A, No. 28 (1978) 2 E.H.R.R. 213. *Klaas* v. *Germany* Series A, No. 269 (1993) 18 E.H.R.R. 305.

[116] For further discussion of these and the other cases mentioned above see below, p. 168 ff.

[117] Ress in Maier (ed.), *op. cit.*, note 81, p. 233; H. Stöcker, "Wirkungen der Urteile des Europäischen Gerichtshofs für Menschenrechte in der Bundesrepublik" [1982] *Neue Juristische Wochenschrift* 1905, at p. 1908; See also Tomkins, above p. 39 ff.

the country concerned only allows partial reparation for the breach. This implies that decisions of the European Court of Human Rights cannot be directly applicable and enforceable in Germany:[118] if that were the case, the need for compensation under Article 50 of the ECHR would not arise.[119] Furthermore, it has to be kept in mind that there are three different ways in which Germany can act against the Convention: administrative acts, statutes and court judgments. Whereas administrative acts can be set aside comparatively easily, changing statutes requires the cooperation of the legislature. Judgments inconsistent with the Convention are an even more difficult issue because to annul them would at the same time undermine the doctrines of *res judicata* and of the independence of the judiciary.[120] Still, in spite of these problems (and except for past violations of the ECHR such as wrongful detention), Article 50 should only be seen as a subsidiary remedy, as otherwise a country could "follow" decisions of the European Court of Human Rights only by paying compensation. This would reduce the protection of rights afforded by the ECHR to the level of a farce.[121]

Three areas of enforcement need now to be discussed in more detail: First, decisions of the Court where German statutory provisions have been held to be in contravention of the Convention; secondly the question whether such decisions can force Germany to reopen a case and revise domestic judgments;and thirdly the influence of the case law of the ECHR on German case law.

2. GERMAN STATUTORY PROVISIONS HELD TO BE IN VIOLATION OF THE ECHR

Perhaps the clearest example of changes in German law following a decision of the European Court of Human Rights is that of *Luedicke, Belkacem and Koc*.[122] The three applicants had requested the service of interpreters in criminal proceedings brought against them. Under the then German law, the person who was convicted had to pay the cost of the criminal proceedings

---

[118] See R. Bernhard, "Einwirkungen der Entscheidungen internationaler Menschenrechtsinstitutionen auf das nationale Recht" in K. Hailbronner (ed.), *Festschrift für Karl Doehring* (Berlin, 1989), 23 at p. 28.

[119] *Cf.* Ress in Maier (ed.), *op. cit.*, note 81, at p. 246.

[120] *Cf.* Guradze, *op. cit.*, note 80, p. 247 ff.

[121] *Cf.* Stöcker, *op. cit.,* note 117, p. 1908.

[122] Series A, No. 29 (1978) 2 E.H.R.R. 149. 41 of the 138 references to decisions of the Court and the Commission until 1993 are to this case: see Uerpmann, *op. cit.*, note 104, at p. 139.

against him or her. This included fees for interpreting which according to a 1975 amendment were part of the costs of the proceedings. Following their conviction, the applicants had to pay the costs of interpreting. Although Article 6.3 (e) of the ECHR declares that "Everyone charged with a criminal offence has the following minimum rights:…to have the free assistance of an interpreter if he cannot understand or speak the language used in court", the German courts held that this Article did not preclude the recovery of such costs *following* conviction. In doing so they gave the ECHR provision a very restricted meaning, narrowing it to free interpretation only during the procedure, thereby allowing charges for the translation afterwards. When the European Commission and the Court found that this understanding was not in line with the ECHR, the relevant German provisions then had to be amended.[123] The amendment duly came into force on 1 January 1981,[124] inserting a second sentence in No. 1904 of the table of costs of the *Gerichts-kostengesetz* (legal costs act), providing for free interpretation only in criminal proceedings. Even when the case was still pending before the European Court, the German authorities had arranged for the suspension of the recovery of costs in similar cases.[125] Indeed even before the European Court's judgment, the decision of the European Commission had already caused several courts to hold that Article 6.3 (e) precluded recovery of the costs of an interpreter even following conviction.[126]

In 1984, the European Court decided in *Öztürk*[127] that because of Article 6.3 (e), interpretation fees could also not be charged in cases of *Ordnungs-widrigkeiten* (administrative offences such as the disregarding of traffic regulations). These are minor criminal offences which are tried in summary administrative proceedings because the legislator has decriminalised them.[128] The European Court had to decide on a case where the appellant (Öztürk) had committed a minor traffic offence which had been dealt with by the administrative authorities. He appealed, thereby causing a public hearing of his

---

[123] See Kleinknecht and Meyer, *op. cit.*, note 81, p. 1776.

[124] Amendment of 18 August 1980, BGBl, vol. I, p. 1503, at p. 1507.

[125] *Cf.* A. Drzemczewski, *European Human Rights Convention in Domestic Law* (Oxford, 1983), p. 18; *ibid.*, "The Authority of the Organs of the European Human Rights Convention in Domestic Courts" [1979] *Legal Issues of European Integration* 1. See also Stöcker, *op. cit.*, note 117, p. 1907 and Ress in Maier (ed.), *op. cit.*, note 81, p. 282.

[126] *Cf.* Ress in Maier (ed.), *op. cit.*, note 81, referring to Landgericht Frankfurt Beschluß 27 July 1978; Landgericht Bonn Beschluß 16 August 1978 and Amtsgericht Berlin-Tiergarten [1978] *Neue Juristische Wochenschrift* 2462.

[127] *Öztürk* v. *Germany* Series A, No. 73 (1984) 6 E.H.R.R. 409.

[128] Riedel, in Starck (ed.), *op. cit.*, note 87, p. 211.

case in court. During this hearing Öztürk required an interpreter. He then withdrew his appeal and accepted the previous decision of the administrative authorities. When he was charged with the costs of interpreting, he appealed, relying on Article 6.3 (e) of the ECHR. Although again a literal application of the Article was favoured by the German courts, the European Court of Human Rights decided that if in criminal proceedings the accused was exempted from interpretation costs, then this also had to be the case even though the offence was considered less criminal by the legislature and had been made subject only to administrative proceedings.[129]

The decision to treat these administrative offences as criminal in this way has been criticised.[130] Even while the case was pending, Vogler argued that such a view ignored the legislative decision by Germany to decriminalise this area of law.[131] He considered that once an offence did not carry the moral and ethical stigma of criminality, the need for protection by guaranteeing free interpretation had been significantly diminished, particularly when compared to a criminal procedure.[132] Germany did not immediately amend her legislation, apparently hoping for the European Court on Human Rights to change its mind on this matter.[133] The statute was eventually changed in 1989, five years after the decision by the European Court of Human Rights, and it now includes administrative or regulatory defences in the free interpretation provision.[134] Some German courts had however followed the decision in *Öztürk* even before that,[135] not charging for the costs of interpretation in administrative offences, whereas other courts[136] had applied the same legislation as before until the amendment went through. Lappe ob-

---

[129] *Ibid.*

[130] See for example Frowein in Delmas-Marty and Chodkiewitz (eds.), *op. cit.*, note 94, p. 123.

[131] Vogler, *op. cit.*, note 92, p. 647.

[132] *Ibid.*

[133] Kühl, *op. cit.*, note 97, at pp. 602–603; Frowein in Delmas-Marty and Chodkiewitz (eds.), *op. cit.*, note 94, p. 123.

[134] *Gerichtskostengesetz* (legal expenses act) *Anlage I* (table of costs), as amended on 15 June 1989, BGBI vol. I p. 1082.

[135] See F. Lappe, "Entwicklung des Gerichts im Jahre 1985" [1986] *Neue Juristische Wochenschrift* 2550 at p. 2555, notes 67 and 68, referring to decisions by the Landgericht Düsseldorf Jur. Büro 1985, 427 and Landgericht Stuttgart Jur. Büro 1985, 1069.

[136] Landgericht Nürnberg Fürth Jur. Büro 1985, 429 [1991] *Europäische Grundrechte Zeitung 185*. See also the F. Lappe, "Entwicklung des Gerichts im Jahre 1986" [1987] *Neue Juristische Wochenschrift* 1860, at p. 1865, note 89, referring to a decision of the Landgericht Osnabrück Jur. Büro 1986, 1224.

served in 1986 that not charging the cost of interpretation in the case of administrative offences was winning recognition from the German courts, but he did not give sufficient references to make this observation more than a mere opinion.[137]

The 1989 reform was not embarked upon willingly by the authorities. Following *Öztürk*, Germany had only agreed to the right of individual complaint to the Commission and the court for a period of three instead of (as previously) five years.[138] In the case of *Lutz*[139] in 1987, concerning the applicability to administrative offences of the presumption of innocence under Article 6.2, the European Court of Human Rights still did not change its view that administrative offences were criminal under Article 6. After this decision, Germany's hope for a different decision had begun to seem somewhat unrealistic. The European Commission added to the pressure by accepting another application against being charged with the costs of interpreting in administrative offences.[140] This was in spite of Article 27.1(b) of the ECHR which sets out that an application is not admissible if the Commission has already decided on a similar question. This seems to have been a way of dealing with Germany's refusal to alter her legislation despite being bound by the decision under Article 53 ECHR, as it was clear that further evidence of continuing breaches of the convention would not promote her international image.[141]

Another area of German law where alterations became necessary because of the ECHR has been the law relating to the length of criminal and civil proceedings. Although this is often more a matter of the facts of the case than of law, and although in *Wemhoff*[142] Germany was not found in breach of the Convention as far as the "reasonable time" rule of Article 5.3 was concerned, the law of criminal as well as of civil procedure was amended in the early 1960s.[143] §§ 121 and 122 StPO (Act of Criminal Procedure) were added to the statute, requiring that detention on remand was not thenceforth

---

[137] Lappe, 1986, *op. cit.*, note 135, at p. 2555.

[138] See *Bekanntmachung of 5 March 1987 zu den Art. 25, 46 und 63 der Konvention zum Schutze der Menschenrechte und Grundfreiheiten und zum Protokoll Nr. 4 dieser Konvention*, referring to a declaration with effect from 1 July 1986, BGBl vol. II (1987) p. 213.

[139] *Op. cit.*, note 112.

[140] 5 March 1986, reported in [1986] *Europäische Grundrechte Zeitung* 444.

[141] See also Kühl, *op. cit.*, note 97, at pp. 605 and 639.

[142] *Op. cit.*, note 114.

[143] For the criminal law see Ress in Maier (ed.), *op. cit.*, note 81, 236 at p. 276.

to exceed six months. Any detention exceeding this time limit had to be permitted by a superior court, and further detention had to be reconsidered every six months.

The "reasonable time" rule in Article 6.1 of the ECHR seems also to have influenced German law. This right is not explicitly guaranteed by the German constitution, but is deduced from the inviolability of the dignity of man under Article 1.I and the *Rechtsstaatsprinzip* or rule of law under Article 20.[144] In 1976,[145] the law of civil procedure was changed significantly in order to shorten the duration of proceedings.[146] However, even after these changes Germany has been found to be in breach of Article 6.1.[147] This does not necessarily show that the procedural laws of Germany violate the ECHR. First, as already mentioned, the length of proceedings is influenced by the circumstances of the case as well as by the relevant statutes. Secondly, shortening the proceedings can also have the effect of truncating the other rights of the parties at the same time.[148] It has, however, been suggested that the German constitution and the *Bundesverfassungsgerichtsgesetz* be amended in such way as to allow an individual constitutional complaint to the Federal Constitutional Court in cases of alleged violations of the ECHR.[149]

Finally a note on two further areas of law where amendments have already been made to the law or where changes might eventually become inevitable in order to comply with the ECHR. Firstly, the presumption of innocence in Article 6.2 of the ECHR. As is the case with the due process rules of Article 6.1 (and, more specifically, Article 5.3), discussed previously, this principle is not explicitly guaranteed under the German constitution, but is generally held to be included in Articles 1 and 20 of the consti-

---

[144] *Cf.* Kühl, *op. cit.*, note 97, at pp. 620–1.

[145] *Gesetz zur Vereinfachung und Beschleunigung gerichtlicher Verfahren, Vereinfachungsnovelle*, 3 December 1976 BGBl, vol. I, p. 3281.

[146] Generally speaking, evidence that Germany has changed her legislation *because* of the ECHR is rare. In many cases the ECHR is only referred to as the reason for a change in law if the German constitution is silent on the issue in question: see Kühl, *op. cit.*, note 97, at p. 620.

[147] *Bock* v. *Germany, op. cit.*, note 108 (divorce proceedings lasted more than nine years); *Deumeland* v. *Germany, op. cit.*, note 108; *Eckle* v. *Germany, op. cit.*, note 108 (criminal proceedings lasted for 20 years); *König* v. *Germany, op. cit.*, note 108 (action to decide whether medical practitioner was authorised to practise and run a clinic took nearly 11 years).

[148] Kühl, *op. cit.*, note 97, p. 633.

[149] *Ibid.*, p. 635.

tution (dignity of man and *Rechtsstaatsprinzip*). German law allows the non-prosecution of minor offences and the discontinuation of proceedings if there is no public interest in the prosecution and if the hypothetical level of guilt of the accused is low enough.[150] It is suggested that a violation of the presumption of innocence cannot be seen in this provision as the guilt of the accused in such instances is purely hypothetical.[151] Connected with the question whether German law always observes Article 6.2 ECHR when discontinuing criminal proceedings is the question of who in such cases has to pay the costs. In 1978, the European Commission "was informed of the Federal Government's intention...to draw attention of the *Länder* judicial authorities to the need of the courts to respect the principle of the presumption of innocence embodied in Article 6.2 of the Convention when setting out reasons for decisions relating to expenses under § 154 and § 467 IV StPO".[152] The very duty to pay the expenses even if the proceedings have been discontinued has been felt to violate the presumption of innocence[153] as the decision as to costs could amount to the equivalent of a conviction.[154] However, the European Court of Human Rights has decided in *Englert*[155] as well as *Lutz*[156] and *Nölkenbockhoff*,[157] in each case by a majority of 16 votes to one, that the Convention does not oblige Germany, where a prosecution has been discontinued, to indemnify a person "charged with a criminal offence" for any detriment that he or she may have suffered and that there is no breach of Article 6.2 of the ECHR in such a situation.[158] Accordingly, in none of these cases did the Court find a breach of the Convention.

---

[150] § 153 *Strafprozeßordnung*.

[151] See also Kühl, *op. cit.*, note 97, p. 615. Frowein in Delmas-Marty and Chodkiewitz (eds.), *op. cit.*, note 94, p. 124 sees § 153 *Strafprozeßordnung* as a breach of Article 6.2 of the ECHR.

[152] According to Drzemczewski, 1979, *op. cit.*, note 125, p. 19, referring to a report of the commission adopted on 11 May 1978.

[153] Kühl, *op. cit.*, note 97, p. 618; Frowein in Delmas-Marty and Chodkiewitz (eds.), *op. cit.*, note 94, p. 127; Riedel, in Starck (ed.), *op. cit.*, note 87, p. 212.

[154] Frowein, *ibid.*, p. 126.

[155] *Op. cit.*, note 112.

[156] *Op. cit.*, note 112.

[157] *Op. cit.*, note 112.

[158] For a discussion of the three cases see Stock-taking on the European Convention on Human rights, A periodic note on the concrete results achieved under the Convention, Supplement 1987, by the Secretary of the European Commission of Human Rights (Strasbourg, 1988), pp. 44–47.

The second area where the possible need to amend German legislation may be discussed involves the right of self-defence under § 32 *Strafgesetz-buch* (criminal code), which constitutes a justification for what would otherwise be a criminal offence. Under Article 2.2 of the ECHR, causing the death of some other person for the purpose of self-defence is only allowed if absolutely necessary. German doctrine, however, also sees self-defence as a justification for causing the attacker's death in order to protect one's property. The right to self-defence in this situation does not include causing the attacker's death if the value of the property to be protected is low. Such a right to self-defence could surely be vulnerable to restriction under Article 2.2.[159] A more general question is whether the ECHR only grants protection against the state or whether it can also be applied as between two persons. Neither the European Court of Human Rights nor the Federal Constitutional Court have as yet answered this question.[160]

3. REOPENING A CASE AND REVISION OF A JUDGMENT AFTER A DECISION OF THE EUROPEAN COURT OF HUMAN RIGHTS

The case of *Pakelli*[161] caused extensive discussion in Germany[162] on the extent to which a decision by the European Court of Human Rights could force Germany to change her rules relating to the reopening of criminal proceedings. Mr. Pakelli, a Turkish National, was sentenced in Germany to two years and three months imprisonment for an offence against the Narcotics Act and for tax evasion. The applicant had been refused the appointment of an official defence counsel to act on his behalf in the hearing of his appeal against conviction before the *Bundesgerichtshof* (federal court) and he went on to allege a breach of Article 6.3 (c) of the ECHR. As we have seen, this provision lays down that everyone charged with a criminal offence has the minimum right to defend him- or herself in person or through legal assistance of his or her own choice. Should he or she not be able to afford legal assistance, it has to be given free when the interests of justice so require.

---

[159] *Cf.* Kühl, *op. cit.*, note 97, at pp. 624 and 626.

[160] *Cf. The Practice of European Countries where direct effect is given to the European Convention on Human Rights in internal law.* Written observations presented by Sir Vincent Evans to the Colloquy on Human Rights held in Athens 21–22 September 1978 (Strasbourg 1978), p. 62.

[161] *Pakelli* v. *Germany, op. cit.,* note 108.

[162] See for example E. Schumann, "Menschenrechtskonvention und Wiederaufnahme des Verfahrens" [1964] *Neue Juristische Wochenschrift* 753, at p. 756, who is of the opinion that Germany has to change its law of criminal procedure in order to be able to reopen proceedings if a judgment is held by the Strasbourg Court to infringe the ECHR.

Both the European Commission and the Court held that the applicant's right to legal assistance referred to all stages of the proceedings and that Germany was therefore in breach of the Convention. Mr. Pakelli sought a reopening of his case in Germany. As there is a consensus that decisions of the European Court on Human Rights do not lead to an automatic annulment of a judgment by a court,[163] the question arose whether the finding of an infringement by the Court could nevertheless oblige Germany to make good the violation of human rights suffered by the appellant by reopening the procedure. On a more general note, only the reopening of the procedure could lead to full compensation in the case of a judgment contradicting the Convention, whereas the non-execution of a judgment infringing human rights under the ECHR or the pardon of a person convicted in violation of the ECHR would mean a lesser degree of reparation.[164]

German procedural law, however, as Mr. Pakelli soon discovered, provides for the reopening of criminal proceedings only on very narrow grounds. One of these covers the situation where new relevant facts emerge,[165] but a decision by the European Court does not amount to a new fact within the meaning of this provision.[166] A proceeding may also be reopened if the statutory provision on which it is based is ruled to be void by the *Bundesverfassungsgericht* (Federal Constitutional Court) or if the court lays down that the statutory provision in question is only in accordance with the German constitution if interpreted in a way prescribed by the *Bundesverfassungsgericht*.[167] Infringement of the ECHR by the judgment against Pakelli without the appointment of an official defence counsel was not sufficient for a reopening of procedure under this provision of the *Bundesverfassungsgerichtsgesetz*. When Mr. Pakelli appealed to the *Bundesverfassungsgericht*, a committee of three judges rejected his appeal in a summary preliminary examination.[168] Although this may not appear to be a decision in

---

[163] *Cf.* K. Kühl, "Der Einfluß der Europäischen Menschenrechtskonvention auf das Strafrecht und auf das Strafverfahrensrecht der Bundesrepublik Deutschland: Teil I" (1988) 100 *Zeitschrift für die gesamte Strafrechtswissenschaft* 406, at p. 423, note 103.

[164] *Cf.* Ress in Maier (ed.), *op. cit.*, note 81, p. 240.

[165] See § 359 *Strafprozeßordnung* (code of criminal procedure) and, more especially, § 359 no. 5.

[166] See C. H. Schreuer, "The Impact of International Institutions on the Protection of Human Rights in Domestic Courts" (1974) 4 *Israel Yearbook on Human Rights* 60, at p. 64.

[167] *Cf.* § 79.I, *BVerfGG*.

[168] Pakelli-Beschluß, 2 BvR 336/85, 11 October 1985, (1986) 46 *Zeitschrift für ausländisches öffentliches Recht und Völkerrecht* 289.

support of the impact of the ECHR, it does contain a number of aspects favourable to its role in the legal system of Germany.

First, the committee of three judges held the complaint to be admissible. This is worth noting because in order for an individual constitutional complaint to be admissible, the applicant has to claim that one of his or her basic rights has been violated. The committee decided that the right to free development of one's personality under Article 2.I of the German constitution could be violated by Germany ignoring a general rule of public international law under Article 25 of the constitution. This can be seen as a move on the part of the *Bundesverfassungsgericht* towards treating a violation of the ECHR as an infringement of basic rights.[169] (Having said that, the *Bundesverfassungsgericht* in a later decision[170] confirmed their previous view that an individual constitutional complaint was not admissible if supported only by the allegation of a violation of rights protected under the ECHR.) Secondly, although the committee of three judges decided that Pakelli's individual constitutional complaint had to be rejected because there was no obligation to follow the European Court of Human Rights by reopening the procedure, it stressed that they did not want to decide the issue whether *e.g.* Germany has to stay the execution of a judgment if its legal basis has been ruled to be against the ECHR. Until the present day, however, Germany has neither changed her code of criminal procedure to include a decision by an international institution in the reasons for reopening a case nor does she appear to be planning such a change.[171]

4. THE INFLUENCE OF THE CASE LAW OF THE ECHR ON GERMAN CASE LAW

Contrary to the provisions of the ECHR, which are referred to comparatively often in German case-law,[172] the decisions of the court are referred to only extremely rarely.[173] The ECHR and its case-law have their greatest impact on

---

[169] *Cf.* J. A. Frowein, "Anmerkung zur Pakelli-Entscheidung des Bundesverfassungsgerichts" (1986) 46 *Zeitschrift für ausländisches öffentliches Recht und Völkerrecht* 286.

[170] 13 January 1987, decision by the *BVerfG* vol. 74, 102 at p. 121.

[171] *Cf.* Kühl, *op. cit.*, note 163, at p. 424.

[172] Drzemczewski, 1983, *op. cit.*, note 125, p. 112 even states that in Germany, the provisions of the ECHR are invoked before courts more often than in any other contracting state. Until 1993, the Convention had been referred to by the courts about 682 times: see Uerpmann, *op. cit.*, note 104, at p. 137.

[173] Drzemczewski, 1979, *op. cit.*, note 125; Schreuer, *op. cit.*, note 166, p. 73; Kühl, *op. cit.*, note 163, p. 430; Ress in Maier (ed.), *op. cit.*, note 81, p. 256. Uerpmann, *op. cit.*, note 104, has observed, at p. 138, that until 1993, there were 138 references to decisions of

the German legal system when they lead to changes in statutory provisions.[174] Of the many possible reasons for this lack of importance of the case-law of the European Court, the most convincing seems to be that German judges hold the case-law of the *Bundesverfassungsgericht* to be very important. As it is often thought that human rights are sufficiently protected by the German constitution,[175] the decisions of the European Court of Human Rights appear therefore to lose their importance when compared with the case-law on the German constitution.[176] Another explanation offered for the decisions of the European Court of Human Rights being seldom referred to is the lack of adequate information and a general unfamiliarity with the published materials.[177] Even as late as 1993, there was no official German translation of the judgments of the court, although decisions relevant to German law are mostly published in journals.[178]

As far as decisions by German courts are concerned, it is extremely difficult to give an account of how many of them refer to the provisions of the ECHR. This is due to the fact that neither the official publications nor other legal journals have a reliable index dealing with such references.[179] According to a survey made by Kühl in 1988,[180] by that year there had been more than 300 decisions referring to the ECHR. More than two-thirds of the judgments were by criminal courts, and 60 of these were by the criminal law division of the *Bundesgerichtshof* (Federal Supreme Court). Peak years for the number of references to the ECHR were 1982 and 1985/6. By far the largest number of references is to Article 6 of the ECHR.[181] The general im-

---

either the Court or the Commission or both, 41 of which were to *Luedicke, op. cit.*, note 122. Of the case-law of the Court, only 35 decisions have been mentioned, most of them involving Germany: Uerpmann, *ibid.*

[174] See Lappe, 1987, *op. cit.*, note 136, p. 1865.

[175] See also Drzemczewski, 1983, *op. cit.*, note 125, p. 111.

[176] *Cf.* Frowein in Delmas-Marty and Chodkiewitz (eds.), *op. cit.*, note 94, p. 125.

[177] Schreuer, *op. cit.*, note 166, p. 75; Drzemczewski, 1979, *op. cit.*, note 125, p. 17; Ress in Maier (ed.), *op. cit.*, note 81, p. 257; Uerpmann, *op. cit.*, note 104, at pp. 170–171.

[178] Principally the *Europäische Grundrechtszeitung*. See generally Frowein in Delmas-Marty and Chodkiewitz (eds.), *op. cit.*, note 94, p. 125.

[179] Kühl, *op. cit.*, note 163, p. 425–426.

[180] *Ibid.*

[181] BGH (Beschluß) 29 July 1964 [1964] *Neue Juristische Wochenschrift* 2119 (Article 6.2, no breach); OLG Karlsruhe 20 January 1972 [1972] *Neue Juristische Wochenschrift* 1907 (Article 6.1, no breach); *BVerfG* Beschluß 29 May 1990, 2 BvR 254, 1343,/88 [1990] *Neue Juristische Wochenschrift* 2741 (Article 6.2, breach); BFH 27 August 1991 [1992] *Neue Juristische Wochenschrift* 1472 (Article 6.2, no breach); BFH Beschluß 13 September 1991 [1992] *Neue Juristische Wochenschrift* 1527 (Article 6.1, no breach); BGH 29

pression is that references are mostly to procedural rights, and even then that the relevant provision is rarely held to have been violated. Of those decisions in which an application of the provisions of the ECHR has worked in favour of the party relying on it, a recent decision by the *Oberlandesgericht Düsseldorf* is worth mentioning.[182] The court decided that a violation of the "reasonable time rule" of Article 6 of the ECHR meant that the criminal proceedings in question had to be ended. This ruling stands in marked contrast to a decision by the *Oberlandesgericht Karlsruhe* in 1972,[183] where after an appeal by the *Staatsanwaltschaft* (public prosecution) the *Oberlandesgericht* reversed the decision of a lower court and proceedings were started again because the *Oberlandesgericht* felt that in spite of Article 6 ECHR, the length of the proceedings did not constitute an obstacle to the continuation of the trial.

Two further cases where the application of the ECHR has worked in favour of the injured party are a decision by the *Bundesverfassungsgericht* of 1990[184] and a decision by the *Bundesgerichtshof* (Federal Supreme Court) in 1991.[185] In the 1990 decision, the *Bundesverfassungsgericht* had to decide on an individual constitutional complaint alleging the violation of the presumption of innocence by a lower court. The lower court had terminated criminal proceedings under § 153.II *Strafprozeßordnung*, which as we have seen permits the discontinuation of a trial if there is no public interest in the prosecution and if the hypothetical level of guilt of the accused is low. The lower court (*Amtsgericht*) had ordered the accused to pay the costs of the trial under §§ 464, 467 I and IV *Strafprozeßordnung* and in the reasons it gave for this order it had implied that the accused was guilty of fraud even though no such guilt had been established during the trial. The *Bundesverfassungsgericht* held that the presumption of innocence under Article 6.2

October 1991 [1992] *Neue Juristische Wochenschrift* 1118 (Article 6.1, no breach); BGH Beschluß 6 November 1991 [1992] *Neue Juristische Wochenschrift* 849 (Article 6.3(c), breach); BGH 7 November 1991 [1992] *Neue Juristische Wochenschrift* 1245 (Article 6, no breach); OLG Düsseldorf Beschluß 29 January 1992 [1992] *Neue Juristische Wochenschrift* 1183 (Article 6.2, no breach).

[182] OLG Düsseldorf Beschluß v. 26.8.1987, XII 29/87 [1988] *Neue Juristische Wochenschrift* 2751 (NStZ 1988, 427).

[183] OLG Karlsruhe 20 January 1972 [1972] *Neue Juristische Wochenschrift* 1907.

[184] *BVerfG* Beschluß 29 May 1990, 2 BvR 254, 1343/88 [1990] *Neue Juristische Wochenschrift* 2741. Pronouncements by the *BVerfG* on the Convention are—even if only *obiter dicta*—relatively rare, *cf.* Riedel, in Starck (ed.), *op. cit.*, note 87, p. 217.

[185] BGH Beschluß 6 November 1991, 4 StR 519/91 [1992] *Neue Juristische Wochenschrift* 849.

of the ECHR was infringed but based its actual decision on the more general *Rechtsstaatsprinzip* contained in the German constitution.[186]

In the 1991 decision, the *Bundesgerichtshof* held that Article 6.3 (c) of the ECHR had been infringed by a court which had appointed a different defence counsel to act for the accused when it had become apparent that the accused's counsel would not be in a position to come to the trial. Although the time gap until a trial is continued after an adjournment must as a rule be not more than 10 days,[187] which is a rather short period of time, the *Bundesgerichtshof* held that not enough effort had been made to try the case within the time limit and with the counsel chosen by the accused. It held that the lower court (*Landgericht*) had not sufficiently taken into account the fact that the accused had relied especially on his defence counsel and that she was the person best informed on the details of the case. The *Landgericht* could also within the ten day period have set another date for the trial as its timetable was not fully occupied with other trials. Finally, the reasons given by the *Landgericht* for not fixing a date suitable to the defence counsel within the period permitted were not convincing. Although the only times suitable to counsel as well as the court were respectively four and five days after the present trial, it would have been possible to summon at least three of the five witnesses because at the time in question they were detained in prison and thus were easy to get hold of.

Trying to find out whether German case law has been influenced by decisions of the European Court of Human Rights means facing even greater difficulties than when attempting to detect the application of provisions of the ECHR by German courts—there is not even an unreliable index but no index at all on this subject in official publications and legal journals. It is difficult to estimate how far books and articles on the Court's case-law have indirectly influenced German case-law simply on account of having been read by the judges in question.[188] German decisions on civil law and criminal law (though not on the law of criminal procedure) have remained untouched by the Convention because of the lack of conflicting topics in these areas. It has to be stressed,[189] however, that the principles developed by the Court have in some cases been adopted without reference to its case-law. It is also true of course that an explicit reference to decisions by the Court does not

---

[186] See also Oberlandesgericht Köln, Beschluß 30 October 1990, 2 WS 528/90 [1990] *Neue Juristische Wochenschrift* 506 (Article 6.2 ECHR, breach).

[187] See § 229.I *Strafprozeßordnung* (act of criminal procedure).

[188] Uerpmann, *op. cit.*, note 104, at p. 158.

[189] *Ibid.*, at p. 169.

mean that it has necessarily been followed. The only conclusion to be drawn from this is that the case-law on the ECHR is of little more than marginal importance in Germany.[190] Academic references to the influence of the case-law of the ECHR on the decisions of the German courts have to remain vague. Lappe mentions that the decision in the case of *Öztürk* has caused German courts to follow the view of the Court, but, as we have already noted, he fails to give more than two decisions in support of these propositions.[191] Ress[192] wants to note a change towards increased recognition of the rulings of the European Court of Human Rights since the decision in the case of *Luedicke et. al.*[193] Hopes of a move towards the increasing importance of the ECHR following decisions of the *Bundesverfassungsgericht* have failed to materialise: although the *Bundesverfassungsgericht* in 1987 expressly referred to the decisions of the Commission on Articles 3 and 4.2 of the ECHR in order to decide to what extent obligations to work are justified,[194] in a study conducted by Kühl, there were until 1988 less than 20 decisions containing references to the case-law on the ECHR.[195] This stands in stark contrast to the number of cases containing references to the Convention itself (see earlier).

Still it may be possible to read between the lines a change towards greater recognition of the ECHR in two decisions well known to EC lawyers—*Solange I* and *Solange II*.[196] Reversing its previous opinion,[197] the *Bundesverfassungsgericht* decided that a court could not any longer stay proceedings under Article 100.1 of the German constitution by requesting the *Bundesverfassungsgericht* to decide whether the (EC) provision to be applied by the court violated basic rights under the German constitution. The *Bundesverfassungsgericht* held that the values of the ECHR were at that

---

[190] This conclusion is however not drawn by Uerpmann, *ibid*.

[191] See Lappe, 1986, *op. cit.*, note 135, p. 2555 notes 67 and 68, referring to decisions by the Landgericht Düsseldorf Jur. Büro 1985, 427 and Landgericht Stuttgart Jur. Büro 1985, 1069.

[192] In Maier (ed.), *op. cit.*, note 81, p. 277.

[193] *Luedicke, Belkacem and Koc* v. *Germany, op. cit.,* note 108 (recovery of costs of interpreter).

[194] *BVerfG* 13 January 1987. See *BVerfGE* vol. 74, p. 102, at p. 121.

[195] Kühl, *op. cit.*, note 163, p. 430.

[196] Beschluß 22 October 1986, *BVerfGE* vol. 73, p. 339 *ff*. See also R. Herzog, "The Hierarchy of Constitutional Norms and its Function in the Protection of Basic Rights" (1992) 13 *Human Rights Law Journal* 90 at p. 93.

[197] As in Beschluß of 29 May 1974, *BVerfGE* vol. 37, p. 271.

stage accepted by the majority of member states,[198] thus making the protection by the German constitution no longer necessary. This judgment shows an increasing acceptance of the function of the ECHR by the German Federal Constitutional Court.[199]

Among the few examples of the case-law of the European Court of Human Rights being referred to by German courts are references to *Wemhoff*[200] and to *Lutz*[201] and *Nölkenbockhoff*.[202] The *Oberlandesgericht Düsseldorf* commented in 1992[203] that an agreement between Germany and the applicant in the case 12748/87 under Article 28(b) ECHR was not binding on other courts. What is more, a recent decision by the *Bundesverfassungsgericht* on Article 10 of the German constitution (on privacy) neither mentions the corresponding provision in the ECHR (Article 8) nor any case-law on this provision of the ECHR. This is rather surprising, particularly if we have regard to what the case was concerned with:[204] The German Telecom had, on the request of one of its customers, kept the customer's telephone line under surveillance. This included monitoring from where calls were made to the extension in question. The facts were as follows: The applicant (A) had filed an individual constitutional complaint against the data as described being used in a court proceeding against her. These court proceedings had been started by the present girlfriend (B) of A's former boyfriend. B had been receiving anonymous calls over a considerable period of time. She suspected that A was the caller whereupon A obtained a court order forbidding the repetition of this allegation. After this, B arranged to have her telephone monitored by the German Telecom. It then turned out that the anonymous calls were indeed coming from A's flat. In the court case that followed, A was convicted and required to pay damages. She then lodged an individual

---

[198] See H. Säcker, *Das Bundesverfassungsgericht*, 4th ed. (Bonn, 1989), p. 36.

[199] Kühl, *op. cit.*, note 163, p. 429.

[200] *Wemhoff* v. *Germany, op. cit.*, note 114. OLG Karlsruhe 20 January 1972 [1972] *Neue Juristische Wochenschrift* 1907, referring to EGMR Band I p. 121, at p. 180 but rejecting further comparison to *Wemhoff* without any arguments; OLG Stuttgart [1974] *Neue Juristische Wochenschrift* 284.

[201] *Lutz* v. *Germany, op. cit.*, note 112.

[202] *Nölkenbockhoff* v. *Germany , op. cit.*, note 112. *BVerfG* Beschluß 29 May 1990, 2 BvR 254, 1343/88 [1990] *Neue Juristische Wochenschrift* 2741 (Article 6.2) (referring to *Lutz* and *Nölkenbockhoff*); OLG Köln Beschluß 30 October 1990 2 WS 528/90 [1990] *Neue Juristische Wochenschrift* 506, referring to *Lutz* and *Nölkenbockhoff*.

[203] OLG Düsseldorf Beschluß 29 January 1992 [1992] *Neue Juristische Wochenschrift* 1183.

[204] *BVerfG* Beschluß 25 March 1992, 1 BvR 1430/88, reported at [1992] *Computer und Recht* 431.

constitutional complaint against the use of the data obtained by monitoring the incoming phone calls on her "rival's" telephone.

The question arose whether the *Fernmeldeordnung*, the regulation in force at the time of the incident dealing with such interceptions, was sufficient as a statutory regulation under Article 10.2 of the German constitution. The problem was that although the *Fernmeldeordnung* mentioned that a service to monitor incoming phone calls on an extension was available to customers, the *Bundesverfassungsgericht* held this not to be sufficient to justify an infringement of another customer's privacy of telecommunications, protected under Article 10.1 of the German constitution. However, the *Bundesverfassungsgericht* nevertheless held Article 10.1 of the German constitution not to have been infringed. This may appear less outrageous if we consider some further details of the case. The *Bundesverfassungsgericht* decided that although the *Fernmeldeordnung* was not sufficient to justify the infringement, use of the data was permitted as otherwise until the change of the *Fernmeldeordnung* a victim of anonymous calls would be left unprotected. Even if this result does not leave much room for criticism, it is most remarkable that nowhere in the whole decision was there any reference to Article 8 of the ECHR or to any of the case-law on this Article, some of which is of German origin.[205]

Conclusion

Trying to draw a conclusion from the recognition of the ECHR in Germany on the one hand and the decisions on the ECHR by the European Court of Human Rights on the other, it seems that although the ECHR is (maybe apart from procedural rights) not very prominent in Germany, cases like *Markt Intern*[206] show that the European Court of Human Rights is also sometimes reluctant to interfere: with the help of the casting vote of the President, the court held that although commercial speech was covered by Article 10 ECHR, the infringement in this case was "necessary in a democratic society". Even though it is implied that the court did not find the measures taken necessary, it held that it should not substitute its own evaluation for that of the national courts.[207] Similarly in the case of *Vogt*,[208]

---

[205] See *Klaas* v. *Germany, op. cit.*, note 115.

[206] *Op. cit.*, note 113.

[207] *Ibid.*, p. 176.

[208] *Op. cit.*, note 111.

in which the Court by 10 votes to 9 held Article 10 of the ECHR to be violated, the question was whether the removal of the appellant from her post as a civil servant which she held as a teacher of German and French was "necessary in a democratic society" as a protection against Ms. Vogt's influence in view of her active membership of the German Communist party. Whereas a narrow majority held that there had been no evidence of Ms. Vogt's political ideas influencing her work and that therefore her dismissal under the "Radikalenerlass" violated her right to freedom of expression, the dissenting opinions, especially that expressed by Judge Jambrek, showed the difficulty the Court had in judging on such sensitive matters. In spite of the fact that Germany was held to have infringed the Convention in this case, a certain reserve on the part of the Court is still discernible which may well be interpreted as its recognition of the altogether exemplary protection of human rights in Germany.

5.   IRELAND

Leo Flynn

Part I: General Constitutional Background

Like most member states of the Council of Europe, Ireland has a written constitution. It was adopted in 1937 and, though intended to further the process of disengagement from the United Kingdom, it was largely a continuation of the 1922 constitution of *Saorstát Éireann* (the Irish Free State) adopted following the 1921 Anglo-Irish Treaty. The 1937 constitution set up the organs of the state on a classical "separation of powers" model, with the government, the courts and the *Oireachtas* (legislature) given exclusive responsibility for the exercise of executive power (Article 28.2), the administration of justice (Article 34.1), and the enactment of legislation (Article 15.2) respectively. The constitution may be amended only with difficulty. What is required is an Act of the *Oireachtas* followed by a referendum of the people in which the majority of those voting approve the change. Laws passed by the *Oireachtas* which are inconsistent with the constitution are prohibited (Article 15.4). This general prohibition is fleshed out by Article 34.3.2 which enables the High Court, and, on appeal, the Supreme Court, to adjudicate on the constitutional validity of laws. The High Court may also examine the compatibility of pre-1937 laws under Article 50, which continues in force such laws "to the extent to which they are not inconsistent" with the constitution, and Article 34.3.1 which gives it jurisdiction to "determine all matters and questions". The constitution also contains a special procedure for the constitutional review of bills by the Supreme Court before they are signed into law by the president. The president, whose position is similar to that of a constitutional monarch, may, after consultation with the council of state, refer any bill to the Supreme Court on the question of whether it is repugnant to the constitution (Article 26). If the Supreme Court finds that the proposed legislation is not inconsistent with any provisions of the constitution then future challenges in reliance on the constitution by private liti-

C. A. Gearty (ed.), European Civil Liberties and the European Convention on Human Rights, 177–215.
© 1997 *Kluwer Law International. Printed in the Netherlands.*

gants are precluded (Article 34.3.3). This power is exercised infrequently[1] and the Supreme Court has pointed to the disadvantages in its Article 26 jurisdiction, not the least of which is the abstract nature of the inquiry.[2] Its use of this power has, however, been the occasion of controversy in the past, most notably when a presidential reference of security legislation led to critical remarks by a member of the government which, in turn, precipitated the president's resignation.[3] Legislation passed by the *Oireachtas* benefits from a presumption that it is constitutional,[4] as do bills referred under Article 26.[5] Pre-1937 law, whether common law or statute, enjoys no such presumption.[6]

The legislative machinery put in place by the constitution, the *Oireachtas*, consists of a bicameral parliament and the president. The lower house of the *Oireachtas*, the *Dáil*, is directly elected by voters using a single transferable vote in multi-seat constituencies. The upper house, the *Seanad*, lacks a clearly defined function. Each house has equal, legal power in the process of legislation but the *Seanad* has few powers in relation to the government, and in the case of conflict between the upper and lower houses, it is the will of the *Dáil* that prevails (Article 23). The mode of selection of the members of the *Seanad* also reduces its influence. All the elected senators, forty-nine out of a total of sixty, are chosen as representatives of some group in Irish society, such as agriculture or commerce or university graduates. Almost all the voters for these vocational panels are members of the *Oireachtas* or are local government politicians, and the effect of this is to give the members of the

---

[1] There have been nine Article 26 references made: *In re Article 26 and the Offences against the State (Amendment) Bill 1940* [1940] I.R. 470; *In re Article 26 and the School Attendance Bill 1942* [1943] I.R. 334; *In re Article 26 and the Electoral (Amendment) Bill 1961* [1961] I.R. 169; *In re Article 26 and the Criminal Law (Jurisdiction) Bill 1975* [1977] I.R. 129; *In re Article 26 and the Emergency Bill 1976* [1977] I.R. 159; *In re Article 26 and the Housing (Private Rented Dwellings) Bill 1981* [1983] I.R. 181; *In re Article 26 and the Electoral (Amendment) Bill 1983* [1984] I.R. 268; *In re Article 26 and the Matrimonial Home Bill 1993* [1994] I.R. 305; and *In re Article 26 and the Regulation of Information (Services outside the State for the Termination of Pregnancies) Bill 1995*, [1995] 2 I.L.R.M. 81.

[2] *In re Article 26 and the Housing (Private Rented Dwellings) Bill 1981, op. cit.*, note 1.

[3] See *In re Article 26 and the Emergency Bill 1976, op. cit.*, note 1. For a description and comment on the affair, see D. Morgan, "The Emergency Powers Bill References–I" (1978) 13 *Irish Jurist (new series)* 67.

[4] *Pigs Marketing Board* v. *Donnelly* [1939] I.R. 413.

[5] *In re Article 26 and the Offences against the State (Amendment) Bill 1940, op. cit.*, note 1.

[6] *The State (Sheerin)* v. *Kennedy* [1966] I.R. 379.

Dáil a strong voice in the composition of the *Seanad*. The remainder of the senators are nominated by the Taoiseach, who is the head of the government. The *Dáil* nominates the Taoiseach who in turn nominates other members of the government for approval by the *Dáil*. The constitution states that "The Government shall be responsible to Dáil Éireann" (Article 28.4.1) but the reality is usually that the government controls the *Dáil*. This control is normally based on the reliable majority which the government party or parties hold. Dominance by the government is further strengthened by the "peculiar effectiveness"[7] of party discipline in Ireland. Accordingly, the government, through its constitutional powers and its control of party machinery, enjoys a great deal of freedom without significant constraints from either house of the *Oireachtas*.

The 1937 constitution contains an express guarantee of certain fundamental rights. Articles 40 to 44 set out rights necessary for the individual to have an acceptable life in a democratic, constitutional state. These cover such civil liberties and political rights as freedom of speech, freedom of assembly and the freedom to practise religion. The rights covered do not extend very far in the direction of economic, social or cultural rights although Article 45 does contain "Directives of Social Policy" which are expressed to be non-justiciable and which are directed only at the *Oireachtas*. The state is bound to respect the rights in Articles 40 to 44 and, as with other Articles of the constitution, any law which conflicts with them cannot stand.[8] The 1922 constitution, which contained a short list of similar rights, could be amended by an Act of the *Oireachtas*. The Irish courts treated those rights in a positivist fashion, holding that they could be amended in the ordinary way.[9] However, the rights guaranteed by the 1937 constitution have been read as stating, in an inevitably incomplete and imprecise fashion, rights which are inherent in the person by natural law, or in the citizen by virtue of the nature of the state. This natural law view would imply that there may be some rights possessed by individuals which are not expressed in the constitution's text. It has been held that such unenumerated fundamental rights are inherent in the general phrase "the personal rights of the citizen" found in Article

---

[7] D. Morgan, *Constitutional Law of Ireland* (Dublin, 1985), p. 81.

[8] It is clear from the debate on the draft constitution in the *Dáil* that Mr. de Valera, who as the head of the government was largely responsible for drafting the 1937 constitution, expressly intended the fundamental rights to be mere "headlines to the legislature" which it might ignore. See Dáil Eireann Parliamentary Debates, vol. 67, cols. 1784–6 (3 June 1937); Dáil Eireann Parliamentary Debates, vol. 68, cols. 216–7 (9 June 1937).

[9] *The State (Ryan)* v. *Lennon* [1935] I.R. 170.

40.3.1 of the constitution.[10] In the landmark High Court judgment of Kenny J. in *Ryan* v. *Attorney-General*, rights such as a right to bodily integrity, a right to marry, and a right to free movement (and to a passport) were found by the court to enjoy constitutional status even though they were not expressly stated in the text of the constitution.[11] Because the fundamental personal rights are antecedent to the constitution and are not derived from it, they may also be invoked by persons who are not citizens.

The development of the courts' jurisprudence on fundamental personal rights resulted in a startling expansion of judicial activism from the late 1960s onwards. For the most part, the rights which have been recognised have formed part of a liberal political agenda which would have had difficulty in achieving sufficient support from the major political parties necessary to have been adopted through the legislative process. Rights recognised since the decision in *Ryan* have included the right to marital privacy,[12] the right of unmarried mothers to the custody of their children,[13] the right of accused persons to legal assistance,[14] and the right of prisoners to medical treatment.[15] These developments might have occurred eventually in the form of Acts of the *Oireachtas* but it was the judicial branch that took the strain of adapting the legal environment to a changing social and economic context. For example, recognition of a right to marital privacy in *McGee*'s case led the Supreme Court to declare unconstitutional section 17 of the Criminal Law Amendment Act 1935 which provided that to sell, or import any contraceptive device was a criminal offence. Legislation on contraception was eventually passed in 1979, six years after *McGee* was decided, and after an earlier unsuccessful attempt at family planning legislation which had been defeated when several members of the government which had introduced the measure, including the Taoiseach, voted against it on the ground that any liberty whatsoever in this field was unacceptable.[16] At times, however, the courts have made it clear that they are neither anxious nor particularly willing to assume this role of legislator in response to social change. In *Attor-*

---

[10] *Ryan* v. *Attorney-General* [1965] I.R. 294.

[11] [1965] I.R. 294. The passage was obiter dicta though the suggestions of Mr Justice Kenny have been largely vindicated in the subsequent case-law.

[12] *McGee* v. *Attorney-General* [1974] I.R. 284.

[13] *G.* v. *An Bord Uchtála* [1980] I.R. 32.

[14] *State (Healy)* v. *Donoghue* [1976] I.R. 325.

[15] *State (C)* v. *Frawley* [1976] I.R. 365.

[16] See B. McMahon, "The Law relating to Contraception in Ireland" in D. Clarke (ed.), *Morality and the Law* (Cork, 1982), p. 120.

ney-General v. *X*,[17] which involved the right of a fourteen-year-old rape survivor to travel outside the state to obtain a medical termination of her pregnancy, the members of the Supreme Court castigated the failure of the legislature to enact the appropriate legislation to give effect to a constitutional amendment on the issue of the right to life of the unborn. McCarthy J. said, "It is not for the courts to programme society; that is partly, at least, the role of the legislature. The Courts are not equipped to regulate these procedures."[18] He went on to add in his conclusion that "the failure of the legislature to provide for the regulation of [the constitutional amendment] has significantly added to the problem [of abortion.]"[19]

The independence of the judiciary is expressly guaranteed by Article 35.2 which states that "all judges shall be independent in the exercise of their judicial functions and subject only to this Constitution and the law". There are several points at which judicial independence may be compromised and at the first, that of appointment, it has been said that it is maintained "in spite of, rather than because of, the rules governing appointment".[20] Judges are appointed by the president, acting on the advice of the government (Article 35.1 and Article 13.9), and while the judges appointed have usually been supporters of the political party in power, there is no evidence that party favouritism has been a factor in judicial decisions.[21] Judges are required to make a declaration on entry into office promising to "uphold the Constitution and the laws" and to execute the office "without fear or favour, affection or ill-will towards any man" (Article 34.5). Once appointed, a judge is not eligible to be a member of either house of the *Oireachtas* or to hold any other paid appointment (Article 35.3), though the remuneration of a judge may not be reduced while he or she remains in office (Article 35.5). Judges may not be removed from office except for stated misbehaviour or incapacity, and to do so requires resolutions passed by both houses of the *Oireachtas* (Article 35.4) In addition to the constitutional mechanisms which underpin judicial autonomy, the judges' right to protect their independence is supported by their ability to punish contempt of court of their own motion and in their own discretion. Criminal contempt of court has been held to form a necessary exception to the rule in Article 38.5 as to trial

---

[17] [1992] 1 I.R. 1.

[18] *Ibid.*, at p. 83.

[19] *Ibid.*, at p. 85.

[20] Morgan, *op. cit.*, note 7, p. 188.

[21] P. Bartholomew, *The Irish Judiciary* (Dublin, 1971), ch. 2.

by jury for all serious cases.[22] In addition to the direct constitutional safe-guards of judicial independence, indirect protection is provided by Article 34.1 which provides that, subject to exceptions, justice may be administered only in courts manned by these judges.

The judiciary has been exposed, at least potentially, to pressure insofar as they have taken up non-judicial public office. The possibilities for the government to influence judicial views was demonstrated when a sitting judge of the High Court was removed from his position as head of the Law Reform Commission in 1992. However, this did not prevent continued extra-judicial statements of the views which had provoked the original action by the government.[23] Less dramatic attempts to exercise influence on members of the judiciary can be seen in the pressure put on another sitting High Court judge by those opposed to abortion, arising out of her membership of the Irish Council for the Status of Women. As the chairperson of the Council she had written to the government concerning a proposed constitutional amendment dealing with travel to other jurisdictions for services lawfully available there, including terminations of pregnancy. Subsequently she was asked by an anti-abortion group to remove herself from a case she was hearing involving the provision of abortion-related information. The judge refused. On appeal, the Supreme Court held that while there was no suggestion of actual bias, the issue of objective bias had not been considered by her and that as the interpretation of the other party in the original case might correspond with the views she had expressed, she should have discharged herself.[24] Too much should not be made of these examples. For the most part, the judiciary is careful to regulate its own behaviour to diminish the scope for political influence on the behaviour of its members.

Members of the executive and legislative branches are extremely sensitive to suggestions that the judiciary is not wholly independent. The claim by the chairman of the *Dáil* Public Accounts Committee in 1994[25] that judges are not sufficiently independent because politicians are responsible for their appointment and promotion was met with angry and acrimonious responses from other members of the Dáil, including a former minister for

---

[22] *The State (Director of Public Prosecutions)* v. *Walsh* [1981] I.R. 412.

[23] For an example of the judge's controversially expressed opinions, see R. O'Hanlon, "The Judiciary and the Moral Law" (1993) 11 *Irish Law Times (new series)* 129.

[24] *Dublin Well Woman Centre Ltd. and others* v. *Ireland, Attorney-General and S.P.U.C. (Ireland) Ltd.* [1995] 1 I.L.R.M. 408.

[25] *State (Summers Jennings)* v. *Furlong* [1965] I.R. 70; *Wadda* v. *Ireland* [1994] I.L.R.M. 126, 135. See M. Tynan, "Independence of judges raised" *Irish Times*, 11 March 1994.

justice.[26] This incident is consistent with an overall unwillingness on the part of members of other branches of government to pass comment, let alone criticise, the decisions made by the judicial branch.[27]

Part II: The European Convention on Human Rights in Irish Law

Although the constitution affirms that the state accepts the generally recognised principles of international law as its rules of conduct in its relations with other states (Article 29.3), Ireland has a dualist approach to the place of international law in its internal legal order. International law does not enter into the domestic legal order until it is incorporated and gives rise to no rights or obligations which may be presented to an Irish court until such incorporation has occurred. Article 29.6 expressly provides that "no international agreement shall be part of the domestic order of the State save as may be determined by the Oireachtas." International agreements have been given force as domestic law in a number of ways. Ireland's accession to the European Communities required an amendment to the constitution so that EC law, a self-described "new legal order of international law",[28] would be treated as superior to all domestic law.[29] Subsequently, constitutional amendments were required to allow the ratification of the Single European Act[30] and the Treaty of European Union[31] so that the transfer of competences by the state and the subsequent exercise of those powers could not be challenged under the constitution.[32] Of course, to the extent that the norms of

---

[26] See Tynan, *Ibid.*

[27] See, generally, C. A. Gearty, "Democracy and a Bill of Rights: Some Lessons from Ireland" in K. D. Ewing, C. A. Gearty and B. A. Hepple (eds.), *Human Rights and Labour Law: Essays for Paul O'Higgins* (London and New York, 1994), p. 188, especially at p. 215.

[28] Case 26/62 *Van Gend en Loos* v. *Nederlandse Administratie der Belastingen* [1963] E.C.R. 1, at p. 12.

[29] Article 29.4.3 of the constitution.

[30] Article 29.4.4 of the constitution.

[31] Article 29.4.5 of the constitution.

[32] The adequacy of the formula used in these amendments was successfully challenged in the High Court, though later upheld on appeal in *Meagher* v. *Minister for Agriculture* [1994] I.L.R.M. 1. The Supreme Court interpreted the phrase "acts done...necessitated by membership of the Communities" as allowing statutes to be amended by ministerial regulation for the purposes of implementing EC directives. The Court took a highly deferential view as to the use of executive power at the expense of the status of the *Oireachtas*. See, generally, D. R. Phelan, "'Necessitated' by the Obligation of Membership? Article 29.4.5.

European Community law are determined by reference to the European Convention on Human Rights, the Irish courts would be obliged to enforce those rights which are derived from the Convention, albeit through the medium of EC law. Thus, as one commentator has noted, "The present position under Irish law is that the scope and nature of the fundamental rights protection enjoyed by an individual will depend on whether or not the issue causing concern is governed by EEC law."[33] This state of affairs has led to the observation that Ireland now has three constitutions, namely, the constitution, the Treaty of Rome and the European Convention on Human Rights.[34]

However, constitutional amendments are rarely required in order to bring international law into the Irish municipal legal order so that ordinary legislation or other mechanisms will suffice to give effect to international legal instruments. Acts of the *Oireachtas* have made agreements such as the treaties governing the European Communities and the Vienna Conventions on Diplomatic and Consular Immunities part of domestic law. In respect of other agreements, such as the Geneva Convention on Prisoners of War, the approach taken has been for the *Oireachtas* to authorise compliance with them by ministers when making regulations. Another method of giving domestic force to international agreements has been to enact a law which gives effect in Irish legislative form to the obligations which the agreement involves. For instance, the Genocide Act 1973, gives effect to the UN Convention on Genocide. In the absence of some such measure, neither the courts nor the other organs of the state are bound to comply with such instruments. Accordingly, in *Application of Woods*[35] the Supreme Court considered, obiter, that Article 4 of the UN Universal Declaration of Human Rights, to which Ireland is a signatory, does not form part of the domestic law of Ireland.

In addition, the question of whether the government should bring international agreements into domestic law is not one which the courts will consider. Ireland was one of the original signatories of the European Convention for the Protection of Human Rights and Fundamental Freedoms (the

---

of the Constitution" (1993) 11 *Irish Law Times (new series)* 272.

[33] J. Gallagher, "The Constitution and the Community" (1993) 1 *Irish Journal of European Law* 129, at p. 140.

[34] J. Temple Lang, "The Widening Scope of Constitutional Law", in D. Curtin and D. O'Keeffe (eds.), *Constitutional Adjudication in EC and National Law—Essays for the Hon. Mr Justice T. F. O'Higgins* (Dublin, 1992), p. 229 at p. 245.

[35] [1970] I.R. 154.

ECHR Convention). The ECHR Convention, together with its First Protocol, was ratified in 1953 and at the same time Ireland made declarations which granted its nationals the right of individual petition (Article 25) and accepted the compulsory jurisdiction of the European Court of Human Rights (Article 46).[36] The declarations were to run for an indefinite period of time, unlike the majority of declarations made by high contracting parties at that time. However, no steps have been taken to incorporate the Convention into the Irish domestic legal order and there is no part of the constitution which requires incorporation. The Court of Criminal Appeal explicitly reiterated this in *The People* v. *McKeever*[37] holding that the failure to lay the ECHR Convention before the *Oireachtas* was not a matter for the courts. Although there is no international law obligation to incorporate the text of the Convention into municipal law,[38] there are arguments of a pragmatic and political nature for doing so. Despite this, there has been an almost universal party political silence in Ireland on the advantages and disadvantages which such incorporation would offer, in sharp contrast to the periodic debates which this issue generates on the other side of the Irish sea.[39] At the time of writing, a commission under the chairmanship of Dr. T. K. Whitaker is considering whether the constitution should be amended to reflect changes in Irish society. One option which is being considered is whether particular Articles from the European Convention might be inserted into the constitution by way of substitution of certain existing provisions. This might amount to a partial incorporation of the Convention. However, in the absence of the final reports from the Commission,[39A] it is difficult to predict what it may propose, and even more difficult to identify the likely reaction of the major political parties in Ireland.[40]

---

[36] A. Drzemczewski, *European Human Rights Convention in Domestic Law: A Comparative Study* (Oxford, 1983), p.170.

[37] Unreported judgment of 11 July 1992.

[38] See, *e.g.*, *Lithgow and others* v. *United Kingdom* Series A, No. 102 (1986) 8 E.H.R.R. 58. See generally Drzemczewski, *op. cit.*, note 36, pp. 40–53.

[39] For the British position, see Gearty, pp. 77–83 above. As far as Ireland is concerned, note, however, that incorporation has been called for by certain non-party political groups: see S. Bailey (ed.), *Human Rights and Responsibilities in Britain and Ireland: A Christian Perspective* (London, 1988), p. 197.

[39A] The Final Report of the Review Group is analysed briefly at p. 215.

[40] One of the government parties has indicated in its submission to the Whitaker Commission that it would favour reforms which would strengthen human rights guarantees in line with international law and this would, presumably, include the European Convention on Human Rights: see "Labour suggests specific powers for President", *Irish Times*, 4

Despite being unincorporated, the ECHR Convention has been raised in arguments before the Irish courts from time to time. It was first relied on in *In re O Láighléis*[41] where internment provisions in the Offences against the State (Amendment) Act 1940, were challenged as violating Articles 5 and 6 of the Convention. Because the 1940 Act had been the subject of an Article 26 reference to the Supreme Court when it was a bill, it was immune from subsequent constitutional scrutiny. The Supreme Court held that the compatibility or otherwise of the Act with the Convention had no bearing on the validity of the legislation for the purposes of Irish domestic law. Maguire C.J. said, "The Court cannot accept the idea that the primacy of domestic legislation is displaced by the State becoming a party to the Convention...."[42] The Chief Justice went on:

> The insuperable obstacle to importing the provisions of the Convention for the Protection of Human Rights and Fundamental Freedoms into the domestic law of Ireland—if they be at variance with that law—is [Article 15.2.1 which provides] that "the sole and exclusive power of making laws for the State is hereby vested in the Oireachtas: no other legislative authority has power to make laws for the State". Moreover, Article 29, the Article dealing with international relations, provides at s. 6 that "no international agreement shall be part of the domestic law of the State save as may be determined by the Oireachtas".
>
> The Oireachtas has not determined that the Convention on Human Rights and Fundamental Freedoms is to be part of the domestic law of the State, and accordingly this Court cannot give effect to the Convention if it be contrary to domestic law or purports to grant rights or impose obligations additional to those of domestic law.[43]

This decision made clear that the Convention itself was not a binding source of law to be enforced by Irish courts. The same is true of the European Court of Human Rights' decisions made under the Convention, even where such decisions have directly involved the compatibility with the Convention of exactly the law that is before the Irish courts. In *Norris* v. *Attorney-General*[44] the plaintiff sought to rely on a decision of the European Court of Human Rights that laws in Northern Ireland criminalising male homosexual

---

August 1995, p. 4. The provisional report on Article 29 makes no recommendations on changing the status of international law in Irish domestic law: see Constitutional Review Group, *Provisional Report on International Relations* (Dublin, 1995), pp. 2–6.

[41] [1960] I.R. 93.

[42] *Ibid.*, at p. 125.

[43] *Ibid.*, at pp. 124–125.

[44] [1984] I.R. 36.

conduct were incompatible with the Convention.[45] The Northern Ireland law had been set out in Victorian legislation which still applied in the Republic of Ireland. Before the Supreme Court, counsel argued on Norris' behalf that because Ireland had confirmed and ratified the Convention, a presumption had arisen that the constitution itself was compatible with it, and that in considering the consistency with the constitution of a pre-1937 law (Article 50), regard should be had to whether such laws were consistent with the Convention. The majority of the Supreme Court did not accept the argument (the minority did not consider this point), and expressly adopted the remarks of Maguire C.J. in *O Láighléis'* case. O'Higgins C.J., on behalf of the majority in *Norris*, took the view that to accept the submission that the constitution was compatible with the Convention "would be contrary to the provisions of the Constitution itself and would accord to the Government the power, by an executive act, to change both the Constitution and the law."[46]

In addition to their general inability to employ the European Convention and the Strasbourg decisions under it as binding sources of law, Irish courts are unable to apply decisions of the European Court of Human Rights even where the judgments have been made against the state itself. In *E* v. *E* [47] the defendant in a family law dispute had been refused legal aid and, claiming that he could not pay for it himself, invoked the decision of the European Court of Human Rights in *Airey* v. *Ireland*[48] where the state had been found in breach of its Convention obligations in a similar context. He argued that this decision bound the state and could be given effect by domestic proceedings within the state. O' Hanlon J. in the High Court rejected this submission and held that the issue of whether the legal aid scheme put in place by the state went far enough to satisfy the criteria of the *Airey* case could only be decided by the European Court of Human Rights itself.

> [Counsel for the defendant] argued that a judgement of the European Court [of Human Rights] in proceedings in which the State was a party, bound the State for the future and could be given effect to in later proceedings brought against the State in the domestic courts. I am unable to accept that this contention is correct. [Because the issue as to whether the funding provided by the State for civil legal aid complies with the *Airey* decision is strongly disputed], it appears to me to be a dispute which should properly be determined by the procedure provided for in the European Convention.[49]

---

[45]   *Dudgeon* v. *United Kingdom* Series A, No. 45 (1981) 4 E.H.R.R. 149.

[46]   [1984] I.R. 36, at p. 66.

[47]   [1982] I.L.R.M. 497.

[48]   Series A, No. 32 (1979) 2 E.H.R.R. 305. See further below, Part III, section 1.

[49]   [1982] I.L.R.M. 497, at pp. 499–500.

The tenor of the judgment makes it clear that even if the facts were not "strongly disputed", the court would not have applied the decision in *Airey* to the case in hand. It is clear from this that neither the Convention nor the decisions of the European Court of Human Rights are a binding source of law in the Irish domestic legal order.

Even though the Convention does not constitute binding domestic law, it is of legal significance in the state's internal legal order. For instance, the parliamentary draftsman office must, in drafting any legislation, be satisfied that the proposed bill will not operate, when enacted, in a manner which is inconsistent with the international obligations of the state, including those arising under the Convention.[50] The Convention has also been highly influential in the formulation of the recommendations of the Law Reform Commission in its work, such as in its studies on libel and contempt of court.[51] However, the Convention is more something to be noted in these settings than a binding guide in the preparation of new legislation. For example, in its consultation paper on the crime of libel, the Law Reform Commission, having established a need to re-define the offence of blasphemous libel for domestic reasons, went on to add that "any legislation we propose might be arguably in contravention of those provisions of the European Convention on Human Rights, as interpreted by the Court, which require a law restricting freedom of expression to be formulated with sufficient precision to enable a citizen to regulate his conduct."[52] Notwithstanding this possible conflict, it went on to set out its proposed new offence. Similarly, when an interdepartmental committee established in 1993 was considering the legal treatment of refugees in Irish law, it referred exclusively to the 1951 UN Convention relating to the status of refugees and to its 1961 Protocol, and to the law and practice in other EU member states, but it did not mention the European Convention on Human Rights as a relevant source of law.[53]

Although the Convention is not itself binding on the courts in Ireland, it is, as we have already observed, cited to them in argument and referred to in judicial decisions from time to time. Often such reference may be little more

---

[50]   E. J. Donelan, "The Role of the Parliamentary Draftsman in Preparing Legislation in Ireland" (1992) 14 *Dublin University Law Journal (new series)* 1, at p. 5.

[51]   See, *e.g.*, Law Reform Commission, *Consultation Paper on Contempt of Court* (Dublin, July 1991), pp. 261–266; Law Reform Commission, *Consultation Paper on the Crime of Libel* (Dublin, August 1991), pp. 88–92, 173.

[52]   *Consultation Paper on the Crime of Libel, ibid*, p. 173.

[53]   Inter-Departmental Committee on Non-Irish Nationals, *Interim Report on Applications for Refugee Status* (Dublin, 1993).

than a "belt and braces" exercise, with the Convention being used to under-line the significance of a constitutionally guaranteed right. In *D.P.P.* v. *Gaff-ney*,[54] for instance, Article 8 of the Convention was employed to echo and reinforce Article 40.5 of the constitution guaranteeing the inviolability of the dwelling. A similar invocation of provisions of the European Convention as a support for domestic constitutional provisions occurred in *O'Domhnaill* v. *Merrick*[55] where the Supreme Court considered a challenge to the Statute of Limitations 1957 based on the assertion that the statute placed an unfair burden on a person being sued to defend him- or herself from a delayed claim. Henchy J., delivering the majority judgment of the Supreme Court, referred to the "implied constitutional principles of basic fairness of proce-dures", and to the ratification by the state, prior to the enactment of the Stat-ute of Limitations, of the European Convention on Human Rights. Article 6.1 of the European Convention entitles everyone to a fair hearing within a reasonable time in the determination of his civil rights. Henchy J. expressed no opinion as to the construction and interpretation of the legislation in the light of the European Convention. When the issue of constitutional fairness was next considered in a similar context, in *Celtic Ceramics Ltd.* v. *IDA*[56] O'Hanlon J. referred to *O'Domhnaill* v. *Merrick* and other Irish cases on constitutional fairness in order to address the problem of an excessively de-layed civil action, without making any reference to the impact of Article 6.1 of the European Convention.

This technique of marshalling the provisions of the Convention to sup-port judicial interpretation of the protection of rights which are already guaranteed in the constitution was taken further in *O'Leary* v. *Attorney-General*[57] where legislation was challenged as shifting the burden of proof onto an accused and depriving such a person of the protection of the pre-sumption of innocence. Costello J. in the High Court had no difficulty in construing the constitution and the common law tradition as conferring on every accused a protected right to the presumption of innocence. He then went on to say that, "This right has now widespread, and indeed enjoys uni-versal, recognition", and proceeded to quote Article 6.2 of the European Convention on Human Rights, as well as Article 11 of the UN Universal Declaration of Rights, Article 8(2) of the Inter-American Convention on

---

[54]   [1987] I.R. 177.

[55]   [1984] I.R. 151.

[56]   [1993] I.L.R.M. 248.

[57]   [1993] 1 I.R. 102. There was a similar approach taken on the issue of self-incrimination in *Heaney and McGuiness* v. *Ireland* [1994] I.L.R.M. 420.

Human Rights and Article 7 of the African Charter on Human and Peoples' Rights. The relevant provisions of all of these documents were treated in *O'Leary* as providing the plaintiff's case with strong support. The court went on to consider if such a right was an absolute one, incapable of restriction and found that under the Irish constitution it could be restricted in certain circumstances, including the creation, as here, of a rebuttable presumption of fact. This conclusion was supported by reference to the jurisprudence of the European Commission of Human Rights on the correct construction of Article 6 of the European Convention. Reference was also made by the judge to Article 29 of the UN Universal Declaration, section 1 of the Canadian Charter of Rights and Freedoms and to the jurisprudence of the United States' Supreme Court on the due process clause of the fifth amendment on this point.

It is clear that Irish judges are entitled to construe the constitution in the light of contemporary standards of human rights' protection,[58] and because of this references to international norms and decisions from other jurisdictions with comparable, constitutionally enshrined guarantees of rights are not uncommon.[59] The European Convention on Human Rights enjoys no special role in these cases. If anything, such judicial references to the European Convention as one of a number of international documents on human rights seem intended simply as evidence of the high level of protection of rights afforded by the Irish constitution. Speaking for the majority of the Supreme Court in *Re R. Ltd.*,[60] Walsh J. said:

> This fundamental principle [of the public administration of justice] was made part of the fundamental law of the State by Article 34 of the Constitution in 1937. More than a decade later the same fundamental principle was incorporated in certain international instruments dealing with human rights....[The Universal Declaration of Human Rights and the American Declaration of the Rights and Duties of Man of 1948] were followed by several international Conventions incorporating the same principle among which are Article 6(1) of the European Convention on Human Rights 1950 and the International Covenant on Civil and Political Rights 1966, Article 14(1).[61]

There is no indication in these decisions that the Convention has anything unique or authoritative to offer the Irish legal system. The Irish constitution

---

[58] See *State (Healy)* v. *Donoghue* [1976] I.R. 325.

[59] For instance, in *Murphy* v. *Attorney-General* [1982] I.R. 241, the High Court and the Supreme Court considered decisions from the Italian Constitutional Court and the German Federal Constitutional Court on the point at issue.

[60] [1989] I.R. 126.

[61] *Ibid.*, at p. 135.

has express provisions dealing with human rights, and the judicial creativity which has been a feature of constitutional adjudication in Ireland since *Ryan* has been formally based on the text of the constitution itself. The European Convention's role in this setting is that of the minor, supporting player, whose words support those of the protagonist but, for the most part, add little, if anything, of value.

However, the Convention and decisions of the European Court of Human Rights may have had more impact than this merely rhetorical invocation in some judicial decisions, influencing the weight which Irish courts have accorded to decisions from other jurisdictions. O'Hanlon J. in *Desmond* v. *Glackin (No. 1)* held that the decision of the European Court of Human Rights in *Sunday Times* v. *U.K. (No. 1)*[62] was relevant in considering if the House of Lords' statement of the law in *Attorney-General* v. *Times Newspapers*,[63] a persuasive authority of considerable importance for an Irish court, should be taken as a correct statement of the law of contempt in Ireland. He went on to say:

> As Ireland has ratified the Convention and is a party to it, and as the law of contempt of court is based…on public policy I think it is legitimate to assume that our public policy is in accord with the Convention or at least that the provisions of the Convention can be considered when determining issues of public policy. The Convention itself is not a code of legal principles which are enforceable in the domestic Courts, as was made clear in *In Re O Láighléis*, but this does not prevent the judgment of the European Court from having a persuasive effect when considering the common law regarding contempt of court in the light of the constitutional guarantees of freedom of expression contained in our Constitution of 1937. Henchy J expressed the view in *State (D.P.P.)* v. *Walsh and Connelly*[64] that there was a presumption that our law on contempt is in conformity with the Convention, particularly Articles 15 and 10(2).[65]

In a later case on contempt, *Wong* v. *Minister for Justice*[66], Denham J. quoted the views of O'Hanlon J. that the Convention and the Strasbourg court's jurisprudence must be treated as persuasive in Irish law without expressly adopting them, or indeed commenting on them, herself. Budd J. also quoted these views in his very full judgment on contempt of court in *PSS* v.

---

[62] Series A, No. 30 (1979) 2 E.H.R.R. 245.
[63] [1974] A.C. 273.
[64] [1981] I.R. 412, at p. 440.
[65] [1993] 3 I.R. 1, at pp. 28–29.
[66] [1994] I.R. 223.

JRS (otherwise C)[67] but made no comment in relation to them. In general, however, the reliance by the Irish courts on the Convention's provisions and on the decisions of the Court of Human Rights has been selective and has rarely gone beyond an unadorned invocation of the text of the Convention. Such exceptions as do exist to this general pattern are probably best treated as anomalous.

Apart from its limited role in the issue of determining which substantive rights are protected in the Irish legal order, the ECHR Convention has also been invoked in support of certain forms of judicial reasoning. In *Kearney* v. *Minister for Justice*,[68] Costello J. in the High Court considered the validity of restrictions imposed on prisoners' correspondence. In establishing a right to communicate he referred exclusively to case-law dealing with the Irish constitution. However, in order to show that the right could properly be restricted he referred, in addition to those Irish cases and to decisions both of the United States' Supreme Court and the Canadian Supreme Court, to *Golder* v. *U.K.*[69] and *Silver* v. *U.K.*[70] He considered that neither of these cases was particularly relevant to the facts in the instant case but went on to observe of the decisions:

> [I]t is worth noting that they both make clear that some interference with prisoner's correspondence is permitted by the European Convention on Human Rights and Fundamental Freedoms and that in assessing whether an interference is permissible regard could be had to the ordinary and reasonable requirements of imprisonment.[71]

The same process of supporting a style of judicial reasoning without close attention to the substantive rights at issue can be seen in *O'Leary* v. *Attorney-General*[72] where the validity of a statute creating a rebuttable presumption of fact was considered. As we have already noted neither the Convention nor the decisions of the European Court of Human Rights were examined closely. The judge was content to note that the Irish courts' approach to the limitation of rights conformed with the practice of the European Court of Human Rights. There was no detailed examination of the question of the justification of such limits, of the concept of necessity or of any of the central features of the Convention structure in this field. The

---

[67] Unreported judgment of 22 May 1995.

[68] [1986] I.R. 116.

[69] Series A, No. 18 (1975) 1 E.H.R.R. 524.

[70] Series A, No. 61 (1983) 5 E.H.R.R. 347.

[71] [1986] I.R. 116 at p. 121.

[72] [1993] 1 I.R. 102.

same result was contemplated in both systems and this seems to have been used without more to support the fashion in which the Irish judge approached the matter.[73]

Despite the occasional dicta, therefore, the Convention cannot be said to have implanted itself in Irish judicial minds. Further evidence of this may be garnered from the fact that there is a series of cases in which issues which could have been viewed in the light of the Convention's provisions have been dealt with in exclusively domestic terms. In these cases, reference to the constitution alone was sufficient to resolve the issue at stake and the matter ended in the Irish courts. In *State (Lynch)* v. *Cooney*[74] the status of a ministerial order, forbidding a statutory authority from broadcasting the election address of a specified political party, Sinn Féin, on RTE, the national radio and television network, was challenged. The challenge succeeded in the High Court but that decision was reversed on appeal. According to the Supreme Court, there was no breach of the applicant's right to free expression under Article 40.6 of the constitution which allows for the control of this freedom based on the need to uphold public order and morality and which obliges the state not to allow organs of public opinion to be used to undermine public order and morality or the authority of the state. The European Convention on Human Rights was not referred to at any stage in the judgments.[75] In a number of later cases concerning the validity of the ban on members of Sinn Féin being broadcast on RTE, *State (Lynch)* v. *Cooney* was considered. In *O'Toole* v. *RTE (No. 2)*[76] the Supreme Court held that RTE's interpretation of the ministerial order as excluding the transmission of any interview with a member of Sinn Féin in any capacity (in this case, as the representative of a group of striking workers) was overbroad and went beyond the scope of the original order. The Supreme Court considered arguments based on several constitutionally guaranteed rights and on the

---

[73] See further K. Duffy, "Pre-Trial Publicity, Prejudice and the Right to a Fair Trial" (1994) 4 *Irish Criminal Law Journal* 113. The author notes (at pp. 141–142) that the approach of the Irish courts on fair procedures may be supported by reference to the European Convention on Human Rights.

[74] [1982] I.R. 337.

[75] As already observed, see *O'Leary* v. *Attorney-General, op. cit.*, note 57; *Murphy* v. *Attorney-General, op. cit.*, note 59. This silence can hardly have been due to any reluctance on the part of the judiciary to refer to authorities from courts outside the Irish legal system. In the High Court in *The State (Lynch)* v. *Cooney*, O'Hanlon J. had cited Privy Council cases on written constitutions in former colonies in the course of dealing with some of the issues in the case.

[76] [1993] I.L.R.M. 458.

scope of its earlier decision in *State (Lynch)* v. *Cooney* but there was no reference to the European Convention on Human Rights, either by the members of the Court or by counsel for either side. A few months later, in *Brandon Book Publishers Ltd.* v. *RTE*,[77] RTE's refusal to accept for transmission an advertisement by Gerry Adams, the President of Sinn Féin, for a book of short stories which he had written was challenged by the publishers of the book. RTE took the view that while the ministerial order could not be interpreted to prohibit the broadcasting of interviews with "foot-soldiers" of Sinn Féin on innocuous matters, this license did not extend to the leader of the Party. Carney J, in the High Court, found that it was a matter in which the judgment of the Broadcasting Authority of RTE should not be upset by the Court because it had a greater expertise in the area and because the decision was not reviewable. Again, Irish decisions on the broadcast ban were examined but there was total silence on the implications for such a policy of the European Convention on Human Rights.[78]

Similarly, in *King* v. *Attorney-General*[79] the Supreme Court considered the compatibility with the constitution of an offence which allowed for conviction on proof that the accused was a suspected person or a reputed thief who was frequenting or loitering in certain types of places indicated in the Act. The Supreme Court unanimously found the section unconstitutional. Henchy J. said:

> In my opinion, the ingredients of the offence and the modes by which its commission may to be proved are so arbitrary, so vague, so difficult to rebut, so related to rumour or ill-repute or past conduct, so ambiguous in failing to distinguish between apparent and real behaviour of a criminal nature,…that it is not so much a question of ruling as unconstitutional the type of offence we are now considering as identifying the particular constitutional provisions with which such an offence is at variance.[80]

The same issue has arisen in the European Court of Human Rights. In the *Sunday Times* case, the European Court held that the law must be adequately accessible and that "a norm cannot be regarded as a law unless it is formulated with sufficient precision to enable the citizen to regulate his conduct: he must be able—if need be with appropriate advice—to foresee to a degree that is reasonable in the circumstances, the consequences which a given

---

[77] Unreported judgment of 16 July 1993.

[78] See note 92 below for the outcome of a challenge to the ban before the Strasbourg authorities.

[79] [1981] I.R. 233.

[80] *Ibid.*, at p. 257.

course may entail".[81] The Irish Supreme Court did not make use of the provisions of the European Convention or its case-law interpreting those provisions because the Irish constitution provided a sufficiently high degree of protection for the rights in question.[82] This functional parity of the Irish constitution and the European Convention may not always be evident; in such cases, applications from the Irish system to the European Commission could be expected, though such applications are not always forthcoming. Thus in *O'Reilly* v. *Moroney and the Mid-Western Health Board*,[83] a Supreme Court decision on the involuntary admission of patients to be treated for mental illness, the issues were discussed without any reference to the relevant European Convention jurisprudence, such as *Winterwerp* v. *Netherlands*.[84] There is a general consensus amongst Irish commentators that the Irish legislation which is currently in place on involuntary detention does not conform with the requirements of the European Convention.[85]

The absence of reliance on the Convention in the Irish courts does not mean that it has been without political effect. The European Convention on Human Rights has on a number of occasions been invoked by the executive as a reason for introducing legislation, even in the absence of an action taken against the state for failure to observe its obligations. For instance, when the minister for justice introduced the bill which became the Interception of Postal Packets and Telecommunications (Regulation) Act 1993 into the *Seanad* in May 1992, he referred to the judgment of the European Court of Human Rights in the *Malone* case[86] as a reason for proposing the new

---

[81] *Op. cit.*, note 62, at para. 49. See also *Malone* v. *United Kingdom* Series A, No. 82 (1984) 7 E.H.R.R. 14, which is to similar effect.

[82] See also *Fajujona* v. *Minister for Justice* [1989] I.L.R.M. 234, where the issue of the deportation of parents of Irish children was considered without reference to comparable cases on the European Convention on Human Rights such as *Abdulaziz* v. *United Kingdom* Series A, No. 94 (1985) 7 E.H.R.R. 471 and *Berrehab* v. *Netherlands* Series A, No. 138 (1989) 11 E.H.R.R. 322. See K. Costello, "The Irish Deportation Power" (1990) 12 *Dublin University Law Journal (new series)* 81, at p. 87.

[83] Unreported judgment of 16 November 1993.

[84] Series A, No. 33 (1979) 2 E.H.R.R. 387.

[85] T. Cooney, "Psychiatric Detainees and the Human Rights Challenge to Psychiatry and Law: Where do we go from here?" in L. Heffernan (ed.), *Human Rights: A European Perspective* (Dublin, 1994), ch. 4.4; A. Connelly, "The Convention and Ireland: An Overview" in Heffernan, *ibid.*, p. 45; A-M. O'Neill, "*O'Reilly* v. *Moroney and the Mid-Western Health Board*: Highlighting the Case for Mental Health Reform" (1994) 12 *Irish Law Times (new series)* 211.

[86] *Op. cit.*, note 81.

statutory scheme.[87] In his speech, the minister said that "apart from the intrinsic merits of placing our interception system on a statutory basis, it is also necessary to do so owing to the decision of the European Court of Human Rights in the case of Malone against the United Kingdom....The present Bill takes full account of the requirements of the provisions of the Convention on Human Rights." He added that "[i]t is important to note that under section 2 [of the Bill] the power to authorise interceptions will be much more restrictive against the Executive than is required under the European Convention on Human Rights". However, some members of the *Seanad* noted that the proposed legislation had domestic origins, referring to cases brought in the High and Supreme Courts by journalists whose telephones had been tapped[88] by a predecessor of the minister who had been from the same political party. This was indirectly referred to by one senator when he praised the bill as providing a "a statutory format which takes cognisance of the High Court and Supreme Court decisions. It has also taken cognisance of the well known case of *Malone...*".[89] A more acerbic view was taken by an independent senator who praised the journalists and the court decisions which had established a right to privacy in Irish domestic law. He went to say, "I want to make the point that none of us is deceived by the Minister's coy reference to *Malone* v. *U.K.* We are thankful to the [Irish] courts for the insistence on [the journalists'] right to privacy as one of the unenumerated personal rights and we see this Bill as a development of that court position."[90] This last perspective may well reflect the political realities of the European Convention's domestic significance more accurately than the minister's speech.

This impression of peripheral importance is fortified by the number of parliamentary debates in which there has been no mention made of the European Convention on Human Rights in contexts in which it would have been relevant if it has been considered important by those participating. For instance, in the wake of the decision in *O'Toole* v. *RTE (No. 2)* the minister recommended that the banning order be allowed to lapse without renewal. When his failure to renew the order was debated in the *Dáil* in February 1994, the Minister made references to the constitution and to Article 19.2 of

---

[87] Seanad Eireann Parliamentary Debates, vol. 132, cols. 755–757 (6 May 1992) (Deputy P. Flynn).

[88] The decisions are reported at *Kennedy* v. *Attorney-General* [1987] I.R. 587.

[89] Seanad Eireann Parliamentary Debates, vol. 132, col. 787 (6 May 1992) (Senator D. O'Donovan).

[90] *Ibid*, col. 789 (Professor J. A. Murphy).

the United Nations' Covenant on Civil and Political Rights to justify removing this restriction on freedom of expression.[91] He made no reference to the European Convention on Human Rights; nor did any of the other speakers in the debate.[92] As with the courts, one is left with the impression that neither the European Convention nor the decisions taken by the European Court of Human Rights under the Convention are influential in the formulation of executive policy or in the shaping of legislative debate in Ireland. Although the Convention has been invoked in these settings from time to time when the state has not been brought before the Court, these references add little, if anything, to domestic legal considerations on these occasions.

Part III: The Effect of Judgments of the European Court of Human Rights in the Irish Legal Order[93]

I.   THE *AIREY* CASE[94]

Josie Airey was a married woman with four children who wanted to obtain a judicial separation from her husband. Judicial separation proceedings were heard in the High Court but, because of her low income, Ms. Airey could not afford to retain a solicitor and she was not in a position to proceed with the case without legal advice and representation. At this time there was no provision for civil legal aid in Ireland. Ms. Airey made a complaint to the European Commission of Human Rights and ultimately her case was heard by the European Court of Human Rights. The Court held by a majority that the failure of Ireland to institute an accessible legal procedure in family law matters amounted to a breach of Article 6.1 (by five votes to two) and Article 8 (by four votes to three). It found that Article 6.1 comprised a right for Ms. Airey to have access to the High Court in order to petition for judicial

---

[91]   Dáil Eireann Parliamentary Debates, vol. 438, cols. 232–233 (1 February 1994) (Deputy M. D. Higgins).

[92]   This may have been because the European Commission of Human Rights had decided in 1991 that complaints made by Irish journalists and producers in relation to the section 31 banning order were unfounded: *Purcell* v. *Ireland*, Application No. 15404/89 (1991) 12 *Human Rights Law Journal* 254. See generally, E. Hall, *The Electronic Age: Telecommunication in Ireland* (Dublin, 1993), ch. 26.

[93]   See Connelly, *op. cit.*, note 85, at pp. 34–47, who ultimately adopts a less critical analysis than that advanced here.

[94]   *Op. cit.*, note 48. For comment see G. Whyte, "And Justice for Some" (1984) 6 *Dublin University Law Journal (new series)* 88; M. Cousins, "Access to the Courts" (1992) 14 *Dublin University Law Journal (new series)* 51.

separation. The possibility that she might conduct her case in person without the assistance of legal advice did not exhaust her right because the rights protected by the Convention must be practical and effective. The Court noted that High Court proceedings for a judicial separation order were complicated and difficult. The Court found that legal assistance would not be required in all civil cases; this would depend on the complexity of the procedure and on other factors. Article 8 was breached because effective respect for private or family life obliged the state to make the means of protection constituted by a judicial separation order effectively available, where appropriate, to anyone who might wish to employ it. That protection was not effectively available to Ms. Airey.

The Irish government responded to the Court's decision against it by establishing a civil legal aid scheme by way of the "Scheme of Civil Legal Aid and Advice", introduced on a non-statutory basis by the minister for justice in 1980.[95] Legal aid is provided only through salaried lawyers and the scheme is managed through a non-statutory Legal Aid Board.[96] The scope of the scheme is extremely limited. It excludes several areas of law, including defamation and property disputes, and it also excludes tribunal representation. These formal restrictions limit the access of individuals to justice, a situation made more difficult by severe funding restrictions which have meant that in practice the scheme has provided only a restricted family law service.[97] It is arguable that the current Scheme of Civil Legal Aid and Advice fails to satisfy the criteria which were laid down in *Airey* and that Ireland remains in breach of its obligations under the Convention. The geographical extent of the scheme is limited and there is a long waiting list for legal advice and assistance. In arguments made by proponents of a more extensive system, reference is made to the state's obligations in respect of civil legal aid under the European Convention,[98] but this argument has not proved persuasive to the legislature.

---

[95] For an outline of the scheme's operation, see T. Dalton, "The Civil Legal Aid Scheme" (1989) 83 *Incorporated Law Society of Ireland Gazette* 137. For a more recent, comparative perspective, see M. Cousins, "Civil Legal Aid in France, Ireland, the Netherlands and the United Kingdom—A Comparative Study" (1993) 12 *Civil Justice Quarterly* 154.

[96] M. Cousins, "Neither Flesh nor Fowl—The Status of the Scheme of Civil Legal Aid and Advice" (1992) 10 *Irish Law Times (new series)* 41.

[97] Some 98 per cent. of the casework is related to family law disputes: see Legal Aid Board, *Report 1992* (Dublin, 1994).

[98] See Free Legal Advice Centres (FLAC), "Submission to the Council of Europe on the Crisis in Legal Aid in Ireland" (1990) 8 *Irish Law Times (new series)* 289.

However, even though arguments based on the European Convention and on the *Airey* case have not been useful in later debates about the extent of civil legal aid available in Ireland, there has been some judicially led expansion of the scheme. To the extent that courts have been involved in this process, they have based their decisions solely on the Irish constitution and the unenumerated rights which have been found to enjoy protection under it. In *Forrest* v. *Legal Aid Board*[99] O'Hanlon J. found that the requirement that an applicant be "reasonably likely to be successful in the proceedings" could not apply where the proceedings concerned the welfare of children of a marriage in an action ancillary to a judicial separation. In such proceedings one could not properly speak of winners and losers and cases of this type fell into a completely different category from conventional disputes between litigating parties which have to be resolved by the courts. Given the nature of such proceedings, he found that special interests of the type contemplated in *State (Healy)* v. *O'Donoghue*,[100] a case establishing a constitutional right to legal aid in criminal cases, were present and ordered that legal aid could not be denied in such cases. This approach was expanded by Lardner J. in *B.S.* v. *Laney*[101] where the applicant was refused civil legal aid in wardship proceedings. Applying the reasoning in *Forrest* v. *Legal Aid Board* and *State (Healy)* v. *O'Donoghue,* Lardner J. held that the Legal Aid Board could not refuse an application of this type on the grounds of insufficient information, saying that "it is…necessary that this should be done in order that the constitutional requirement that the Courts should administer justice with fairness be given efficacy". These cases make no reference to any source of law other than those under the Irish constitution, neither by way of guidance nor as authority. Given the family-centred basis of the cases, one might have thought that there was a double reason to refer to the European Convention here. The absence of any reference says much about the Convention's significance in Irish law.

There has been a recent move to place this mixture of administrative measures and judicial decisions on a sounder legislative footing. In 1995 the minister for equality and law reform introduced a civil legal aid bill to the *Seanad*. In his speech the minister referred to the genesis of the existing scheme but it is noticeable that he gave more credit to a domestic source, the report of the Pringle committee in 1979, than to *Airey*'s case.[102] However,

---

[99] Unreported judgment of 4 December 1992.

[100] See [1976] I.R. 325 at p. 350.

[101] Unreported judgment of 10 February 1993.

[102] Seanad Eireann Parliamentary Debates, vol. 141, col. 2125 (16 February 1995) (Deputy

speaking in reply to the minister, another senator was keener to identify the role of the European Court of Human Rights when she noted that, "[i]t is 20 years since the European Court of Human Rights found in favour of Mrs Airey by deciding that our legal system did not then provide proper and adequate access to the law in that we did not have a proper system of civil legal aid. It is obvious that the Government of that time did not readily accept that judgment with delight because, after all, it took them a further six years to establish a basic administrative scheme of civil legal aid."[103] Another senator went so far as to suggest that, "[i]t might be a good idea if in the preamble to the Bill we said, 'An Act to comply with our obligations pursuant to the European Convention on Human Rights.' That might be a tribute to Mrs. Airey and to all those people who have had recourse to the European Convention on Human Rights, and it might be an acknowledgement of that Convention."[104] That suggestion was not taken any further. In conclusion, one can say that while the decision of the European Court of Human Rights may have been important in activating domestic law reform there is, at best, only limited official recognition of the case as a source of change.

2.   THE *NORRIS* CASE[105]

David Norris, a leading member of several homosexual law reform organisations, brought a challenge to Victorian legislation which was still applicable in Ireland criminalising same-sex sexual acts between men.[106] Norris sought to have this legislation struck down as contrary to his rights protected by the Irish constitution. He was aware of his sexual orientation at an early age and of public and state attitudes, including the sanction of the criminal law. This environment caused him anxiety and distress, leading to nervous illness which required medical care and counselling. After his recovery he publicly declared himself a homosexual and helped to found the Irish Gay Rights Movement. From that time on he was involved in law reform groups.

M. Taylor).

[103]   *Ibid.*, 2156–2157 (Senator A. Gallagher).

[104]   Seanad Eireann Parliamentary Debates, vol. 142, cols. 32–33 (22 February 1995) (Senator M. Mulcahy).

[105]   Series A, No. 142 (1988) 13 E.H.R.R. 146. For comment see A. Connelly, "Irish Law and the Judgment of the European Court of Human Rights in the *Dudgeon* Case" (1982) 4 *Dublin University Law Journal (new series)* 25; C. A. Gearty, "Homosexuals and the Criminal Law—The Right to Privacy" (1983) 5 *Dublin University Law Journal (new series)* 264.

[106]   Offences Against the Person Act 1861, ss. 61 and 62; Criminal Law Amendment Act 1885, s.11.

He was never prosecuted for having engaged in homosexual activities, and nor were any of those involved in the law reform groups with which he was associated. Though his cross-channel mail had been opened by the authorities in 1976, that practice had not continued. His main claim was that criminalisation of consensual sexual activity between men in private infringed a right to privacy which was, he claimed, constitutionally protected though the right was not to be found on the face of the constitution's text. He also argued that it breached expressly guaranteed rights to equality before the law on account of the fact that, while all sexual activity between men was criminal, sexual activity between women was subject to no criminal sanction. His case was unsuccessful in the Irish courts. His action failed in the High Court. In dismissing his appeal, the Supreme Court was split three to two on the ground of privacy. However, he was ultimately successful in an action before the European Court of Human Rights,[107] with the Strasbourg court holding by a majority of eight to six that the applicant's right to privacy under Article 8 of the ECHR had been infringed.

Ireland failed to liberalise its law for almost five years, with successive governments strongly resisting change, until finally in June 1993 the fresh political climate created by the formation of a new Fianna Fáil/Labour coalition government was reflected in the enactment of the Criminal Justice (Sexual Offences) Act 1993. In introducing the legislation to the *Dáil* the Minister for Justice explained that while such action was mandated by the decision of the European Court of Human Rights "it would be a pity to use that judgment as the sole pretext for the action we are now taking so as to avoid facing up to the issues [of individual dignity and human rights] themselves".[108] She reiterated this position when introducing the bill into the *Senad*, saying "I am not introducing this Bill simply because of the requirement of compliance with the judgment in the European Court of Human Rights in the case brought by Senator Norris although that requirement is certainly there. This Bill stands on its own merits as a fundamental development in human rights which will put an end to unwarranted intrusion over a very long period into the private life of adults and which is recommended by both the Second Commission on the Status of Women and the Law Re-

---

[107] *Op. cit.* note 105. The decision was not unexpected inasmuch as the European Court of Human Rights had previously ruled that the same legislation which remained in force in Northern Ireland was an infringement of an applicant's human rights: see *Dudgeon* v. *United Kingdom* Series A, No. 45 (1981) 4 E.H.R.R. 149.

[108] Dáil Eireann Parliamentary Debates, vol. 432, cols. 1971 (23 June 1993) (Deputy M. Geoghan-Quinn).

form Commission."[109] Although the minister was keen to locate domestic sources for the legislation, other speakers in that debate were less confident in local ability to generate reform in this area. One senator from the government benches admitted as much when she said, "I believe that this legislation would not be before us if [Senator Norris] had not been a Member of the Oireachtas *and* had not taken his case to Europe".[110]

3. THE *JOHNSTON* CASE[111]

Until 1995 the constitution of Ireland prohibited divorce.[112] Those persons who lived together in a stable relationship following the breakdown of the marriage of one of them were unable, during the lifetime of the other party to that marriage, to marry each other in Ireland. They were not recognised as a family for the purposes of the constitution. In particular such unmarried cohabitants had no legal duty to support each other and had no mutual statutory rights of succession. The old law was that because they were illegitimate, any children of such a union had succession rights which were inferior to those of legitimate children. Under this legal arrangement the mother of an illegitimate child was to be sole legal guardian and the children could not be jointly adopted by their parents nor be legitimated by their subsequent marriage.[113] There were several unsuccessful challenges under the Irish constitution to the legislation which conferred this inferior status on such children.[114] In 1986 the government introduced into the *Seanad* the Status of Children Bill which had the stated purpose of removing as far as possible provisions in existing law which discriminated against children born outside marriage. Prior to the introduction of this legislation, Roy

---

[109] Seanad Eireann Parliamentary Debates, vol. 137, col. 254 (29 June 1993) (Deputy M. Geoghan-Quinn).

[110] *Ibid.*, col. 300 (Senator C. Honan). Emphasis added.

[111] Series A, No. 112 (1986) 9 E.H.R.R. 203. For comment see K. Dillon, "Divorce and Remarriage as Human Rights: The Irish Constitution and the European Convention on Human Rights at Odds in *Johnston* v. *Ireland*" (1989) 22 *Cornell International law Journal* 63.

[112] Article 44 as originally drafted. An amendment, which was to have permitted divorce, was rejected in a referendum by the people (26 June 1986). An amendment permitting divorce in limited circumstances was passed by referendum in November 1995.

[113] See W. Duncan, "Supporting the Institution of Marriage in Ireland" (1978) 13 *Irish Jurist (new series)* 215; Comment, "Succession Rights of Illegitimate Children" (1984) 2 *Irish Law Times (new series)* 63.

[114] See *Re Estate of N.W.* unreported judgment of 29 May 1979, McWilliam J.; *O'B.* v. *S.* [1984] I.R. 316.

Johnston, Janice Williams-Johnston and their daughter, Nessa, applied to the European Commission of Human Rights on 16 February 1982, complaining of the absence of provision in Irish law for divorce and for the recognition of the family life of persons who, after the breakdown of the marriage of one of them, were living in a relationship outside marriage.

Roy Johnston, an Irish citizen, and Janice Williams-Johnston, a British citizen, lived together in Ireland with their daughter, Nessa Williams-Johnston, who was born in 1973. Mr. Johnston had married in 1952 and he and his wife had agreed to separate in 1965, subsequently concluding a formal separation agreement. There were three children from that marriage. He had lived in a stable relationship with Ms. Williams-Johnston since 1971 and supported her and their daughter. He had made provision for Ms. Williams-Johnston, their daughter and his other children in his will. In their complaint to the European Commission on Human Rights they relied on Articles 8, 9, 12 and 13 of the Convention and also on Article 14 (taken in conjunction with Articles 8 and 12). The Court held that the inability of Mr. Johnston to divorce under Irish law and the subsequent inability of Ms. Williams-Johnston and Mr. Johnston to marry did not give rise to a violation of Article 8 or Article 12 of the Convention. It said that,

> The Court is not oblivious to the plight of the first and second applicants. However, it is of the opinion that although the protection of private or family life may sometimes necessitate means whereby spouses can be relieved from the duty to live together, the engagements undertaken by Ireland under Article 8 cannot be regarded as extending to an obligation on its part to introduce measures permitting the divorce and the remarriage which the applicants seek.[115]

Concerning Nessa, the Court held that an effective respect for family life imposed on Ireland a positive obligation to improve her legal situation. The Court held that she should be placed, legally and socially, in a position akin to that of a legitimate child and that, at the time the complaint was initiated, her legal situation differed considerably from a legitimate child. This absence of an appropriate legal regime reflecting Nessa's natural family ties amounted to a failure to respect her own and her parents' family life amounting to a violation of Article 8 as regards all three applicants.[116]

---

[115] *Op. cit.*, note 111, at para 57.

[116] See generally J. Andrew and A. Sherlock, "Family Life and the Constitutional Ban on Divorce in Ireland" (1987) 12 *European Law Review* 393; A. Drzemczewski and C. Warbrick, "The European Convention on Human Rights" (1986) *Yearbook of European Law* 430–432.

This decision was handed down in December 1986. The bill introduced to the upper house of the *Oireachtas* by the Irish government in May 1986 was enacted as the Status of Children Act 1987. The main parts of the Act came into force on 14 June 1988. The purpose of the Act was expressed to be to equalise the rights under the law of all children whether born within or outside marriage. This objective was achieved by setting out the general principle that in this and all future legislation relationships were to be determined without regard to whether or not the parents of any person were married to each other. The Act was, in fact, based on the Irish Law Reform Commission's *Report on Illegitimacy*.[117] It removes the discrimination formerly faced by children in the position of Nessa Williams-Johnston so that the Irish government has now remedied its breach of its obligations under the Convention.[118] Once again, it is questionable to what extent the judgment against Ireland lay at the root of the reforms undertaken. The minister for justice said, when he introduced the legislation in the *Dáil* in May 1987, that "this Bill is a major piece of reforming legislation, which will bring an important area of our family law fully into line with present day standards of social justice. It also has implications on the international plane. [He referred to the outcome in *Johnston*]...The enactment of this Bill and the consequential changes in revenue law to which I referred earlier will remedy that breach."[119] It is fair to observe that the timing, if not the contents, of the 1987 Act was influenced by the *Johnston* litigation. In fact, the opposition spokesperson on the subject responded to the minister by noting that "whereas in a decision relating to the rights of children on intestacy when a parent dies without making a will our Supreme Court held it was justifiable under our Constitution to discriminate against children, the European Court of Human Rights took an entirely different view".[120] He made reference to the Report of the Law Reform Commission and to the persistent campaigning over 15 years of various pressure groups as sources of this legislative action but concluded by saying, "I suspect if it were not for the *Johnston*

---

[117] Law Reform Commission Report No. 4 (Dublin, 1982).

[118] For an overview of the legislation's implications see C. Lehane, "The Law relating to the Status of Children born outside Marriage and their Property Rights" (1989) 83 *Incorporated Law Society of Ireland Gazette* 402–408; 443–447.

[119] Dáil Eireann Parliamentary Debates, vol. 372, cols. 2507–2508 (20 May 1987) (Deputy G. Collins).

[120] *Ibid.*, col. 2511 (Deputy A. Shatter).

case in the European Court we might still not have measures such as this before the House".[121]

4. THE OPEN DOOR COUNSELLING CASE[122]

Open Door Counselling and the Dublin Well Woman Centre were counselling clinics which both provided pregnant women with non-directive information about abortion facilities outside Ireland. In 1985 the Society for the Protection of Unborn Children (SPUC) brought a private action in the High Court restraining the clinics from providing such information. The Supreme Court issued an injunction in 1988 against the defendants, restraining them, their servants or agents from assisting pregnant women to travel abroad to obtain abortions by providing them with information about abortion clinics abroad.[123] The decision was based on the eighth amendment to the constitution which provides that "the State acknowledges the right to life of the unborn and, with due regard for the equal right to life of the mother guarantees in its laws to respect, and, as far as practicable, by its laws to defend and vindicate that right" (Article 40.3.3). The clinics, two counsellors employed by the Dublin Well Women Centre, and two Irish women of childbearing age, made a complaint to the European Commission of Human Rights. Their case was eventually heard by the European Court of Human Rights which held that the injunction prohibiting non-directive abortion counselling was a violation of the applicants' right to freedom of expression (Article 10). The central issue for the Court was whether the restriction of the applicants' freedom to receive and impart information was justified under Article 10.2, and it found that it was not necessary in a democratic society for the protection of the legitimate end which it purported to uphold, namely the protection of morals. This holding that the injunction was overbroad and disproportionate to the end advanced was based on several factors, the most important of which was that the injunction was absolute. It imposed a perpetual restraint on the provision of information to pregnant women irrespective of their age, state of health or their reason for seeking such information. The European Court of Human Rights noted the Irish government's concession that the injunction could not legally prevent access to such information by those women who were not prohibited by the Irish constitution from having an abortion.[124] That concession came about because, shortly before

---

[121] *Ibid.*, col. 2512.

[122] Series A, No. 246 (1992) 15 E.H.R.R. 244.

[123] *Attorney-General (S.P.U.C.)* v. *Open Door Counselling* [1988] I.R. 593.

[124] *Op. cit.*, note 122, at para. 25.

the European Court had given its ruling on the case, the Irish Supreme Court had held in *Attorney-General* v. *X and Others*[125] that the eighth amendment to the constitution permitted lawful termination of pregnancy where the life of the woman was at risk, including a risk of suicide.

In the debate which surrounded and followed the *X* case,[126] the Irish government proposed three constitutional amendments, one of which guaranteed the right to provide and receive information about services lawfully available in other states, including abortion services. The result in the referendum on this proposed "information amendment" brought Irish law into line with the requirements of Article 10 as set out by the Court in *Open Door*.[127] However, it is worth noting that the debate prior to that referendum was couched largely in domestic terms. To the extent to which factors originating outside the state played any role at all, the main "foreign" influence on the shape of the exchanges which took place was probably EC law. European Community law had become relevant by virtue of the addition of a Protocol to the Treaty of European Union[128] which purported to insulate Article 40.3.3 of the Irish constitution from the impact of EC law. The Protocol was added to the Treaty in the wake of the decision of the Court of Justice of the European Communities in *S.P.U.C.* v. *Grogan*[129] to the effect that abortion is a service within Articles 59 and 60 of the Treaty of Rome. The absence of any sustained reference to the European Convention on this point may be explicable on the basis of the intensely introspective soul-searching undertaken by the Irish polity following the *X* case;[130] nonetheless, it confirms the impression that the European Convention's importance in the domestic legal and political environment is, essentially, a marginal one, contingent on the interaction of more weighty domestic considerations.

---

[125] *Op. cit.*, note 17.

[126] See generally A. Connelly, "The Constitution" in A. Connelly (ed.), *Gender and the Law in Ireland* (Dublin, 1993), at pp. 4, 10–13; F. Murphy, "Maastricht: Implementation in Ireland" (1994) 19 *European Law Review* 94; A. Smyth, "The 'X' Case: Women and Abortion in the Republic of Ireland, 1992" (1993) 1 *Feminist Legal Studies* 163; E. O'Reilly, *Masterminds of the Right* (Dublin, 1992).

[127] Article 40.3.5: 'Subsection 3 of this section shall not limit freedom to obtain or make available, in the State, subject to such conditions as may be laid down by law, information relating to services lawfully available in another State.' This amendment was approved by over 60 per cent. of the those voting in the referendum.

[128] See D. Curtin, "The Constitutional Structure of the Union: A Europe of Bits and Pieces" (1993) 30 *Common Market Law Review* 17, at pp. 47–49.

[129] Case C–159/90 [1991] 3 C.M.L.R. 849. See Persaud, *post*, pp. 382–384.

[130] See A. Smyth (ed.), *The Abortion Papers: Ireland* (Dublin, 1992).

This impression is largely confirmed by the parliamentary debates which accompanied the passage of legislation to give effect to the relevant constitutional amendment. The minister for health brought a Regulation of Information (Services outside the State for Termination of Pregnancies) Bill, 1995 before the *Dáil* in March 1995, and set out the background to the legislation, referring to the state's obligations under the European Convention on Human Rights in doing so.[131] Apart from the occasional passing reference to the judgment in *Open Door*, there was virtually no mention of the European Convention on Human Rights during the *Seanad* debates which focused almost exclusively on the constitutional and EC law points. Unusually, there was a more detailed speech made in the *Dáil* when an opposition deputy raised the spectre of Article 10 in relation to the restrictions on information contemplated by the bill. She argued that the Irish provisions introduced a disproportionate penalty where they restricted freedom of speech.[132] However, this point went completely unanswered in the remainder of the debates; the point being simply not referred to by any other speaker.

5.   THE *PINE VALLEY DEVELOPMENTS* CASE[133]

The *Pine Valley Developments* case involved applicants, a number of natural and legal persons, who had bought land and applied for planning permission to develop the area. Permission to undertake the development was refused by the minister for the environment but his decision was successfully challenged by the applicants in the Supreme Court.[134] Section 6 of the Local Government (Planning and Development) Act 1982 passed in the wake of *Pine Valley (No. 1)*, dealt with the "gap" which the case was perceived to have created in the zoning and planning law. It retrospectively validated all planning applications whose legality had been compromised by the decision of the Supreme Court. However, the case of the applicants themselves was expressly exempted from section 6; this exclusion was explained by the minister for the environment when he introduced the legislation as necessary to avoid interference with the progress through the courts of a second case

---

[131] Dáil Eireann Parliamentary Debates, vol. 450, cols. 6–10 (2 March 1995) (Deputy M. Noonan). The Minister made an almost identical speech when he brought the Bill before the Senate: Seanad Eireann Parliamentary Debates, vol. 142, cols. 824–828 (13 March 1995).

[132] Dáil Eireann Parliamentary Debates, vol. 450, cols. 51–53 (2 March 1995) (Deputy L. O'Donnell).

[133] Series A, No. 222 (1991) 14 E.H.R.R. 319.

[134] [1984] I.R. 407.

brought by the applicants.[135] The Irish courts jealously guard their exclusive right under the constitution to administer justice (Article 34.1) and in the past they have struck down as unconstitutional legislation which has purported to interfere with cases in progress.[136] There can be no doubt that the decision to draft section 6 in this fashion was constitutionally proper. However, the second case, seeking damages for the wrongful decision of the minister, was unsuccessful so that the applicants were left without a remedy in Irish law.[137] The European Court held that the applicants were victims of discrimination in the enjoyment of their property rights, contrary to Article 14 of the Convention read in conjunction with Article 1 of the First Protocol, in that the Local Government (Planning and Development) Act 1982 had retrospectively validated all planning permissions in the relevant category other than theirs. Following its decision in *Pine Valley Developments Ltd.*, the European Court of Human Rights reached a further decision on the issue of affording just satisfaction to the injured parties in accordance with Article 50 of the Convention.[138] The Court required Ireland to pay, within three months, pecuniary damages and interest, the total amount of compensation under this head being assessed on an equitable basis, and to pay nonpecuniary damages in addition to costs and expenses in respect of the domestic and the Strasbourg proceedings. This case gave rise to no issue of general importance. The only remedy necessary was payment of compensation to the applicants who were the only persons affected by the legislation in question, and this payment was made by the state shortly after the date of the judgment against it.

6. THE *KEEGAN* CASE[139]

Article 41 of the Irish constitution states that the state recognises the family as the natural primary and fundamental unit group of society and as a moral institution possessing inalienable and imprescriptible rights antecedent and superior to all law. Article 42 also acknowledges the role of the family as the primary and natural educator of the child and the state can only interfere

---

[135] 337 Dáil Eireann Parliamentary Debates, vol. 337, cols. 2467–2469 (14 July 1982) (Deputy R. Burke).

[136] See most famously *Buckley* v. *Attorney-General* [1950] I.R. 67.

[137] [1987] I.R. 23.

[138] See Series A, No. 246–B (1993) 16 E.H.R.R. 379.

[139] Judgment of the European Court of Human Rights, 26 May 1994. See P. Ward, "The Irish Family outside Marriage and the European Convention on Human Rights—*Keegan* v. *Ireland*" (1994) 12 *Irish Law Times (new series)* 168.

with the rights of parents where the parents for physical or moral reasons fail in their duty to their child or children. The family protected by Articles 41 and 42 is based on marriage.[140] The protection enjoyed by the marital family is extensive; for example, the courts have ordered the return of children from their adoptive parents to their birth parents who had married after the adoption order was made, even though considerable periods of time had elapsed in the interim.[141] The rights of children born outside marriage[142] and of unmarried mothers[143] do enjoy constitutional protection, but only under Article 40.3.2 which permits these rights to be abrogated or surrendered. However, the Supreme Court has held that the natural father of a child born outside marriage has no constitutionally protected rights.[144] The Status of Children Act 1987 improved the position of the natural father to some extent but it gives natural fathers no more than a bare right to apply to be appointed guardian.

Keegan was the natural father of a daughter who was born outside marriage. He and the natural mother had lived together for several months and planned the pregnancy. However, the natural mother subsequently broke with him and returned to her family. After the birth of the child, her mother decided to place her for adoption; the preliminary steps of this process were carried out without notice to Keegan and without his consent. He subsequently sought to be appointed the child's guardian under section 6A of the Guardianship of Infants Act 1964;[145] it was only as the child's guardian that he could veto the proposed final adoption order, but his application was unsuccessful.[146] It was held that section 6A gave him a right to apply for guardianship but did not give him a right to be appointed guardian. The test laid down by the Supreme Court in dealing with Keegan's application was that such applications should be refused unless it were shown that custody with the father would be not inconsiderably better for the child's welfare

---

[140] See *State (Nicholau)* v. *An Bord Uchtála* [1966] I.R. 164.

[141] See *M.* v. *An Bord Uchtála* [1977] I.R. 375 (child returned to birth parents having been in care of his adoptive family for six years). See also *K.C. and A.C.* v. *An Bord Uchtála* [1985] I.L.R.M. (child returned to birth parents having been with prospective adoptive parents for two years).

[142] *M.* v. *M.* unreported judgment of 2 December 1982 (High Court).

[143] *G.* v. *An Bord Uchtála* [1980] I.R. 32.

[144] *State (Nicholau)* v. *An Bord Uchtála*, *op. cit.*, note 140; affirmed in *K.* v. *W.* [1990] 2 I.R. 437.

[145] Inserted by Status of Children Act 1987, s. 12.

[146] *K.* v. *W.*, *op. cit.*, note 144; *K.* v. *W. (No. 2)* [1990] I.L.R.M. 791.

than custody with the prospective adoptive parents. Keegan applied to the European Commission of Human Rights on the ground that his rights under Articles 6, 8 and 14 of the Convention were violated by Irish law. The Commission found that the test laid down by the Supreme Court for guardianship was virtually insurmountable in order for the natural father to win custody against the adoptive parents. The Court in turn held that Ireland was in breach of its Convention obligations. It found that Article 8 of the Convention had been breached; the father in this case had established a family life and his right to respect for his family life had been violated when the child had been placed for adoption without the knowledge or consent of the father. In addition, there had been a breach of Article 6 of the Convention in that the father had no involvement or standing in the adoption hearing and this had not been remedied by allowing the father to apply for guardianship. The Court found that the right to apply for guardianship was irrelevant to the issue of adoption as the child had been placed before there was any hearing as to guardianship.

The response of the Irish government to *Keegan* thus far has been to do nothing. This has placed *An Bord Uchtála* (the Irish Adoption Board) in a difficult situation and in some cases it is not willing to make any adoption order.[147] Another result of *Keegan* has been to cause delays in adoptions in Ireland because the social workers and adoption societies have changed their practice to ensure that the father of a child being put up for adoption is informed of the proposed adoption.[148] The minister for health and the attorney-general are said to be considering what legislation should be brought forward. The initial response of *An Bord Uchtála* was that existing placements had to be reviewed to ensure that natural fathers were informed of intended adoptions and given an opportunity to be heard in this matter. In addition, all future placements could only proceed with the knowledge and consent of the natural father, even where he was a minor or married, and the Board took the view that this applied even where it was against the wishes of the mother that he be informed. The Board also took the view at that time that if the mother did not give the father's name and address, the placement for adoption should not proceed. It subsequently modified this approach and indicated that, pending legislation, placements for adoption and adoptions could go ahead even where the mother refused to cooperate in contacting the natu-

---

[147] D. Brown, *Paper delivered to Conference on the European Convention on Human Rights*, University College, Cork, 4 February 1995, at p. 5.

[148] M. Cahill and L. Siggins, "Court ruling on rights of the father causing major delays in adoptions", *Irish Times* 16 November 1994, p.1.

ral father. This may give rise to practical difficulties if there is a significant delay before new legislation is passed into law, and the practice would be, at best, dubious under the European Convention. Finally, while it is not clear at present what form the new legislation will take, it is certainly the case that any new arrangement will mark a major shift in the legal status of natural fathers in Irish law. The *Keegan* case reflects that limited notion of the family and familial rights under the Irish constitution, and any Convention-inspired developments will be a step to extending protection to those persons who are not protected under the Irish constitution.[149] However, it may be that any new legislation will be officially traced back to the 1982 Law Commission *Report on Illegitimacy* which had proposed a more favourable regime for natural fathers than that finally established by the Status of Children Act 1987. A (suspect) genealogy of this kind would certainly be consistent with the response of the Irish government to previous decisions against it from the European Court of Human Rights.

Conclusion

The continued failure of successive Irish governments to incorporate the European Convention on Human Rights means that it has no direct effect in Irish domestic law. It does not give rise to rights capable of being enforced by an individual in the Irish courts. This failure does not, in itself, preclude the possibility of a substantially influential role for the Convention in the local political and legal order. However, except in the cases taken against the state itself (and even then, to a limited extent), there is little sign of the Convention developing such a status. It is difficult to assess the degree of influence which the Convention does enjoy and any attempt to do so is, inevitably, controversial. In advocating an ongoing and significant place for the Convention in Ireland one can point to many occasions where it was referred to as part of the reasons given to justify decisions taken both by the judicial and the executive arms of government. However, this is a distorted representation; there are also many decisions where no reference was made to the European Convention in situations where it would have been not merely appropriate but actually obvious to do so. This pattern of regular omission undermines any depiction of the Convention as a consistently important factor in the calculations of Irish decision-makers. In addition, it is questionable whether the use which is made of the European Convention and the

---

[149] Brown, *op. cit.*, note 147, at p. 7.

judgments of the European Court of Human Rights in any way influences the outcomes of the decisions in which they feature.

It can be convincingly claimed that these decisions are wholly determined by domestic factors, primarily the constitution and the case-law of the Irish courts, and that the European Convention is employed as little more than a secondary argument to validate these decisions. In none of the cases or legislation considered in which the European Convention was referred to was the Convention to the foreground as a reason for arriving at a particular conclusion. This analysis holds good both for cases where substantive rights were considered and for those where the mode of reasoning involved in a given decision was subjected to scrutiny. As a result, any evaluation of the Convention in the Irish domestic order turns primarily on one's assessment of the human rights protection occasioned by domestic sources. Given the essentially reflexive role of the European Convention one might say that it has legitimated the failure of the Irish state to accord adequate human rights protection to those within its jurisdiction. Equally, one may present the European Convention as an external vindication of the norms which have been developed and protected within the Irish legal order. Either way, the Convention is quite detached from the Irish context.

There are a few cases where the Convention is indisputably relevant to the shape of Irish human rights' protection. However, these are the exceptional cases in which a complaint brought against the state under the European Convention has been upheld. Even here, the extent of the Convention's relative influence is disputable; the decisions of the European Court of Human Rights may require that a given national measure be struck down but they do not draft the successor to that law. The Irish experience has been that both the timing and the precise shape of that replacement, if any, seems to turn more on domestic considerations than on the actions of the European Court. The narrow role of the European Convention is illustrated by the limited accessibility to Ireland's underfunded civil legal aid scheme and the long, domestically-inspired delay in implementing the *Norris* decision with the final decision being to adopt an equal age of consent rather than the British approach to the issue of consensual homosexual sexual activity. The situations mentioned above are ones in which domestic political considerations were determinative of the eventual response. The Convention may have been invoked from time to time in these situations but, from the perspective of individual citizens, one would be wiser to pay more attention to Dublin than to Strasbourg. Irish reaction to *Johnston* and *Open Door* shows that though the Convention may be used to force law reform, it is debatable whether it is more influential than the recommendations of the Irish Law

Reform Commission or than the decisions of the Irish courts. *Open Door* is particularly interesting here; there is no suggestion that the prospect of a decision against Ireland resulted in the constitutional amendment on the provision of information related to terminations of pregnancy. That painful episode had more to do with the aftermath of the *Attorney-General* v. *X* and the state's international obligations played little part in the moral and social deliberations which preceded the referendum.

A survey of the role of the European Convention in Irish law provokes the question why it has failed to achieve a more prominent place in the domestic legal order. There is little in the Irish response of the insular hostility to any bill of rights which is a feature of some strands of British reaction to the Convention. Nor can it be simply that the Convention is not of domestic origin. Ireland is a small jurisdiction whose situation and common history renders reference to the decisions from other jurisdictions useful and positively difficult to avoid. The developments in Irish constitutional adjudication in the last thirty years have been marked by an increased willingness to refer to human rights documents and decisions from other parts of the world. It may be that differences in the style of drafting and interpreting of the Convention have made it harder for Irish lawyers to work with it than with comparable documents and decisions from the common law world. This is not to overlook the occasional references to German and Italian jurisprudence that one finds in arguments to the Irish courts on constitutional issues.[150] A more prosaic reason, which returns obliquely to the earlier demand to assess the adequacy of Irish human rights' protection, is that the Convention adds little of note to the Irish constitution from the perspective of Irish lawyers and judges. The one notable exception is the protection of family life because of the more extensive definition of "family" accepted under Article 8 of the European Convention;[151] this would explain why family related issues have featured so strongly in the cases decided against Ireland. In that sense, it is, for the most part, simply not useful in this jurisdiction at this point in time. That is not to diminish the real contribution made in Ireland by the European Court of Human Rights and European Convention. However, to place it in context requires one to keep one's attention firmly and primarily focused on the Irish constitution and on the decisions of the Irish courts. Unless there is a move towards a full or partial incorpo-

---

[150] See above, note 59.

[151] See C. Lysaght, "The Status of International Agreements in Irish Domestic Law" (1994) 12 *Irish Law Times (new series)* 171, at p. 172.

ration of the European Convention into the Irish constitution, this situation is most unlikely to change.

Addendum

The Final report of the Constitution Review Group was published in May 1996. The Convention has proved to be a significant influence in its deliberations, more so than other international human rights instruments. Although the Review Group decided against direct incorporation of the Convention into the constitution, it recommended drawing on the Convention where a right is not protected by the constitution, or where the standard of protection of such rights is superior to those guaranteed by the constitution, or the wording of such a right might be improved. Most interestingly, it proposed introducing a catalogue of protected statuses into the equality clause (Article 40.1), and replacing the bare text of Article 40.3.1 and the judicially created category of unenumerated personal rights with a comprehensive list of fundamental rights, both drawing on, *inter alia*, the Convention for this purpose. If the Irish government responds positively to these and other suggestions, there may be a sea-change in the status of the Convention in Irish law. However, given the dearth of reform to emerge from the proposals of a similar group almost thirty years ago[152] a more cautious approach seems reasonable.

---

[152] *Report of the Committee on the Constitution*, Pr 9817 (Dublin, 1967).

6. SWEDEN

Iain Cameron

Part I: General Constitutional Framework

Sweden is a unitary state with a constitutional monarchy. It has a unicameral legislature and the system of government is parliamentary. There are four documents in Sweden which have constitutional status: the Freedom of the Press Act (*Tryckfrihetsförordningen*, TF), the Freedom of Expression Act (*Yttrandefrihetsgrundlag*, YGL), the Instrument of Government (*Regeringsformen*, RF) and the Succession Act (*Successionsförordningen*, SO). The Succession Act deals only with the issue of succession to the throne. The other three documents all contain important human rights provisions. The Freedom of the Press Act (1949:105)[1] and the Freedom of Expression Act (1991:1469) deal, respectively, with the printed and electronic media. They provide *inter alia* for a special system of criminal responsibility for crimes committed by means of the printed or electronic media (defamation, breaches of the Secrecy Act etc.) and for the right to jury trial for those accused of committing such offences. They prohibit censorship and lay down the right to communicate official information to the press for publication, even secret information, subject to certain narrowly defined exceptions.[2]

---

[*] I would like to thank Lena Marcusson for her comments on part of this article. Helpful remarks were also made by Thomas Bull. Any errors remaining are my own.

[1] References to the Swedish statute book (Svensk författningssamling, SFS) are by year followed by the relevant number. Translations of the constitution come from the official English edition unless otherwise stated. References to a constitutional provision are by chapter and article number, *e.g.* RF 11:14. An Article can have several paragraphs which are in turn divided into subparagraphs. The Swedish form of citation of a constitutional provision appears rather cumbersome in English, but this is preferable to inventing my own form of citation (which in the long run would be misleading to both Swedish and foreign readers), thus, RF 2 kap. 1§ 1st. 1.p is translated RF 2:1, paragraph 1, subparagraph 1.

[2] For a discussion in English of the provisions of the Act insofar as they relate to informants, see L. Marcusson, "Freedom of the Press. Rights and Freedoms of Informants" in U. Göransson (ed.), *Modern Legal Issues: An Anglo-Swedish Perspective* (Uppsala,

C. A. Gearty (ed.), *European Civil Liberties and the European Convention on Human Rights*, 217–265.
© 1997 *Kluwer Law International. Printed in the Netherlands.*

The Acts in question are very detailed. In comparison to other European countries Sweden is unusual both in giving constitutional status to, and such detailed and strong protection of, these particular forms of expression. Swedish protection of freedom of information is probably stronger than in any other European state, and forms an important part of the country's system of constitutional control.

Other human rights are set out in Chapter 2 of the Instrument of Government (1974:152). The Instrument of Government was adopted in 1974, totally replacing the earlier version from 1809. It sets out, in 13 chapters, basic rules governing parliament and government, their composition, relationship inter se, law-making, budgetary and treaty-making powers, the functions and competence of the courts and the administrative agencies, constitutional control mechanisms and emergency powers. Chapter 2 was a late addition to the original drafts of the new Instrument of Government. The Social Democratic government of the day saw little need for constitutional protection of human rights, beyond that provided by the Freedom of the Press Act.[3] It was reluctant to do anything which could hinder its programme of legislative reforms, and considered that, in any event, the sole meaningful protection of fundamental freedoms lay in the democratic process.[4] Nonetheless, opposition from the centre/right parties, and to a certain extent from the radical left, forced a retreat on this point. The Social Democratic scepticism nonetheless resulted in a limited number of rights being included in the chapter and a very weak system of protection of these rights. The ECHR (hereafter, the Convention) had little, or no significance, in the drafting process. The rights were formulated so as to provide little, if any, restraint on the possibility of a parliamentary majority to limit them. They were split into two categories: "absolute" and "relative" rights. The category of relative rights—which included the usual civil rights of freedom of speech, assembly, association etc., but only applied to Swedish citizens—could be restricted by an ordinary statute. Absolute rights could only be al-

---

1993). Where possible, I have tried to refer to literature in English.

[3] The Freedom of the Press Act was part of the reason why it took until 1974 for Sweden—which has always been a strong champion of human rights in other countries—to write such rights into its own constitution. The Act is firmly established in the Swedish legal culture, having antecedents which go back to 1766. The opinion is still occasionally expressed that Sweden could manage quite well without Chapter 2 as long as the Freedom of the Press Act continued to apply.

[4] For an exhaustive discussion of the different positions taken by the political parties in 1974, 1976 and 1979, see K. Algotsson, *Medborgarrätten och regeringsformen* [Citizens' rights and the Instrument of Government] (Stockholm, 1987).

tered by constitutional amendment.[5] A few absolute rights were included in Chapter 2 of the Instrument of Government such as the prohibitions of the death penalty and of retroactive criminal law. But, as shown below, the process of constitutional amendment is in Sweden a relatively easy one.

There was general dissatisfaction with the weak position of rights in the original Instrument of Government. An all party committee which reported even before the new Instrument had entered into force, recommended a number of changes in 1975. The new centre/right government which came to power in 1976, ending almost 40 years of Social Democratic rule, made a number of alterations to Chapter 2. These introduced new relative rights and general substantive conditions which have to be satisfied before relative rights can be restricted. The general conditions provide basically that a restriction may only be imposed for a purpose which is acceptable in a democratic society, may never exceed the bounds of what is necessary with regard to its purpose, may never go so far as to constitute a threat to freedom of opinion, which is a cornerstone of democracy and may never be made only on the basis of a political, religious, cultural or similar belief. Specific conditions were also introduced for restrictions to the freedoms of speech, assembly and association. Not all relative rights were covered by these conditions. In particular, these did not apply to the right to property. This right was formulated in a negative sense, providing only for compensation "on grounds determined by law" when expropriation occurred. The impact of the general substantive conditions was, furthermore, severely limited by the very narrow view taken by the legislative history—which has guided the subsequent approach of both parliament and the courts to interpretation of the rights—to the concept of a "restriction" of a human right. A "restriction" was said to be primarily aimed at measures backed by physical sanctions (*e.g.* criminalisation of conduct). Thus, if someone was refused state employment because of the expression of a political opinion this was not to be seen as a restriction of his or her freedom of expression.[6]

The 1976 reform also provided that aliens present in Sweden were to enjoy, in certain cases, equality of protection with Swedish citizens. In other

---

[5] The provisions of the Freedom of the Press Act, and, since 1991, the Freedom of Expression Act, being constitutional documents, are "absolute rights".

[6] SOU 1975:75 p. 104. References to *travaux préparatoires* are either to the number of the commission responsible for investigating the law, *Statens offentliga utredningar* (SOU) and the year of its report, or to the draft bill put before parliament together with its accompanying documentation, (*proposition,* prop.) or to the report of the Parliamentary Committee on the Constitution on the bill (KU).

cases, the protection is either weaker—the material conditions do not apply to laws which apply exclusively to aliens—or does not exist at all (*e.g.* the right to freedom of movement within the Realm does not apply to aliens). Thus, there are two parallel systems of protection in Chapter 2; for aliens and for Swedish citizens. It should, however, be stressed that legislation which provides for differential protection is in practice relatively rare.

No system of entrenchment of relative rights was introduced in 1976, this being a source of disagreement between the Social Democrats and the centre/right parties. A compromise solution was, however, later achieved and 1979 saw the introduction of the "qualified legislative procedure". In essence this provides that a statute which restricts certain relative rights can (subject to certain minor exceptions) be delayed by a minority of MPs for a period of one year, the idea being that during this year opposition both within and without parliament can be mobilised. The procedure does not apply to all relative rights, *e.g.* the right to property is not covered. Nor does it apply automatically, but only when a group of at least 10 MPs propose it. Should it not be proposed, the statute is passed by simple majority. Even if it is proposed, such a proposal can be overruled by a 5/6 majority of the MPs in parliament.[7]

Another change which was made in 1979 was the formal recognition of the possibility for both courts and administrative agencies to review, in concrete cases, the constitutionality of statutes and subordinate legislation. A cautious practice of constitutional review had gradually developed during the early twentieth century. However, the competence of the courts to engage in this was, and is, viewed with deep suspicion by the left wing parties, who were unwilling to confirm its existence by a constitutional provision. They eventually accepted it, but subject to a major limitation. This limitation stipulates that a law (*lag*) passed by parliament or an ordinance (*förordning*) passed by the government must be "manifestly" in breach of a constitutional provision before a court or administrative agency can refuse to apply it in the case before it (RF 11:14).[8] No such limitation applies to subordinate legislation issued by administrative agencies on delegation by

---

[7]   This is a simplified explanation. The political compromise which resulted in the qualified procedure makes it rather complicated.

[8]   The Swedish system of constitutional review is unusual in that the power of review is vested not just in courts in general (unlike, *e.g.*, the German and Italian systems which are concentrated in a specialised court) but also in administrative agencies. This can be partly explained by the quasi-independent role administrative agencies have in the Swedish system (see below Part III, section 1).

the government which conflicts with higher norms. The final change which was made in 1979 was the reinstatement of the requirement to submit a legislative proposal involving human rights to the Law Council (*lagrådet*). The Law Council consists mainly of a number of justices from the Supreme Court and Supreme Administrative Court. It engages in a relatively wide form of abstract constitutional review, considering not simply the compatibility of the proposal with the constitution, but also with the legal system as such. The requirement to place all legislative proposals before the Law Council was abolished in 1971 over the protests of the centre/right parties and replaced with a discretion to do so. The amendment in 1979 does not make the referral requirement absolute, but strong reasons must be given for not complying with it.

The last important series of amendments to Chapter 2 was effected in 1994. These changes added certain new (albeit weak) rights, amended and improved the protection of the right to property so as to correspond with its formulation in the Convention and provided for a quasi-constitutional status for the Convention. This last point will be dealt with later in this chapter.

Having sketched out the history of Chapter 2, a few general points can now be made regarding the means by which the human rights set out in Swedish constitutional documents are protected. First, the system of entrenchment is relatively weak. As mentioned above, all relative rights can be restricted by a statute passed by simple majority, unless the qualified legislative procedure applies to the right in question and that procedure is actually invoked. This procedure has been threatened on a few occasions but has been used very rarely. Its main significance is that it encourages political compromises. Restriction of absolute rights requires constitutional amendments, but this is a relatively simple process in Sweden. In general, all that is required is two votes by simple majority in two different parliamentary sessions. There must be an intervening general election and a period of nine months must pass between the first and second votes. It is possible for a minority of one-third of all MPs to require a referendum to be held on a constitutional amendment, but this is rare.[9] Second, having said this, the preventive control in Sweden is relatively strong in practice. Considerable efforts are usually made to achieve a consensus among the political parties regarding constitutional amendments. Moreover, the legislative process in general is more open than in, *e.g.*, the UK. The input of interest groups and academic lawyers to legislation depends upon the circumstances, but can

---

[9] This is a simplified explanation. The detailed procedure for amendment of constitutional documents is set out in RF 8:15.

often be considerable. Abstract review of a bill provided by the Law Council usually focuses on technical matters, but criticism has been made of legislative proposals on the basis of Chapter 2 and the European Convention.[10] While not binding on the government, such criticism provides valuable ammunition to the political opposition in securing changes to the proposal.[11]

Third, the role of the Parliamentary Ombudsman (*Justitieombudsmannen*) should be mentioned. The decisions of the Ombudsman in the Swedish system are not binding, but are nonetheless highly influential in maintaining and improving standards of good public administration.[12] Under the Ombudsman Act (1986:765) one of the particular functions of the Ombudsman is "to ensure that the courts and administrative agencies observe the requirements of the Instrument of Government concerning objectivity and impartiality and that citizens' basic human rights are not infringed". The constitutional provision in question, RF 1:9, states that all courts and public authorities "shall observe in their work the equality of all persons before the law and shall maintain objectivity and impartiality". This is used by the Ombudsman to widen the otherwise very narrow concept of what constitutes a restriction on human rights.[13] There are usually a few cases every year in which the Ombudsman criticises public authorities for infringing human rights, mainly rights under the Freedom of the Press Act, but occasionally also rights under Chapter 2.

Fourth, the "manifest" restriction on the power of the courts to engage in concrete constitutional review has meant that there have been very few cases indeed in which the courts have screwed their courage to the sticking post

---

[10] See generally, K. Algotsson, *Lagrådet, rättsstaten och demokrati under 1900-talet* [the Law Council, the Rule of Law and Democracy during the Twentieth Century] (Stockholm, 1993) (with English summary).

[11] *E.g.* the debate on the Planning and Building Act in 1985, Algotsson, *ibid.* pp. 221–231.

[12] There are four Parliamentary Ombudsmen. While decisions are not binding, it should be noted that, in extreme cases of abuse of power, the Ombudsman can prosecute individual civil servants for breach of official duty.

[13] *E.g.*, youth branches of political parties are entitled to apply for (modest) financial contributions from local authorities, the sum in question being assessed on the basis of the number of members. In order to prevent abuse, a local authority required, before paying out the contribution, the disclosure of the names of the members of youth parties. The Ombudsman found that this, while not directly covered by the prohibition on being forced to disclose a political opinion (RF 2:2) nonetheless came very close to it. As public authorities at all times should have objective grounds for their actions, he recommended that alternative means of preventing abuse should be found: JO *Ämbetsberättelse* [Official Report of the Ombudsman] 1979–80, p. 375.

and refused to apply a statute or an ordinance.[14] The courts are traditionally deferential to parliament in the Swedish system. There is no space here to discuss in detail why this is so, but a few reasons, or possible reasons, may be mentioned. One is the influence of the Scandinavian school of legal philosophy in the first part of the twentieth century. This school saw law merely as a tool of social control and was sceptical of the very notion of a "right". Another explanation lies in the existence of the abstract review carried out by the Law Council. If the Law Council has not criticised, or even questioned, a provision in a bill, then it is very difficult for a court subsequently to hold that the same provision is "manifestly" in breach of the constitution. Many years of uninterrupted rule by the Social Democratic Party has also had its effect on the legal culture.[15] The Social Democrats have emphasised the democratic process and have been hostile to any hint of explicit policy-making by the courts. Having said this, deference to the democratic will cannot explain the fact that not only laws but also ordinances are protected from review. The formal explanation for this is that under RF 8:13 the government has its own primary area of legislative competence, *i.e.* it does not simply exercise powers delegated by parliament. In any event, this special status granted government ordinances is probably unusual in international comparison. It has the paradoxical result that judicial challenges to subordinate legislation issued by the government is much less common in Sweden, where the courts ostensibly have the right of constitutional review, than in, *e.g.*, the UK, where they do not.

Judicial deference to the parliament (and, indirectly, the government) also makes its presence felt in the statutory interpretative methods used by the courts. The normal methods can, loosely, be described as subjective, objective and teleological. The subjective method involves placing reliance on the very detailed legislative history in an attempt to discern the will of the legislator. The objective method focuses on the text. The teleological

---

[14] *RÅ 1982 1:74*, *RH 102:84*, *RÅ 1993:10*. See also the decisions of the lower courts referred to at the end of this section and the decision of the Jönköping Administrative Court of Appeals noted on p. 242 and p.255. Cases from the courts of appeal are cited from the official series *Rättsfall från hovrätterna* (RH) and cases from the Supreme Administrative Court (*Regeringsrätten*) are cited from the official series RÅ. Lower court decisions are unreported in Sweden. For a useful recent discussion in English of constitutional review in Sweden generally, see B. Holmström, "The Judicialization of Politics in Sweden" (1994) 15 *International Political Science Review* 153.

[15] The SDP has governed, either as the sole party of government or the major party in a coalition government during the years 1936–1976 and 1982–1991. It was returned to office again in 1994. The next general election is due to be held in 1998.

method (which comes in objective and subjective variations) attempts to ascertain the main purpose(s) of a statute by having regard to its "normal" field of application. It then applies these purposes to "hard cases". While it is probably fair to say that the courts pick and choose between these methods, the subjective method is common. The very detailed legislative history enables parliament to draft legislation in a relatively general way, knowing that the courts will refer to the legislative history to flesh out the statute.

The way judges are picked for the higher courts can also explain, to some extent, the cautious approach of the Swedish judiciary to constitutional review. The judiciary in Sweden is a career judiciary. On the other hand, there is no prohibition on judges being politically active. Many judges, before they obtain a tenured post, have served a considerable amount of their time in government departments, usually drafting legislation. While this provides them with valuable insights into the legislative process, it is open to the criticism that it gives them a one-sided, and restricted, view of the judicial function. This criticism is strengthened by the fact that all senior judges—a category which includes all Supreme Court and Supreme Administrative Court judges, as well as the presidents of the courts of appeal—are appointed purely at the discretion of the government.[16] It is not unknown for politicians who are legally qualified to be appointed to senior judicial office. Having said all this, I should add that, relatively recently, there have been a few decisions of lower courts refusing to apply laws. As I will discuss below, the incorporation of the Convention and Swedish membership of the EU may well also mean that the courts will become more willing to—or at least, feel more obliged to—engage in constitutional review.[17]

---

[16] Many of the circa 1,000 judges serving in Swedish courts—around 40 per cent.—do not have tenured positions. This obviously raises questions regarding the independence of the judiciary. All tenured judges (some 600) are appointed by the government, but in practice, as far as lower judges are concerned, the government follows the recommendations of an independent commission on judicial appointments. The senior judges—over 100 of the 600 positions—are appointed purely at the discretion of the government. There is, however, a constitutional convention when appointing Supreme Court and Supreme Administrative Court justices to consult first with the existing justices in the court to which the appointment is to be made.

[17] In 1991 a district court found a law to be in breach of the (very weak) constitutional right to property (RF 2:18): see below Part II, section 2. This judgment was reversed on appeal. In 1995 there have been two judgments of district courts finding the Political Uniforms Act (1947:164) in breach of the constitutional right to free speech (RF 2:1 p. 1). The judgments have been confirmed by the appeal courts. Proposals to replace the law have been made.

Before leaving the subject of the constitutional background, a few words should be said about the content of the substantive rights. I will not summarise the catalogue of rights as it now appears in Chapter 2. Instead, the full text is set out in an appendix to this chapter. I will, however, make a few brief comparisons between the rights in Chapter 2 and the rights in the European Convention and its protocols, as they have been interpreted in the Convention organs' case law.

First, there is, naturally enough, a great deal of overlap between the two catalogues as regards the rights protected. Where there appear to be differences in formulation, or in the limits to which a right is subject, these differences are usually of little significance, bearing in mind Convention case law. One possible exception is the fact that, while RF 2:6, like Article 8, protects "home and correspondence", there is no corresponding protection of "private and family life". On the other hand, it is also clear that, in a few respects, Chapter 2 probably goes further than the Convention, at least as it at present has been interpreted, *e.g.* RF 2:14 provides for less restrictions on the right of assembly as compared to Article 11; RF 2:10 prohibits (subject to certain exceptions) retroactive tax legislation; and RF 2:11 prohibits the establishment of a court to try an offence already committed or otherwise to consider a specific case. Second, like the Convention, the rights in Chapter 2 are against the State.[18] Again, like the Convention, there are some minor exceptions, *e.g.* the protection of property in RF 2:18 is subject to *allemansrätt,* the right of everyone to cross private land, a right exercisable against individuals and the intellectual property rights protected in RF 2:19 (insofar as a formal requirement for a statute can be said to be protection) are aimed primarily at other individuals. Third, the provisions against racial and sexual discrimination, RF 2:15 and 2:16 respectively, are formulated differently from Article 14 of the Convention. Unlike the latter ("discrimination...such as..."), the former provisions exhaustively specify prohibited criteria for discrimination. Thus, under RF 2:15 discrimination based on nationality is legitimate. On the other hand, RF 2:15 and 2:16 prohibit discrimination in general, in all legislation and subordinate legislation, *i.e.* not simply discrimination in relation to the rights set out in Chapter 2.[19] In addition RF 2:16 expressly permits positive discrimination, although this may also be

---

[18] The term *"de allmänna"* encompasses not only central government, but also local government.

[19] *Cf.* Article 26 of the ICCPR as interpreted by the Human Rights Committee in the cases *Zwaan de Vries, Broeks and Danning* v. *Netherlands,* Communications 172, 180 and 184/84.

permissible under Convention case law. The discrimination provisions, and Chapter 2 in general, must also be seen in the light of RF 1:9. This resembles the Convention safeguards of proportionality and *detournement de pouvoir* but goes further. Fourth, as already mentioned, Chapter 2 is complemented by very detailed, and extensive, provisions relating to freedom of expression and freedom of information. Fifth, the very narrow approach taken to what is a "restriction" of a human right may be contrasted with the more realistic approach taken by the Convention organs which do not accept that restrictions are limited to physical sanctions or measures intended to operate as restrictions.[20] Finally, as already mentioned, Chapter 2 provides for two different systems of protection, for citizens and aliens. This can be contrasted with the standard rule in Article 1 of the Convention ("secure...to everyone") which is subject only to the limited qualification set out in Article 16.[21]

Part II: The Legal Status of the Convention in Swedish Law

1. THE CONVENTION BEFORE 1995

Sweden signed the European Convention on Human Rights (ECHR) on 28 November 1950. On 2 March 1951, a bill for approval of the Convention was submitted to parliament.[22] Under Chapter 12, section 1 of the Instrument of Government of 1809, treaties had to be submitted to parliament for approval if they dealt with matters of major importance or otherwise fell within the competence of parliament (*e.g.* because they required legislation). The bill contained an extremely summary (two page) comparison of the Convention provisions and Swedish law which was followed by the relevant minister's opinion that "a review of the Convention articles shows that...there appears to be no obstacle to Sweden ratifying the Convention".[23]

---

[20] For a recent example, see *Vogt* v. *Germany* Series A, No. 323 (1995) 21 E.H.R.R. 205, on which see above, E. Voss, pp. 174–175.

[21] It should be noted that the Court has interpreted this article very restrictively in *Piermont* v. *France* Series A, No. 314 (1995) 20 E.H.R.R. 301.

[22] Prop. 1951:165.

[23] The "analysis" of Article 6—subsequently to cause major problems for Sweden—amounted to one sentence: "The provisions in Article 6 on legal guarantees are completely covered by the Code of Judicial Procedure" Prop. 1951: 165 at p. 12. See also H. Danelius, "Judicial Control of the Administration—a Swedish Proposal for Legislative Reform" in F. Matscher and H. Petzold (eds.), *Protecting Human Rights: the European Dimension* (Köln, 1988).

The conclusion was, thus, that there was no need for legislation.[24] Sweden ratified the Convention on 4 February 1952. A declaration under Article 25 was made at the same time. By contrast, it was not until 1966 that Sweden recognised the competence of the Court to decide cases under Article 46. The main reason for the delay was the opposition of Östen Undén, foreign secretary during a large part of the period in question, who considered that the settlement of disputes over human rights was a matter of politics rather than of law.

Whereas, as we have seen, the Convention was not drawn upon when drafting the original version of Chapter 2, it did have some significance as a "source of inspiration" to the work of the commission which proposed the amendments to the chapter made in 1976.[25] It is obvious that the formulation of the general material conditions set out in RF 2:12 owes much to the "accommodation clauses" in Articles 8–11. Nonetheless, the Commission rejected the option of incorporating the Convention at the constitutional level, and deliberately refrained from using exactly the same language as the Convention articles. It did this mainly because it found the drafting to be alien to Swedish legal traditions and so likely to cause difficulties in interpretation.[26] Apart from this indirect influence, it is probably fair to say that the Convention was largely ignored by the legislator up until the early 1980s. Nor did the Convention achieve much attention in legal doctrine or in the case law. An exception to this were the so-called "transformation judgments" in the early 1970s.

It is now generally accepted that Sweden is a "dualist" state, but this point was not in fact settled before three cases decided, respectively, by the Labour Court, the Supreme Court and the Supreme Administrative Court in 1972, 1973 and 1974.[27] The first case concerned the Swedish Engine Drivers Union's attempt to force the national railway company to conclude a collective agreement with it. The second case was brought by a member of the

---

[24] The same conclusion was reached regarding the subsequent ratification of additional Protocols 1, 4, 6 and 7. A reservation was, however, made to Article 2 of Protocol 1. It is interesting to note that the same complacent position was taken in 1989 when the UN Convention on the Rights of the Child was ratified. Recently there have been protests that Swedish legislation, or at least its application, is contrary to this Convention.

[25] SOU 1975:75, p. 99, Prop. 1975/76: 209, p. 85.

[26] SOU 1975: 75, p. 98

[27] *AD 5/1972, p. 75, NJA 1973, p. 423* and *RÅ 1974, p. 121*. Swedish cases from the Supreme Court (*Högsta domstolen*) are cited from the semi-official Supreme Court Reports, NJA. The cases from the Labour Court (*Arbetsdomstolen*, AD) are cited from the official series, AD.

same union after a wage settlement had granted train drivers who were members of another union a retroactive wage increase. In both cases the argument was made, *inter alia*, that the measures were in breach of Article 11 of the ECHR. The third case was brought by parents concerned that posters advertising films which were hung in a school hall (used in the evenings by a cinema group) could have a deleterious effect on their children. The argument was made that the refusal of the local school authority to order removal of the posters was in breach of their parental rights relating to their children's education under Article 2, Protocol 2 of the ECHR. In all three cases, the courts stated that before a treaty could create direct rights and duties for individuals in Swedish law it had first to be converted into Swedish law. As parliament had not incorporated[28] or "transformed" the Convention into Swedish law, but had simply stated at the time of ratification that it considered existing Swedish law fully satisfied its requirements, the Convention did not create such direct rights.

Critics have attacked these judgments, arguing that constitutional practice regarding the conversion requirement for treaties was by no means clear or uniform and it did not prove that Sweden was a "dualist" state.[29] It is also interesting to note that, in comparison with the UK, there is no democratic reason why some act of conversion should be required. Under the old Instrument of Government, the Swedish parliament had given its consent to the ratification of the Convention. The new Instrument of Government also retains the requirement of parliamentary approval of treaties which require legislation or the allocation of public funds or are otherwise of significance (RF 10:2). The argument against automatic effect following on ratification—and such an argument has been made in the doctrine, not by the courts—is legal security (foreseeability) *i.e.* that individuals are unable adequately to understand treaties drafted in unfamiliar language and terms. Such an argument is obviously stronger in relation to treaties which impose duties on individuals, rather than rights.[30] The Convention has some *dritt-*

---

[28] On the one hand, the term "incorporation" (in Swedish "*inkorporering*") creates the risk of confusion with the doctrine of "automatic incorporation" of customary international law. On the other hand, the use of the term to signify a legislative act which stipulates that the original text of a treaty should apply as national law now appears to be generally accepted in both Swedish and English doctrine.

[29] One of the main critics has been Sundberg, see *e.g.* "Om mänskliga rättigheter i Sverige" [On Human Rights in Sweden] [1986] *Svensk Juristtidning* 660 and "Folkrätt och folkvett" [International Law and Common Sense] [1988] *Svensk Juristtidning* 401.

[30] The term "legal security" comes closer to the meaning of *rättssäkerhet* than "foreseeability" which is only part of the concept. For a comparative discussion of the po-

wurkung, but not much, so the legal security argument is not very strong. Nonetheless, the issue must now be regarded as settled.[31]

The three cases can also be criticised for their failure to examine properly the requirements of the Convention. The Supreme Court decision in particular was disappointing. It was, and is, incorrect to say that Article 11 of the Convention requires employers to enter into collective agreements with trade unions. But the Supreme Court did not say this. Instead it stated that, if parliament had considered that the Convention demanded this, then it would have amended Swedish law to bring it into line with the Convention. As it did not do so, then the Convention could not require this. Such an approach to the Convention undermined the whole purpose of the principle of interpretation that national law be interpreted in accordance with treaty commitments (*fördragskonform tolkning*) and made it into a formality as it took the position in practice that Swedish law can never be in conflict with the Convention. But it is the European Court of Human Rights which is the final arbiter of what the Convention requires, not the Swedish parliament. In addition this approach ignored one special feature of the Convention, namely that the requirements of the Convention can expand as a result of the dynamic method of interpretation applied by the Convention organs. The judgment of the Supreme Administrative Court in *RÅ 1974 p. 121* can also be criticised for the negative effect it had on the principle that national law be interpreted in accordance with treaty commitments. The court simply stated that administrative agencies were not bound by the Convention. But by failing to clarify this point it implied that administrative agencies were not even obliged to *examine* what the Convention demands in a particular case. Worse, there was the risk that some agencies concluded from the judgments that they were obliged *not* to examine the Convention.[32]

In any event, the Convention was largely ignored in Swedish legal circles during the 1970s. The labour law cases brought before the Court, the *Swedish Engine Drivers* and *Schmidt and Dahlström* cases, were both won by the Swedish government.[33] Another case which could have gone to the Court

---

sition of the Scandinavian states on this point, see S. Jensen, *The ECHR in Scandinavian Law* (Copenhagen, 1992), pp. 177–180. See also the Norwegian report on the issue of incorporation which recommends "sector monism" as regards human rights treaties in general, *Lovgivning om menneskerettigheter* [Legislation on Human Rights] NOU 1993:18.

[31] Although an exception is now obviously made for EC law with direct effect, see below Part II , section 2C.

[32] The judgment was criticised for this reason by, *e.g.*, Professor Hilding Eek, *Juridikens Källmaterial* 8th ed. (Stockholm, 1975), at p. 56.

[33] Series A, Nos. 20 and 21 (1976) 1 E.H.R.R. 617 and 632.

was settled after being declared admissible by the Commission.[34] It was not until the *Sporrong and Lonnröth* case in 1982, in which the Court ruled that Swedish expropriation legislation was in breach of Article 1, Protocol 1 and Article 6, that the ECHR achieved any prominence in political and legal circles in Sweden.[35] Following this case, people dissatisfied with the protection of human rights in general, and the "high tax society" and weak recognition of the right to property in particular, seized upon the Convention as a basis with which to criticise legislation and government policy.[36] A number of attempts were made to challenge before the Convention organs controversial Social Democrat legislation affecting property.[37] There were also a number of attempts by the centre/right political parties to incorporate the Convention. All of the attempts at incorporation failed due to opposition from the Social Democrats.

Notwithstanding the greater attention being devoted to the ECHR in Sweden from 1982 onwards, there is no evidence during the 1980s that Swedish administrative agencies consulted the Convention either when issuing subordinate legislation (*föreskrifter*) or when taking decisions in individual cases.[38] Of course, this was probably more for practical than dogmatic reasons, *i.e.* the Convention organs' case law was neither generally available nor translated into Swedish. It is difficult to criticise this position, as the Ombudsman, whose task it was to oversee agencies' performance of their functions, also took the view that, while it was desirable to try to interpret national law in accordance with the Convention, agencies were not *obliged*

---

[34] *Karnell and Hardt* v. *Sweden*, App. No. 4733/71, 14 *Yearbook of the European Convention on Human Rights* p. 664. The case concerned a religious group which wished to provide religious education for the children of its members, and wanted a corresponding exemption from state religious education classes (Article 2, Protocol 1).

[35] Series A, No. 52 (1982) 5 E.H.R.R. 35.

[36] One should mention, in particular, the important role played by Professor Jacob Sundberg in spreading knowledge of, and interest in, the Convention. On the other hand, Sundberg's use of the Convention to attack Social Democratic ideology is unlikely to have improved the willingness of the Social Democratic establishment to incorporate the Convention.

[37] *E.g.* the taxation legislation on pension funds (*löntagarfonderna*), *Svenska management AB* v. *Sweden*, App. No. 11036/84, 45 D.R. 211 (1985). It should be pointed out here that organised housing and business interests lay behind the *Sporrong-Lönnroth* case. See J. Sundberg (ed.), *Sporrong-Lönnroth, en handbok* (Institute for Offentig och Internationell rätt, Stockholm, 1985).

[38] This requirement, often called the rule of instruction in Scandinavian doctrine, is examined in more detail by Jensen, *op. cit.*, note 30, especially pp. 159–171.

to follow the Convention and so they could not be criticised for failing to take account of it.[39]

On the other hand, during this same decade, the restrictive view the Supreme Court and the Supreme Administrative Court had taken of the value of the Convention slowly changed. It gradually became accepted that it was a source of law from which the Swedish courts could and should draw inspiration. It was clear that the Convention, and the judgments of the Court, were not as such binding on the Swedish courts, but at the same time it was implicitly recognised that it was foolish to be dogmatic about the issue. Milestones in this development were the European Court's judgments which found Sweden to be in breach of the Convention, particularly in the *Sporrong and Lonnröth, McGoff, Ekbatani* and *Pudas* cases.[40] While all these cases required legislative reform, rather than a simple change in judicial interpretative methods, the courts realised (notwithstanding their traditional deference to the legislature) that if they continued to interpret national law totally without reference to the Convention, then there was bound to be a risk that even in other areas Swedish law would be incompatible with the Convention organs' case law. Such cases would, sooner or later, end up in Strasbourg, Sweden would be found in breach of the Convention and it would thus probably be required to amend its laws. It would save everyone involved a good deal of time and expense if the Swedish courts, where this was at all possible, interpreted domestic law so as to be compatible with the Convention in the first place.

Thus, beginning in the early 1980s,[41] the higher courts began referring, first to the Convention, and then also to the Convention organs' case law as a means of interpreting the requirements of Swedish law. The cases involved

---

[39] See Dnr 2477–1990, JO ämbetsberättelse 1991/92 p. 153. The Ombudsman noted, however, that it is part of his function to draw the attention of parliament to discrepancies between the Convention and Swedish law when it is appropriate to do so. It is interesting to note here the very different approach taken on this issue by the Danish Ombudsman who, even before incorporation, actively encouraged administrative agencies to play close attention to the Convention. See N. E. Holm, "The Danish Ombudsman and the ECHR" [1986] *Scandinavian Studies in Law* 75.

[40] See below, Part III. It can also be assumed that Supreme Court Justice Danelius and Supreme Administrative Court Justice Palm, members, respectively, of the Commission (since 1985) and of the Court (since 1988) have influenced these developments.

[41] Even before the *Sporrong and Lönnroth* case there had been a case in which the Convention was invoked, and (at least) not dismissed as totally irrelevant. In *NJA 1981, p. 1205,* the Supreme Court in refusing to annul a clause in a contract providing for obligatory arbitration (and excluding the jurisdiction of the courts) nonetheless considered that Article 6 could be used to interpret the meaning of the Instrument of Government.

a great variety of legal issues. A few examples will suffice to give a picture of this development. In *NJA 1984, p. 903*, the Supreme Court, referring to Article 6, refused to extradite a person to Italy who had been convicted there in absentia. In *NJA 1989, p. 131* the Supreme Court examined whether a restriction on freedom of movement of terrorist suspects (*kommunarrest*) constituted a "deprivation of liberty" within the meaning of Article 5.4. In doing so, it referred extensively to the ECHR decision in *Guzzardi* v. *Italy*.[42] Following the *Ekbatani* case in 1988, the Supreme Court and Supreme Administrative Court allowed appeals based on the fact that a party to a case in a lower court had been refused an oral hearing.[43] The Convention thus came to be used not simply passively, to confirm the reasonableness of a restriction on human rights, but actively, *i.e.* Swedish laws were being interpreted as far as possible to conform to the Convention. The Convention also began to play a role in abstract constitutional review. During the 1980s the Law Council began referring to the Convention organs' case law in assessing the constitutionality of legislative proposals.[44]

Of course, the principle that national law be enacted and interpreted in accordance with treaty commitments can be a real safeguard or a mere formality depending, first, on how much time and effort the Law Council and the courts devote to investigating what the Convention really requires in a given case and second, the status that such a principle is given by the courts compared to other principles of interpretation. As regards the first point, the Law Council, the Supreme Court and the Supreme Administrative Court have occasionally made relatively detailed investigations of the requirements of the Convention. By referring not simply to the Convention but also to the Convention organs' case law, the Law Council has encouraged the legislator to pay attention not only to the letter of the Convention but also to its spirit. However, while some members of the Law Council have knowledge of the Convention case law, others do not. The quality of the scrutiny is, therefore, dependent on which group within the Law Council is assigned the proposal, as well as the amount of time that is at its disposal. Similarly, the extent of knowledge of the Convention varies considerably as regards the judges in the Supreme Court and Supreme Administrative Court. Nonetheless, these courts have in general encouraged the lower courts and ad-

---

[42] Series A No. 39 (1980). The Supreme Court found that *kommunarrest* did not violate the Convention. The Commission came to the same conclusion in *Aygun* v. *Sweden*, App. No. 14102/88, 63 D.R. 195 (1989).

[43] Below Part III, section 1. See also *NJA 1988, p. 572, NJA 1989 p. 131, NJA 1990 p. 636.*

[44] See Algotsson, *op. cit.*, note 10, at pp. 345–9.

ministrative agencies to study not simply the Convention, but the Convention case law as well.

As regards the second point, as already mentioned, the Swedish courts often apply the subjective/historical method of interpretation as well as the objective (textual) and teleological methods. It is still uncertain exactly how the principle of interpretation in accordance with treaty commitments should be weighed against other principles of interpretation. In *NJA 1992, p. 532*, the issue was whether a trial in which one of the chief witnesses for the prosecution was unavailable for cross-examination was "fair" within the meaning of Article 6 of the ECHR. The Supreme Court ruled, with detailed reference to Convention case law, that it was not. Supreme Court Justice Lind noted in a separate opinion that the courts should prefer an interpretation of national law which conforms with the Convention even over contrary views expressed in the legislative history to the statute, in doctrine or even in earlier judgments of the higher Swedish courts. In Justice Lind's opinion, only the textual approach had a higher status: the courts may interpret a national law in a way which conflicts with the requirements of the Convention only when it was totally clear from the wording of the national law that such a result was intended.[45] While this opinion was obiter, it is undoubtedly the case that the Convention, even before its incorporation in Swedish law, was beginning to be taken very seriously by the Swedish courts.

2. THE INCORPORATION OF THE ECHR CONVENTION INTO SWEDISH LAW

A. The Background to the Incorporation of the Convention

In 1991, a government commission, the Committee on Rights and Freedoms (hereafter, the Committee) was appointed to investigate whether additions should be made to the catalogue of rights in RF Chapter 2. The Committee was also asked to consider a number of other questions, namely whether the courts' power of constitutional review in RF 11:14 should be strengthened, whether Sweden should incorporate the Convention and whether a more general right of access to courts for the review of administrative decisions

---

[45] But see below, Part II, section 2B, regarding the variant of this principle suggested by the Supreme Court in its comments on Prop. 1993/94: 117. According to this approach, even the objective principle could give way in case of a conflict.

should be introduced.[46] The Committee reported on these issues in 1993 and 1994.[47]

The Committee recommended incorporation. There were a number of reasons for this. Firstly, while there is no requirement in the Convention that it be incorporated, it is undoubtedly the best way to go about realising the rights protected in the Convention, as it would oblige Swedish courts and administrative agencies to have regard to the Convention without having to rely on their good will in applying the principle that legislation be interpreted to accord with treaty commitments. Secondly, incorporation would hopefully mean less issues going to Strasbourg (and less defeats there). Thirdly, Finland and Denmark had already incorporated the Convention and Norway and Iceland were likely to do so. Incorporation would thus bring Sweden into line with the practices of the other Nordic countries. Fourthly, and probably most importantly, there was the EU aspect: The Convention is part of the general principles of EC law.[48] Sweden was, in 1993, part of the European Economic Area and was thus obliged to apply EC law, albeit indirectly. Sweden was also contemplating membership of the EU. Incorporation of the Convention would avoid the awkward and inconsistent situation where Swedish courts and administrative agencies were obliged to have regard to the Convention when applying EC law, or national law connected to EC law, but not when applying "pure" national law.[49] Finally, it was felt that incorporation would also, hopefully, have a general pedagogical effect on Swedish political, social and legal thinking and Swedish administration, fostering a respect for individual rights.[50]

In Sweden, the main argument against incorporation has usually (although not always) come from the Social Democratic Party. The Social Democrats have feared, not without reason, that such a reform would involve a shift of power to the courts at the expense of the executive and of the democratically elected legislature. The question of incorporation was thus intimately connected with the question of the scope of the power of

---

[46] Kommittédirektiv 1991:119. Utvigad skydd för grundläggande fri och rättigheter samt ökade möjligheter till domstolsprövning av normbeslut och förvaltningsbeslut.

[47] Fri- och Rättighetsfrågor, inkorporering av Europakonvention, [Issues concerning rights and freedoms, incorporation of the European Convention] SOU 1993:40 del B. The Committee reported on the issue of administrative appeals in Domstolsprövning av förvaltningsärenden [Judicial review of administrative matters], SOU 1994:117.

[48] See I. Persaud, below, ch. 9.

[49] The awkward problem of constitutional review in relation to conflicts between EC law and other national law is examined below, Part II, section 2C.

[50] See below, the conclusion to this chapter.

constitutional review. Put bluntly, the issue was which of the three organs of government was to have the final say as regards the scope of human rights, in particular the scope of the right to property.

The delicacy of this issue can be illustrated by a district court case from 1991 concerning the introduction in 1985 of the statutory right to fish in coastal waters with hand held tackle.[51] The court held that this law constituted an expropriation of the owner's exclusive fishing rights. By failing to provide for compensation for loss of future earnings it was manifestly in breach of the protection against expropriation without compensation (RF 2:18). The court accordingly refused to apply the law but instead ruled that compensation was payable under the Expropriation Act (1972:719). In reaching this judgment the court referred to the Convention, although it did not base its reasoning on it.[52] This was sensible as the Commission had in fact ruled in 1989 that the introduction of free fishing was not an expropriation, nor a denial of the free enjoyment of possessions, but a "control on use" which fell within the state's margin of appreciation.[53] The Swedish district court decision was reversed on appeal. Later, the Supreme Court in a similar case went out of its way to disapprove of the reasoning of the district court, stating that the law on the introduction of the right of free fishing was not in breach of RF 2:18, or at least, not manifestly in breach of it.[54]

B. The Legal Status of the Convention today

It came as no real surprise that the Committee on Rights and Freedoms reached a political compromise whereby the Convention was to be incorporated, but the existing limits on the power of constitutional review were to be maintained. Moreover, the Committee was careful to stress that the primary responsibility for ensuring that Swedish law continued to be in conformity with the changing requirements of the Convention lay on the legislature, not on the courts.[55] There was also agreement among all the political parties that the Convention should not be given constitutional status, but instead should be incorporated in an ordinary law. The supposed reason for this was to avoid the risk of confusion which might be caused by two paral-

---

[51] Act on compensation for interference with fishing rights (1985:139).

[52] Linköpings tingrätt, Dom nr DF 33, 1991–11–13 (handredskapsfiske målet).

[53] Banér v. Sweden, App. No. 11763/85, 60 D.R. 128 (1989).

[54] See NJA 1992, p. 337.

[55] SOU 1993: 40, del B p. 126. This was also stressed in identical terms in the bill (Prop. 1993/94: 117 p. 36) and the report of the Committee on the Constitution (1993/94 KU 24, p. 17.

lel catalogues of rights having the same constitutional status.[56] After a short debate, this law was enacted on 5 May 1994 and entered into force on 1 January 1995.[57] The Act provides that the Convention and Protocols One to Eight shall, in their authentic texts (*i.e.* English and French) apply as Swedish law. A new Swedish translation was made of the Convention because of certain problems with the old text. This was also appended to the Act, but it does not formally speaking have the status of law, although in practice this will be the text which is used by Swedish courts and administrative agencies.

While there was little debate on the desirability of the law, the legislator recognised that there was a difficulty involved in only giving the Convention the status of an ordinary law. The problem would inevitably arise of it coming into conflict with other laws, passed either before or after 1995. How should such a conflict be handled when both norms would have the same status? The principle that laws should be interpreted in accordance with treaty obligations, recognised by the Supreme Court and the Supreme Administrative Court, would provide some protection. Similarly, the *lex posterior* rule of interpretation would give the Convention[58] precedence where it conflicted with any earlier law. On the other hand, this principle also meant that the courts would be expected to give precedence to a later law in a case in which a conflict arose between this law and the Convention. While it was true that the legislative process, and in particular the scrutiny of bills by the Law Council, would be able to identify in advance provisions in bills which were likely to be in breach of the Convention (so preventing conflicts before they arose), it was also clear that the scope of the Convention was so wide that some conflicting provisions were bound to get through. A similar problem would arise in relation to the *lex specialis* rule of interpretation: as the Convention rights were expressed in such general terms, other statutory provisions were very likely to appear to be *lex specialis* in comparison.

---

[56] SOU 1993: 40 del B p. 127. The somewhat contradictory point was also made that application of the *lex posterior* principle would mean that the Convention was to be preferred to RF Chapter 2 in the case of a conflict.

[57] Lag (1994:1219) om den europeiska konventionen angående skydd för de mänskliga rättigheterna och de grundläggande friheterna [Act on the European Convention on Human Rights], since amended by SFS 1995:462, incorporating Protocol 9.

[58] Of course, constitutionally speaking, the conflict would be between the law which incorporates the Convention and another Swedish law, not between the Convention as such and a Swedish law. For the sake of simplicity, however, I will refer simply to the "Convention". There was no discussion in the *travaux préparatoires* of the principle *lex posterior generalis non derogat lege priori speciali*, although see below, note 59.

The solution that was reached was that a new provision, RF 2:23, should be added to the constitution. This provision also entered into force on 1 January 1995. It provides that "a law or other regulation may not be issued in conflict with [the Convention]". This provision does not, as such, give the Convention constitutional status. Nor does it create a new category of laws midway between the constitution and ordinary laws. Instead, it means that a law or other regulation which conflicts with the Convention, also conflicts with the constitution. In this respect RF 2:23 resembles the anti-discrimination provisions in RF 2:15 and 2:16. As with all such conflicts, the normal rule on constitutional review in RF 11:14 therefore applies. In other words, the courts, and administrative agencies, should refuse to apply a regulation which conflicts with the Convention, although if this regulation is in the form of a law or an ordinance, then the conflict with the Convention must be "manifest". Laws or ordinances which conflict with the Convention but do not manifestly conflict it should thus be applied. This also means that, despite the fact that the Convention has the status of law, and thus is constitutionally superior to an ordinance, an ordinance which conflicts with it can be preferred as long as the conflict between it and the Convention is not manifest. This will usually be the case where the ordinance is very specific and the requirements of the Convention are vague.[59]

The legislature saw the rule in RF 2:23 as a last resort. It was stated repeatedly in the legislative history that the courts should make every effort to apply the other principles of legal interpretation so as to avoid conflicts with other national laws. In this respect, the legislature drew special attention to the principle that national laws should be interpreted in accordance with treaty commitments, and even to a new variant of it proposed by the Supreme Court in its comments on the legislative bill. The Supreme Court stated that treaties on human rights were not simply ordinary treaties[60] and such treaties, because of their special character, should be given particular weight should a conflict arise between them and national laws. The exact

---

[59] The *travaux préparatoires* to RF 11:14 indicate that, in general, the more vaguely the superior rule is formulated, the less likely the conflict with an inferior rule will be seen to be manifest. See SOU 1978:34, p. 109.

[60] The Supreme Court was presumably referring here to the established jurisprudence of the European Court that the Convention involves more than simply reciprocal rights and duties between the contracting states, but creates a form of common European public order for the benefit of individuals. See, *e.g.*, *Ireland* v. *United Kingdom* Series A, No. 25 (1978) 2 E.H.R.R. 25, at para. 239. See also the Advisory Opinion of the International Court of Justice regarding the *Reservations to the Genocide Convention*, ICJ Rep. 1951, at p. 16.

scope of this new principle was not made clear. It could be taken to mean that the judge should be prepared to diverge even from the objective principle of interpretation and strain the wording of a law so as to find it in conformity with, *inter alia*, the Convention.

In any event, it is clear from the *travaux préparatoires* that one of the overriding concerns of the legislator was to maintain, as far as possible, the existing balance of power between the courts and parliament and the executive. It was made plain that the primary responsibility for ensuring that Swedish law is in continuing compliance with the Convention lies with the legislature. The courts were explicitly discouraged from going so far as to refuse to apply other legislation on the basis of the Convention. It is interesting to note here how the Danish legislature, in the *travaux préparatoires* to the Danish incorporation statute, goes out of its way to make the same point.[61] The Norwegian legislature is less negative, reflecting the more liberal approach to constitutional review in that country, although caution is still advocated, especially regarding review on the basis of Articles 8–11. Obviously, opinions can vary as to whether a restriction is "necessary in a democratic society" and the Norwegian *travaux préparatoires* stress that the courts should not be over eager to set themselves above the legislature when it comes to judging the issue.[62] In any event, it is fair to say that, notwithstanding the different traditions of constitutional review in the Scandinavian states, the Scandinavian parliaments, naturally enough, are not interested in giving the courts any more power.

To return now to the particular solution adopted in Sweden, the complicated sequence of interpretative operations to be performed by a court faced with a possible conflict between the Convention and another Swedish law can be represented by the diagram which follows. This diagram, I should

---

[61] The original Danish report stated that the Danish courts should apply a (rebuttable) presumption that Danish legislation was in accordance with the Convention, and, in civil cases at any rate, should normally not, *proprio motu*, take up the issue of compatibility with the Convention (*Den europaeiske Menneskerettighedskonvention og dansk ret* (bet. nr. 1220, Copenhagen, 1991), pp. 149–50). The subsequent *travaux préparatoires* accepted a slightly more active role for the courts, admitting the possibility of constitutional review on the basis of newer judgments from the European Court which the legislature had obviously not had access to when legislating (FT 1991–2, tillaegg A sp. 5467–5469). See further T. Jensen, "Domstolskontrollen med overholdelse af grundrettigheder" [Constitutional review on the basis of human rights] *Ugeskrift for Retsvaesen* (1995), p. 241.

[62] NOU 1993: 18 (*op. cit.*, note 30), at pp. 85–6.

stress, is my own attempt to simplify and explain how the instructions set out in the *travaux préparatoires* should be applied. It has no official status.

Solving conflicts between the Convention and other Swedish laws and ordinances

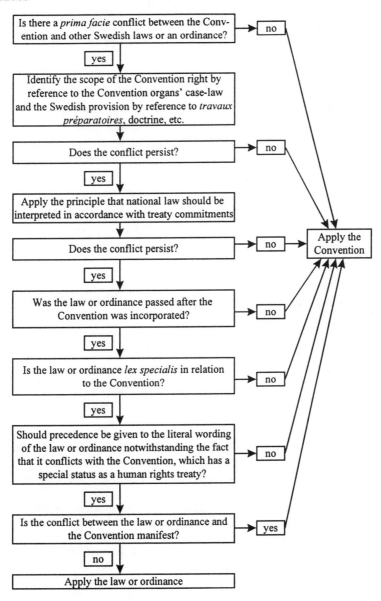

There is still a great deal of uncertainty surrounding this ingenious political compromise. It is, however, clear that little confidence can be given to the view expressed by the Committee on Rights and Freedoms that there are no existing Swedish laws which conflict with the Convention.[63] The Committee only carried out a superficial examination of Swedish law on this point (and indeed, on most of the other points it was asked to look at).[64] It is true that the rights in the Convention are of a minimum nature and that in some respects the present constitutional rights enjoyed in Sweden exceed this minimum level. It is also true that Convention case law can be difficult to interpret and apply. Nonetheless, as the Committee was well aware, the teleological interpretative method applied by the European Court mean that conflicts which it has not foreseen will undoubtedly arise. I do not think that it is realistic to expect that even the majority of such conflicts can be solved by the legislature or by the government issuing new laws or ordinances. Of course, conflicts which would entail major policy discussions and extensive law reform are, and should remain, the responsibility of the legislature. But, whether they like it or not, the Swedish courts will probably be asked by the parties in disputes to use RF 2:23 to resolve minor, but still inescapable, conflicts between the Convention and other Swedish laws and ordinances. Notwithstanding the principle *jura novit curia* ("the court knows the law"), which is applied in much Swedish procedural law, it will in practice be up to the lawyers in the case to bring such possible conflicts to the attention of the courts.

Much will depend on how the courts view the "manifest" requirement in the final stage of the review process. Logically, a provision which cannot be reconciled with the requirements of the Convention by the use of the interpretative methods set out above must be "manifestly" in conflict with them. On the other hand, it will invariably be the Convention case law which a

---

[63] SOU 1993:40, del B, p. 126. Though to be fair, the Committee expressed some doubts concerning the lack of a general right to an oral hearing before the courts (at p. 56) and the limited possibilities for obtaining damages from the state when a breach of the Convention is committed (at p. 78).

[64] *Ibid.* pp. 25–109. The report was a singularly poor piece of work. The level of independent analysis can be shown by the fact that, after publication, the Ministry of Justice attached a correction sheet apologising for the fact that sections of the report had been copied, without attribution, from the standard Swedish introductory textbook on human rights, H. Danelius, *Mänskliga rättigheter,* 5th ed. (Stockholm, 1989). In fairness to the secretary to the committee, who was responsible for writing the report, it should be said that he was probably given the political compromise and told to produce legal argumentation in support of it.

Swedish provision cannot be reconciled with, not the wording of the Convention itself. The legal status of this case law in the national legal order has not been subject to any official examination. The act of incorporation does not, formally speaking, give the European Court of Human Rights pre-eminence in the domestic judicial hierarchy. On the other hand, there is, in any event, no doctrine of *stare decisis* in Swedish procedural law. The lower Swedish courts follow the judgments of the higher courts not because they are bound to do so, but because they either find the legal reasoning in them convincing or because they accept that reasons of procedural economy in practice oblige them to follow them (*i.e.* if they do not, the case will be appealed and the finding reversed). The Swedish courts have, thus, found no great difficulty in the past in drawing directly upon judgments of the European Court of Human Rights as a source of law.[65] Nonetheless, as far as constitutional review in the future is concerned, an important practical and legal distinction should be drawn between cases before the European Court concerning Sweden and cases concerning other states. Under Article 53, only the respondent state is bound by a judgment of the Court. Nonetheless, many cases concerning other states obviously have had major implications for Sweden and Swedish legislation (*e.g.* the *Benthem* case, on which see below Part III). A faithful attempt to follow the spirit of the Convention means that the Swedish courts should look at cases dealing with foreign law and should "translate" both the facts of the case and the legal ruling of the European Court to the corresponding Swedish legal conditions.[66] They have, of course, done this before. But it is one thing to employ a foreign case to interpret Swedish law, when there is an opening to do so. It is another thing to use such a case in order to refuse to apply a Swedish law. So far (up to September 1996, the proof stage of the book) the question of constitutional review on the basis of the Convention has arisen only once. Rather surprisingly in

---

[65] Support for this in the future can also be drawn from the fact that the *travaux préparatoires* (SOU 1993:40) stress that Swedish courts should look at the Strasbourg case law. This position can be contrasted with the curious wording of the Icelandic act of incorporation which expressly states that decisions of the Commission, Committee of Ministers and Court are not binding in domestic law. The purpose of this provision is, however, apparently not to deny these decisions their status as a source of law, but to exclude a decision on just satisfaction under Article 50 being exigible in Iceland.

[66] This task is often made more difficult by the fact that the European Court is usually very careful to stick closely to the facts of the case in question which diminishes the *erga omnes* effect of its judgments. For a discussion of this and other related points, see I. Cameron, "Protocol 11 to the ECHR: the European Court of Human Rights as a Constitutional Court" (1995) 15 *Yearbook of European Law* (forthcoming).

view of the traditional reluctance of Swedish courts to engage in constitutional review, an administrative court of appeal found invalid on the basis of Article 6 an ordinance (1994:1715) which provided for no right of appeal to a court from an administrative decision to pay or not pay an agricultural subsidy (Jönköping KR, decision in case 2442-1996, unreported). The ordinance post-dated the law on incorporation. The court also found—controversially and in direct conflict with an earlier decision of the Supreme Administrative Court—that the administrative courts were competent to hear the appeal. In doing so they also had to set aside, or rather, rewrite, a provision in the Administrative Courts Act (1971:289). The court was undoubtedly influenced by the unsatisfactory situation caused by an earlier conflict between the Supreme Court and the Supreme Administrative Court (dealt with below) as well as the influence of EC law on the subject, in particular the principle of access to judicial remedies. It remains to be seen whether the reasoning of the court—which is undoubtedly the best solution to the issue—will be adopted by other courts.

C.   Constitutional review, the Convention and Swedish membership of the EU

The final issue which should be dealt with in this part of the chapter is the question of the relationship between Swedish law on the one hand and the Convention as a part of EC law on the other. As already mentioned, the incorporation of the Convention was intimately connected with the question of possible EU membership. After the referendum approving Swedish membership in November 1994, the *riksdag* definitively approved a legislative proposal to amend RF 10:5, the provision which allows the transfer of legislative power to the EU. As is well known, the ECJ has taken the view that EC law has precedence even over the provisions of national constitutions which protect human rights. This has been accepted by the member states, but only on the condition that EC law provides an equivalent protection for national systems of human rights. The Swedish riksdag therefore decided to follow the German example and write in such a condition to its membership of the EU.[67] This is intended as a political signal to the EU, and the ECJ in particular, to develop and maintain a high degree of protection of human rights in EC law. The implication is that so long as such a high degree of

---

[67]   On the general point about the EU and human rights, see Persaud, below, Chapter 9. As far as the Swedish law discussed in the text is concerned, the relevant part of RF 10:5 reads "Parliament can transfer legislative power to the EC as long as these have a system of protection for human rights and freedoms equivalent to that which exists in the Instrument of Government and the European Convention".

protection exists, the Swedish courts will not question the validity of EC law on the basis that it conflicts with the human rights set out in RF Chapter 2 or (more likely) the Freedom of the Press and Freedom of Expression Acts.

I turn now to the other side of the coin, namely the possibility, indeed the obligation, EU membership gives the Swedish courts to question the validity of national law insofar as it is considered to be in conflict with EC law. The important point to note here is that the restrictions in RF 11:14 do not apply in such a case. Thus, where a Swedish law or ordinance is found to conflict with the provisions of the EC constitutive treaties, or a regulation or decision or directive with direct effect, the Swedish courts do not have to ask themselves the further question whether it conflicts manifestly with EC law, but rather, having established that the conflict exists, they are required to give precedence to EC law.

What about the position where a decision or directive does not have direct effect, and has not been implemented? In such cases, the Swedish courts must interpret and apply relevant national law in the light of the unimplemented decision or directive, which in turn must be applied in accordance with the general principles of EC law, including the Convention. The same applies to directives and decisions which have been implemented into the Swedish legal system and so have become ordinary "national" laws. Finally, the Swedish courts are also obliged to have regard to the general principles of EC law, including the Convention, when applying *national* laws or ordinances which otherwise *fall within the scope of EC law*, i.e., which constitute exceptions to rights which individuals have under EC law, e.g. to freedom of movement.[68] All these cases can be seen as applications of a special, and particularly powerful, variant of the principle that national law should be interpreted in accordance with treaty commitments. The point is that where the wording of such a national law or ordinance in fact makes it impossible to give it an interpretation which complies with EC law, then it is in violation of EC law and so should not be applied. The restriction in RF 11:14 would not apply in such a case either. Thus, the conclusion is that it is only in conflicts between "pure" national law and the Convention that the restriction in RF 11:14 would apply. Conflicts between Swedish law and human rights as a part of the general principles of EC law are likely to be rare. Nonetheless they are by no means impossible, especially in the area of availability of judicial remedies to challenge administrative decisions.[69] If

---

[68] See *SPUC* v. *Grogan* Case C–159/90, (1991) E.C.R. I–4722.

[69] See below, Part III, section 1. See further regarding this requirement of community law, E. García de Enterría, "The Extension of the Jurisdiction of National Administrative Courts

such conflicts do occur, the Swedish courts will be faced with applying two different systems of constitutional review.

Part III: The Impact in Sweden of the Case-Law of the European Court of Human Rights

1.   THE IMPACT OF THE CASES BEFORE THE EUROPEAN COURT

The most common complaints against Sweden can be divided into five broad areas: judicial review of administrative decisions; violations of property rights; taking of children into care; procedural safeguards in civil and criminal trials; and matters concerning aliens. At the time of writing, the Court has dealt with 31 cases against Sweden. In 21 of these Sweden has been found in violation of one or other provision of the Convention. There have been a number of negative judgments from the Court which have led to important changes in Swedish law. The most significant change has probably been regarding the question of access of an individual to a court to determine a dispute he or she has with the administration. At the time they ratified the Convention, many states, Sweden included, made the mistake of assuming that "civil rights and obligations" in Article 6.1 of the ECHR referred to the sphere of *private law, i.e.* to rights and obligations which individuals have vis à vis other individuals.[70] As the ordinary courts have jurisdiction over such disputes, the requirement that disputes over such rights or obligations be settled by tribunals which are "independent" (of the parties and the executive), "impartial" and whose proceedings are "fair" was not regarded as a problem. The situation in Sweden was, and is, different for disputes which individuals have concerning their *public law* rights and obligations (*i.e.* rights or duties which they have vis à vis the state or local government). In Sweden, as in the majority of Convention states, many legal disputes between the state/local government and individuals (apart from those concerning *criminal law*) are not settled in the ordinary courts. Unlike a number of other Convention states, however, Sweden in 1950 did not have a complete parallel system of administrative courts. Instead, the majority of disputes an individual had with an administrative agency, even those of a predominantly legal character, were settled by a superior administrative

---

by Community Law: the Judgment of the Court of Justice in *Borelli* and Article 5 of the EC Treaty" (1993) 13 *Yearbook of European Law* 19 and Andersson, *infra* note 105.

[70]   Prop. 1951:165. See Prop. 1990/91:176, p. 3.

agency. The final appeal was often to the government itself.[71] Between the 1950s and the 1970s the system of administrative courts was expanded greatly. Nonetheless, there was still no general right for an individual to bring an administrative dispute before a court. The jurisdiction of the administrative courts was limited to specific areas.

The problem for Sweden was that the European Court at an early stage stated that Article 6.1 was applicable to all proceedings "the outcome of which is decisive for private rights and obligations".[72] The Court stated that "civil rights and obligations" was an autonomous concept. The application of the Article could not be allowed to depend on whether the national legal system classified the right in question as "public" or as "private". It was on the cards that the Swedish system of appeals to the government would, insofar as these concerned "civil rights or obligations", be in violation of Article 6. Sure enough, the Court in *Sporrong and Lönnroth* found a violation of Article 6, as well as of Article 1 of Protocol 1.[73] Nonetheless, the Swedish government of the day was obviously reluctant to extend further the scope of judicial review of administrative action. It chose to take a minimalist approach to the judgment and no steps were taken to correct the situation regarding access to a court.[74] Sweden paid the penalty for its legislative inac-

---

[71] The Swedish system of executive control over the administration is the direct opposite of a system of ministerial responsibility. While the government exercises strong control over administrative agencies in a variety of different ways (in particular through budgetary means and the issuing of general ordinances), it is constitutionally prohibited from issuing directives to agencies on how to interpret or apply the law in individual cases (RF 11:7). On the other hand, the government can still, ultimately, decide individual cases where it is the final instance of appeal. The prohibition on government involvement in individual cases was part of the background to the *Cruz Varas* decision, Series A, No. 201 (1989) 14 E.H.R.R. 1, in which a Chilean asylum seeker had been deported back to Chile notwithstanding a request from the Commission under Rule 36 of its Rules of Procedure to stay execution of the deportation.

[72] *Ringeisen* v. *Austria* Series A, No.13 (1971) 1 E.H.R.R. 455. See also *Golder* v. *UK* Series A, No. 18 (1975) 1 E.H.R.R 524 in which the Court stated that Article 6.1 implied a *right of access to a tribunal* to determine one's civil rights and obligations

[73] The remedy of "reopening" (*resning*) before the Supreme Administrative Court or Supreme Court was found to be of an extraordinary nature, and thus not sufficient to satisfy the requirements of Article 6. This has been criticised by certain Swedish commentators who consider that the conditions to be satisfied before the courts will reopen a case are not so onerous in practice.

[74] If any further confirmation was needed of the inadequacy of Swedish law in this respect, it came with *Benthem* v. *Netherlands* Series A, No.97 (1985) 8 E.H.R.R. 1, on which see below Klerk and de Jonge, pp. 131–132. See further J. Sundberg (ed.), *Laws, Rights and the European Convention on Human Rights* (Colorado, 1986), pp. 85–98.

tion when it lost, in quick succession, a number of cases on the issue in Strasbourg beginning in 1987. One of these cases in particular, *Pudas*, resulted in a great deal of publicity in Sweden regarding the Convention.[75]

Legislation was eventually introduced in 1988 which provided for a right of judicial review of certain administrative cases decided by an administrative agency or by the government as a final instance of appeal. The law was initially passed for a trial period until 1991. It has since been made permanent.[76] The law does not give a general right of access to a court. It applies only to cases in which there is no other available judicial remedy and in which the administrative decision imposes a burden on an individual. The intention behind the legislation was to cover the category of "civil rights and obligations" but this term was not used because it was considered that its unfamiliarity could cause Swedish lawyers difficulties. Instead, the law refers to the areas of public activity covered by RF 8:2 and 8:3. These provide that delegation of legislative power in certain areas—particularly those involving burdens for the individual—should be approved by statute. This has the consequence that, *e.g.* decisions to refuse permission to engage in a particular business activity are subject to review whereas decisions to withhold a benefit, *e.g.* a social security payment or admission to a higher educational course, are not. It has been pointed out that the exclusion of decisions involving benefits from review is not without its difficulties, particularly in view of the *Deumeland* and *Feldbrugge* cases.[77] In addition to this general restriction, decisions by certain quasi-judicial tribunals and decisions con-

---

[75] Pudas had had his driving licence taken away by a County Administrative Board without being able to challenge this before a court. Pudas' father went on hunger strike outside the parliament in protest against this. Other cases concerning different areas but raising the same issue were *Bodén* v. *Sweden* Series A, No. 125 (1987) 10 E.H.R.R. 367; *Tre Traktörer AB* v. *Sweden* Series A, No. 159 (1989) 13 E.H.R.R. 309; *Allan Jacobsson* v. *Sweden* Series A, No. 163 (1989) 12 E.H.R.R. 56; *Mats Jacobsson* v. *Sweden* Series A, No. 180A (1990) 13 E.H.R.R. 79; *Skärby* v. *Sweden* Series A, No. 180B (1990) 13 E.H.R.R 90; *Zander* v. *Sweden* Series A, No. 279-B (1993) 18 E.H.R.R. 175.

[76] Lag (1988:205) om rättsprövning av vissa förvaltningsbeslut. Re-enacted and amended by SFS 1991:342 and SFS 1994:719. Werling-Nerep, "Rättsprövning av förvaltningsbeslut" [1991] *Förvaltningsrättslig tidskrift* p.129 and "Rättsprövningslagen—utgör den ett lyckat försök att anpassa Svensk rätt till Europakonventionen Art 6(1)?" in E. Nerep and W. Werling-Nerep (eds.), *Festschrift till Jacob Sundberg* (Stockholm, 1994) (hereafter Werling-Nerep, 1994). The Act was made permanent by SFS 1996:420.

[77] *Duemeland* v. *Germany* Series A, No. 100 (1986) 8 E.H.R.R. 448; *Feldbrugge* v. *Netherlands* Series A, No. 99 (1986) 8 E.H.R.R. 425. See further Werling-Nerep, 1994, *op. cit.*, note 76, p. 134 and the recent dispute between the Supreme Court and the Supreme Administrative Court discussed below in Part III, section 2.

cerning matters regarded as predominantly of a policy nature are excluded from review, notwithstanding the direct impact that these could have in the area of "civil rights and obligations".[78] Originally, all applications for review were directed to the Supreme Administrative Court. Due to the burden of work this resulted in, the law was recently amended to provide that the appeals from administrative agencies should be directed to the local administrative court of appeal, with the Supreme Administrative Court retaining the function of reviewing cases decided by the government. The procedure is largely written, although another amendment which has been made from the original system is to provide for oral hearings, where a party requests this and it is not manifestly unnecessary.[79] The scope of the review—something of a novelty for Swedish law—has some similarities with the English system of judicial review. It is not limited to simply checking the strict legality of the decision but can, depending on the nature of the decision being reviewed, extend to such matters as whether the agency has evaluated facts properly and even how appropriate the decision is. Issues of "purely political discretion" are nonetheless excluded from the court's jurisdiction.[80] The review has a cassation effect: a successful application is remitted back to the agency in question for a new decision. Reactions to the new power of review have, in general, been positive. Although a number of cases dealt with have been of a trivial character, in other cases the Supreme Administrative Court has looked at both the legality and the appropriateness of decisions of significance for the individual. A number of decisions have been overruled. [81] The existence of this review mechanism will, hopefully, strengthen awareness of the importance of the principles of legality in administrative decision making.[82]

---

[78] It is not by any means clear that all of these tribunals would satisfy the requirements of Article 6. Certainly, not all of them are regarded as "courts" in Swedish constitutional law: see Werling-Nerep 1994, *op. cit.*, note 76, p. 135.

[79] See Prop. 1995/96: 133. It is stated there that the situations in which an oral hearing is "manifestly unnecessary" should be determined by reference to the Convention organs' case law. The lack of an oral hearing in this procedure was the reason for a finding of a violation in *Fredin* v. *Sweden (no. 2)* Series A, No. 283-A (1994).

[80] For a general analysis of this problem, see L. Marcusson, "Laglighets- och lämplighetsprövning—en titt i bakspegeln och framåt" [Review of legality and discretion] [1992] *Förvaltningsrättslig Tidskrift* 121.

[81] See Prop. 1990/91: 176, p. 4–5. For an example see *RÅ 1990 ref. 59*.

[82] The question of a general right of access to judicial review—recommended by a commission of inquiry appointed under the centre/right government of 1991–94 (see above, note 47) is still a live issue (see below Part III, section 2). This is another area of Swedish law

While the majority of cases concerning Sweden have concerned the lack of access to a court to determine civil rights and obligations, a number of other issues have also arisen. I will here only deal with the most important of these.[83] The *McGoff* case concerned the length of the period a person suspected of a crime could be detained on the orders of a prosecutor before being brought before a court competent to order release or continued detention. The period in question—15 days—was, predictably enough, found to be in violation of Article 5.4. As a result of the judgment, amendments were made providing for a maximum period of four days.[84]

The *Ekbatani* case concerned the lack of an oral hearing in proceedings before a criminal court of appeal.[85] The Court ruled that, because the court of appeal had refused Ekbatani an oral hearing and because this testimony concerned matters central to the case itself (*i.e.* Ekbatani's guilt or innocence), he had not received a "public hearing".[86] Amendments were subsequently made to the Code of Judicial Procedure requiring appeal courts in criminal cases to hold oral hearings on the request of a party unless this is manifestly unnecessary.[87]

---

in which the influence of EC membership will probably be felt.

[83] In addition to the legislative changes noted in the text, amendments have also been made to the Expropriation Act as a result of the *Sporrong-Lönnroth* case (SFS 1988: 206) and to the Acquisition of Land Act as a result of the *Håkansson and Sturesson* case (SFS 1991: 669). For highly critical surveys of the developments concerning the Convention and Swedish law in general in the 1980s, see J. Sundberg, *Human Rights in Sweden, the Annual Reports 1982–84* (Institute för Offentlig och Internationell rätt, Stockholm, 1985); *Human Rights in Sweden, the Annual Reports 1985, 1986, 1987, 1988* (Colorado, 1987, 1988, 1989, 1991).

[84] Code of Judicial Procedure (*Rättegångsbalken*, RB) 24:12. For the background to the *McGoff* and *Skoogström* cases—the latter being resolved by a friendly settlement—see J. Sundberg, *Om rätt, rättskällor och rättstillämpning. Ett textpaket* (Stockholm, 1991), pp. 4–13.

[85] Series A, No.160 (1988).

[86] The requirements of the Convention in this respect were further clarified in the subsequent cases of *Helmers* v. *Sweden* Series A, No. 212-A (1991) 15 E.H.R.R. 285; *Fejde* v. *Sweden* Series A, No. 212-B (1991) 17 E.H.R.R. 14; *Jan Åke Andersson* v. *Sweden* Series A, No. 212-C (1991) 15 E.H.R.R. 218.

[87] See now RB 51:13. The question of oral hearings has arisen subsequently in a number of other cases before the Swedish courts (below Part III, section 2) This is because, traditionally, appeal court proceedings were, notwithstanding the fact that these normally involved a new trial rather than simply an appeal on a point of law, largely written in nature. Unless there were reasons for doing so, new oral hearings with witnesses and the parties were not normally held.

A number of cases have concerned the right to family life under Article 8. To date, the question of custody over children has resulted in five cases before the Court and four findings of violations.[88] The breaches found have, however, mainly concerned the manner of implementation of Swedish legislation, rather than the laws as such and only one legislative reform has been made as a result of these cases (on access to a court to review a decision by the social authorities, made after taking a child into care, to restrict a parent's access to the child).

The well-known *Leander* case concerned files held by the security police.[89] The applicant had been denied employment in the public service as a result of secret information held on him (*personalkontroll*).[90] He wished to have access to this information. The Court found, by a majority, that there had been no violation of either Article 8 or Article 13. The judges in the minority argued that there was a violation of Article 13 because there was no mechanism or institution capable, in practice, of periodically or on specific complaint, checking the accuracy and appropriateness of the information stored in the secret files. Although no violation of the Convention was found, the criticism expressed by the minority of the Court was one of the reasons why *personalkontroll* has been the subject of a number of later official investigations. Some reforms have been made to the system, although the criticism made by the judges in the minority still holds true today.

The *Langborger* case was a typically Swedish example of the rights of collectives being given precedence over the rights of individuals. The applicant in this case complained about the composition of the Housing Court (*bostadsdomstolen*) because representatives for the landlords' and the tenants' associations sat as judges. Normally these representatives would "cancel each other out" but Langborger was in dispute with both these associations and the Court agreed with him that in the circumstances he had not received a trial by an "impartial tribunal".[91] Amendments have subsequently

---

[88] *Olsson* v. *Sweden* Series A, No. 130 (1988) 11 E.H.R.R. 259; *Eriksson* v. *Sweden* Series A, No. 156 (1989) 12 E.H.R.R. 183; *Margareta and Roger Andersson* v. *Sweden* Series A, No. 226 (1992) 14 E.H.R.R. 615; *Rieme* v. *Sweden* Series A, No. 226-B (1992) 16 E.H.R.R. 155; *Olsson* v. *Sweden (no. 2)* Series A, No. 250 (1992) 17 E.H.R.R. 150. The long-drawn out struggle of the Olsson family to regain custody of their children was concluded by the Supreme Court in *NJA 1993 p. 666* which confirmed that custody should remain with the foster parents.

[89] Series A, No. 116 (1987) 9 E.H.R.R. 433.

[90] See generally, D. Töllborg, *Personalkontroll* (Stockholm/Lund, 1986).

[91] *Langborger* v. *Sweden* Series A, No.155 (1989) 12 E.H.R.R 416.

been made to the composition of the Court where a party's interests are in conflict with both the landlords' and tenants' associations.[92]

The Court also found a violation of the right to trial by an impartial tribunal in the *Holm* case.[93] The applicant had sued for defamation the author of a book published by a company owned by the Social Democratic Party (SDP). It being a case under the Freedom of the Press Act it was tried by a jury. Jury members are chosen at random from a list provided by the political parties in the locality. Potential jury members are thus usually politically active for their respective parties. Members of the SDP happened to be in a majority on the jury and the author was acquitted. This judgment has led an official inquiry to propose that a constitutional amendment be made removing the right to jury trial in cases where the composition of the jury gives rise to doubts as to whether the trial will be fair.[94] The case is interesting in that it shows that there is scope for conflict between constitutional documents and the Convention—an issue which, as we have seen, was conveniently ignored by the Committee on Rights and Freedoms.[95]

Lastly, mention should also be made of the *Gustafsson* case.[96] This case concerned the negative right of freedom of association under Article 11; more specifically, it raised the question whether there is an obligation on the state to take positive measures to protect this right. Gustafsson was a restaurant owner who had suffered a boycott and blockade from a trade union which wanted him to sign a collective agreement. Gustafsson argued before the Convention organs that, in taking this action, the union was not representing any members employed by him. His employees were satisfied with pay and working conditions. The union was rather wishing, in general, to strengthen the collective bargaining system. Judicial remedies were, however, unavailable in Swedish law to prevent or minimise the effect of the boycott and blockade. The Commission, by 13 votes to 4, ruled that, in the circumstances, the union's acts were disproportionate and the state was therefore obliged under Article 11 to make available legal remedies to Gustafsson. In the proceedings before the Court, the Swedish government

---

[92] Housing Court (Amendment) Act (1991:636).

[93] *Holm* v. *Sweden* Series A, No. 279–A (1993) 18 E.H.R.R. 79.

[94] Domaren i Sverige inför framtiden [the Judge in Sweden in the Future] SOU 1994:99, p. 315 ff.

[95] This simply stated glibly that where the Convention went further than the constitution, the former should be applied: SOU 1993:40, p. 128.

[96] *Torgny Gustafsson* v. *Sweden*, App. No. 15573/89, report adopted 10 January 1995, judgment of 25 April 1996.

(which had reverted to SDP control since the Commission report) led new evidence which cast some doubt on the claims made by the applicant, and accepted by the Commission, that the union action was unjustified. The Court ruled by a majority that Article 11 was applicable to the case but that it had not been violated. It was obvious that the majority of the Court was reluctant to interfere with the Swedish system of labour law which grants considerable autonomy to the trade unions' and employers' associations to regulate labour relations by means of collective agreement.

2.   THE EFFECT OF CASES IN THE NATIONAL LEGAL SYSTEM

In Part II, section 1, a number of cases were mentioned in which the Swedish courts during the late 1980s and early 1990s had interpreted national law in the light of the Convention and Convention case law. There is now a fairly large body of case law from the Supreme Court and Supreme Administrative Court dealing with the Convention. There are also a small number of cases from the appeal courts and the specialised courts in which the requirements of the Convention are considered. The Act incorporating the Convention only entered into force on 1 January 1995, and there have been relatively few cases up to the time of writing (April 1996).

There is no need to go into detail concerning the case law before 1995. Many of the cases to date have concerned the question of the right to an oral hearing before the appeal courts in both civil and administrative cases.[97] Many cases before the Supreme Administrative Court referring to the Convention have concerned the Act on Judicial Review of Certain Administrative Decisions and have only indirectly involved the Convention itself.[98] In addition to the cases referred to in Part II, section 1, one further example will suffice to give an idea of the breadth of impact of the Convention on the national legal order. *NJA 1993, p. 566* concerned an appeal made by a person convicted of sexual exploitation of a minor. His lawyer requested the verbatim record of the trial at first instance. According to Chapter 9 section 16 of the Secrecy Act (1980:100), evidence in trials for sexual crimes is not to be disclosed outside of the actual trial. Under Chapter 14 section 9 of the Act secret information can, however, be disclosed subject to a condition set

---

[97]   *E.g. RÅ 1990:75; RÅ 1990 note 492; NJA 1991 p. 514; RÅ 1991, note 160; NJA 1991, p. 188; NJA 1992, p. 363; NJA 1992, p. 513; NJA 1993, p. 103; NJA 1993 p. 109; NJA 1993 p. 111; NJA 1994, p. 290; RH 1994:8.* Of course, even where a case was remitted back and an oral hearing was held, this did not mean that the lower court was convinced of the applicant's arguments. In many of these cases, the original finding was confirmed.

[98]   *E.g. RÅ 1993, note 599; RÅ 1993, note 475;* and *RÅ 1993, note 300.*

by the relevant authority, in order to ensure that the information is not disclosed to the detriment of the individuals it concerns. The lower courts permitted disclosure to the lawyer but subject to the reservation that the evidence could only be used for appeal purposes before the Swedish courts. The lawyer appealed against this on the basis that she was considering submitting an application on the subject to the European Commission of Human Rights. The Supreme Court allowed the appeal. First, it considered that proceedings before the Commission are confidential. Should the matter go to the Court, there was the possibility under the Court's rules of procedure of keeping evidence confidential. Second, it would be incompatible with the Convention principle of equality of arms if the lawyer was unable to refer to such evidence, as the Swedish government, in its reply to the Commission, was permitted under Chapter 1 section 3 st 3 to do so. Third, it was contrary to the spirit of Article 25.1 to hinder the effective exercise of the right of individual application.

To turn now to the decisions since 1995. Notwithstanding the established case law of the Supreme Court and the Supreme Administrative Court emphasising the need for oral hearings when a party requests it, there are still cases concerning this issue.[99] There has also been at least one example of a court deliberately choosing to ignore the Convention. In an unreported case from a county administrative court concerning the custody of children, the court ruled that, since the *travaux préparatoires* to the Act incorporating the Convention had stated that the government's view was that the Care of Children Act (1990:52) was in accordance with the requirements of the Convention, it would decide the issue only on the basis of the Act.[100] This is an echo of the dreadful decision in *NJA 1974, p. 423* (above, Part II, section 1) which, if followed by other courts would deprive the Convention of any significance in practice. It is possible that the real reason for such a ruling can probably be sought in a degree of judicial laziness and/or in a lack of time available to the tribunal that considered the case.

In *RÅ 1995 note 156* the issue was whether the denial of asylum and deportation of a family of aliens because of the fact that the father had been convicted of a criminal offence was a "collective expulsion" forbidden by Article 4, Protocol 4. The Supreme Administrative Court, referring to the fact that the determination of whether or not members of the family should be permitted to stay had been made on an individual basis, found no violation of the Article.

---

[99] See *RÅ 1995 note 184*; *RÅ 1995 note 179*.
[100] *LR i Skaraborg 1995–02–22*; *Ö 1274–94*; *Ö 915–94*; and *Ö 3059–94*.

All the other reported cases have concerned one or other aspect of Article 6. In *HR 1995:32*, the court of appeal ruled that a policeman did not have to disclose the name of an informant who had given information which was part of the basis of the prosecution's case against a person accused of complicity in embezzlement. The court considered the Convention case law on the issue of anonymous witnesses (embraced within the fair trial guarantees in Article 6) but concluded that, since the information in question formed only a small, and relatively insignificant part of the prosecution's evidence, ordering disclosure of the name of the informant, so as to allow cross-examination of him, would, in the circumstances, be a disproportionate measure.

In *HR 1995:66* a company had failed to send in its accounts for the last two years to the Patent and Registration Board. In accordance with Chapter 13 section 4a of the Joint Stock Companies Act (1975:1385), the Board applied to the district court for the company to be entered into liquidation. The company argued against the Board's decision on the basis that its failure to send in its accounts was due to circumstances outside its control, namely that its accounts were at the time being scrutinised by the tax authorities. This fact had been communicated to the Board by the tax authorities. The legislation, and established case law, however, gave the court no discretion to take into account any excuses a company threatened with liquidation on this ground might have. The district court therefore issued the liquidation order. The court of appeal nonetheless allowed the company's appeal against this judgement, invoking Articles 6 and 13 of the Convention. It considered that, in such an important area of civil rights or obligations, the requirement of an effective remedy meant that courts must be able to take into account extraordinary circumstances which had the potential to excuse a failure to comply with legislative requirements. This judgment is an example of—for Swedish standards—a rather bold approach to the Convention, using it to create a remedy where none previously existed.

NJA 1995, p. 322 concerned the building of an international bridge between Malmö and Copenhagen. A number of fisherman who trawled in the waters in question had made representations in the Water Court concerning the construction work. Later, they applied for their court expenses to be paid. The issue before the Supreme Court was whether they could be seen as "parties affected by construction" within the meaning of the Water Act (1983:291). The Court considered that the *travaux préparatoires* to the Act and subsequent practice showed that they could not, and that there was no indication either that they would be seen as being possessors of a "civil right" within the meaning of Article 6.

Finally, an interesting example can be given of a conflict between the Supreme Court and Supreme Administrative Court regarding interpretation of the Convention. *NJA 1994, p. 657*, concerned a dispute over who was entitled to a farming subsidy, the old or new owner of a farm. The Farm Board had paid the subsidy to the trustee in bankruptcy of the estate, rather than the new owner. The relevant legislation provided that there was no appeal from the decision of the Farming Board. The issues were first, whether, notwithstanding the provision that there was to be no appeal, the new owner of the farm had a right of access to a court to determine the issue on the grounds that the matter fell within the concept of "civil right" in Article 6 and second, if so, which courts were competent to determine the issue, the general courts or the administrative courts. The case did not fall within the scope of the Act on Review of Certain Administrative Decisions because it dealt with a benefit. The Supreme Court, with some hesitation, considered that the dispute did concern a civil right, but concluded that it was more appropriate that the administrative courts decide the case, primarily because the dispute largely concerned administrative law. The court reached this conclusion notwithstanding the established practice that, failing specific provision to the contrary, the general courts are competent to hear all disputes concerning private law. The case was then heard by the administrative courts, culminating in the Supreme Administrative Court.[101] This court reached the conclusion that, while there were some arguments in favour of the view that the case fell within the category of disputes over "civil rights", it was not certain that this was in fact the case. There was therefore no reason to provide a judicial remedy to the plaintiff. Two dissenting judges took the view that, even if it had been shown that the matter concerned a civil right, the Supreme Administrative Court would have no jurisdiction because, in all cases before the administrative courts, it is necessary to found such jurisdiction on a specific law bestowing such competence.

The regrettable conflict of jurisdiction between the two courts in this matter has led to a lively, indeed, at times an acrimonious, debate in the legal journals.[102] It can be speculated as to why the Supreme Court reached the decision it did. It was undoubtedly an approach which diverged from previously established practice. On the other hand, it may, on the merits, be the

---

[101] *RÅ 1995 ref. 58.*

[102] See R. Lavin, "Domstolskompetens enligt artikel 6 i Europakonventionen" [The competence of the Courts under Article 6 ECHR] [1995] *Juridisk tidskrift* 731, H. Strömberg, "Delade meningar om allmän förvaltningsdomstols kompetens" [Differing views on the competence of the administrative courts] [1995] *Förvaltningsrätt tidskrift* 211.

best approach to the issue. Article 6 means that a number of disputes previously decided by administrative agencies must now be determined by a court. There is no logical reason why all of these cases should be heard by the general courts when there exists a satisfactory system of administrative courts to share this work. But whether or not this argument has merit in general, it can still be argued that the Supreme Administrative Court, as the final instance of appeal, should have accepted that it had jurisdiction in the specific case. It was open to it to hedge this acceptance around with restrictions, to minimise its precedent effect. Of course, it is not certain that the Convention organs will regard the matter as falling within Article 6, but this is probably the case. The plaintiff was, in any event, forced to go to Strasbourg and this was one of the things incorporation was expressly intended to avoid. (The government subsequently paid her a large sum in a "friendly settlement" and the application was withdrawn).The dissenting opinions given in the judgment of the Supreme Administrative Court are also interesting as showing a failure to understand the changes necessarily entailed in Swedish administrative law by the incorporation of the Convention. Article 6 is a general empowerment to the courts to create a judicial remedy where the case concerns "civil rights", notwithstanding any previous restrictions to the contrary in Swedish law. These opinions reveal the difficulties certain more traditionalist judges may still have in coming to terms with the Convention.

Finally, as already mentioned on page 242 in a very recent case also concerning the right of access to a court to challenge an administrative decision on an agricultural subsidy, an administrative court of appeal has not followed the same line as the Supreme Administrative Court in *RÅ 1995, ref. 58*. It was careful to distinguish the two cases, although in substance the two issues are the same.

Some Concluding Comments Regarding the ECHR Convention and Swedish Legal Culture

It is evident that the Convention, even before its incorporation, has had a considerable effect on certain areas of legislation. While incorporation must increase the impact the Convention will have, it is too early to say how great this impact will be. Whatever changes that are likely to emerge will be gradual rather than dramatic. They are likely to be part of a general, if slow, "Europeanisation" of legal thinking occasioned principally by membership of the EU. Three tentative points may, however, be made by way of a conclusion to this chapter.

First, the point of departure for the relationship between the Convention and national law is Article 60; the Convention provides only minimum protection. It is evident that, in several areas, *e.g.* freedom of expression and freedom of information, Swedish law goes further, or much further, than the Convention demands. On the other hand, the provisions of Chapter 2 of the Instrument of Government, while important as preventive controls on the legislative process, are seldom invoked by the courts. Nor is there much discussion in the doctrine on the subject of the constitutional interpretation of human rights. This situation can be contrasted with the position in many other Convention states where there is a large body of constitutional rights case law and a lively ongoing debate on constitutional rights and interpretative methods. Thus, in some other Convention states which have incorporated the Convention, the Convention case law is often used merely to supplement constitutional rights. Naturally enough, constitutional courts are more at home interpreting their own constitution rather than the Convention. Thus, even when a case from the Court is relevant in interpreting the scope of a right under the incorporated Convention, and that right is relevant in a case before it, a constitutional court may instead choose to base its judgment on a constitutional right, even when this involves a wide interpretation of the constitution.[103] This situation can be contrasted with that of the Netherlands where constitutional review can only occur on the basis of treaties. The Dutch courts have, on occasion, gone further than the Convention organs in their interpretation of the Convention.[104] Neither situation is likely to apply in Sweden. There is no substantial pre-existing body of domestic constitutional case law into which the Convention case law can be fitted, but equally RF 11:14 and the Swedish judicial culture will tend to discourage the Swedish courts from using the Convention actively, and going beyond, or predicting, the case law of the Convention organs. Nonetheless, it may be that the Swedish courts, in time, will overcome their reluctance to subject the views of parliament and the government to the necessity for, and the

---

[103] See, *e.g.*, the practice of the German constitutional court, *BVerfG* 74, 358, noted in J. Polakiewicz and V. Jacob-Feltzer, "The European Human Rights Convention in Domestic Law: the Impact of the Strasbourg Case-Law in States Where Direct Effect is Given to the Convention" (1991) 12 *Human Rights Law Journal* 65 at p. 80. See generally, E. Voss, below, Ch. 4.

[104] *E.g.*, in basing a right for homosexual couples to adopt children on Article 8. See further below Y. Klerk and E. J. de Jonge, Ch. 3.

proportionality of, a particular restriction on human rights. Certainly, the coexistence of two (or, with EC law, three) overlapping but slightly different rights catalogues and ways of interpreting rights will be uncomfortable in the long run. Even now it is difficult to see how the artificial approach the *travaux préparatoires* to the Instrument of Government take to the question of a "restriction" of human rights can survive.

Secondly, there are a number of unresolved problems regarding the effect the Convention has had on Swedish law. One of these has already been noted above, *i.e.* the correct application of Article 6 to the system of judicial review of administrative action. The approach of the minority in *RÅ 1995 ref. 58* illustrates that it is one thing for Swedish lawyers to use the Convention as a ground for, or at least, an additional reason for, giving other Swedish legislation a restrictive or extensive interpretation. It is perceived as quite another matter to use it as an independent ground for recognising a right which a Swedish statute governing the area has purposely omitted or, worse, has contradicted. Here, it is not a question of interpreting a right given by national law, but of "completing" it. This is something with which Swedish judges are, so far, relatively unfamiliar. On the other hand, the approach of the Court of Appeal in *HR 1995:66* and the decision of Jönköping KR in case 2442-1996 shows that some, at least, of the judges are keen to rise to the challenge.[105] Another unresolved issue is whether the "reopening" of an earlier domestic decision is possible after a negative judgment in the European Court. The position at Swedish law is unclear.[106] As this would strengthen greatly the impact of the Convention I consider that there are strong policy arguments in favour of this, at least in criminal cases. The relevant provisions of the Code of Judicial Procedure (RB 58:1 and 2) do not exclude it. While it must be conceded that there is no unanimity among the Convention states on this issue, some states at least allow it, and among them are the Scandinavian states of Norway and Denmark.[107]

---

[105] For a discussion of a similar point in the context of EC law, see T. Andersson, "Effective Protection of Community Rights in Sweden" in I. Cameron and A. Simoni (eds.), *Dealing with European Integration* (Uppsala, 1996).

[106] There was a very short discussion of the issue in SOU 1993: 40, del B, pp. 77–8. See also J. Sundberg, "Implementing the ECHR in Sweden: The Boll Case Discussion" in *Laws, Rights and the European Convention on Human Rights, op. cit.*, note 74, at p. 69.

[107] As regards the diversity on the issue, see the study prepared by the committee of experts: "The ECHR: Institution of review proceedings at the national level to facilitate compliance with Strasbourg decisions" (1992) 13 *Human Rights Law Journal* 71. For the Norwegian legislation see Tvistemalsloven §407 (13 August 1915, No. 6 as amended) and Straffprocessloven §391 (22 May 1981, No. 25). These laws have not yet been applied.

Thirdly and finally, I can make the simple observation that genuine respect for human rights in the national order depends on a wide variety of factors. The technical legal aspect (*i.e.* the content and status of laws guaranteeing individual rights) is only one of these. The practical problems involved for administrators and lawyers in interpreting and applying the Convention at the national level should not be underestimated. One of the things which makes the Convention interesting for academics is the fact that, as an autonomous system, it cuts across normal national legal categorisations. A Convention case which concerns one area of legislation can have major implications for quite another area. For judges, prosecutors, police officers, social workers and others, new and (relatively) unpredictable sources of law are not always welcomed. Here the fact should be noted that the Convention—like important parts of EC law—is largely a case law system. While case law is obviously an important source of law in the Swedish legal system, Swedish lawyers are more used to seeking guidance in extensive *travaux préparatoires* rather than in distinguishing cases in the common law way. While it is easy to understand and draw the implications of cases concerning Sweden, as already mentioned, many other cases are also relevant, or potentially relevant to Sweden. But judgments in cases concerning foreign law have to be "translated" to be understood in Swedish legal conditions. This is no easy task. It is not only a question of altering (or supplementing) one's way of legal reasoning. There is also the more basic question of accessibility. While the Convention is readily available in Swedish translation, there is no official translation of the body of Court or Commission case law. A readily available database, RIXLEX, has summaries of the first two hundred cases, but nothing else. No steps have yet been taken to facilitate courts' access to the ever growing body of case law.[108] Nor have any systematic measures yet been taken to educate "target" groups of public servants. Until something is done about the basic issues of education and access to information, the Convention is not likely to obtain the attention it deserves.

For the Danish law, see Retsplejelov §977 (Law of 10 November 1992). This provision was applied following *Jersild* v. *Denmark* Series A, No. 298 (1994) 19 E.H.R.R. 1.

[108] The way the majority of Swedish lawyers have of keeping themselves up to date with Convention developments is to read the occasional summaries of Court case law published by Hans Danelius in the leading journal, *Svensk juristtidning*. While valuable in themselves, these are no substitute for proper access to the original source.

Appendix

Relevant sections of the Instrument of Government 1974

What follows is largely taken from the official translation. I am, however, responsible for translating the amendments made in 1994 (*i.e.* to Articles 18, 20, 21 and 22.)

CHAPTER 2. FUNDAMENTAL RIGHTS AND FREEDOMS

Art. 1. All citizens shall be guaranteed the following in their relations with the public administration:

1. freedom of expression: the freedom to communicate information and to express ideas, opinions and emotions, whether orally, in writing, in pictorial representations, or in any other way;
2. freedom of information: the freedom to obtain and receive information and otherwise acquaint oneself with the utterances of others;
3. freedom of assembly: the freedom to organise or attend any meeting for information purposes or for the expression of opinions or for any other similar purpose or for the purpose of presenting artistic work;
4. freedom to demonstrate: the freedom to organise or take part in any demonstration in a public place:
5. freedom of association: the freedom to unite with others for public or private purposes; and
6. freedom of worship: the freedom to practise one's own religion either alone or in company with others.

In the case of the freedom of the press and the equivalent freedom to express oneself on radio, television, film, video etc. the provisions of the Freedom of the Press and Freedom of Expression Acts shall apply. The Freedom of the Press Act also contains provisions concerning the right of access to public documents.

Art. 2. All citizens shall be protected in their relations with the public administration against all coercion to divulge an opinion in any political, religious cultural or other similar connection. They shall furthermore be protected in their relations with the public administration against all coercion to participate in any meeting for the formation of opinion or in any demonstration or other expression of opinion or to belong to any political association, religious congregation or other association for opinions of the nature referred to in the first sentence.

Art. 3. No record about a citizen in a public register may be based without his consent solely on his political opinions.

Citizens shall be protected to the extent determined in detail by law against any infringement of their personal integrity resulting from the registration of information about them by means of electronic data processing.

Art. 4. There shall be no capital punishment.

Art. 5. All citizens shall be protected against corporal punishment. All citizens shall likewise be protected against torture or any medical influence or intervention for the purpose of extorting or suppressing statements.

Art. 6. All citizens shall be protected in their relations with the public administration against any physical violation also in cases other than those referred to in Articles 4 and 5. Citizens shall likewise be protected against physical search, house searches or other similar encroachments and against examination of mail or other confidential correspondence and against eavesdropping, telephone-tapping or recording of other confidential communications.

Art. 7. No citizen may be deported or refused entry to Sweden

No citizen who is resident in Sweden or who has been resident in Sweden may be deprived of his citizenship unless he becomes at the same time a national of another state, at his express consent or because he has taken employment in the public service. It may however be prescribed that children under the age of eighteen shall have the same nationality as their parents or one of their parents. It may furthermore be prescribed that, in pursuance of an agreement with a foreign state, a person who has been a national also of the other state from birth, and who is permanently resident there, shall forfeit his Swedish nationality at or after the age of eighteen.

Art. 8. All citizens shall be protected against deprivation of liberty in their relations with the public administration. They shall also in other respects be guaranteed freedom of movement within the Realm and freedom to depart Sweden.

Art. 9. Where a public authority other than a court has deprived a citizen of his liberty for committing a criminal offence or because he is suspected of having committed such an offence, he shall be entitled to have the matter tested before a court of law without undue delay. This shall not, however, apply where the issue concerns the transference to Sweden of responsibility for executing a penal sanction involving deprivation of liberty which has been imposed in another state.

If, for reasons other than those referred to in the first paragraph, a citizen has been forcibly taken into custody he shall likewise be entitled to have the matter tested before a court of law without undue delay. In such a case, examination before a tribunal shall be equated with examination before a court of law, provided that the composition of the tribunal is governed by rules of law and it is laid down that the chairman of the tribunal must be currently, or shall have been previously, a permanent judge.

If an examination under the first or second paragraph has not been referred to an authority which is competent according to the provisions laid down therein, the examination shall be carried out by a court of general jurisdiction.

Art. 10. No penalty or other penal sanction may be imposed in respect of an act which was not subject to any penal sanction at the time it was committed. Neither may a more severe penal sanction be imposed than that which was prescribed when the act was committed. The provisions thus laid down with respect to penal sanctions apply likewise with respect to confiscation or any other special legal effects attaching to criminal offences.

No State taxes, charges or fees may be levied except insofar as they were in force when the circumstance arose which occasioned the liability for the tax, charge, or fee. Should the Riksdag find that specific reasons so warrant, it may be provided under an Act of law that State taxes, charges, or fees shall be levied even although no such act had entered into force when the aforementioned circumstance occurred, provided that the Government or a Committee of the Riksdag had submitted a proposal to this effect to the Riksdag at the time concerned. For the purposes of the foregoing provision, any written communication from the Government to the Riksdag announcing that a proposal of this nature will be forthcoming shall be equated with a formal proposal. The Riksdag may furthermore prescribe that exceptions shall be made from the provisions of the first sentence if it considers that this is warranted by specific reasons connected with war, the danger of war, or severe economic crisis.

Art. 11. No court may be set up to try an offence already committed, or for a particular dispute or otherwise for a particular case.

Proceedings in the courts shall be open to the public.

Art. 12. The rights and freedoms referred to in Article 1, sub-paragraphs 1–5, in Articles 6 and 8, and in Article 11, second paragraph, may be restricted by law to the extent provided for in Articles 13–16. After authorisation in law, they may be restricted by statutory order in the cases referred to in

Chapter 8, Article 7, first paragraph, sub-paragraph 7, and in Chapter 8, Article 10. Freedom of assembly and the freedom to demonstrate may similarly be restricted also in the cases referred to in Article 14, first paragraph, second sentence.

The restrictions referred to in the preceding paragraph may be imposed only to achieve a purpose acceptable in a democratic society. The restriction may never exceed what is necessary having regard to the purpose which occasioned it, nor may it be carried so far as to constitute a threat to the free formation of opinion as one of the foundations of democracy. No restriction may be imposed solely on grounds of political, religious, cultural or other such opinions.

Government bills of the nature referred to in the first paragraph or Government bills for the amendment or repeal of such legislation, shall, if not rejected by the Riksdag, be held in suspense for a period of not less than twelve months from the date on which the first report of a Riksdag Committee on the Bill was submitted to the Chamber of the Riksdag, on a motion by no fewer than ten members. The above provision notwithstanding, the Riksdag may approve the bill if no fewer than five sixths of those voting concur.

The third paragraph of the present Article shall not apply to any bill prolonging the life of legislation for a period of up to two years. Nor shall the said paragraph apply to any bill concerned exclusively with

1. prohibition of the disclosure of matters of which a person may have acquired knowledge in the public service, or in the performance of official duties, when secrecy is called for having regard to interests under Chapter 2, Article 2 of the Freedom of the Press Act;
2. house searches and similar intrusions; or
3. deprivation of liberty imposed as a penal sanction for a specific act or omission.

The Committee on the Constitution decides on behalf of the Riksdag whether the present Article, third paragraph, is applicable in respect of a specific bill.

Art. 13. Freedom of expression and freedom of information may be restricted having regard to the security of the Realm, the national supply, public safety and order, the integrity of the individual, the sanctity of private life, or the prevention and prosecution of crime. Freedom of expression may also be restricted in economic activities. Freedom of expression and freedom of information may otherwise be restricted only where particularly important reasons so warrant.

In judging what restrictions may be made by virtue of the preceding paragraph particular regard shall be paid to the importance of the widest possible freedom of expression and freedom of information in political, religious, professional, scientific and cultural matters.

The issuing of rules and regulations which govern in detail a particular manner of disseminating or receiving information without regard to its content shall not be deemed to restrict freedom of expression or freedom of information.

Art. 14. Freedom of assembly and the freedom to demonstrate may be restricted for the purpose of preserving public safety and order at the meeting or demonstration, or having regard to the circulation of traffic. These freedoms may otherwise be restricted only out of regard for the security of the Realm or for the purpose of combating an epidemic.

Freedom of association may be restricted only in respect of organisations whose activities are of a military nature or the like, or which involve the persecution of a population group of a particular race, skin colour, or ethnic origin.

Art. 15. No Act of law or other statutory instrument may entail the discrimination of any citizen because he belongs to a minority on grounds of race, skin colour, or ethnic origin.

Art. 16. No Act of law or other statutory instrument may entail the discrimination of any citizen on grounds of sex, unless the relevant provision forms part of efforts to bring about equality between men and women or relates to compulsory military service or any corresponding compulsory national service.

Art. 17. Any trade union or employer or association of employers shall be entitled to take strike or lock-out action or any similar measure unless otherwise provided by law or arising out of an agreement.

Art. 18. Every citizen's right to property is secured in that be obliged to relinquish his property to the public administration or to an individual by means of expropriation or by any other similar measure or accept that the public administration restricts the use of land or buildings except where this is necessary to satisfy important public interests.

Every citizen whose property is requisitioned by means of an expropriation order or by any other similar measure shall be guaranteed compensation for his loss. Such compensation shall also be guaranteed where the public administration restricts the use of land or buildings in such a way that the use of the immovable property is significantly obstructed or damage results which is considerable in relation to the value of the immovable property. The compensation shall be determined according to conditions laid down in law.

Everyone shall have access to nature in accordance with the right of commons (*allemansrätten*) irrespective of what is set out above.

Art. 19. Authors, artists and photographers shall own the rights to their works in accordance with provisions laid down in law.

Art. 20. Limitations in the right to engage in business activity or to a profession may only be imposed to protect important public interests and never only to give economic advantages to certain people or companies.

Art. 21 All children obliged by law to attend school have the right to free basic education in public school. The public administration shall also be responsible for ensuring that higher education facilities exist.

Art. 22 A foreigner within the Realm shall be equated with a Swedish citizen in respect of

1. protection against all coercion to participate in any meeting for the formation of opinion or in any demonstration or other expression of opinion, or to belong to any religious congregation or other association (Article 2, second sentence);
2. protection of personal integrity in connection with electronic data processing (Article 3, second paragraph);
3. protection against capital punishment, corporal punishment and torture and against medical intervention aimed at extorting or preventing statements;
4. the right to have any deprivation of liberty on account of a criminal offence or on grounds of suspicion of having committed such an offence tested before a court of law (Article 9, first and third paragraphs);
5. protection against retroactive penal sanctions and other retroactive effects of criminal acts and against retroactive taxes, charges or fees (Article 10);
6. protection against the establishment of a court to try a particular case (Article 11, first paragraph);
7. protection against discrimination on grounds of race, skin colour, ethnic origin, or sex (Articles 15 and 16);
8. the right to take strike or lock-out action (Article 17); and

9.   protection against expropriation or by a similar measure as well as against restrictions imposed on the use of land or buildings (Article 18);

10.   the right to education (Article 21)

Unless otherwise provided by special rules of law, a foreigner within the Realm shall be equated with a Swedish citizen also in respect of

1.   freedom of expression, freedom of information, freedom of assembly, freedom to demonstrate, freedom of association, and freedom of worship (Article 1);

2.   protection against all coercion to divulge an opinion (Article 2, first sentence);

3.   protection against physical violations also in cases other than those referred to in Articles 4 and 5, against physical search, house searches, or other similar intrusions, and against violations of confidential communications (Article 6);

4.   protection against deprivation of liberty (Article 8, first sentence);

5.   the right to have any deprivation of liberty for reasons other than a criminal offence or suspicion of having committed such an offence tested before a court (Article 9, second and third paragraphs);

6.   public court proceedings (Article 11, second paragraph);

7.   protection against violations on grounds of opinion (Article 12, second paragraph, third sentence); and

8.   the rights of authors, artists, and photographers to their works (Article 19).

9.   the right to engage in business activity or in a profession (Article 20)

With respect to the special provisions referred to in the second paragraph of the present Article, the provisions of Article 12, third paragraph; fourth paragraph, first sentence; and fifth paragraph shall apply.

Art. 23 No law or other statutory instrument may be issued which is in conflict with the obligations undertaken by Sweden in the European Convention on Human Rights and Fundamental Freedoms.

7.   FRANCE

Eva Steiner

Part I: General Constitutional Background

France ratified the European Convention on Human Rights in 1974[1] and recognised the right of individual petition in 1981.[2] We may immediately question why France, the country of the 1789 Declaration of the Rights of Man and the Citizen, waited so long to ratify the Convention and then such a further length of time before giving to individuals the right of individual complaint. Many factors—legal, constitutional and political—hindered the process of ratification and these will be considered later. However, it may be pointed out here that, by virtue of Article 55 of the current French constitution of 1958, treaties and agreements, once ratified, have superior authority over parliamentary statutes. Although the application of Article 55 was the subject of litigation in each of France's three supreme judicial bodies, it is now established that ratification enables parties to rely on the Convention in domestic law and empowers French courts to apply it in preference to existing statutes. Before examining further the legal and constitutional implications of ratification and the attitude to these issues adopted by the French courts, we must first put our subject in context by looking briefly at the constitution, the court system and the position of the judiciary in France.

1.   THE CONSTITUTION AND THE CONSTITUTIONAL PROTECTION OF CIVIL LIBERTIES IN FRANCE

Since the 1789 Revolution France has had an unbroken tradition of written constitutions (14 in total). As far as the current 1958 constitution is concerned, its primary purpose is, in accordance with De Gaulle's views, the reinforcement of executive power and the limitation of parliamentary sovereignty. Indeed, parliamentary supremacy is restricted in two ways in the

---

[1]   Law of 31 December 1973 and Decree of 3 May 1974.

[2]   Decree of 9 October 1981, renewed by further Decrees on 23 December 1986 and 14 May 1990.

C. A. Gearty (ed.), *European Civil Liberties and the European Convention on Human Rights*, 267–305.
© 1997 *Kluwer Law International. Printed in the Netherlands.*

1958 document: first, parliament no longer enjoys legislative sovereignty and shares its legislative function with the government. Article 34 of the constitution lays down an exhaustive list of matters on which parliament alone may legislate. Article 37 then expressly specifies that any other matters than those listed in Article 34 fall within the sphere of executive power.[3] Secondly, this restriction of parliamentary power is enforced by an organ newly created by the 1958 constitution, the *Conseil Constitutionnel*, which has jurisdiction over claims that parliament has overstepped the bounds of its law-making authority. Before 1958 legislative power in parliament was not checked by any formal constitutional limit[4] but by the persistent lack of any stable majority. The end of constitutional parliamentary supremacy was seen in 1958 as a *révolution juridique* which was in breach of the traditional idea of democracy based on J. J. Rousseau's *Contrat Social* (1762) according to which legislative enactments may only proceed from the expression of the popular will and national sovereignty and may not be subjected to limit or control.[5]

It seems that this constitutional transformation has given an added dimension to the protection of civil liberties in France, in three ways in particular: first, according to Article 34 of the constitution, only parliament can establish the rules concerning the system of basic civil liberties and their protection. These cover civic rights and duties, fundamental safeguards of civil liberties, nationality, civil status, criminal law, criminal procedure, the system of courts and the judiciary. Secondly, like most governmental action, the enactments of the executive power passed under Article 37 are subjected to the control of the *Conseil d'Etat*, which is the highest administrative court in France.[6] In order to test the legality of governmental action the *Conseil d'Etat* has over the years developed an independent source of legislation—

---

[3] Parliament alone may legislate on civil rights, the determination of crimes and misdemeanours and criminal procedure (Article 34). However, civil procedure and the determination of petty offences known as "contraventions" fall, amongst other matters, within the sphere of executive power (Article 37).

[4] For the constitutional position before 1958, see J. Bell, *French Constitutional Law* (Oxford, 1992), pp. 20–29.

[5] See for example P. Durand "La décadence de la loi dans la Constitution de la Veme République" J.C.P. 1959, Section I, 1470.

[6] See the following cases decided by the *Conseil d'Etat*: *Conseil d'Etat*, 26 June 1959, *Syndicat Général des Ingénieurs Conseil*, Rec. 394, and *Conseil d'Etat*, 12 February 1960, *Sté Eky*, D. 1960 J. 123. In both cases the *Conseil d'Etat* held that regulations under Article 37 were to be regarded as *actes administratifs* and as such subject to the principle of legality.

the general principles of law—the content of which very often derives from the 1789 Declaration. Amongst these principles are the principle of equality of citizens before the law and freedom of opinion,[7] but also more specific rights like the principle of *publicité des débats* according to which cases must be heard in open court.[8] In the 1959 case of *Syndicat Général des Ingénieurs Conseils*,[9] the *Conseil d'Etat* held that executive action under Article 37 must be in accord with the general principles of law. Thirdly, one of the more unexpected aspect of the 1958 transformation has been that the *Conseil Constitutionnel*, which as we have seen was primarily created to ensure that parliament would keep within its constitutionally prescribed bounds, has become since a decision of July 16, 1971 a primary protector of civil liberties in France.[10]

This 1971 decision, which has been described as the French *Marbury* v. *Madison*, concerned a government bill designed to amend the Law of Association of July 1901 and to introduce administrative control over the registration of associations.[11] The *Conseil Constitutionnel* found the measure unconstitutional on the ground that it was in breach of the principle of freedom of association. The *Conseil* based its decision on the preamble to the 1958 constitution, the legal value of which had been a matter of debate before 1971. The preamble incorporates by reference the 1789 Declaration of the Rights of Man,[12] the social and economic rights listed in the preamble to the constitution of 1946[13] and the "fundamental principles recognised by the Laws of the Republic". In the *Conseil's* view, freedom of association, was one of these "fundamental principles". This is a rather vague concept which recurs several times in subsequent decisions of the *Conseil*.[14] It is very flexi-

---

[7] On which see the case-law and bibliography quoted in A. De Laubadère, J. C. Vénézia and Y. Gaudemet, *Traité de Droit Administratif* 11th ed. (1990) vol. 1, nos. 864–869.

[8] *Conseil d'Etat*, 4 October 1974, *Dame David*, D. 1975 J. 369.

[9] *Op. cit.*, note 6.

[10] See generally B. Nicholas, "Fundamental Rights and Judicial Review in France" [1978] *Public Law* 82–101 and 155–177; R. J. Cummins, "Constitutional Protection of Civil Liberties in France" (1985) 33 *American Journal of Comparative Law* 721.

[11] For the background, see Nicholas, *ibid.*, pp. 87–92.

[12] The Declaration affirms principles such as equality under law; freedom of speech and of the press; the right to liberty, property, and security; and also the presumption of innocence.

[13] These rights include the right to work; to form labour unions; and to strike. Also included are the right to education and to health protection.

[14] See J. Rivero, "Les principes fondamentaux reconnus par les lois de la République: une nouvelle categorie constitutionnelle?" D. 1974 *Chronique* p. 265. See also Bell, *op. cit.*,

ble in the sense that it can exist without specific reference to any particular law. Since 1971, the 1958 preamble has been treated as giving binding constitutional force to the texts and principles that it mentions. The *Conseil* has referred frequently to the 1789 Declaration[15] and to the 1946 preamble[16] in its case-law and these cannot be seen any more as mere declarations of intent.

The impact of the 1971 decision on the French legal system has however been limited by the manner in which constitutional review is carried out in France: ordinary judges do not function as constitutional judges and the *Conseil Constitutionnel* has exclusive competence when it comes to ensuring the conformity with the constitution of parliamentary statutes. There is, in France, a strong feeling against a general control over the constitutionality of legislation by the courts, a tradition which is rooted in ancient suspicion about the judiciary derived from the practices of the royal courts of the *Ancien Régime*.[17] Furthermore the courts themselves have steadily refused to assume the role of constitutional judges.[18] However, the control by the *Conseil Constitutionnel* is only applied to Acts of parliament. The legality of executive and administrative regulations can be examined by the administrative courts and, to a certain extent, by civil and criminal courts.[19] An added complication is that the *Conseil Constitutionnel* does not perform its functions as a judicial body. Its nine members do not have the status of judges and are nominated in equal number by the president of the Republic and the presidents of the two houses of parliament. There are no criteria for membership of the *Conseil* but if one looks at the appointments to the *Conseil* since 1959, parliamentary, governmental and legal experience can be

---

note 4, pp. 68–71 which cites the case-law.

[15] See the decision of 16 January 1982 on nationalisation discussed in Bell, *op. cit.*, note 4, at pp. 274–275 and the decision of 23 July 1975 on equality before justice discussed by the same author, *ibid.*, at pp. 352–353.

[16] See the decision of 25 July 1979 on trade union rights discussed in Bell, *op. cit.*, note 4, at pp. 322–323.

[17] These courts, known as "Parlements", had for many years exercised quasi-legislative power by passing regulations on matters which were not covered by custom or royal ordinance. On this point see A. West, Y. Desdevises, A. Fenet, D. Gaurier and M. C. Heussaff, *The French Legal System* (Fourmat, 1992), pp 12–13.

[18] See *Cass. Crim.*, 26 February 1974, D. 1974, J. 273; *Conseil d'Etat*, 22 February 1946, S. 1946, 356 and more recently, *Conseil d'Etat,*, 21 December 1990, D. 1991, 283.

[19] On this question see West et. al., *op. cit.*, note 17, at p. 85 under "preliminary reference" and also at pp. 171–175. As far as criminal courts are concerned, Articles 111–115 of the new 1992 criminal code allow these courts to deal with the legality of administrative regulations when this matter is in issue during criminal proceedings.

seen to have shaped the nominations.[20] The *Conseil* not being part of the judiciary, access to it as set out in the constitution, Article 61, is strictly limited. At present, no reference to the *Conseil* can be made by an individual.[21] Originally only the president of the Republic, the prime minister, and the president of either house could refer a bill to the *Conseil*. However this was widened in 1974, following a constitutional amendment, to enable a reference to be made by a group of 60 members of either house of parliament. This has led to an increase in references to the *Conseil*[22] and has been used in recent years by the opposition parties as a mean to challenge many major government reforms.[23]

The constitution has been amended on several occasions since 1958. In 1992 President Mitterrand set up a committee—the Vedel Committee—to consider a more comprehensive revision of the constitution with the view to redefining executive power so as to give a more dynamic role to parliament and greater involvement to ordinary citizens. The recommendations made by the Committee have not yet been implemented apart from those strengthening the independence of the judiciary and those which made it easier to prosecute members of the government. Moreover, following the 1995 presidential elections, the French parliament passed constitutional reforms which represented the most significant constitutional change since the introduction in 1962 of direct universal elections for the presidency. The new reforms, which dealt with referendum procedure and the assembly of parliament were aimed at narrowing the gap between parliament and the French people.[24]

2.   COURTS AND JUDGES

A distinctive aspect of the French legal system is the existence alongside the ordinary civil and criminal judiciary headed by the *Cour de Cassation* of

---

[20] See Bell, *op. cit.*, note 4, pp. 34–41 for discussion of the composition of the *Conseil Constitutionnel*.

[21] A government bill was introduced in 1989 in order to amend the constitution on this question. It would have allowed, under certain conditions, a right of individual reference to the *Conseil Constitutionnel*. The bill failed to obtain Senate support. A further bill was introduced in 1993 following the recommendations made by the Vedel committee but no constitutional amendment has yet taken place on this point.

[22] Between 1959 and 1974, nine decisions were handed down by the *Conseil*. Between 1974 and 1984, there were 79 such decisions.

[23] For example, the 1981 nationalisations, the 1986 denationalisations and the 1990 bill which sought to grant special status to Corsica and to recognise the existence of the Corsican people.

[24] See "Le projet de réforme de la Constitution", *Le Monde*, 22 June 1995, p. 8.

separate administrative courts, which are headed by the *Conseil d'Etat*. These decide most legal disputes to which the government is a party. Although the existence of separate administrative courts was originally designed to free the executive from interference from the judiciary,[25] today the emphasis is placed on the advantages that accrue from referring disputes arising out of governmental action to judges specialised in the problems of public administration. The separation between ordinary and administrative courts has led to inevitable jurisdictional disputes[26] and to divergence between the case-law produced by the two supreme courts.[27] However disparity of case-law between ordinary and administrative courts should not be exaggerated for, most of the time, each of them decides on different areas of law and, in the event that they have both authority to interpret and apply the same rules of law, the conflict between them has very often been ended by legislative intervention or by an agreement between the courts themselves after a re-examination of their mutual positions.[28]

The French judiciary is a career judiciary with law graduates able to choose to try to become judges. However, while members of the ordinary courts are graduates from the *Ecole Nationale de la Magistrature* (ENM), administrative judges are graduates from the *Ecole Nationale d'Administration* (ENA). Entry to both schools is open to any student with a law degree, who, after a training period and final examinations, will be offered a position whose rank will depend on the performance achieved at these examinations.

According to Article 64 of the 1958 constitution, the president of the Republic is the guarantor of the independence of the judiciary. Although, generally, the political views of judges play no part in their promotion, appointments to the higher echelons of the judiciary (*e.g.* to the presidency of the *Cour de Cassation* or the *Procureur General* (Public Prosecutor) at the Paris Court of Appeal) are highly political and follow the changeover of po-

---

[25] See West et. al., *op. cit.*, note 17, pp. 22–24.

[26] In 1872 the *Tribunal des Conflits* was specially created to resolve any conflicts of jurisdiction between the two court systems.

[27] See D. Tallon, "The Constitution and the Courts in France" (1979) 27 *American Journal of Comparative Law* 567–75 (part 2).

[28] For examples of legislative intervention, see the Law of 31 December 1957 whereby litigation relating to loss caused by motor vehicles belonging to the administration, which would otherwise have been within the competence of the administrative courts, had been assigned to the ordinary courts. On the question of the enforceability of statutes inconsistent with international agreements where an agreement between the courts has been reached, see generally Part II, below.

litical power between the parties.[29] Generally judges cannot be removed or even promoted against their will. However this constitutional protection applies only to judges who actually try the cases.[30] The protection does not extend to the *Magistrats du parquet* who are the actual prosecutors. They must obey the orders of those above them all the way up to the minister of justice. The minister may require a prosecution to be commenced in a given case and, more generally, he or she may determine prosecution policies, particularly by issuing circulars. Failure to follow the orders of a superior may lead to disciplinary sanction or a transfer.[31] Moreover, in recent years investigating magistrates (*juges d'instruction*)[32] have been at odds with the government particularly in cases concerning financial scandals in which political parties have been involved.[33] Often such a dispute has ended with the removal of the file from the investigating magistrate involved and the passing of it to another.[34]

In matters of career advancement and discipline, the task of the *Conseil Superieur de la Magistrature* (CSM) should be noted. The role of the CSM

---

[29] See *Le Monde*, 11 February 1994 on the appointment of the new *Procureur Général* of the Paris Court of Appeal.

[30] In 1980 the *Conseil Constitutionnel* affirmed that the independence of administrative judges is a fundamental principle recognised by the laws of the Republic: Decision no. 80–119 of 22 July 1980, Validation of Administrative Decisions *Recueil des décisions du Conseil Constitutionnel* 46. Members of the lower administrative courts (but not the *Conseil d'Etat*) have also been recognised as independent by the Law of 6 January 1986.

[31] See the Review, "*Pouvoirs*" (1981) no. 16 on the judiciary, especially: P. Lyon-Caen, "L'expérience du Syndicat de la magistrature", at pp. 55–68; J. L. Bodiguel "Qui sont les magistrats français?", at pp. 31–41; and J. Libman "La politisation des juges", at pp. 43–53.

[32] The purpose of an "instruction" is to carry out in serious criminal cases a judicial investigation into the facts referred to the *juge d'instruction* by the public prosecutor or by the victim.

[33] For example the judge Jean-Pierre in the *Urba* case as related in *Tempête sur la Justice* (Paris, 1992) by the former Minister of Justice H. Nallet. This also occurred when, after election irregularities in both the presidential and legislative elections of 1988, legislation was passed in 1989 amnestying those who had been involved in irregularities in relation to the funding of political parties. This gave rise to considerable controversy amongst judges. After former members of parliament were held to be beneficiaries of the Amnesty Law, judges in the lower courts did consider that there was a case of unequal treatment before the law and took the opportunity to pass low sentences on other criminals. More recently, the series of prosecutions against politicians and sometimes members of the government in respect of further allegations of corruption have increased the tension between the executive and the judiciary.

[34] Article 34 of the code of criminal procedure provides for the possibility of replacing a particular *juge d'instruction* "in the interest of the good administration of justice".

is to assist the president of the Republic in guaranteeing the independence of the judiciary, with particular responsibilities in respect of appointments, advancement and discipline. It thus advises the president on who should be appointed as a judge.[35] The fact that the members of the CSM were appointed by the president of the Republic had been the subject of controversy in recent years. In July 1993 the 1958 constitution was amended on this point. Although the CSM is still presided over by the president of the Republic[36] its members are not appointed by him or her anymore. The new CSM consists of members elected from the ranks of the judiciary, one nominee of the president of the Republic and one nominee of each the two houses of parliament under terms set out in an organic law.[37]

The way judges are recruited in France explains why they tend to be young, men or women in equal numbers, and from different social and ethnic backgrounds. These may appear to be important factors influencing the way in which they decide cases. In addition, the fact that they go directly from law study into their careers may result in an approach to the law which is mostly governed by the theoretical education they have received. This factor also influences their manner of thinking, working and deciding cases.

3.   THE ROLE OF THE JUDICIARY

In the constitution the judiciary is seen as an "authority" rather than a power (Article 65). This constitutional view of the judiciary is supported by the French approach to the principle of separation of powers, which dates back to the Revolution, and by reference to which the judiciary has always been perceived as a rival to the executive. The revolutionaries established a body of rules, which are still in force today, whereby they prevented the judiciary from interfering in the spheres of the executive and legislature. Indeed by the Law of 16–24 August 1790, they organised a separation of ordinary and administrative courts by removing the jurisdiction of the ordinary courts in respect of administrative activity. Furthermore, they limited the role of the courts to that of applying to individual cases the rules emanating from the legislature. In such a system there was no place for a rule of binding precedent and this has been confirmed by Article 5 of the civil code which pro-

---

[35]   Article 65 of the 1958 constitution.

[36]   It has been said that the president is acting here rather as an arbitrator in the functioning of the different institutions of state than as a representative of the executive power.

[37]   Organic Laws are those which are so described by the constitution, such as those dealing with the status of judges. Here it concerns the Law no. 94–100 of 5 February 1994 completed by a Decree dated 9 March 1994.

vides that the judges are forbidden from making general or regulatory decisions in respect of the cases coming before them. If for these reasons case-law cannot be regarded as a formal source of French Law, it has, however, a persuasive value. Behind the facade of interpretation the judge may, very often, create law especially in cases where the law is silent, unclear or insufficient.[38] Moreover, the existence of a judicial hierarchy means that, even in the absence of judicial precedent, decisions given by the supreme courts are unlikely to be overruled by lower courts.

Part II: The European Convention on Human Rights in Domestic Law

We have already noted that in 1974 France incorporated the Convention within its domestic law, and that, following the presidential elections of 1981, she finally recognised the right of individual petition. As far as ratification is concerned, Article 55 of the 1958 constitution provides that duly ratified treaties should have precedence over ordinary statutes. This is generally only insofar as such treaties have been respected by France's treaty partners. However this condition of reciprocity is understood to apply only to international agreements which impose reciprocal obligations upon the states that have become parties to them (*traité-contrat*); in the case of treaties aiming to provide objective rules intended to bind the signatory states in the treatment of their own nationals (*traité-loi*), as is the case with the Convention, it would seem that the reciprocity provision does not apply.[39] We begin this section by considering some of the reasons that delayed France's acceptance of the ECHR framework. Then we look at the litigation on the status of treaties (including the ECHR) in French law, litigation that has occurred despite the apparent willingness of those who drafted the 1958 constitution to give treaties superiority over statutes. Finally in this section, we examine how the ECHR has been applied and enforced by the French courts after its ratification and consequent entry into the country's domestic law.

---

[38] Article 4 of the civil code states that a judge would be in breach of the obligations of his or her office if he or she fails to reach a decision on the grounds of the silence, lack of clarity or insufficiency of the written Law.

[39] B. Nicholas, *op. cit.*, note 10, p. 157. See also G. A. Bermann, "French Treaties and French Courts" (1979) 28 *International and Comparative Law Quarterly* 458–490, especially at pp. 465–469.

1. THE FACTORS WHICH HAVE HINDERED THE PROCESS OF RATIFICATION

Article 55 of the constitution makes ratification a matter of great importance. It was feared that ratification would, by incorporating the Convention into the French legal system, lead to a continuous interaction between European law and domestic law, followed by a series of amendments to domestic law in order to conform to the provisions of the Convention. In addition to that, the case-law that had grown up around Article 55 had shown that the principle of superiority was not easy to apply, especially in cases of conflict between a treaty and a subsequent statute.[40] It was also argued that there was an overlap between the provisions of Article 15 of the Convention, which authorises the states to take exceptional measures in times of war or other public emergency, and those of Article 16 of the French constitution, which provides that in times of grave crisis threatening the institutions of the Republic, the president may intervene and take "whatever measures are required by the circumstances". It was feared that Article 15, by providing that the states concerned should keep informed the secretary general of the Council of Europe, had the potential to hinder decisions of the president of the Republic issued under Article 16. However, many authors pointed out that the information required by Article 15 would not constitute an *a priori* control over presidential decisions and would, therefore, not interfere with the power of the president in the way that was feared.

It was also said that Article 2 of the first additional protocol to the Convention, in providing that "no person notwithstanding his religious believes shall be denied the right to education" was inconsistent with the fact that France was a secular state. This basic principle originates in a law of 1905 separating church from state, and has been restated in Article 2 of the 1958 constitution, which provides that France is a secular Republic. This implies that the Republic should remain neutral in matters of religion. However, on the question of schooling the application of this principle has not been easy. France has always been divided over the issue of whether or not private schools, which are usually religious, should be publicly funded.[41] Indeed, in the early 1950s, when the first debate on ratification took place, the most virulent opponents of ratification of the Convention were those who op-

---

[40] See the discussion on Article 55 of the 1958 constitution at section II of this Part, below.

[41] In December 1993, the revision by parliament of the 1850 Falloux Law, which had constrained local authorities from financing the investment costs of private schools, provoked more controversy.

posed state-aided schools. The 1959 Debré Law partially solved the dispute by granting state moneys to private schools while introducing at the same time measures to ensure a degree of state control over them.[42] This compromise removed an obstacle to ratification by setting a legal framework for freedom of education. However the question of secular education has remained a source of social and political controversy in recent years, not least because it has frequently come into confrontation with the religious rights of minorities.[43]

The greater part of the pre-1974 debate about the advisability of ratification surrounded the rules concerning the safeguards for people in custody after arrest. Article 5.3 of the Convention provides that "Everyone arrested...shall be brought promptly before a judge". The time allowed under French law for custody in respect of ordinary suspects (24 hours which could be extended for a further 24 hours) seemed to be in keeping with the requirement of reasonable time set forth in the ECHR. However, until 1986, the law provided for a maximum period of six days in offences against state security and terrorism. This appeared to conflict with Article 5.3. The Law of 9 September 1986 has finally reduced to four days the period of custody in this situation. This new time-limit should be sufficient to bring the law within the requirements of Article 5.3, as it has been interpreted by the European Court of Human Rights.[44]

It was at the political level that resistance to ratification was strongest. The French government, which in the 1950s had been involved in the Algerian conflict, did not wish to expose itself to an international organisation which might interfere in the internal affairs of the state. More generally, ratification was hindered by the French conception of unitary national sovereignty. A number of politicians pointed out that ratification would have the effect of transferring sovereignty away from the nation to an international organisation. However, since the 1958 constitution the concept of national sovereignty had changed in response to the fact that parliamentary supremacy had itself been restricted.[45] Surprisingly, despite this fact, the *Conseil*

---

[42] On the Debré law, see Bell, *op. cit.*, note 4, at pp. 151–154.

[43] See the case of the "Muslim scarf" in the *Conseil d'Etat* decisions of 2 November 1992, D. 1993, 108–111 and 10 March 1995, *Le Monde*, 13 March 1995. See further E. Steiner, "The Muslim Scarf and the French Republic" (1995–96) 6 *King's College Law Journal* 146.

[44] *X. v. Netherlands*, Decision of the European Commission of Human Rights, 6 October 1966; *Duinhof and Duijf* v. *Netherlands* Series A, No. 79 (1984) 13 E.H.R.R. 478; *Brogan* v. *United Kingdom* Series A, No. 145–B (1988) 11 E.H.R.R. 117.

[45] Articles 34 and 37 of the 1958 constitution, discussed in Part I above.

Constitutionnel has taken, as recently as 1991, a rather conservative view with regard to national sovereignty and the law of the European Communities, holding that, because national sovereignty is unitary and cannot be divided, no transfer of sovereignty is possible.[46]

In this context, it is perhaps unsurprising that once ratification had occurred, there should have been this further wait until 1981 for the right of individual petition to be recognised by France. This delay was the object of criticism since this right, which can rightly be described as the cornerstone of the European system of protection, was designed to furnish an international remedy in situations where the national remedy was inadequate. Prior to 1981, successive governments put forward two main reasons to justify the delay. One reason was the assertion that human rights were already adequately protected by national remedies in France. A second was that the application of the Convention by the courts should first be tested domestically before making available international remedies. These objections were overridden following the 1981 presidential elections. Indeed, the right of individual petition was part of the socialist candidate's platform in the run-up to that election.

2. THE PLACE OF THE CONVENTION IN THE FRENCH LEGAL SYSTEM: ARTICLE 55 OF THE 1958 CONSTITUTION

Article 55, which makes duly ratified treaties superior to ordinary statutes, is merely an application of the principle according to which enacted laws in France are categorised according to a "hierarchy of norms" (*hiéarchie des normes*). In such a system constitutional laws have greater value than treaties[47] which in turn are superior to parliamentary statutes. Each of the authorities which enact laws must abide by the principle of the hierarchy of norms. This is a very important aspect of the French doctrine of *Etat de droit* whereby public authorities are required to act in accordance with legal

---

[46] *Conseil Constitutionnel* decision of 30 December 1976, D. 1977, 201. The case dealt with the constitutionality of the introduction of the principle of the election of members of the European Parliament by universal suffrage. On the facts the *Conseil* held that no transfer of sovereignty had occurred. This view was confirmed in 1991 in a case in which the *Conseil* was asked to determine the constitutionality of a statute authorising the ratification of the Shengen agreement (Decision of 25 July 1991). However, in respect of the Maastricht treaty the *Conseil* took the view that "transfers of competence" was possible in the context of the development of the European Community: *Conseil Constitutionnel,* 9 April 1992, J.C.P., 1992, Section II, 21853.

[47] If a treaty is contrary to the constitution this requires the amendment of the latter before ratification may be proceeded with.

norms, thus being subject to and not above the law. However, enforcing the rule of superiority of treaties under Article 55 has not proved an easy task and has been the subject of litigation in each of France's three supreme judicial bodies.[48] The 1975 abortion bill gave the *Conseil Constitutionnel* an opportunity to take a view on the provision. The abortion legislation was referred to the *Conseil* by members of the national assembly on the basis of its possible breach of Article 2 of the Convention which provides that "everyone's right to life shall be protected by law". In its decision dated 15 January 1975, the *Conseil* declared itself incompetent to deal with the question of whether a statute was in conformity with a treaty.[49] The grounds for the decision were that the *Conseil's* jurisdiction under Article 61 of the constitution was confined to the question whether a statute was in conformity with the constitution. Whether or not it was in conformity with a treaty was a different question which could not be dealt with by the *Conseil*. Decisions under Article 61, the *Conseil* said, were "absolute" in the sense that a statute which is not in conformity with the constitution simply cannot be enacted at all. However, the rule of superiority of treaties provided in Article 55 was, in contrast to Article 61, only "relative and contingent", being itself conditional on reciprocity. It is clear that what the *Conseil* meant was that a statute which was contrary to a treaty could not be held unconstitutional because the reciprocity provision made it only "relatively" and not "absolutely" defective. This argument was not beyond criticism. As we have already observed, the concept of reciprocity seems largely alien to the ECHR, a convention which was designed primarily to bind the signatory states in the treatment of their own nationals.[50] The 1975 decision was also criticised because of its refusal to ascribe a constitutional value to treaties. It enabled the legislature to pass statutes not in conformity with ratified treaties, therefore rendering ineffective the protection supposedly afforded by Article 55. Despite these criticisms the *Conseil* has confirmed its position in subsequent decisions.[51]

---

[48] For further details, see Bermann, *op. cit.*, note 39.

[49] *Conseil Constitutionnel*, 15 January 1975, D. 1975 J. 529.

[50] Bermann, *op. cit.*, note 39, pp. 465–469; Nicholas, *op. cit.*, note 10, p. 157.

[51] Decision of the *Conseil Constitutionnel* of 3 September 1986, Rec. 135 in which the *Conseil* held that it was within the competence of the ordinary courts to implement Article 55. However, prior to ratification, the *Conseil Constitutionnel* may determine if treaties are in conformity with the constitution (Article 54 of the 1958 constitution): see decision 22 May 1985, Rec. 15.

Since a conflict between a treaty and a statute is not a constitutional question and, therefore, not within the competence of the *Conseil Constitutionnel*, it must necessarily be within the competence of the ordinary courts. In fact, the ordinary courts, turning the abortion law ruling to their advantage, have decided to review the conformity of legislation with existing treaties under Article 55. However, while the rule superiority did not affect the resolution of conflicts where a treaty was later in time than the statute said to be in opposition to it, the superiority of treaties over subsequent statutes became the subject of divergence between the ordinary and the administrative courts. The *Cour de Cassation*, in the case of *Société Jacques Vabre*,[52] decided to give priority to Article 95 of the EC Treaty over a subsequent incompatible parliamentary statute on import duties, applying Article 55 to the case. However, the *Conseil d'Etat*, in a first ruling took a different view in similar circumstances,[53] considering that it was not its role to intervene in the province of the legislature by holding parliament to account for adopting statutes contrary to international agreements. But in the recent case of *Nicolo*,[54] the *Conseil d'Etat* has eventually reached an agreement with the *Cour de Cassation* by deciding that the provisions of the EC Treaty take precedence over a subsequent incompatible statute delimiting the constituencies for the elections to the European parliament. This decision was generally welcomed as it brought consensus to the courts over what had until then been a contentious issue. Although case-law on this matter has predominantly been concerned with the EC Treaty, there has now been a similar resolution in favour of the ECHR,[55] as Article 55 does not distinguish between international and EC law in its statement of the rule of superiority.

3. THE RECEPTION OF THE ECHR BY THE JUDICIARY

A. *Preliminary comments*

One of the most important effects of the case-law concerned with Article 55 is that the parties to a case coming before the courts have come to rely increasingly on the ECHR. This has been mainly so in the sphere of criminal procedure. The length of criminal proceedings is indeed a problem in France. However, in recent years, the ECHR has been used in various other areas including contract law, protection for aliens, telephone tapping, taxa-

---

[52] Cassation Chambre Mixte 24 May 1975, p. 497.
[53] In *Scat Gal des fabricants de semoule*, D. 1968, 285. See also *Conseil d'Etat*, decision of 31 October 1980, D. 1981, 38–43 (the abortion case).
[54] *Conseil d'Etat*, 20 October 1989, J.C.P. 1989, Section II, 21371.
[55] For example the two decisions at *Conseil d'Etat*, 21 December 1990, D. 1991, 283–286.

tion, civil proceedings, the right to privacy, abortion, surrogacy and transsexuals. In theory, parties to a case may also rely on the 1789 Declaration which is a constitutional norm and which, by reference to the principle of the hierarchy of norms, has a binding effect on the judges. Two main reasons justify recourse to the Convention rather than to the 1789 Declaration. The first is constitutional and arises from the fact that, as has already been noted, French judges cannot review statutes by reference to a constitutional norm, here the 1789 Declaration. However, the administrative courts have regard to such norms when adjudicating on administrative activity. In such a case it is not a matter of constitutional review but a matter of legality. This means that administrative activity must comply with the law in general and this includes constitutional norms.[56] In contrast the ordinary and administrative judges are able to give priority to the ECHR over an incompatible parliamentary statute. The second reason for reliance on the ECHR is to be found in the differing scope of the two texts being considered. The ECHR is wider than the 1789 Declaration, particularly in the area of criminal procedure. Articles 5 and 6 of the Convention provide very specific and detailed guarantees which are not to be found in the Declaration. Furthermore, the Declaration does not provide for certain rights to be found in the European Convention such as, for example, those set out in Articles 8 and 12. As a result these Articles have been frequently used in domestic law.[57]

To summarise, then, we may say that fundamental rights in France are protected in three ways:

1. By constitutional review undertaken by the *Conseil Constitutionnel* for which, since the 1971 leading case, the 1789 Declaration has been the favoured source of civil liberties. The *Conseil Constitutionnel* will not, however, scrutinise statutes for compatibility with France's treaty obligations.
2. By the administrative courts when adjudicating on administrative activity by reference to the "general principles of law". The administrative courts will also take into account the ECHR when adjudicating on administrative action.
3. By the application of the ECHR by the civil and criminal courts. There is no doubt that for the courts the Convention is part of domestic law and has to be applied directly.[58] Even in circumstances where the parties have

---

[56] On the principle of legality, see West *et al.*, *op. cit.*, note 17, pp. 171–175.

[57] The cases are discussed below at text to note 71 ff.

[58] *Respino*, decision of 3 June 1975, Bull. Crim. no. 141, 382; *Glaeser*, decision of 30 June 1976, D. 1977, 1–4. Both cases were decided by the *Cour de Cassation*, Criminal Divi-

not referred to it the judges have used it in the process of reaching their decisions.[59] However, case-law shows also that judges have reduced the effect of the Convention by interpreting it restrictively. It is to this last point that we now to turn.

B. Case-Law

As we have already observed, most of the case-law concerned with the Convention is in the sphere of criminal procedure. Three principal issues have been addressed before the criminal courts: first detention on remand exceeding the "reasonable time" provided for in Article 5.3; secondly, the question of fair trial by an independent and impartial tribunal" (Article 6.1); and thirdly, the right to defence (Article 6.3). Most of the time the Criminal Division of the *Cour de Cassation* has dismissed appeals to it on these issues. Indeed, the *Cour de Cassation* has limited the scope of the guarantees accorded in Articles 5 and 6 by constructing these texts narrowly. Some striking examples of this strict approach will now be illustrated. In the *Milone* case decided by the *Cour de Cassation* in 1985, the defendant complained that his right to have his case heard by an impartial tribunal under Article 6.1 had been breached owing to the fact that, after termination of a first investigation due to irregularities in the proceedings, a second investigation had been initiated by the same investigating magistrate (*juge d'instruction*) who had undertaken the first one. The *Cour de Cassation* dismissed the appeal.[60] According to the Criminal Division of the *Cour* the requirement for an impartial tribunal was not concerned with pre-trial proceedings (*e.g.* investigation) but only with trial proceedings. A similar view had been taken one year previously by the Criminal Division[61] in a case where a defendant, who had been committed for trial, complained that the judge who had been sitting in the indictment division of the Court of Appeal (*Chambre d'Accusation*) during the pre-trial proceedings, was also to be found sitting in the trial court. The *Cour de Cassation* decided that there was no infringement of Article 6.

The grounds for the two decisions seem to rest on the term "judgment" which appears as the first word in the second sentence of Article 6.1 which states that: "In the determination of his civil rights and obligations or of any

---

sion.

[59] *Boeuf*, decision of the *Cass. Crim.* 5 June 1980, Gaz. Pal. 1981, I, 6–8.

[60] *Milone*, decision of the *Cass. Crim.* 29 January 1985, D. 1985, I.R., 107.

[61] Decision of the *Cass. Crim.* 14 June 1984, D. 1985, I.R., 66. See also decision of the *Cass. Crim.* 20 December 1984, D. 1985, 541.

criminal charges against him, everyone is entitled to a fair and public hearing within a reasonable time by an independent and impartial tribunal established by law. Judgment shall be pronounced publicly...". Although the *Cour* is not explicit in its decisions, it appears, however, that it has indeed relied on this term to reduce the range of what precedes it in the first sentence of Article 6.1.[62] In French criminal law the word *jugement* applies only to trial courts. Courts dealing with investigation (*juge d'instruction* and *Chambre d'Accusation*) which only decide if the accused should be sent for trial, give *ordonnances* and *arrêts* as opposed to *jugements*.

In the 1986 *Villemin* case,[63] the defendant was charged with murder and was remanded on detention. He submitted an application for his release. His application was dismissed by the examining magistrate and, on appeal, by the indictment division of the Nancy Court of Appeal. The defendant filed an appeal before the Criminal Division of the *Cour de Cassation* relying *inter alia* on Article 5.1 (c) of the ECHR claiming that he possessed all the necessary guarantees that he would appear for trial and that, therefore, his detention could not be justified. His argument was that this provision in the ECHR restricted such detention to situations where either its purpose was to bring "an accused person before the competent legal authority on reasonable suspicion of having committed an offence" or where it was judged "reasonably...necessary to prevent his committing an offence or fleeing after having done so". He claimed that none of these circumstances applied to his case. The *Cour de Cassation* dismissed the appeal on the grounds that the provisions of Article 5.1 (c) were only concerned with the conditions under which a person, having been arrested by the police, is remanded on custody with the view to appearing before the examining magistrate. It held that the provision did not apply to the decisions taken by the examining magistrate concerning detention on remand.

On the question of the reasonableness of the length of detention on remand provided for by Article 5.3, the *Cour de Cassation* in the *Lamarque* case[64] decided that a reasonable time and length of detention were not questions of law which would be dealt by the *Cour de Cassation*, but were rather merely questions of fact which, under French law, fell to be dealt with in the lower courts. This last decision reflects a practical reluctance on the part of

---

[62] On the notion of *tribunal impartial* before the French courts, see also J. Pradel, "La notion européenne de tribunal impartial et indépendant selon le droit français" [1990] *Revue Sciences Criminelles* 692–706.

[63] *Cass. Crim.* 3 January 1986, D. 1986, 137–138.

[64] *Cass. Crim.* 6 March 1986, D. 1986, 315–317.

French judges to give precedence over domestic law to the ECHR. In the same decision the *Cour* did not hesitate to show the merit of French criminal procedure over and above the safeguards offered by the Convention, stating that "...the provisions of our Code of Criminal Procedure, which strictly define the conditions under which detention on remand may be ordered or continued, far from being incompatible with the provisions of the Convention, offer on the contrary additional guarantees in order to prevent unjustified detention". Indeed, if one compares the wording of Article 5 with the wording of Articles 144 and 145 of the code of criminal procedure, it may be noted that, whereas Article 5.1 (c) only requires a "reasonable suspicion of having committed an offence", the French code imposes additional conditions which makes detention on remand an exceptional measure. For instance, Article 144 provides that, in cases involving less serious criminal offences (*matière correctionnelle*) detention on remand may be ordered only if the sentence risked is equal to or exceeds one year's imprisonment in cases of apprehension *in flagrante delicto*, or two years imprisonment in other cases. Article 144 also lays down the specific circumstances in which detention on remand may be ordered or continued, for example, when the detention on remand of the accused is the sole means of preserving evidence or material clues or of preventing either pressure being brought to bear on the witnesses or the victims, or collusion between the accused and accomplices. Furthermore, Article 145 provides that the order of detention must give specific reasons with reference to the particular circumstances of the case in relation to the provisions of Article 144 and furthermore that the decision as to detention may only be made in chambers after an adversarial hearing in the course of which the investigating magistrate should hear the observations of the accused and of his counsel.

The Criminal Division of the *Cour de Cassation* has also undermined the scope of Article 6.3(c) of the ECHR which states that: "Everyone charged with a criminal offence has the following minimum rights:...(c) to defend himself in person or through legal assistance of his own choosing...". In the *Demoiselle Ouin* case[65] it has been decided that this right does not imply that the defendant has personal access to the file of his or her case. Only his or her counsel has this right if he or she chooses to instruct one. More recently the *Cour de Cassation* held, in conformity with Article 114 of the code of criminal procedure, that the right of individuals charged with a criminal offence to have adequate time and facilities for the preparation of their defence (Article 6.3(b) of the ECHR) does not extend to the passing by their

---

[65] *Cass. Crim.* 9 February 1978, D. 1979, 463–466.

lawyer to them of documents—or copies of such documents—relating to the accusation.[66] This decision followed several disciplinary sanctions against lawyers in France. It has been criticised as considerably restricting the rights of the defence to the extent that defendants are not able to have a complete knowledge of the nature and cause of the accusation against them.

Whereas criminal procedure has been for many years the particular field in which the Convention has been invoked, the courts have also heard cases concerned with other rights protected by the ECHR, particularly those rights guaranteed by Articles 2, 8, 9, 10, 11 and 12. The enthusiasm of certain lawyers in their tendency to invoke the Convention systematically has spilled over into what one French author has referred to as a *fièvre européenne*.[67] On occasion this enthusiasm has been carried too far, as the same author illustrated by referring to the case of *Rouyer* heard in 1983 by the Criminal Division of the *Cour de Cassation*.[68] Here, a teacher, prosecuted for not having paid his taxes claimed as a defence that, as he did not wish to pay for ideological reasons, he should be protected by the provisions of Articles 9 and 10 of the Convention which proclaim the rights to freedom of thought and freedom of expression. Needless to say, the *Cour de Cassation* dismissed his appeal. The same court has also had to deal with other cases where the outcome was predictable owing to the restrictions authorised by the Convention itself. Thus, it was decided that the rights to freedom of peaceful assembly and to freedom of association did not prevent a soldier being convicted under military law for having distributed to his fellow soldiers leaflets inciting them to indiscipline.[69] Indeed, Article 11.2 authorises lawful restrictions on the exercise of these rights by members of the armed forces. This case may be linked with the case of *Tesson*, a conscientious objector, who invoked Articles 10 and 11 of the Convention in order to avoid the duties he had to perform in substitution of his military service.[70] In dismissing his appeal, the *Cour* referred to Article 4.3(b) of the Convention which allows complete latitude to the member states in so far as service exacted of conscientious objectors in place of military service is concerned. It has also been decided that the right of the customs authorities to require the production of papers and documents and the power to search houses (Articles 64, 65, 65–1 and 454 of the customs code) are not incompatible

---

[66] The case is reported in *Le Monde*, 2 and 3 July 1995.

[67] J. Mestre, [1992] *Revue Trimestrielle de Droit Civil* 88 (no. 9).

[68] *Cass. Crim.* 19 May 1983, Bull. Crim. 367–369.

[69] See *Cass. Crim.* 23 January 1985, Bull. Crim. 36; D. 1986, I.R., 107.

[70] *Cour de Cassation*, 4 March 1980, D. 1980, 330–333.

with the right to respect for private life and correspondence protected by Article 8 of the Convention.[71] Article 8.2 provides that there may be interference by a public authority with the exercise of this right so long as the interference is in accordance with the law and amounts to a measure which is necessary in a democratic society in the interests of the economic well-being of the country or for the prevention of disorder or crime. It was this provision which the *Cour* relied on.

French courts have had to address themselves to other contentious questions. Article 8 of the ECHR has arisen in cases concerning creditors who have sought to obtain the addresses of debtors whose residents were currently not known to them. According to the *Cour de Cassation*, seeking the address of a debtor did not amount to a breach of Article 8 as long as the objective was to protect "a right legally or judicially recognised", as when, for example, there was a court order against a debtor providing for a certain sum to pay.[72] One of the most controversial areas has been telephone tapping. In the past the *Cour de Cassation* had always taken the view that telephone tapping ordered by an examining magistrate in the course of a criminal investigation was not in breach of Article 8.[73] Although there was no provision in French Law permitting telephone tapping, the *Cour* considered such conduct to be covered by Article 81 of the code of criminal procedure which states that: "The investigating magistrate shall undertake in accordance with the law all investigative measures as he deems useful for the establishment of the truth". The view taken by the *Cour* was heavily criticised. Indeed, it was argued that since Article 81 did not specifically mention telephone tapping, the measure was therefore not "in accordance with the law" within the meaning of Article 8.2 of the ECHR. Furthermore, incorporating

---

[71] *Cass. Crim.* 21 November 1983, Bull. Crim. no. 304; *Crémieux and others, Cass. Crim.* 21 January 1985, D. 1986, I.R., 107. In this last case the defendants applied to the European Commission. The case ended with the European Court of Human Rights judgments dated 25 February 1993 in *Crémieux v. France* Series A, No. 256–B (1993) 16 E.H.R.R. 357; *Funke v. France* Series A, No. 256–A (1993) 16 E.H.R.R. 297; and *Miailhe v. France* Series A, No. 256–C (1993) 16 E.H.R.R. 332, in which it was decided that there had been a violation of Article 8 of the ECHR. Indeed, at the material time, the rule applicable to the case was Article 64 of the customs code. This Article did not make house searches and seizures subject to judicial authorisation. However, the 1986 Budget Act completed later by the 1989 Budget Act amended Article 64. Under the 1986–1989 reforms every search must now be authorised by a judge's order.

[72] *SA Locumiviers v. Hospices Civils de Lyon, Cass. Civ.* 1, 19 March 1991, D. 1991, 568–571.

[73] *Kruslin*, 23 July 1985, Bull. Crim. no. 275; *Cass. Crim.* 15 March 1988, Bull Crim. no. 226; *Cass. Crim.* 19 June 1989, Bull. Crim. no. 261.

telephone tapping within the scope of Article 81 was not in accordance with the general rule according to which criminal provisions must be construed strictly. (As we shall see presently, new legislation on telephone tapping was introduced in 1991 following judgments given by the European Court of Human Rights against France on this issue.[74])

Transsexuals have also alleged that the refusal by the French courts to recognise their true sexual identity was in breach of Article 8. They argued that, by failing to allow the indication of their sex to be corrected in the civil status register and on their official identity documents, the authorities were forcing them to disclose intimate personal information to third parties. In the past, some lower courts and courts of appeal had granted applications for amendment of entries in civil status registers relating to sex and forenames.[75] However the *Cour de Cassation* had, until recently, taken a more conservative view. In two judgments given in 1987[76] the *Cour* decided that the refusal to rectify the applicant birth certificate was justified by the fact that the change of sex was not caused by a factor extraneous to the will of the person concerned. In 1990 the *Cour de Cassation* stated that in its judgement, "transsexualism, even when medically acknowledged, cannot be regarded as a true change of sex, as the transsexual, although having lost certain characteristics of his original sex, has not thereby acquired those of the opposite sex...".[77] However, following the judgment given by the European Court of Human Rights on 25 March 1992 in *B. v. France*, the *Cour de Cassation* has agreed to overrule its own case-law on this question.[78]

Another question French courts have had to address with respect to the ECHR has been abortion. The controversy concerning abortion was not settled with the 1975 decision given by the *Conseil Constitutionnel*.[79] It arose once more in 1980 and again in 1991 before the *Conseil d'Etat*. In the 1980 case the plaintiff wished to challenge an abortion undertaken by his estranged wife. He brought proceedings against the hospital which had per-

---

[74] See the *Kruslin* and *Huvig* judgments, discussed in Part III, section 3 below.

[75] See TGI Aix-en-Provence, 6 March 1991 [1991] *Revue Trimestrielle de Droit Civil* 706; TGI Perigueux, 10 September 1991, J.C.P. 1992, section IV, 129; CA Colmar, 15 May 1991, J.C.P. 1992. section IV, 434.

[76] *Franquet and Botella, Cass. Civ.* 3 and 31 March 1987, D. 1987, 445.

[77] *Mme X. Cour de Cassation, Civ. 1*, 21 May 1990, D. 1991, 169.

[78] *René X* and *Marc X*, two decisions of the Full Assembly of the *Cour de Cassation* given on 11 December 1992, J.C.P. 1993, Section II 21991. For *B. v. France* Series A, No. 232–C (1992), see Part III, section 2 below.

[79] See above note 49.

formed the abortion alleging that it had been carried out in breach of Article 2 of the ECHR which declares that "Everyone's right to life shall be protected by law." The administrative court dismissed his action. He then appealed against the judgment to the *Conseil d'Etat* which upheld the decision of the lower court.[80] In the 1991 case, the *Conseil d'Etat* dismissed the appeal of two anti-abortion associations which had challenged as contrary to Article 2 the decision of the minister of health authorising the commercial sale of the abortion pill in France.[81] Whereas, in the first case, the grounds for dismissal were that the administrative judge would not give at that time priority to an international agreement over a subsequent parliamentary statute (in this case the 1975 legislation on abortion), in the second case, the *Conseil* justified its decision by saying that : "the 1975 Law on abortion [to which the Minister's decision referred] guarantees in its Article 1 respect for any human being from the beginning of his life except in cases of necessity and within the strict conditions laid down in the law itself. In those circumstances the 1975 law is not incompatible with the provisions of the Convention".

Finally, French courts have heard cases in which Article 12 of the ECHR has been invoked. In 1989 and in 1991 the *Cour de Cassation* decided that the right to marry and to found a family did not justify the making of surrogacy agreements which were otherwise illegal in that they constituted a sort of disposal of the human body which was not authorised by law and which was contrary to public policy.[82] It has also been decided that the provisions of the criminal code which make it an offence for the husband of a prostitute to live off her immoral earnings[83] are not in breach of the same Article.[84] The *Cour de Cassation* has also rejected an argument based on Article 12 which has been raised by transsexuals, who have relied on the provision to claim that the refusal to rectify their civil status has had the effect of wrongly preventing them from getting married.[85]

---

[80] *Conseil d'Etat* 31 October 1980, D. 1981, 38–43.

[81] *Conseil d'Etat* 21 December 1990, D. 1991, 283–286.

[82] *Alma Mater case, Cour de Cassation* 13 December 1989, D. 1990, 273; *Procureur Général v. Mme. X* Ass. Plen. 31 May 1991, D. 1991, 417.

[83] Article 334(2) and (3) of the criminal code.

[84] Crim. 4 June 1980, D. 1981 I.R., p. 143.

[85] *H.* v. *Procureur Général de Rouen* Civ. 1, 10 May 1989, D. 1989, I.R., p. 22.

Part III: The Effect of ECHR Judgments in the French Legal System

After France finally recognised the right of individual petition in 1981, French law could finally be questioned before the European Commission and the European Court of Human Rights. If we include all Article 50 cases as well as substantive applications, by the end of 1995, no fewer than 74 cases involving France have been considered by the European Court of Human Rights with the bulk of the cases having been heard in the last four years. Before considering the impact of the ECHR judgments on French law, we should recall that decisions given by the European Court are not as such binding on French domestic courts. The *Cour de Cassation* has on several occasions confirmed this.[86] It is of course also the case that the Convention itself provides for derogations from and restrictions to the rights and liberties set out in the document.[87] As a result of this, and somewhat paradoxically, French laws which are restrictive of liberty have been able to find in the Convention a fresh source of legitimacy. This has been emphasised by the fact that the European Court has on occasion interpreted the Convention restrictively in much the same way as the French courts.

A striking example is the case of *Sainte-Marie* v. *France*.[88] Mr Sainte-Marie, a member of IPARRETARRAK, a clandestine Basque separatist movement, was charged with various offences concerned with the unauthorised possession of certain categories of weapons. He complained that his case had not been heard by an impartial tribunal within the meaning of Article 6.1. He alleged a violation of Article 6.1 insofar as the Criminal Division of the Court of Appeal which had convicted him had not been an impartial tribunal because two of its members had sat previously in the indictment division of the same court which had ruled on his application for release. In its judgment dated 6 November 1986, in conformity with its existing case-law, the *Cour de Cassation* decided that this was not a ground for quashing the decision: "no statutory provisions prohibit on pain of nullity the members of the indictment division which has given such a ruling from subsequently sitting in the Criminal Appeals Division before which the case comes." Furthermore, the *Cour* went on to assert, "such participation is not

---

[86] See for example, *Cass. Crim* 3 February 1993, pp. 515–516; *Cass. Crim* 4 May 1994, D. 1995, 80–81.

[87] See generally M. Delmas-Marty and C. Chodkiewitz (eds.), *The European Convention for the Protection of Human Rights: International Protection Versus National Restrictions* (Dordrecht, 1992), especially ch. 3 on France, by R. Koering-Joulin and P. Wachsmann.

[88] Series A, No. 253–A (1992) 16 E.H.R.R 116.

contrary to the requirement of impartiality laid down in Article 6 of the European Convention…". In its judgment the European Court echoed this approach, holding that: "the mere fact that a judge has already taken pre-trial decisions in the case, including decisions relating to detention on remand, cannot in itself justify fears as to his impartiality. Only special circumstances may warrant a different conclusion. The European Court agreed, therefore, that the case did not reveal any breach of Article 6.

With this warning in mind, let us now turn to the cases. The main areas of ECHR activity insofar as France has been concerned have been in relation to custody and detention on remand, transsexuals, telephone-tapping, aliens, the reasonableness of the length of proceedings and fair trial. We will now deal with each in turn.

1. CUSTODY AND DETENTION ON REMAND

As far as crucial issues like the length of custody and detention on remand in criminal proceedings are concerned, it may be said that France, after a number of reforms of the law of criminal procedure,[89] has made a continuing effort to conform to the provisions of the ECHR. Since the Law of 17 July 1970, enacted before ratification, detention orders must include specific reasons with reference to the particular circumstances of the case in relation to the provisions of Article 144 of the code of criminal procedure. This is the Article in the code which specifies the particular cases in which detention on remand may be ordered or continued.[90] The 1970 law was also the first step towards a reduction in the length of detentions, thereby making it far less likely that the law would fall foul of Article 5.3 of the ECHR.[91] However, despite the provisions of the code, in practice the length and number of detentions has remained high in France in comparison with other European countries. Thus, on 1 September 1991, there was a rate of 34.8 detentions *per* 100,000 of the population in France, as compared with a rate of 20.2 for the United Kingdom. On 1 May 1994, no fewer than 57,457 individuals were being held in detention on remand.[92] One of the main reasons for this

---

[89] See the Law of 17 July 1970; Law of 6 August 1975; Law of 2 February 1981; Law of 9 July 1984; Law of 30 December 1987; and Law of 4 January 1993 amended by the Law of 24 August 1993.

[90] The Law of 6 July 1980 has extended the provisions of Article 144, which was originally set for less serious criminal offences (*délits*), to serious criminal cases (*crimes*).

[91] The relevant provisions are Articles 145(1), 145(2), 194(2) and 567(2) of the code of criminal procedure.

[92] For these statistics, see "Le Nouveau Code de procédure pénale : la détention provisoire" *Le Monde*, 4 June 1993; and *Le Monde,* 11 May 1994.

high rate is said to be the key role played by the *juges d'instruction* (investigating magistrates) in the criminal proceedings. The *juges d'instruction*, who are responsible for charging the suspects and ordering detentions on remand, have over the years over-used these powers. Indeed, the need to order or to continue the deprivation of liberty on the ground of the disturbance of public order caused by an offence, as set out in the code of criminal procedure, has always been assessed by the *juges d'instruction* in a purely abstract way, taking into consideration only the gravity of the offence.

The situation brought about by such an approach led to the setting up, at the request of the minister of justice, of a Committee on Criminal Justice and Human Rights, known as Delmas-Marty Committee. This body reported in June 1990 that there was an urgent need for a root and branch reform of criminal procedure in France, particularly having regard to the requirements of the ECHR.[93] Before the reforms took place, the European Commission and the European Court of Human Rights had begun to deal with applications in which it was alleged that the length of detention in various cases had been excessive and that Article 5.3 of the ECHR had been breached. In the cases of *Kemmache*,[94] *Letellier*[95] and *Tomasi*[96] the judges of the European Court decided unanimously that France had violated Article 5.3 for the following reasons:

> It falls in the first place to the national judicial authorities to ensure that, in a given case, the pre-trial detention of an accused person does not exceed a reasonable time. To this end they must examine all the circumstances arguing for or against the existence of a genuine requirement of public interest justifying, with due regard to the principle of the presumption of innocence, a departure from the rule of respect for individual liberty and set them out in their decisions on the applications for release....
>
> The Court accepts that, by reason of their particular gravity and public reaction to them, certain offences may give rise to public disquiet capable of justifying pre-trial detention, at least for a time. In exceptional circumstances this factor may therefore be taken into account for the purposes

---

[93] On the reform movement in general, see H. Trouille, "A Look at French Criminal Procedure" [1994] *Criminal Law Review* 735.

[94] Series A, No. 218 (1991) 14 E.H.R.R. 520.

[95] Series A, No. 207 (1991)14 E.H.R.R. 83.

[96] Series A, No. 241–A (1992)15 E.H.R.R. 1.

of the Convention, in any event in so far as domestic law recognises—as in Article 144 of the French Code of Criminal Procedure—the notion of disturbance to public order caused by an offence.

However, this ground can be regarded as relevant and sufficient only provided that it is based on facts capable of showing that the accused's release would actually disturb public order. In addition detention will continue to be legitimate only if public order remains actually threatened; its continuation cannot be used to anticipate a custodial sentence.[97]

In short, for the European Court of Human Rights, decisions to order or to continue detention are legitimate only if investigating judges assess the need to order or to continue the deprivation of liberty from a "subjective" point of view by taking into account the facts of the case capable of showing that the accused's release would actually prejudice public order. In the cases under consideration the European Court noted that the French courts had ruled on the issue from a "purely abstract point of view taking into consideration only the gravity of the offence".[98]

The European Court decisions adverse to France on this Article 5 issue have had a considerable effect on criminal proceedings in France. First, the case of *Letellier* was immediately followed by a circular dated 1 October 1991 issued by the minister of justice and intended to give recommendations to French judges on the question of the length of detentions in the light of the *Letellier* judgment. Secondly, the *Tomasi* judgment was instrumental in accelerating the reform of criminal procedure which eventually took place in 1993.[99] Tomasi was an active member of a Corsican political organisation. He was suspected of having taken part in an attack in February 1982 against the rest centre of the European Legion in Corsica. In March 1983 he was charged and remanded in custody. He spent five years and nearly seven months in detention before being acquitted in October 1988, after which he was immediately released. In its judgment the European Court unanimously condemned France for a violation of Article 5.3. The judgment was all the more damning in that France was also unanimously condemned under Article 3 of the ECHR for the ill-treatment which the applicant had suffered during his police custody. Furthermore, under Article 50, the applicant was

---

[97] *Letellier, op. cit.*, note 95, paras. 35 and 51.

[98] *Ibid.*, para. 51.

[99] For the impact of *Tomasi*, see the case notes by J. F. Renucci, D. 1993, Sommaire, 383–384 and F. Sudre, *Revue Sciences Criminelles* 1993, 33.

awarded the considerable sum of one million French francs in damages and costs.

The 1993 reform of the code of criminal procedure[100] was aimed at achieving compliance with the terms of the European Convention and flowed not only from these European Court decisions but also from the recommendations made three years before by the Delmas-Marty committee. The new provisions concerning detention on remand may be summarised as follows:

i)   New Article 77 of the code of criminal procedure states that police officers may take into custody (*garde à vue*) only persons who are under reasonable suspicion of having committed or attempted to commit an offence. This new version of Article 77 is drafted in similar terms to Article 5.1(c) of the European Convention.

ii)   According to new Article 63(4), everyone is entitled to a meeting with a lawyer following a period of 20 hours in police custody. However this provision is not intended as a step by which the lawfulness of the arrest may be challenged in court as provided in Article 5.4 of the Convention. Rather it is designed to improve the rights of the defence at this stage in the procedure.

iii)   One further innovation of the 1993 reform is the consolidation of the presumption of innocence as a civil right in the French legal system. Apart from Article 9 of the 1789 Declaration of the Rights of Man, which states that "every individual is presumed innocent until found guilty", a new Article 9(1) is introduced into the civil code according to which "everyone has the right to respect for his presumption of innocence". The courts may, on the basis of this text, order for a statement of retraction and, where appropriate, award damages in compensation. This reform was welcomed. Indeed the recent condemnation of France by the Strasbourg Court in the 1995 case of *Allenet de Ribemont* where the applicant complained that the French police had referred to him in a press conference as one of the instigators of a murder although he had not yet been charged, showed that under the old regime the presumption of innocence was not adequately protected in France.

---

[100] A first law reforming the code of criminal procedure was enacted on 4 January 1993; however by the time this reform came into force, new elections had taken place and the new majority in parliament decided to amend the Law of January 1993. This was accomplished when a new Law was passed on 24 August 1993.

iv)   Finally, while the *juge d'instruction* is still invested with authority to order or continue detention on remand,[101] according to new Article 187(1) of the code of criminal procedure, in the case of an appeal against an order for detention on remand, the indictment division of the Court of Appeal may suspend the execution of this order pending its decision on the lawfulness of the detention.[102]

Further reforms are expected following the 1995 presidential elections. The new minister of justice, Jacques Toubon, has declared his intention to reform the law on criminal procedure in respect of detention on remand and appeals against decisions given by courts of assizes. As far as detention on remand is concerned the notion of disturbance of public order set-out in Article 144 of the code of criminal procedure is expected to be narrowed in order further to restrict the power of the investigating judge. In respect of courts of assizes, which try serious offences in France, appeals will be introduced against their decisions. So far no appeal lies against a decision given by a court of assizes the reason being that the jury of nine is considered to be the representative of the French people and thus to be sovereign in respect of its decisions. For years criticism has been voiced against this particular criminal procedure in France and it does appear to be in conflict with Article 2 of the seventh protocol of the European Convention which provides for an appeal against any conviction by a criminal court, which protocol was ratified by France in 1986. There can be little doubt that if these reforms are introduced they will contribute to making French criminal procedure much more consistent with the ECHR.

2.   TRANSSEXUALS

B. v. France[103] is the key decision. B was a transsexual who was born a male but who subsequently underwent gender reassignment surgery and started to live as a woman. She applied to the French courts for rectification of civil status. The application was dismissed in accordance with the then current case-law of the *Cour de Cassation* on this issue.[104] The applicant brought her case before the European Court of Human Rights, complaining that the refusal by France to recognise her true sexual identity was a breach of Article

---

[101] The first version of the 1993 reforms (see note 100, above) had removed this power from the *juge d'instruction* in favour of a collegiate authority, *la chambre d'examen des mises en détention provisoire*.

[102] The practice is called *référé-liberté*.

[103] Series A, No. 232–C (1992) 16 E.H.R.R. 1.

[104] See above notes 75–78 for the French case-law.

8 of the ECHR. She argued that by failing to allow the indication of her sex to be corrected in the civil status register and on her official identify documents, the French authorities had forced her to disclose intimate personal information to third parties. The applicant stressed that in France an increasing number of official documents indicated sex, including identity cards and birth certificates. As a result, transsexuals were unable to carry out many of the transactions of daily life without disclosing the discrepancy between their legal sex and their apparent sex. The European Court distinguished this case from the earlier British cases of *Rees*[105] and *Cossey*[106] where it had been held in each case that there had been no violation of Article 8. First, the European Court noted that, unlike the English civil status system, birth certificates in France were intended to be updated throughout the life of the person concerned so that it would be perfectly possible to insert a reference to a judgment ordering an amendment of the original sex recorded. Secondly, the Court also noted that, unlike in the UK, whether or not a transsexual could change his or her forename in France did not depend only upon his or her wishes but was also subject, under Article 57 of the civil code, to judicial permission. On the basis of these factors the Court decided that in the case of B. there had been a violation of Article 8. Following this judgment, the *Cour de Cassation* held, in two decisions handed down on the same day in December 1992, that when a transsexual has undergone a sex-change operation and has as a result lost the characteristics of the original sex and acquired those of the opposite sex, the obligation to respect the privacy of such an individual's private life demanded a rectification of his or her birth certificate.[107] Originating from *B. v. France*, this ruling effectively overturned the previously settled case-law of the *Cour de Cassation*, which had mainly stressed the principle of the inalienability of the status of individuals. The case constitutes a striking example of the way in which the European Convention judgments have impacted on French law.

3.   TELEPHONE TAPPING

As far as telephone tapping is concerned, the French courts—and in particular the *Cour de Cassation*—have for many years regarded Article 81 of the code of criminal procedure as providing a legal basis for telephone tapping carried out by a senior police officer under a warrant issued by an in-

---

[105]   Series A, No. 106 (1986) 9 E.H.R.R. 56.

[106]   Series A, No. 184 (1990) 13 E.H.R.R. 622.

[107]   See note 78 above.

vestigating judge.[108] In 1989, in the case of *Baribeau,*[109] the Full Assembly of the *Cour de Cassation* quashed a decision given by the indictment division of the Court of Appeal of Paris which had decided that the interception by the police of the defendant's telephone conversations was lawful in the absence of any request for evidence issued by an investigating judge. According to the *Cour de Cassation*, police officers were not empowered under Article 81 to tap telephone conversations of any accused person in the absence of a request for evidence on commission (*commission rogatoire*) issued by an investigating judge. Therefore, the *Cour* ruled that in this case, telephone tapping lacked a statutory basis and was not "in accordance with the law" within the meaning of Article 8.2 of the Convention. The *Baribeau* judgment meant that Article 81 constituted an adequate and effective statutory basis for telephone tapping within the meaning of Article 8.2 only if it took place on foot of a request for evidence on commission from the investigating judge. Although the explicit reference by the *Cour* to Article 8.2 added greater legitimacy to the *Cour's* view on telephone tapping, it was nevertheless questionable whether the rule set by the *Cour* satisfied the requirements of the Convention, especially as regards the phrase "in accordance with the law". Indeed, according to the Strasbourg case-law the requirement of being "in accordance with the law" must be taken to mean that the law, written or unwritten, must be set out with sufficient clarity to give citizens an adequate indication as to the circumstances in which public authorities may act.[110] This did not appear to be true of the French law, even after the *Baribeau* decision. In view of this, an urgent need for new legislation was voiced in France in order to make French law consistent with the Convention on this issue.[111]

While this debate was proceeding, the European Court unanimously decided in *Huvig*[112] and *Kruslin*[113] to condemn France for a breach of Article 8. This was despite the fact that both cases involved telephone conversations

---

[108] See the leading case of *Tournet, Cass. Crim.* 9 October 1980, D. 1981 J. 332, in which the *Cour* held that telephone tapping was lawful where the operation had been undertaken under the supervision of an investigating judge, without any deception and without jeopardising the rights of the defence.

[109] Ass. Plen. 24 November 1989, D. 1990 J. 34.

[110] *Klass* v. *Federal Republic of Germany* Series A, No. 28 (1978) 2 E.H.R.R. 214 and *Malone* v. *United Kingdom* Series A, No. 82 (1985) 7 E.H.R.R. 14 are the leading cases.

[111] See J. Pradel, "Ecoutes téléphoniques et Convention Européenne des droits de l'Homme" D. 1990 *Chronique* pp. 15–20.

[112] Series A, No. 176–B (1990) 12 E.H.R.R. 528.

[113] Series A, No. 176–A (1990) 12 E.H.R.R. 547.

recorded in pursuance of an order issued by an investigating judge. According to the Strasbourg Court, Article 81 of the French code of criminal procedure did not afford enough adequate safeguards as regards telephone tapping. For instance, under Article 81, nothing obliged the judge to set a limit on the duration of telephone tapping; furthermore, the circumstances in which recordings might or might not be erased or the tapes be destroyed were not specified. The Court concluded by saying that, "In short, French Law, written and unwritten, does not indicate with reasonable clarity the scope and manner of exercise of the relevant discretion conferred on the public authorities....There has therefore been a breach of Article 8 of the Convention."[114]

Just three days after these European Court rulings against France a note from the minister of justice was circulated amongst the judges which was intended to emphasise the circumstances in which telephone tapping could be ordered in the light of the judgments. These instructions had an immediate influence on the case-law of the *Cour de Cassation*. In subsequent decisions the *Cour*, after having restated that Article 81 provided a legal basis for telephone tapping, added to its text further conditions, namely that only the most serious offences could give rise to telephone tapping; that precautions should be taken in order to communicate the recordings for possible inspection by the defence; and that there was an obligation on the judge to set a limit on the duration of telephone tapping as required by the European Court in its judgments.[115] However, the *Cour de Cassation* was criticised for having acted as a legislator by adding supplementary conditions to Article 81.[116] It is true that the principle of separation of powers prevents the French judiciary from making law[117] and, more specifically, that under the current 1958 constitution[118] only parliament can legislate on criminal procedure. The

---

[114] See also the murder case involving Prince J. de Broglie in which the European Court of Human Rights decided (in *A.* v. *France* Series A, No. 277–B (1993) 17 E.H.R.R. 462) that there had been a violation of Article 8 in connection with telephone tapping made by a high ranking police officer acting without the prior authorisation of an investigating judge. However, in this particular case, the government conceded that the interference was not "in accordance with the law" at the material time because it had not been ordered by an investigating judge.

[115] The case of *Bacha, Cass. Crim.* 15 May 1990, J.C.P. 1990 Section II 21541; see also the case of *Rodriguez, Cass. Crim.* 26 November 1990, J.C.P. 1991 Section IV 87 and the case of *Falgon, Cass. Crim.* 3 June 1992, Bull. Crim. no. 219.

[116] See the comments of R. Koering-Joulin, D. 1990 *Chronique*, pp. 187–189.

[117] See above Part I, section 3.

[118] Article 34.

need for new legislation was satisfied by the Law of 10 July 1991 on the interception of telephone conversations. In its Section 1, the Law guarantees the right to respect for everyone's correspondence and for everyone's telephone conversations. It sets out the conditions on which telephone conversations may be intercepted during a judicial inquiry: in cases involving the most serious offences, at the request of an investigating judge, for a period of four months which is renewable. The Law of 10 July 1991 also specifies the precautions that must be taken in order to communicate the recordings intact and in their entirety for possible inspection by the judge or by the defence. It also sets out the circumstances in which these recordings may be erased or the tapes destroyed.[119] In so doing, the 1991 Law has followed the requirements set by the ECHR in its *Huvig* and *Kruslin* decisions. Despite this, the issue of telephone tapping remains a controversial one in France.[120]

4. ALIENS

The cases under this head concern extradition and deportation. As regards the first of these, there are no provisions in the ECHR regarding either the conditions whereby an extradition order may be granted or the procedure to apply before such an order is executed. However, if we look at the case law of the European Commission on Human Rights, an extradition order may conflict with the provisions of the Convention, for example, with Article 3 when there are serious reasons to fear that an individual will be subjected in the requesting state to the treatment described in this Article,[121] or with Article 6 when it appears that the requesting state does not sufficiently protect the rights of defendants. It may be noted that the *Conseil d'Etat* has the responsibility of verifying whether the judges of the requesting state abide by the fundamental rights and liberties of individuals as required by the fundamental principles of the law on extradition.[122] Similarly extradition is now

---

[119] See Article 100(3)–(7) of the code of criminal procedure.

[120] The latest report by the National Commission for the Control of the Interception of Communications (CNCIS) stated that for the year 1994 there were 1,180 non judicial and 10,413 judicial official interceptions of conversations. Furthermore, following the recent *Schuller-Marechal* case, the Head of the Police Service resigned after the Court of Appeal of Paris declared void under the 1991 Act telephone tapping that had been undertaken by the police in the absence of a request by an investigating judge. This case involved a local counsellor threatened with extortion in a story of corruption currently in the course of investigation in France.

[121] *Cf. Soering* v. *United Kingdom* Series A, No. 161 (1989) 11 E.H.R.R. 439.

[122] See *Lujambio Galdenao, Conseil d'Etat* 26 September 1984, J.C.P. 1985 Section II, 20346.

refused if the individual whose extradition is challenged is threatened with the death penalty.[123] In the case of *Memick Fidan*[124] the *Conseil d'Etat* decided that "the application of the death penalty to an individual against whom extradition ha[d] been decided by the French government would be contrary to French public policy". However, in the recent case of *J. Davis-Avlor*, an American citizen prosecuted in Texas for capital murder, the *Conseil d'Etat* has refused to annul the extradition order despite the fact that such an offence is punished by the death penalty in Texas. It seems that diplomatic considerations played a crucial part in the decision of the *Conseil*.[125]

Another important issue related to extradition is that of disguised extradition. If the extradition procedure should appear to be impossible, deportation to another state is ordered where this latter state can more easily permit extradition to the original requesting state. In the case of *Bozano*, which led in 1986 to the first condemnation of France by the European Court of Human Rights, an order for deportation to Switzerland had been issued against the applicant following an unfavourable opinion by the indictment division of the Court of Appeal of Limoges upon Italy's request for an extradition. The Swiss authorities then executed a further extradition order issued by Italy. The European Court considered that France's behaviour constituted an irregular deprivation of liberty within the meaning of Article 5.1(f) of the European Convention. The choice of the Swiss border, which had been imposed on the applicant, clearly showed the real reason behind the decision; in reality, the government had sought not to expel the applicant from French territory but to hand him over to the Italian authorities *via* the Swiss authorities with whom Italy had an extradition agreement. The condemnation of France was undoubtedly one of the factors which led the administrative courts, when dealing with expulsion orders, to reinforce their control over these decisions especially in relation to the host country to which the person is expelled. Thus in 1987, in the case of *Mantumona Buayi*, the *Conseil d'Etat*, in accordance with the government's submissions which referred explicitly to the *Bozano* judgement, considered the question of whether there was a risk of the defendant being prosecuted for political reasons in Zaire, the host country to which it was proposed that he be expelled.[126]

---

[123] The Law of 9 October 1981 has abolished the death penalty in France.

[124] *Revue Française de Droit Administratif* 1987, p. 591.

[125] See *Le Monde*, 18 October 1993, pp. 1 and 12.

[126] *M. Mantumona Buavi, Conseil d'Etat* 6 November 1987, *Revue Française de Droit Administratif,* pp 86–95.

Turning now to deportation generally, the Strasbourg court has had to decide on applications against France by aliens alleging that their deportation from France has been in breach of Article 8 of the ECHR (the right to respect for private and family life) in the sense that such action would if it took place jeopardise the maintenance of their family ties in France. In this respect we should note that, although the French 1945 Ordinance on Aliens does not permit deportation orders to be issued against particular categories of aliens having certain family ties in France, *e.g.* someone married to a French national for at least one year, it does not provide for the general protection of family ties that is afforded by Article 8.[127] Accordingly, in the cases of *Djeroud*[128] and *Beldjoudi*,[129] the applicants alleged in Strasbourg that they had real family ties in France and that the deportation orders made against them would jeopardise the maintenance of those ties. In *Djeroud* a friendly settlement took place before the case came before the European Court, with the authorities deciding to withdraw the deportation order against the applicant who was granted a residency permit for ten years and awarded a sum of 150,000 F.Fr. for damages. No doubt the French authorities took such a decision because only one year previously the European Commission, when dealing with the same case, had taken the view that the deportation of a person from one country where he has lived almost all his life to another country with which his only link was the formal tie of nationality might raise issues not only from the point of view of family life but also with respect to privacy.

In the case of *Beldjoudi* the European Court, in conformity with its 1988 decision in *Berrehab* v. *Netherlands*, ruled that the decision to deport the applicant, if put into effect, would not be proportionate to the legitimate aim pursued under Article 8, whether this aim was the "prevention of disorder" or the "prevention of crime". The Court therefore found a violation of Article 8 from the point of view of respect for the applicant's family life. For years the *Conseil d'Etat* had refused to apply Article 8 to cases concerned with deportation orders.[130] However it seems that the decision of the Commission in the *Djeroud* case in particular has played an important part in the evolution of the *Conseil d'Etat's* case-law. One year before the European Court judgment in the case of *Beldjoudi*, the *Conseil d'Etat*, in dealing with

---

[127] See section 25 of the Ordinance.

[128] Series A, No. 191–B (1991) 14 E.H.R.R. 68.

[129] Series A, No. 234–A (1992) 14 E.H.R.R. 801.

[130] See for example *Touami Ben Abdeslen*, 25 July 1980 Rec. Lebon 1980, 820.

the same case,[131] had not reviewed the deportation order with reference only to the threat to public order as might have been expected on the basis of past precedents, but rather decided, having regard to Article 8, to carry out a complete review of proportionality as to whether the measure taken was proportionate to the legitimate aim pursued. In other words, the *Conseil* accepted that it was relevant to consider whether the interference with family life which followed from the order was not excessive when compared with the public interest that was being safeguarded.[132] Furthermore, a ministerial circular, dated 25 October 1991, set out to strengthen the system for the protection of aliens who are subject of measures of removal from French territory. The circular specifically intended to take into account the recent case-law of the *Conseil d'Etat* and the European Court of Human Rights and to ensure compliance with Article 8.[133]

5. THE REASONABLENESS OF THE LENGTH OF PROCEEDINGS

The reasonableness of the length of proceedings, dealt with in Article 6.1, has been at issue in a number of cases against France heard by the European Court of Human Rights.[134] The length of the proceedings in the French courts is attributable primarily to the fact firstly that in many cases parties are allowed to bring action in court by themselves without legal assistance and secondly, that cases may be referred to the appellate courts at the parties' own discretion. These factors have considerably increased the workload falling on the courts especially the *Cour de Cassation* and the *Conseil d'Etat*. Furthermore the existence of two sets of courts and the difficulty in delimiting their two jurisdictions has contributed to the delay. The cases before the Strasbourg Court have frequently raised the question whether proceedings before the administrative courts having exceeded "a reasonable

---

[131] Though Beldjoudi had in fact submitted his case to the European Court of Human Rights before the *Conseil d'Etat* gave its final decision in the case.

[132] *Beldjoudi*, 18 January 1991 Rec. Lebon 1991, 18–19; see also *Belgacem*, 19 April 1991 *Revue Française de Droit Administratif* 1991, pp. 497–510.

[133] Note however that the 1993 strict "Pasqua" immigration laws have tightened up the rules concerned with the issuing of residence permits and with the deportation of aliens. Moreover terrorist bombing during the Summer of 1995 resulted in the mass deportation of aliens from France.

[134] For example *Ste Stenuit* v. *France* Series A, No. 232–A (1992) 14 E.H.R.R. 509 and *Editions Périscope* v. *France* Series A, No. 234–B (1992) 14 E.H.R.R. 597 which show that Article 6.1 applies not only to individuals but also to corporations. See also *Dobbertin* v. *France* Series A, No. 256–D (1993) 16 E.H.R.R. 558, in which the proceedings lasted 13 years.

time" within the meaning of Article 6.1. In *H.* v. *France*,[135] the applicant complained about the time taken by the administrative courts to try his action for damages against a public hospital. The proceedings lasted for a total of a little over seven years. The proceedings were commenced in the lower administrative court on 14 June 1974 and judgment was delivered on 9 May 1978. These proceedings therefore lasted four years which was undoubtedly a long time. The European Court admitted that it was "not unaware of the difficulties which sometimes delay the hearing of cases by national courts and which are due to a variety of factors. Nevertheless, Article 6.1 requires that cases should be heard within a reasonable time. In so providing the Convention underlines the importance of dispensing justice without delay which might jeopardise its effectiveness and credibility."[136]

The case of *H.* was seen in France as an invitation to the administrative judges to dispense justice without delay.[137] In the 1990 *Gisti* case the *Conseil d'Etat* had to deal with the question of the interpretation of an international agreement in relation to the conditions of residence and employment of Algerian nationals in France. The *Conseil*, in accordance with the government commissioner's submissions referring explicitly to the ECHR, decided not to adjourn the proceedings for a preliminary reference on this point to the minister of foreign affairs as would have occurred under its previous case-law.[138] Indeed, prior to this case, the administrative courts in such circumstances routinely decided to adjourn the proceedings for a preliminary reference to the government as to the interpretation of the treaty, a procedural habit which invariably resulted in considerable delay. By following the government commissioner's submissions, the *Conseil* had certainly in mind a possible subsequent challenge under Article 6.1. It now interprets international agreements itself and, if it does seek the opinion of the executive, it does not regard itself as bound by the opinion that it then receives.[139]

---

[135] Series A, No. 162–A (1989) 12 E.H.R.R. 74.

[136] *Ibid.*, at para. 58.

[137] See the note by J. Tercinet following the report of *Gisti* in J.C.P. 1990, Section II, 21579.

[138] *Gisti, Conseil d'Etat*, 29 June 1990 in *Actualité Juridique Droit Administratif*, 1990, 621.

[139] Despite this development, in the recent case of *Beaumartin* v. *France* Series A, No. 296–B (1994) 19 E.H.R.R. 485, France was condemned for a breach of Article 6.1 (length of proceedings and fair trial) in relation to the *Conseil d'Etat* practice which consisted of referring to a representative of the executive any difficulty encountered in interpreting an international treaty. The case arose before the *Conseil d'Etat*'s change of practice in *Gisti*.

In *X.* v. *France,*[140] the applicant was a haemophiliac who had undergone several blood transfusions and had been infected by HIV. In 1989, X made a preliminary claim for compensation to the minister of health. His claim was rejected. He then filed an application in the Paris Administrative Court for the annulment of the decision and for an order requiring the state to pay compensation. The Court dismissed his claim and X died in February 1992. The proceedings were then continued by his parents. The European Court of Human Rights was eventually to find a breach of Article 6.1. Although the French administrative courts took a normal time to give judgement and although there had been no abnormal delay, this case, like those of other infected haemophiliacs, ought to have been dealt with as a matter of urgency because of the life expectancy of the persons concerned. The *X* case was followed by further condemnations of France by the Strasbourg Court in similar cases related to the length of compensation proceedings brought by haemophiliacs infected with the AIDS virus following blood transfusions.[141] Although public opinion and the scandal surrounding the contaminated blood supplied to haemophiliacs at the Blood Transfusion National Centre played an important part in the improvement of the situation of AIDS victims in France, in particular with the setting up of a compensation fund by the Act of 31 December 1991, the effect of these changes was not to speed up proceedings in the courts which were dealing with applications from infected persons. It is to be hoped that the recent Strasbourg judgments on this issue will have an impact on the French judges dealing with such cases.

6. FAIR TRIAL

Applicants to the European Court of Human Rights have also complained about the lack of a fair trial in the French courts. For example, in the case of *Pham Hoang,*[142] the European Court decided that there was a violation of Article 6.3(c) concerning everyone's right to defend him or herself through legal assistance which is required be given free if the defendant has not sufficient means. Mr Pham Hoang complained that he had been unable to secure the official assignment of counsel in the *Cour de Cassation.* In fact legal representation is not compulsory in criminal cases in France; moreover,

---

[140] Series A, No. 234–C (1992) 14 E.H.R.R. 483.

[141] In *Vallée* v. *France* Series A, No. 289 (1994) 18 E.H.R.R. 589, and *Karakaya* v. *France* Judgment of the European Court of Human Rights, 26 August 1994, the European Court considered that a period of more than four years to obtain a judgment in first instance proceedings far exceeded a reasonable time in cases of this nature.

[142] Series A, No. 243 (1992) 16 E.H.R.R. 53.

at the time of this case, there was no provision dealing with the problem of legal aid for persons like the applicant whose means were insufficient to ensure the exercise of their rights in the criminal courts. However since the case was referred to the European Court in June 1991, after the European Commission had unanimously considered that there had been a violation of the ECHR, it has been provided in the Law of 10 July 1991 that, "Legal aid shall be granted to plaintiffs or defendants in contentious or non-contentious proceeding before any Court. It may be granted for all or part of the proceedings". Following this, a system of legal aid in criminal cases has been set up.

The Strasbourg Court has also heard cases against France on the question of everyone's right to examine or have examined witnesses against him under Article 6.3(d) of the ECHR. In the recent case of *Saidi*[143] the European Court condemned France on this issue. In a judgment delivered in 1988, the *Cour de Cassation* denied the applicant, who had been charged with various drug offences, the right to examine and have examined witnesses against him by the investigating magistrate. However, one year later, the *Cour de Cassation*, anticipating a European condemnation in the *Saidi* case, overruled its previous case-law on this question referring, in particular to the relevant provisions of the ECHR.[144] Finally, in the 1994 *Hentrich* case the European Court stated that the inability of dispossessed purchasers in France reasonably to challenge the pre-emption of their property by the Revenue constituted, according a breach of Article 1 of the first protocol (on property) and of Article 6.1 of the Convention.[145]

Conclusion

The opportunity for French litigants to rely on the European Convention and to apply to the Strasbourg Commission and Court undoubtedly constitute, together with the development since 1971 of a veritable body of constitutional case-law, a truly novel element in recent French law on public liberties. Indeed, the European Convention on Human Rights has become a source of French law together with the constitution and statute law. French judges quote the ECHR more and more often in their judgments, either on

---

[143] Series A, No. 261–C (1993) 17 E.H.R.R. 251. See further *Le Monde*, 6 October 1993.

[144] See *Le Monde, ibid.*

[145] An infringement of the Convention occurred here despite the fact that since 1987 the *Cour de Cassation* has ruled consistently that pre-emption decisions must contain reasons which are capable of being challenged by dispossessed purchasers.

their own initiative or in response to the parties' submissions. Even if the courts have sometimes shown leniency and resistance in construing the Convention, nevertheless, it is the case that in the most recent case-law, a continuing good will on their part towards the European case-law is increasingly in evidence. The overall situation may be summarised as follows:

1.   Following the European Court judgments against it, France has adapted its law (statutes or case-law) to take into account the European Court ruling (on telephone tapping and transsexualism for example).

2.   There has been a spontaneous adaptation of the national law even before the European Court has given its decision affirming a violation of the Convention. This is because the threat of being condemned is sometimes sufficient to cause a change in the law, as was the case in both *Beldjoudi* and *Pham Hoang*.

It should be added that often the cases have ended in the European Court with a friendly settlement, the government conceding its liability.[146] The European case-law concerning other member states has occasionally played a marginal role in the liberal evolution of French Law; for example, the *Dudgeon* case led to the abolition of criminal sanctions against homosexuals in France.[147]

However there are still improvements that can be achieved, notably as regards the length of custody faced by individuals suspected of having committed acts of terrorism, the length of detention on remand, and more generally as regards the length of the proceedings in the courts. Despite this, it can be said that, in recent years, France has shown a capacity to contribute towards the development of a new European public order based on democracy, equality and fundamental rights and freedoms.

---

[146]   See *Djeroud* v. *France, op. cit.*, note 128; *Birou* v. *France* Series A, No. 232–B (1992) 14 E.H.R.R. 738; *Demai* v. *France* Series A, No. 289–C (1994) 20 E.H.R.R. 89; and *Marlhens* v. *France,* Series A, No. 317 (1995) 21 E.H.R.R. 502.

[147]   Law of 4 August 1982.

8.   ITALY

Danilo A. Leonardi[*]

Introduction

The number of decisions involving Italy handed down by the European Court of Human Rights in Strasbourg appears to give substance to the claim that "Italy has not had much regard for the Convention".[1] The country has become the most frequent Strasbourg "offender" in recent years.[2] Despite this it is perfectly obvious that the Italian authorities cannot be accused of engaging in the same type of massive violations of human rights that have taken place in other countries, even not too far away from their territory, such as in the Balkans, or in other parts of the world. The heart of the matter is, however, that the respect due to human rights in a liberal democracy en-

---

[*]   I am most grateful to Professor Andrea Bianchi of the University of Siena for his willingness to discuss the ECHR with me and for his help during my research visit to his University. I am also grateful to Professor Roberto Guerrini with whom I discussed the implications of the ECHR for Italian criminal law and to Dott.sa Patrizia Vigni with whom I talked about various issues concerning the application of the ECHR in Italy. I wish to acknowledge that Professor Bianchi and Dott.sa Vigni have kindly read an earlier draft of this chapter and made valuable comments on it. Many thanks to Lic. Gabriele Gatti of the University of Siena, for his help with the database and CD-ROM searches in Italian domestic case-law, and to Professor Alan Boyle of the University of Edinburgh for putting me in touch with his Siena colleague, Professor Bianchi. I must express my gratitude to Mr. C. M. G. Himsworth (University of Edinburgh) for always making himself available for advice. Many thanks also to Tsutomu Takahashi who has been a patient listener. I should add that I take responsibility for the views expressed in this piece and for any remaining inaccuracies or errors concerning the Italian legal system and the impact of the ECHR in the country.

[1]   A. Bernardi and F. Palazzo, "Italy" in M. Delmas-Marty (ed.), *The European Convention for the Protection of Human Rights; International Protection versus National Restrictions* (Dordrecht, 1992), p. 196.

[2]   The number of cases in which Italy was the respondent government in Strasbourg (excluding Article 50 cases and the one inter-state application) between 1980 and 1995, was 116. The number of lost cases was 81, which represents a loss percentage figure of 70 per cent. of the total number of cases filed against Italy before the European Court of Human Rights.

C. A. Gearty (ed.), European Civil Liberties and the European Convention on Human Rights, 307–345.
© 1997 Kluwer Law International. Printed in the Netherlands.

tails a deep commitment to the safeguarding and enhancement of rights under the rule of law, and it is in respect of this criterion that, on the basis of its setbacks in Strasbourg, the Italian legal system would seem to have failed.

It is the purpose of this chapter to provide an assessment of the overall impact of the ECHR on Italian law. First, the position of the Convention will be considered in the context of the Italian constitutional structure as a whole. A discussion of the use made of the ECHR by the domestic courts will follow, and finally the measures taken for its implementation in the domestic system will be assessed. The latter inquiry will not assume that unfavourable Strasbourg rulings have inexorably resulted in law reform in Italy, since it is clear that, as we shall see presently, implementation may take many different forms.

Part I: The Constitutional Structure of the Italian Republic

Italy adopted a written constitution in 1947[3] establishing a new democratic parliamentary republic which stressed the protection of fundamental rights.[4] The constitution has been termed "rigid" by Italian scholarly writing because it is entrenched: special majorities and procedures are necessary for its amendment.[5] Fundamental rights, however, cannot be overridden by parliament, and arguably, not even by constitutional revision. The Italian constitutional structure comprises the president, the cabinet,[6] a bicameral parliament, the Constitutional Court[7], the judicial power (presided over by the Court of Cassation[8]), the Superior Magisterial Council (the administrative organ of the judiciary, separate from the judicial power), the National Economic and Labour Council, the Court of Audit, the Council of State[9], and the administrative hierarchy of courts.[10] The guardian of the constitution is the Constitutional Court, which can act as a judge of parliament by striking down unconstitutional legislation.

---

[3]   The constitution has been in force since 1 January 1948.

[4]   Constitution, Article 2.

[5]   Constitution, Article 138.

[6]   The policy making authority rests with the cabinet, which is accountable to Parliament.

[7]   *Corte Costituzionale.*

[8]   *Corte di Cassazione.*

[9]   *Consiglio di Stato.*

[10]   See G. Leroy Certoma, *The Italian Legal System* (London, 1985), pp. 137–138.

The constitutionally guaranteed fundamental rights, called "inviolable rights" in the constitution, may be relied upon in any court. Individuals, companies and foreigners enjoy the same fundamental human rights as Italian citizens.[11] The list of constitutional rights is non-exhaustive, but it comprises the substantive right to personal freedom,[12] the inviolability of domicile[13] and of correspondence and other means of private communication,[14] and the right of defence[15] and access to the courts.[16] In addition, legal aid is guaranteed,[17] and the principle of legality is established as a fundamental part of the criminal law.[18] Criminal responsibility is personal, an accused is innocent until proved guilty and punishment is required to be administered in accordance with principles of humanity and with a view to the rehabilitation of the person.[19] The granting of extradition requests is subject to stringent conditions.[20] The constitution also contains other substantive rights, including the right of private property[21] and a fairly comprehensive list of programmatic social rights[22] which includes: family rights[23], health rights,[24] education rights,[25] labour rights,[26] co-operation rights[27] and collaboration

---

[11] Constitution, Article 10 (2), and Civil Code, Article 10.

[12.] Constitution, Article 13 (1).

[13] Constitution, Article 14 (1).

[14] Constitution, Article 15 (1).

[15] Constitution, Article 24 (2).

[16] Constitution, Article 24 (1).

[17] Constitution, Article 24 (3).

[18] Constitution, Article 25: there must be a predetermined forum to hear a case; no judge may be appointed ex-post facto; all punishment must be laid out by law; and so on.

[19] Constitution, Article 27 (3).

[20] Constitution, Article 26.

[21] Constitution, Article 42.

[22] E. Cheli and F. Donati, "Method and Criteria of Judgment on the Question of Rights to Freedom in Italy" in D. M. Beatty (ed.), *Human Rights and Judicial Review: A Comparative Perspective* (Dordrecht, 1994), p. 242.

[23] Constitution, Articles 29–31.

[24] Constitution, Article 32.

[25] Constitution, Articles 33 and 34.

[26] Constitution, Articles 35–50.

[27] Constitution, Article 45.

with company management,[28] company and property rights,[29] and rights relating to credit and savings.[30]

I. THE CONSTITUTIONAL COURT

The Constitutional Court is composed of 15 judges, although, exceptionally, 16 additional members would sit on the Court in a case involving proceedings against the president of the Republic, the prime minister or the ministers. The system of appointments is of some complexity. The 15 ordinary members are appointed as follows: a third is appointed by the president of the Republic, another third by parliament,[31] and the final third is appointed by the supreme courts as follows: three judges are chosen by the Court of Cassation while the Council of State and the Court of Audit appoint one each. Regardless of the organ which makes the actual appointment, all constitutional judges are chosen from among (a) magistrates of the superior ordinary and administrative courts; (b) law professors; and (c) lawyers who had been more than 20 years in practice. An appointment to the Constitutional Court is for nine years from the day the judge is sworn in. Re-election is not possible. The Court chooses its own president among its members. An appointment as president of the Constitutional Court is for three years, although re-election is possible within the president's term of office as constitutional judge. The Court needs 11 judges to function. Cases are decided in chambers by majority voting and in the case of a tie, the president's vote prevails. In addition to the ordinary members, parliament keeps a list of extraordinary judges who would join their ordinary colleagues to hear an accusation filed against the president of the Republic, the prime minister or the ministers.[32] The legislature selects these extraordinary judges following the same procedure used to appoint its share of the ordinary judges, but the qualifications for appointment are those necessary for election to the Senate. In extraordinary cases, a quorum of 21 judges (with the extraordinary appointees in a position of majority) is required.[33]

---

[28] Constitution, Article 46.

[29] Constitution, Articles 41–44.

[30] Constitution, Article 47.

[31] The Constitutional Law 22. 11. 1967 n. 2 calls for a procedure of secret ballot in ordinary sittings: the required majorities vary, two-thirds are necessary to select a judge in the first and second round, while three-fifths are sufficient after the third round.

[32] Constitution, Article 135.

[33] See further T. Martines, *Diritto Costituzionale*, 8th ed. (Milan, 1994), pp. 550–553 and I. Scotto, *Diritto Costituzionale*, 2nd ed. (Milan, 1992), pp. 183–185.

More generally, the drafters of the constitution knew that the unavailability of a control of constitutionality in the previous framework of government had given the fascist regime the leeway to violate the constitution.[34] With this in mind, they devised a system in which an organ independent of the three branches of government was to be entrusted with the jurisdiction to review the constitutionality of laws. The ordinary judiciary was not considered the appropriate branch of government to review the action of the legislature.[35] In this way, the constitution differed from the outset from the United States model, epitomised in the *Marbury* v. *Madison* decision.[36] After a long pause, a law establishing a Constitutional Court was passed in 1953. In due course parliament nominated the judges it was entitled to appoint and in 1956 the Court delivered its first judgment.[37] Unlike the situation in other European countries, the Italian Constitutional Court's rulings are not limited to references which concern the future application of a bill.[38] As in the United States, the control also applies to laws already passed by the legislature which, once declared unconstitutional, cease to have effect as of the day following the publication of the decision.

It has been argued that the Constitutional Court has been educating judges, lawyers and jurists by applying the constitution as a higher law as in the United States, a notion which, in turn, differs from the European tendency to view constitutions and declarations of rights as political rather than as legal documents.[39] Moreover, owing to the fragmentary nature of Italian society, and to compensate for the passivity of other organs in upholding the constitution, the Constitutional Court has actively laboured since its creation to set aside "by blows dealt by decisions"[40] the surviving fascist legislation,[41] so as to enhance the principle of equality and so as also to prod the legislator

---

[34]   See G. Mammarella, *Italy after Fascism; A Political History* 1943–1965 (Notre Dame, Indiana, 1966), p.181.

[35]   See A. Pizzorusso, "Italian and American Models of the Judiciary and of Judicial Review of Legislation: A Comparison of Recent Tendencies" (1990) 38 *American Journal of International Law* 373, at p. 378.

[36]   5 US (1 Cranch) 137 (1803).

[37]   See P. Vercellone, "The Italian Constitution of 1947–48" in S. J. Woolf (ed.), *The Rebirth of Italy 1943–50* (London, 1972), p.128.

[38]   Pizzorusso, *op.cit.*, note 35, at p. 382.

[39]   *Ibid.*, at pp. 385–386.

[40]   This rendering into English of *A colpi di sentenza*, the graphic expression used by Temistocle Martines in *op.cit.*, note 33, at p. 618, is my own.

[41]   See generally Mammarella, *op.cit.*, note 34.

into making operational those social and other programmatic rights,[42] such as the right to a healthy environment, housing[43] and privacy,[44] which are set out in the constitution.[45]

2. THE JURISDICTION OF THE CONSTITUTIONAL COURT IN HUMAN RIGHTS AND ECHR CASES

In Italy, a constitutional question is usually handled as "incidental" to a case. There is no direct form of appeal to the Constitutional Court for a human rights issue. Only the government (central or regional) is allowed to initiate direct constitutional proceedings. As far as non-governmental bodies are concerned, therefore, the incidental control of constitutionality is the only available recourse for that purpose.[46] Clearly the difficulty with this method is that individuals cannot seise the Constitutional Court with a direct claim that their fundamental human rights have been violated by any law or by any act having equivalent force. They must take a collateral route to seek protection.[47] Where a human rights complaint emerges in the course of litiga-

---

[42] In his now classic book *The Italians*, the journalist Luigi Barzini wrote more than three decades ago that the Italian Parliament suffered from the tendency to pass too many laws without paying sufficient attention to the existing body of statute law. He wrote with tongue-in-cheek that legislators apparently believed that new laws would "act like an incantation and ward off [a] particular evil" and consequently, overlaps and contradictory requirements in the laws were not avoided. Equally, as we shall see, to bring the country more into line with the ECHR, some areas of the law may need deep reform and it may be necessary to strike down some laws as the mere passing of new statutes may not suffice to achieve a more effective implementation of the ECHR: see L. Barzini, *The Italians* (London repr., 1987), at p. 104.

[43] See Cheli and Donati, *op.cit.*, note 22, at pp. 244–245.

[44] In the case n. 38 of 1973 the Court resorted to the ECHR to add the right to privacy.

[45] Unfortunately many of the programmatic rules set out in the constitution are still not fully operational, and areas of difficulty worthy of mention are as follows: the national environmental policies, the unsatisfactory access to health care by poor people and the organisational difficulties of the health service in general. See Martines, *op.cit.*, note 33, at pp. 692–693. No doubt problems in these areas could (and do) give rise to ECHR claims in certain circumstances.

[46] See A. Pizzorusso, "Giurisdizione costituzionale e diritti fondamentali" (1981) 36 *Rivista di diritto processuale* 340, at p. 341.

[47] Martines, *op. cit.*, note 33, at p. 567, footnote 14, reports that there is dissatisfaction in Italy with this situation, and some reform projects have advised the setting up of a system of direct access to the Constitutional Court modelled on the German *Verfassungsbeschwerde* or the Spanish (and Latin American) *recurso de amparo*. We should add, however, that it would seem necessary to "constitutionalise" the ECHR first in order to enable a hypothetical claimant of a Convention right to benefit from a system of direct access to the Constitutional Court.

tion, the court before whom the issue is being heard submits the matter to the Constitutional Court for adjudication as a preliminary question.[48]

The European Convention on Human Rights (ECHR) was signed by Italy on 4 November 1950. The first protocol was signed on 20 March 1952, and the Convention was incorporated into the Italian legal system on 4 August 1955.[49] The ECHR cannot prevail over the constitution. Nor can any pre-legislative scrutiny of legislation be based on the ECHR alone. Its effectiveness is limited by its status as ordinary law, acquired through incorporation. If the constitution does not cover an issue or sets out different rules, the ECHR cannot take priority.[50] In common with other internationally recognised human rights principles, the ECHR did not originally enjoy any special legal force[51] in the domestic hierarchy of norms in relation to statutes passed after the date of its incorporation. In theory, domestic courts could disregard the ECHR pleaded before them if the case at hand dealt with an internal law passed after incorporation. The incorporation of the ECHR in Italian law had the effect of allowing the Convention to take priority over opposing laws passed prior to incorporation. The technique of treating the ECHR as an ordinary law weakened considerably its claims for application, as it could not take priority over opposing laws passed after its incorporation. Added to this, the statute of incorporation,[52] did not set out how the ECHR obligations were to be fulfilled or how they were to be implemented as it only "transformed"[53] the Convention into an ordinary law.[54]

Article 10(1) of the constitution states that "Italy's legal system conforms with the generally recognised principles of international law".[55] In 1960, in

---

[48] Constitution, Article 134. See F. Francioni, "Italy and the EC: the Legal Protection of Fundamental Rights" in F. Francioni (ed.), *Italy and EC Membership Evaluated* (London, 1992), at p.192.

[49] Law 4. 8. 1955 n. 848.

[50] See the intervention of Professor Capotorti in A. H. Robertson (ed.), *Human Rights in National and International Law; Second International Conference on the European Convention on Human Rights* (Manchester, 1968), p. 42.

[51] Termed in the Italian *forza di resistenza*, meaning that additional dimension to a law which is necessary for it to prevail over opposing, subsequent, legislation.

[52] *Op. cit.*, note 49.

[53] Article 1 of the Law 4. 8. 1955 n. 848 authorised ratification, which took place on 26 October 1955, and Article 2 ordered its execution into domestic law.

[54] See A Drzemczewski, *European Human Rights Convention in Domestic Law: A Comparative Study* (Oxford, 1980), at p. 146, and Capotorti, in Robertson, *op.cit.*, note 50, at p. 42.

[55] See Pizzorusso, *op.cit.*, note 46, and in addition: E. Cannizzaro, "Trattato (adattamento

Regione Trentino-Alto Adige c. Presidente del Consiglio dei ministri, the Constitutional Court considered the position of international treaties in Italian law. Its conclusion was that Article 10(1) of the constitution covered those generally recognised principles but not "specific pledges undertaken by the State on the international level" (*i.e.* treaties).[56] A domestic statute would not therefore be declared unconstitutional for the sole reason that it was against an international treaty.[57] Clearly this covered the ECHR. There have traditionally been two exceptions to this general rule that incorporated international law had merely the same strength as an ordinary statute. One concerns the treatment of aliens, and the other, EU law. Both enjoyed and still enjoy a status which allows their rules to take priority over any domestic enactment.[58]

The authority for the application of the aliens' exception comes from Article 10(2) of the constitution, which says that "The legal status of foreigners is regulated by law in conformity with international rules and treaties". Judgment n. 120 of 1967 spelled out the conclusion to be drawn from this, namely that "the principle of equality also applies to aliens where respect for these [*i.e.* constitutionally based] fundamental rights is concerned."[59] The case *Perovic* is an interesting example of a lower court applying this exception to the general rule in a way which involved the ECHR. Owing to the special protection afforded by Article 10(2), the Rome Court

---

al)", in *Enciclopedia del diritto* (Milan, 1992), vol. XLIV, at p. 1414. For a more detailed discussion of the *adattamento* of international law, see B. Conforti, *Diritto Internazionale* 4th ed. (Naples, 1992), at pp. 283–328. The English version of the Italian Constitution quoted here is drawn from A. P. Blaustein and G. H. Flanz (eds.), *Constitutions of the Countries of the World* (Dobbs Ferry, New York, 1971), vol. IX.

[56] Decision n. 32 of 1960 (1980–1981) 5 *Italian Yearbook of International Law* 251, at p. 252.

[57] See G. Gaja, "Italy" in F. G. Jacobs and S. Roberts (eds.), *The Effect of Treaties in Domestic Law* (London, 1987), ch. 5, at p. 87. In the 1960s, the issue of the treatment of the German speaking minority in the Upper Adige led to the only interstate application in which Italy has been involved: *Austria* v. *Italy* (1963) 6 *Yearbook of the European Convention on Human Rights* 740. In this case the Committee of Ministers found that Italy was not in breach of the ECHR. The case started in 1960 when Austria filed an application against Italy complaining of Convention violations in proceedings against six criminal defendants of that region accused of murder which had resulted in their conviction before the Italian courts. Austria objected, *inter alia*, to Italy's alleged disregard of anti-discrimination principles: see DH(63) 3.

[58] See *Frontini* v. *Ministero delle Finanze* Italian Constitutional Court [1974] 2 C.M.L.R. 372.

[59] This English version of the relevant part of the judgment is drawn from A. H. Robertson, *Privacy and Human Rights* (Manchester, 1973), at p.118.

of Appeal found that, "the rules of the ECHR in regard to the foreigner en-joy special legal force."[60] For that reason, the court could in this case resort to Article 6 of the ECHR to override the requirement set out in municipal law which insisted on the use of the Italian language in all legal proceed-ings, with the sole exception of the languages of ethnic minorities settled in some regions of the country. The Convention was mentioned in support of the decision to require the service of legal documents in a language which the foreign defendant could understand, but this exception was not extended to all the steps in the prosecution of the action.

As far as what is now the European Union is concerned, Article 11 of the constitution is of particular relevance. It lays down that Italy "condemns war as an instrument of aggression against the liberties of other peoples and as a means for settling international controversies; it agrees, on conditions of equality with other states, to such limitation of sovereignty as may be neces-sary for a system calculated to ensure peace and justice between nations; it promotes and encourages international organisations having such ends in view." Article 11 was inserted in the constitution to facilitate Italy's admis-sion to the United Nations and to other organisations for the promotion of "peace and justice." It opened the way for the country's entering into nu-merous international agreements on human rights and for its adherence to customary international law. The clause was inserted to facilitate external help for reconstruction after the second world war. It was also the product of the work of those who aspired to a European federation and who therefore thought it advisable to prepare Italy constitutionally for any future surrender of sovereign powers to a European union of states.[61] The clause suited equally well the ideals of European integration, Catholic universalism and workers' internationalism, as well as the desire of some delegates to the constitutional assembly for a strengthening of ties with the United States or with what was then the Soviet Union.[62]

It was decided in *Frontini* v. *Ministero delle Finanze*,[63] that Community law took precedence over Italian law due to the application of the principle *lex posterior generalis non derogat specialis"* instead of the usual *ex poste-rior derogat priori*.[64] In that case, the Constitutional Court conceded that the

---

[60]   (1980) 23 *Rivista italiana di diritto e procedura penale* 953, at p. 956.

[61]   See F. Roy Willis, *Italy Chooses Europe* (New York, 1971), at p. 11.

[62]   See A. Pizzorusso, *Lezioni di diritto costituzionale* 2nd ed. (Rome, 1981), at p. 209.

[63]   *Op.cit.*, note 58.

[64]   A. Celotto, "La prevalenza del diritto comunitario sul diritto interno: orientamenti della Corte Costituzionale e spunti di teoria generale" (1992) 37 *Giurisprudenza Costituzionale*

internationalist clause of Article 11 of the constitution[65] implied that the constitutional law-givers were "inspired by programmatic principles of a general value, which were concretely realised in the European Community and other European regional organisations". Moreover, Article 11 was resorted to again to define EU law as an "independent and separate legal system" in *S.p.a. Granital c. Amministrazione delle Finanze*[66] in 1984. At that stage, however, none of this reasoning could be taken to apply to the ECHR. This was made clear in the judgment n. 188 of 1980, *re Lintrami and others*.[67] The case concerned a challenge to the constitutionality of the requirement to appoint a defence attorney set down in Articles 125 and 128 of the (old) Code of Criminal Procedure even in situations where the defendant insisted on carrying out his or her own defence. "The Court cannot but reassert its settled *jurisprudence* which rules out international treaty provisions, even if general, from the scope of Article 10 of the Constitution."[68] In an important passage, the Court added that:

> in the absence of a specific constitutional provision, treaty provisions implemented in Italy have the same force as ordinary statutes. Therefore, the very possibility of raising, under this aspect, a question of constitutionality is barred, even more when [...] treaty provisions are invoked as such as tests for the constitutionality of statutory provisions.[69]

Article 11 was similarly inapplicable as "one cannot single out any limitation to national sovereignty with regard to the specific treaty provisions in question." The solution offered by municipal law was favoured and the court rejected any question of a Convention-based unconstitutionality, as the ECHR was vulnerable on account of its position in the constitutional rank. The *dottrina* (scholarly writings) protested against this state of affairs. They pointed to the apparent inconsistency between the law and the court's method and unsuccessfully argued in favour of giving the ECHR constitu-

---

[afterwards *Giur. Cos.*] 4481, at p. 4488. See further Conforti, *op.cit.*, note 55, at pp. 309–23.

[65] Francioni, *op.cit.*, note 48, at p. 195.

[66] Decision n. 170 of 1984, (1984) 1 *Giurisprudenza Italiana* 1521. The Constitutional Court intended to reach the same conclusion previously adopted by the ECJ, namely that ordinary courts should apply those EU provisions with direct effect irrespective of conflicting national legislation. Contrary to the ECJ's approach, however, the application of EU law was made dependent on rules already existing in Italian law, in particular Article 11 of the constitution and the statute implementing the Treaty of Rome.

[67] (1980) 25 *Giur. Cos.* 1612, at p. 1615.

[68] *Ibid.*, at p. 1627.

[69] *Ibid.*, at p. 1626.

tional status based on an ingenious interplay of Articles 2, 10 and 11 of the constitution. But the case-law appeared solid.

In a later judgment, n. 17 of 1981, the Constitutional Court did not find the ECHR helpful in defining rights granted by the constitution and it based its decision in the case before it entirely on domestic law.[70] In a case concerning the constitutionality of Law 6.2.1980 n. 15,[71] which was challenged in the course of proceedings against the criminal defendant, a Mr. Giuliano Naria, the Court chose not to take the opportunity to make a pronouncement on whether the rules that extended the period of pre-trial detention by a third were in line with the ECHR. Mr. Naria had been held for four years in pre-trial detention. The judgment of 1 February 1982 reaffirmed that the ECHR had the force of an ordinary statute, and held that Article 5.3 of the ECHR was a non self-executing Article, which did not provide clear criteria for assessing the reasonable length of pre-trial detention. The Court concluded that the domestic statute was not unreasonable, and echoing the civilian's concern with the status of a rule in the domestic hierarchy of norms, it went on: "[the ECHR] does not place itself at the constitutional level nor does it contain substantial criteria for want of specificity".[72] The extensive Strasbourg case-law on Article 5 of the ECHR was not resorted to.

The matter was considered yet again in the case n. 315 of 5 July 1990. On this occasion, the Constitutional Court confirmed previous *jurisprudence* and issued the usual denial of the constitutional status of the ECHR when it dismissed the claim of the unconstitutionality of two articles of a 1989 Law[73] made with reference to Articles 3 and 24 of the constitution and Article 6 of the ECHR. The domestic statute in question required lawyers to have a specific authorisation from their clients to challenge a sentence passed *in absentia*.[74] According to the traditional position, the authority of the incorporated ECHR derived from the statute of incorporation and not from the ECHR itself as a piece of legislation, and due to the principle *ex posterior derogat priori*, the ECHR could not enjoy a position of complete firmness against opposing subsequent domestic legislation.

---

[70] (1980–1981) 5 *Italian Yearbook of International Law* 251, at pp. 256–257.

[71] Also known as the "Cossiga Law", which authorised exceptional measures to protect the democratic order and public security against the threat of terrorism.

[72] (1982) 27 *Giur. Cos.* 85, at p. 100.

[73] These Articles had replaced Articles 183 (bis) and 192 (3) of the (old) Code of Criminal Procedure of 1930 (the "Code Rocco").

[74] (1990) 35 *Giur. Cos.* 2017, at p. 2024.

Despite this line of case-law, however, the pressure the ECHR is capable of exercising is significant and the case-law has started perceptibly to change. The tool for the change has been a renewed emphasis on judicial interpretation rather than on the stark question of constitutionality. The provisions of the ECHR have been taken into account for interpretative purposes with the result that international and supranational law have effectively been held to prevail over inconsistent national law, in a way which has not involved the explicit constitutionalisation of the Convention. An important decision in this regard is the case n. 10 of 19 January 1993, *re. Kasim, Noureddin.*[75] Here the constitutionality of Article 555(3) of the Code of Criminal Procedure was challenged in the course of criminal proceedings before a Turin magistrate. The alleged unconstitutionality was grounded on the discrimination suffered by those who do not understand the Italian language. It was argued that their right to prepare their defence was impaired if they were not notified of the accusation against them in a language that they could understand. Both Article 6.3(a) of the ECHR and Article 14.3(a) of the UN Covenant on Civil and Political Rights were invoked. The Constitutional Court, without "constitutionalising" those instruments, nevertheless stated that their provisions had not been repealed by the Code of Criminal Procedure because the rules "derived from a source related to an atypical competence and, as such, were not susceptible of being repealed or modified by the provisions of an ordinary law."[76] The question of unconstitutionality was rejected but it was pointed out that the Code had to be interpreted together with those international rules and the right of defence of Article 2 of the constitution, and as a result, the assistance with interpretation to be given to a criminal defendant included such notification of the proceedings. Although the (new) Code of Criminal Procedure was passed many years after the ECHR's incorporation, the rules of the Convention were made to take priority by this means of interpretation. The national rules of the code were interpreted, therefore, in the light of international rules, and the effect of this was to give them prevalence over the conflicting domestic law.

---

[75] (1993) *Rivista di Diritto Internazionale* [afterwards *Riv. dir. int.*] 255, at p. 256. The case is reflective of a trend in Italian law.

[76] *Ibid.*, at p. 261. *Cf. Perovic, op.cit.*, note 60.

Part II: Relationship between Internal Law and the ECHR

Notwithstanding the formal assertion that the ECHR is directly applicable in Italian domestic law by virtue of its incorporation, the Court of Cassation's position on the self-executing nature of its clauses has only very recently moved away from the traditional stand, according to which the rules of the ECHR were intended solely for the guidance of the legislature because they were mandatory between the member states only. Currently the position has changed as the Court of Cassation has accepted that the ECHR enjoys a "special legal strength" in confrontation with national laws passed after incorporation. At this juncture the position of the ECHR resembles that of EU law before the Constitutional Court, but only insofar as its use as a tool of interpretation is concerned.[77] Indeed, there are no differences of opinion between the Constitutional Court and the Court of Cassation on the refusal of both tribunals to "constitutionalise" the ECHR. The jurisprudence of the Court of Cassation simply does not give the ECHR any constitutional status and in doing so it follows the guidelines of the Constitutional Court on the hierarchical position of the ECHR in domestic law that we have already discussed. For example, in the 1992 case *Di Bella c. Consiglio dell'ordine dei giornalisti*,[78] the applicant invoked Article 6 of the ECHR in the reference of the constitutional issue that was to be made to the Constitutional Court but the Court of Cassation declined to "constitutionalise" the Convention in the "incident of constitutionality"[79] of the case that was eventually allowed to reach the Constitutional Court. *Di Bella* was a challenge to the constitutionality of the closed hearings which had taken place before a Milan first instance court and subsequently before the Court of Appeal. The action involved a disciplinary decision of the Council of the Order of Journalists. The constitutional question which in the end was submitted was whether an article of a domestic statute was compatible with Article 101(1) of the Italian constitution, and the question of its compatibility with Article 6 of the ECHR was not raised.

The "traditional" position concerning the "rank" of the ECHR in domestic law was also applied in a case of 5 July 1985, but on this occasion in fa-

---

[77] The general position with regard to the EU is discussed above at text to note 61 ff. See further P. Vigni, "Il caso Medrano e l'applicazione dei trattati internazionali in Italia" (1995) CVII (III Series, XLIV) *Studi Senesi* 126, at p. 128.

[78] (1993) 43 *Giustizia Civile* 706, at p. 708.

[79] This is an Italian technical term meaning the form of application in which a matter is referred to the Constitutional Court.

vour of the ECHR. The Disciplinary Chamber of the Council of the Judiciary held that the requirement of publicity in Article 6.1 of the ECHR was applicable in this case, which involved a disciplinary action against a magistrate. The ECHR was resorted to in order to strike a balance between on the one hand, the protection of the rights of the magistrate as a citizen and holder of an office which enjoys independence and, on the other hand, the general interest in the *buon andamento* (proper functioning) of the judicial system. The Court chose publicity by declaring that the requirement of a hearing behind closed doors in legislation older than the ECHR had been made void by the Convention.[80] It ruled that "the statutes of adaptation of an international treaty have the same strength of ordinary laws, therefore, they enjoy "repeal force" over laws already in existence that do not conform to them."[81] It is to be noted that the court achieved the application of the ECHR without departing from the traditional principle of *lex posterior derogat priori*.[82] Though this might be thought unsatisfactory by some, the court, as most courts would have probably done in the circumstances, managed neatly to side-step the (wider) concerns of the *dottrina*. It said that "to decide this case it [was] not necessary to dwell on the matter of the 'constitutionalisation' of the norms of the Convention" and it thus avoided a discussion of whether the ECHR could be used either to supplant or to assist in the interpretation of laws passed after Law 4. 8. 1955 n. 848, the law which, as we have seen, marked the incorporation of the Convention into Italian law.

Despite these denials of the "constitutional" status of the ECHR, the Italian courts have been hearing arguments on the scope and meaning of the ECHR provisions in a variety of cases for a number of years. Despite this, the rulings of the European Court of Human Rights have been traditionally deemed to lack domestic effectiveness[83] and moreover, when the judiciary has taken the ECHR into account, it has not been as a *lege perfecta*,[84] *i.e.* capable of supporting a decision on its own. This is because its rules have not been considered self-executing. This aspect of the "traditional" Italian

---

[80] See *Foro Italiano*, 1986, vol. III, 43, at p. 48.

[81] *Ibid.*, at p. 47.

[82] Notes to the decision, *ibid.*, at p. 45.

[83] See J. Polaciewicz and V. Jacob-Foltzer, "The European Human Rights Convention in domestic law: The Impact of the Strasbourg case-law in States where direct effect is given to the Convention" (1991) 12 *Human Rights Law Journal* 65.

[84] See M. Chiavario, "La Convenzione Europea dei diritti dell'uomo ed il suo contributo al rinnovamento del processo penale italiano" (1974) 57 *Riv. dir. int.* 454, at p. 464.

stance was put by the Court of Cassation in a case of 25 January 1986 as follows: "If the programmatic norms [of a treaty] are not respected, they can only give rise to a lawsuit before an international organisation."[85] The Court continued:

> The accused cannot maintain that a rule of the Italian legal system is against the norms of the Constitution because it conflicts with the European Convention on Human Rights. The law that ratified the Convention gives it the value of an ordinary law [...] The Constitution is the fundamental law of the State and it cannot be modified by an international convention.[86]

In *re. Polo Castro*,[87] decided in 1990, the Court of Cassation rejected a leave to appeal because it was filed late. Despite this, some interesting considerations concerning the self-executing rules of the ECHR were set out in the judgment. The facts were that at the request of the Italian ministry of justice, the public prosecutor with the Florence Court of Appeal issued a warrant of arrest against a Mr. Polo Castro on 3 August 1988. The defendant was already under arrest for fraud in Geneva. On 12 August 1988, he was served with this Italian arrest warrant while in prison. He later challenged it, arguing that in the 1983 case *Angelopoulos*, the Court of Cassation had admitted appeals in extradition cases against arrest warrants issued by public prosecutors. The defendant argued that any other pronouncement by the court would be incompatible with Article 5.4 of the ECHR, which states that in case of arrest or detention any person "shall be entitled to take proceedings by which the lawfulness of his detention shall be decided speedily by a court and his release ordered if the detention is not lawful". The finding of the Criminal Division of the Court of Cassation on 8 May 1989, explained that only self-executing rules of the ECHR enjoyed immediate operation in Italy: "if an international rule is like a complete domestic act, with its essential elements, that is, if the act is able to create rights and duties without any other act, the domestic adoption of the international rule is automatic...".[88] The previous position had been to deny entirely the self-executing character of any rule of the ECHR.[89] Unfortunately for the applicant, however, there are also time limits and since the challenge was made *ex tempore*, the Court did not grant leave to appeal. The Court of Cassation, however, cleared up one of the difficulties for the Convention in Italian law, the problem of rec-

---

[85] (1986) 29 *Yearbook of the European Convention on Human Rights* 305.
[86] *Ibid.*
[87] (1990) 73 *Riv. dir. int.* 1037.
[88] *Ibid.*, at p. 1043.
[89] Chiavario, *op.cit.*, note 84, at p. 464.

ognising its direct applicability. The question remained as to what status the ECHR should be granted in the hierarchy of norms and whether this question could be successfully finessed by means of judicial interpretation alone.

This question has now been partly answered in the recent case of *re. Medrano*,[90] decided in 1993, in which the Court of Cassation overturned a deportation order issued against a foreign national after he had served a prison sentence imposed by a Rome magistrate for a drug-related offence. Mr. Medrano, a citizen of the Argentine Republic, successfully challenged the decision ordering him to leave the Italian territory which had been made by a Trento magistrate. The Court of Cassation, citing Strasbourg case-law,[91] quashed the decision and held that the magistrate's discretion had to be exercised consistently with Article 8 of the ECHR. They returned the decision to another lower court of the same hierarchy for a fresh judgment. Supranational law was allowed to take precedence over national law by following the position suggested by a substantial part of the *dottrina*[92] since in this case the application of the security measure of deportation after a drug-related conviction had been set out in a law passed in 1990, which was therefore clearly subsequent to the much earlier legislation incorporating the ECHR. To get round this previously fatal problem, the ECHR was granted a "special legal force"[93] and consequently, it could take priority on grounds of the rule *lex generalis non derogat priori speciali* and the rule of due respect to international law, *pacta recepta sunt servanda*.[94] This granting of priority to the Convention by way of interpretation allowed the Court to escape responsibility for addressing whether the ECHR could now be said to enjoy constitutional rank.[95] Another recent case, dealing with a labour law dispute, *Salemme c. Federazione Italiana Tennis—F.I.T.*,[96] provides a further example of the relevance of the use of the ECHR for interpretative purposes in national law. The Court of Cassation pointed out that Article 6 of the ECHR

---

[90] Case n. 319 of 12 May 1993, (1994) *Cassazione Penale* 439.

[91] *Beljoudi* v. *France* Series A, No. 234–A (1993) 14 E.H.R.R. 801, at para. 74; *Moustaquim* v. *Belgium* Series A, No. 193 (1991) 13 E.H.R.R. 802, at para. 43; *Berrehab* v. *The Netherlands* Series A, No. 138 (1988) 11 E.H.R.R. 322, at paras. 28–29; *Abdulaziz, Cabales and Balkandali* v. *United Kingdom* Series A, No. 94 (1985) 7 E.H.R.R. 471, at para. 67.

[92] See G. Raimondi, "Note to the Case" (1994) *Cassazione Penale* 439, at p. 445.

[93] Termed *forza di resistenza*. See text at note 51, above.

[94] (1994) *Cassazione Penale* 439, at para. 8.2.

[95] See Vigni, *op.cit.*, note 77, at pp. 134–5.

[96] Unreported, on-line system of the Court of Cassation, *L. Sez.* [Labour (law) Division] decision n. 4219 of 13 May 1995.

"must be understood as automatically inserted in the arbitration clauses related to labour disputes."

The ECHR as an ordinary law therefore now appears to enjoy the power to cause the repeal of later laws that do not conform to it.[97] *Medrano* confirms the sea change in judicial attitudes started in the 1988 *Polo Castro* case. *Kasim* seems to confirm the trend. The change came about by recognising the immediate applicability in Italy of the self-executing rules laid out in the incorporated international law which were used to interpret the 1990 legislation in *Medrano*. The Court resorted to interpretation in order to allow for the co-existence of both norms and thus it managed to avoid actually striking down the 1990 law in issue. The Court side-stepped the issue of the constitutional rank of the ECHR and granted it its "repeal force" by means of interpretation.

In contrast to these recent dramatic developments in private law, there is a feature of Italian public law which still prevents administrative courts from hearing argument based on the ECHR. As soon as an issue is considered to affect subjective rights it will be heard by the ordinary courts. If it relates to a legitimate interest, however, it will fall to be dealt with by the administrative courts.[98] Nonetheless, despite the traditional position, the expansive pressures of the ECHR in domestic law are making inroads in this area as well,[99] as may be observed in the following example. The case *Sheldia c. Ministero Interno*[100] was pleaded before a regional administrative tribunal (*TAR*) in the region of Friuli Venezia Giulia. It concerned a petition for political asylum by a citizen of Albania. Among the various international rules

---

[97] See Vigni, *op.cit.*, note 77, at pp. 129 and 136.

[98] This exclusion of "legitimate interests" can be explained only by reference to a characteristic of the Italian legal system, in which a distinction is made between subjective rights (*diritti soggettivi*) and legitimate interests (*interessi legittimi*). A "legitimate interest" involves a legal situation in which individuals by themselves cannot ask a court for the protection of this interest as the Italian state would be the only party interested in claiming it. Article 113 of the constitution prescribes that a legitimate interest is involved when there is a complaint against a rule made in the public interest, and the administrative courts (and the Council of State) are competent to hear such cases. It is often difficult, however, to determine whether a legal relationship involves a "right" or a "legitimate interest". In a sense, the Council of State and the administrative courts are not fully independent, because the Court of Cassation has the final word on issues of jurisdiction. Cases involving violations of subjective rights fall under the jurisdiction of the ordinary courts (and of the Court of Cassation). See generally M. Cappelletti, J. H. Merryman and J. Perillo, *The Italian Legal System: An Introduction* (Stanford, 1967), at p. 116.

[99] See Drzemczewski, *op.cit.*, note 54, at p. 150.

[100] *Foro amministrativo*, 1992, at p. 2021.

which, in typical civilian style, the court found "applied" to the situation, the *TAR* considered that "particularly relevant [was] the ECHR of 4 November 1950 (with its Protocols) which protects the fundamental rights of individuals regardless of citizenship."[101] The petition was, however, rejected on the consideration that from the questioning of Ms. Sheldia it did not appear to the court that she had suffered any specific persecution nor that she would have so suffered on her return to Albania.[102]

Part III: The Effect of the Judgments of the European Court of Human Rights on Italian Domestic Law

The cases discussed in this section are organised according to the areas in which the main Convention failures of the Italian legal system have taken place. Due to the high number of decisions against Italy, and the fact that very many of them are very similar in content, this method has been preferred to one which addresses the case-law in a chronological fashion. Within each problem area, the steps taken towards implementation of Strasbourg law and case-law are discussed. To close the section, some areas where little or no implementation of the Convention has occurred are considered.

A breach of the ECHR can arise partly or wholly from the operation of domestic law, but implementation of a ruling against the government does not necessarily involve the passing of new legislation as other appropriate means may be available, such as changes in court practice, or new interpretations of old laws. Moreover, even if law reform is undertaken partly because of ECHR-inspired pressure, it may be that the Convention in fact plays only a marginal role in achieving the desired final outcome. Furthermore, a legislative initiative may lack sufficient breadth.[103] On top of this,

---

[101] *Ibid.*, at pp. 2021, 2023.

[102] *Ibid.*, at pp. 2021, 2025. In fact, the Italian government took swift and drastic measures involving the expulsion of the Albanian nationals who were seeking refugee status in Italy in the early 1990s. For a brief discussion on the Martelli Law's restrictive approach to granting refugee status vis-à-vis Article 10 (3) of the constitution and the Italian government's insistence on considering those Albanians as "economic refugees" only, see G. Strozzi, *"Profughi albanesi e diritto d'asilo"* (1993) *Riv. dir. int.* 97.

[103] For example, the time-limits set for pre-trial detention by the Law 3. 7. 1970 n. 730, which could be considered a reflection of the principle of reasonableness in Article 5 of the ECHR in the domestic system, and Law 5. 12. 1969 n. 939 and Law 18. 3. 1971 n. 62, regarding modifications introduced to the (old) code of criminal procedure to strengthen the right of defence of the accused and the rights of the suspect during the investigative

the (perhaps undeserved) Italian reputation for a lenient attitude towards compliance with written rules may also prevent, if true, specific changes in the law from having any practical significance. In addition, even if the ECHR is not an influential source of law, domestic law may still evolve in a way which happens to comply with the requirements of the Convention. It should be noted, moreover, that the requirements of compliance may differ with the passage of time. For example, the Italian Law 19. 5. 1975, n. 151[104] was passed as a result of the influence of a European movement towards reform in family law which advocated, among other things, the elimination of the differences between children born in and out of wedlock.[105] In 1979 a law similar to this became a requirement under Convention law.[106] Despite the 1975 measure, a scholar has warned that the Italian system may not still be fully in line with the ECHR requirements in the area.[107]

I.   THE GENERAL PROBLEM OF DELAY

Despite the difficulty in pin-pointing cause and effect, it is clear that the Strasbourg case-law of recent years has led to a public relations crisis for Italy. By showing up the problems of the Italian legal system on a European stage, the ECHR has no doubt caused a measure of embarrassment to the Italian authorities. The unease of the authorities may be inferred from the type of acknowledgements they have made to the European Court or before the Council of Ministers about the steps they have been taking to implement ECHR requirements. In two cases before the Committee of Ministers, for example, the Committee was informed that the Italian government had authorised a sum[108] to improve the technical services of the courts. Legislation has also been changed to facilitate compliance. In *Biondo* v. *Italy*[109] the

---

stage (mentioned in (1972) 15 *Yearbook of the European Convention on Human Rights* 730) would all seem insufficient in view of the Strasbourg case-law in which Italy has been a respondent government.

[104]   This law, entitled *Riforma del diritto di famiglia* is part of the civil code.

[105]   See F. Tortoricci, "Un seminario sulle riforme del diritto di famiglia in Europa" (1975) 2 *Il diritto di famiglia e delle persone* 1585, at pp. 1585 and 1590.

[106]   As a result of *Marckx* v. *Belgium* Series A, No. 31 (1979) 2 E.H.R.R. 330.

[107]   P. A. Pillitu, "La tutela della famiglia naturale nella Convenzione europea dei diritti dell'uomo" (1989) *Riv. dir. int.* 791, at pp. 816–7, footnote 75.

[108]   *Azzi* DH(92) 45 and *Frau* DH(92) 54. See W. Finnie, "Jurisprudence of the European Court of Human Rights 1992" (1993) *Juridical Review* 192.

[109]   Commission application 8821/79. The Committee of Ministers (acting under Article 32 of the ECHR) said in its resolution (DH(89) 30) that there was a breach of Article 6(3)(c) of the ECHR as had been reported by the Commission.

authorities said that some specific measures required by the new Code of Criminal Procedure would allow the Italian system to comply with the Convention in respect of the provision of proper legal assistance. The new code called for the mandatory appointment of a defence lawyer before the Court of Cassation, and if a counsel was appointed by the court, then the appellant had to be notified of this, and of the date set for the hearing 30 days in advance. In a series of cases litigated before the 1995 reforms of the Italian pension system, the European Court observed that Italy had sought to introduce some measures of implementation. All these cases had dealt with the same problem of delay in social security claims: "The Court stresses that special diligence is necessary in employment disputes, which included pensions disputes....Italy moreover acknowledged this by amending, in 1973, the special procedure laid down in this field and by introducing, in 1990, emergency measures intended to speed up the conduct of such proceedings."[110] In all these situations, implementation of the Strasbourg judgments would have an impact beyond the case of the successful applicant, the otherwise "normal", if at times delayed, way[111] of responding to a successful Strasbourg claim.[112] In these cases, the influence of the ECHR in prodding the authorities into raising national standards appears as a force for the improvement of the local legal system.

The picture that emerges from an examination of the number of cases against Italy shows a marked contrast between the 1980s and the first half of

---

[110] Cases involving Italy where the quoted paragraph is used (all these cases were judgments of the European Court of Human Rights, 26 February 1992): *Nibbio*; *Borgese*; *Biondi*; *Monaco*; and *Lestini*. In each case the relevant quote is to be found at para. 18.

[111] The Committee of Ministers may limit itself to acknowledging in resolutions (made under Article 54 of the ECHR) that it is satisfied that the Italian government has paid the applicant's compensation, as in for example, *Artico* DH(80) 3, *Guzzardi* DH(81) 6, *Foti & others* DH(84) 3, *Goddi* DH(84) 6, and *Luberti* DH(85) 9, to name just a few examples. Alternatively, the Committee may recommend that Italy pay compensation under Article 32, as in *Minnitti*, Commission application 9630/81, resolution of the Committee of Ministers DH(89) 7. It is well known, however, that the authorities have been very slow to pay damages due to the fact that apparently no provision for the expenditure involved was made in the national budget.

[112] Sometimes after a decision on the merits is made, the applicant may file a claim in the European Court under Article 50 of the ECHR seeking compensation. In *Foti and others* (Article 50) v. *Italy* Series A, No. 69 (1983), for example, the claim for just satisfaction was decided on 21 November 1983 as follows: in respect of Messrs. Foti and Lentini, their claim was struck off the list; as regards Mr. Gullì, Italy was required to pay his lawyers' fees and expenses; and finally, as regards Mr. Cernerini, Italy had to pay damages. The European Court may dismiss a new claim for just satisfaction, for example, in *Zanghì* (Article 50) Judgment of the European Court of Human Rights, 10 February 1993.

the 1990s. The granting of the right of individual petition in 1973 started the chain of events that led in the first half of the 1990s to a body of Italian case-law characterised by its volume. The number of applications peaked in the late 1980s to the extent that, if 1980 is compared with 1991, the European Court saw an almost eight-fold increase in the number of judgments delivered which involved Italy as the respondent government. The volume of cases centring on allegations of delay in the Italian legal system was clear evidence of the lack of the implementation of the Convention in a wide sense. From 1991 to the end of 1993 an average of almost 70 per cent. of all the Italian cases that reached the European Court concerned delay. The figures break down as follows: in 1991, 45 per cent. of all cases against Italy dealt with delays, but after the 1992 high point with 95 per cent., the number dropped to a still very high 69 per cent. in 1993. The proportion of findings made against the respondent government supports the diagnosis that the administration of justice in the country was in need of a substantial overhaul: 100 per cent. of the findings were against the government in 1991 and 1993, and 88 per cent were against in 1992. In 1991 and 1992, the decisions dealing with Italy represented 53 per cent. of the total decision-making work of the European Court.[113]

Particularly in the peak years for Italian applications in Strasbourg, the figures substantiated the remark made more than a decade earlier by the *dottrina* that "It is not arbitrary to affirm that that problem concerns the Italian justice system as a whole."[114] After the all-time high reached in 1992, the number of Italian decisions started to decline sharply, and in 1995 the level came down to the average of the previous decade. The Court has been clear that it is the responsibility of Italy to avoid further violations of the

---

[113] For example, the following judgments handed down by the European Court on 19 February 1991, all involving Italy, and concerned excessive delay in criminal cases (Article 6.1 ECHR): *Adiletta and others* Series A, No. 197–E; *Alimena* Series A, No. 195–D; *Angelucci* Series A, No. 196–C; *Brigandì* Series A, No. 194–B; *Colacioppo* Series A, No. 197–D; *Ferraro* Series A, No. 197–A; *Ficara* Series A, No. 196–A; *Frau* Series A, No. 195–E; *Girolami* Series A, No. 196–E; *Maj* Series A, No. 196–D; *Manzoni* Series A, No. 195–B; *Mori* Series A, No. 197–C; *Motta* Series A, No. 195–A; *Pugliese (no. 1)* Series A, No. 195–C; *Santilli* Series A, No. 194–D; *Triggiani* Series A, No. 197–B; *Viezzer* Series A, No. 196–B; and *Zanghì* Series A, No. 194–C No breach was found in *Isgrò* Series A, No. 194–A. On civil proceedings, see for example, judgments handed down by the European Court on 24 May 1991 involving violations of Article 6.1 due to excessive duration of civil proceedings: *Caleffi* Series A, No. 206–B; *Pugliese (no. 2)* Series A, No. 206–A; and *Vocaturo* Series A, No. 206–C.

[114] G. Michele Palmieri, "L'esperienza italiana in tema di ricorsi individuali alla Commissione europea dei diritti dell'uomo" (1980) 63 *Riv. dir. int.* 45, at p. 63.

ECHR. In *Zanghì* v. *Italy*, the Court refused to indicate to the Italian authorities how to reduce delays in their national system, although it recognised that Italy had to "redress the situation that has given rise to the violation".[115] In *Caleffi* v. *Italy*[116] the Strasbourg Court declined to grant the applicants' requests to order Italy to publish the decisions in the *Gazzetta Ufficiale* and in the media. As we shall see, in light of the changes now taking place in Italian law, it may be that the reforms undertaken in the Italian administration of justice may have finally begun to render applications to Strasbourg less attractive or necessary as litigious options.

2. DUE PROCESS IN ITALIAN LAW AND THE ECHR

Turning now to the particular issues that have arisen, the Italian body of case-law reveals a recurrent theme: the malaise affecting the concept of "due process" in the local administration of justice. As the European Court has remarked, in *Scuderi v. Italy*,[117] "Article 6.1 imposes on the Contracting States the duty to organise their judicial systems in such a way that their courts can meet each of its requirements." The first Italian case decided by the Court in Strasbourg, *Artico* v. *Italy*[118] was a harbinger of the difficulties that were to come. A breach of Article 6.3(c) of the ECHR was found in the failure of the government to ensure the effectiveness of the applicant's right to legal assistance in his appeal against a conviction for fraud before the Court of Cassation. The Strasbourg organs requested the official file on the case to check on the government's action. This proved impossible. The Commission had to rely mainly on the applicant's assertions and on the documents he produced because:

> when the Commission had asked the Government for certain details about the course of the 1972 and 1973 proceedings before the Court of Cassation, the reply had been that the registry of that Court could not supply them because, after the applications to quash had been declared inadmissible, the files had been returned to the courts from which they originated.[119]

The Italian government's defence was tantamount to raising its own inefficiencies as an excuse for not producing the applicant's file. They sought the dismissal of Mr. Artico's application on grounds of its insufficiency, with the burden of proof being squarely on him to fill in the gaps left by the

---

[115] *Op.cit.*, note 113, at para. 26.

[116] *Op.cit.*, note 113.

[117] Series A, No. 265–A (1994) 19 E.H.R.R. 187, at para. 16.

[118] Series A., No. 37 (1980) 3 E.H.R.R. 1.

[119] *Ibid.*, at para. 29.

authorities' inability to assist. The failure of the national authorities to produce or make over the file was taken as silence, however, and the silence of the administration worked against its case.[120] The justification of "practical difficulties" put forward by the government lawyers did not mislead the European Court: "the Court refuses to believe that the administrative or practical difficulties relied on by the Government are insurmountable in a modern society."[121] Incidentally, the lawyers acting for the government have ever since this case abstained from such arguments which can so easily backfire and which, as one scholar remarked, certainly add little to the prestige of the authorities.[122] In other cases, the government has also tried to justify the delays by invoking the pressure caused by the workload of the national courts and their consequent backlog of cases, as in *Biondi* v. *Italy*.[123] At least since *Vocaturo* v. *Italy*,[124] the European Court has found these domestic reasons not to be admissible as excuses for non-compliance.[125]

The delays result from an unhappy combination of the unacceptable length of cases combined with a heavy backlog of cases in the courts, a problem that is in turn worsened by a system that encourages appeals.[126] Only in the past few years has the Court of Cassation reduced its enormous backlog of cases. Not too long ago, the workload of the domestic courts in general was almost unmanageable, forcing the judges to deal simultaneously

---

[120] As one Italian commentator wryly observed, "It is really comforting to see that the Court did not believe in the existence of such organisational failures in a basic public service as the Italian Government was trying so hard to demonstrate!": T. Scovazzi, "Le prime esperienze dell'Italia davanti alla Corte Europea dei diritti dell'uomo" (1984) 20 *Rivista di Diritto Internazionale Privato e Processuale* 37, at p. 46.

[121] *Op.cit.*, note 118, at para. 30.

[122] Scovazzi, *op.cit.*, note 120, at p. 46.

[123] *Op.cit.*, note 110. See also the other cases cited at that note.

[124] *Op.cit.*, note 113.

[125] For a recent authority on the issue decided in March 1994, this time concerning proceedings before the Court of Audit, see *Muti* v. *Italy*, Judgment of the European Court of Human Rights, 23 March 1994.

[126] See O. G. Chase, "Civil Litigation Delay in Italy and the United States"(1988) 36 *American Journal of Comparative Law* 41, at p. 47. See also B. Lafargue and T. Godefroy, "The situation in European countries from the point of view of delays in the criminal justice system as regards adults: Reports presented to the 9th Criminological Colloquium" (1989) *Criminological Research, Delays in the criminal justice system*, vol. XXVIII (Strasbourg, 1992), at p. 27. The case *F.M.* v. *Italy* Series A, No. 245–A (1994) 18 E.H.R.R. 570, in which the applicant complained of delays in dealing with a disabled person's attendance allowance, was struck off the list in a similar way, although in this case the dismissal was due to the death of the applicant.

with many cases, and denying lawyers many chances of putting requests to the courts.[127] The habits of mind of the Italian legal profession have also apparently played a part in causing this delay, as the lawyers have reportedly frustrated many attempts over the years to speed up all processes[128] (civil, criminal, and so on). On top of this, the processes themselves have been frequently a reflection of local practices.[129]

Alimena v. *Italy*[130] is an example of the idiosyncrasies of a legal system which are unacceptable in the light of the ECHR. The European Court put it in the following way:

> In fact the case was a very simple one. Moreover the applicant's conduct gave rise to hardly any delay. There were, however, long periods of inactivity in the proceedings which the applicant alleged were due to faults inherent in the legal and court system in Italy and for which no satisfactory explanation was given by the Government. It follows that the Court cannot regard as "reasonable" in the instant case a lapse of time of more than seven years and four months.[131]

In this contempt of court case, the Court of Cassation had notified the applicant's lawyer of the date for an oral hearing but had then proceeded to examine and dismiss the applicant's appeal one day before the appointed date. The effect of this was to deprive Mr. Alimena of legal assistance at a stage in which it may have helped to secure his unqualified acquittal rather than one based on insufficient evidence against him. Although the government argued that no damage was directly caused to the applicant, who was eventually acquitted, the procedure was nevertheless in breach of Article 6.3(c) of the ECHR. In fact, the Court of Human Rights observed that although Mr. Alimena may have not "suffered pecuniary damages as a result of the failure to conduct proceedings within a reasonable time", the applicant "must nev-

---

[127] G. Bruno Bruni, "Trial and Court Procedures in Italy" in C. Platto (ed.), *Trial and Court Procedures Worldwide* (London, 1991), at p. 149. Approximately, three to four years are necessary in the first instance, three years are added at the appeal level and perhaps another three to four years in the Court of Cassation. And, we should add, if the case is taken to Strasbourg, the various material and logistic difficulties may stretch the duration for another four to five years before a decision is eventually reached by the European Court of Human Rights.

[128] The idea of speedy trial was not new in Italian law in general, however, and it was, for example, already set out in Article 175 of the code of civil procedure: see V. Esposito, "L'applicazione pratica dei princìpi della convenzione europea dei diritti dell'uomo nel processo penale italiano" (1992) II *Documenti Giustizia* 1057, at p. 1079.

[129] Chase, *op.cit.*, note 126, at p. 58.

[130] *Op.cit.*, note 113.

[131] *Ibid.* at para. 17.

ertheless have suffered a degree of stress which calls for financial reparation."[132]

All the numerous delay cases supply examples of the type of balance and standards of justice the national authorities are expected to follow. Delays produced by inefficiencies of the legal and court system should not be suffered by the applicants. *Messina* v. *Italy*[133] is another case in which the European Court had little difficulty in finding a breach of Article 6.1 of the ECHR owing to the seven year length of the proceedings. In addition, the government was found in breach of Article 8 of the ECHR because of its failure to provide a higher standard of respect for civil rights by ensuring that correspondence reached the applicant while in prison. The provision of a list drawn up by the prison authorities to show that the correspondence had been received at the prison was not sufficient to show that they had discharged their duties and passed the mail on to the applicant. In the instant case, there was no domestic equivalent to Article 6 of the ECHR to which the applicants could have had resort,[134] and although Italy had made a pledge in international law to protect ECHR rights, no sufficiently effective remedies had therefore been made available under Article 13 of the ECHR.[135]

The cluster of decisions processed together by the European Court of Human Rights, particularly in the peak years of 1991[136] and 1992 highlighted in an extraordinary way the inefficiencies of the national administration of justice.[137] The intrinsic value of those cases may seem open to doubt as they were decided in a rubber-stamp fashion. As a source of enlightenment for the Italian parliament or the domestic courts their potential would seem to

---

[132] *Ibid.*, at para. 23.

[133] Judgment of the European Court of Human Rights, 26 February 1993.

[134] Scovazzi, *op.cit.*, note 120, at p. 42.

[135] *Ibid.*, at p. 45.

[136] It should however be noted that 33 of these cases involved rote repetitions of previously used legal formulae.

[137] Judgments handed down by the European Court on 27 February 1992, all of them involving Italy in breaches of Article 6.1 of the ECHR on the ground of the excessive length of civil proceedings were as follows: *Barbagallo*; *Caffè Roversi S.p.a.*; *Cappello*; *Cardarelli*; *Casciarolli*; *Cifola*; *Cooperativa Parco Cuma*; *Diana*; *Gana*; *Golino*; *Idrocalce S.r.l*; *Lorenzi, Bernardini & Gritti*; *Manieri*; *Manifattura FL*; *Mastrantonio*; *Pandolfelli*; *Pierazzini*; *Ridi*; *Ruotolo*; *Serrentino*; *Steffano*; *Taiuiti*; *Tumminelli*; *Tusa*; and *Vorrasi*. The Court did not find a breach of Article 6 in only four of the cases in the batch: *Andreucci*; *Arena*; *Cormio*; and *G*. In 1993, the Court found breaches of Article 6.1 arising out of the length of civil proceedings in the following five cases, all once again involving Italy and all decided on 26 February: *Billi*; *De Micheli*; *Pizzetti*; *Salesi*; *Trevisan*; and (in a sixth decision on 23 November) in *Scopelliti* Series A, No. 278.

be limited and, as a whole, they add little to the evolution of a shared European law of human rights. Their relative lack of importance prompts the serious question whether these cases should have been heard at all by the European Court as they could be said to represent a misuse of (scarce) judicial resources in Strasbourg.[138] Nonetheless, the value of the case-law lay in its potential to inspire legal reform, albeit in an indirect manner.

Since, as Warbrick notes, "[s]tructural features in the national legal system and a lack of resources are the real reason why so many cases arise,"[139] it is tempting to assume that any reform in the "risk area" of procedure at least amounts to an attempt to implement the ECHR. For example, after the *Ciulla* case, parliament passed Law 3. 8. 1988 n. 327, amending an article of a 1956 law in order to abolish the special form of detention which had been at issue in the case: Mr. Ciulla had complained of his detention during the consideration of the applicability to him of a compulsory residence order. The Strasbourg Court found by 15 votes to two that there had been a breach of Article 5.1 of the ECHR and by 13 to four that there had also been a violation of Article 5.5 of the Convention. Articles 314 and 315 of the new Italian Code of Criminal Procedure now confer a right to compensation for wrongful detention under certain circumstances.[140] Equally, the decision in *Bezicheri*,[141] appears to have prompted the changes which eventually materialised in Article 299(3) of the new Code of Criminal Procedure.[142] That Article now requires a judge to rule within five days on any application for release from detention on remand made by an accused and it therefore avoids situations such as the one that led to a violation in *Bezicheri*.[143] In that case, the European Court found, unanimously, that there had been no speedy determination of the applicant's situation and a breach of Article 5.4 ECHR

---

[138] See J. Andrews, "Trial Delays in Italy" (1991) 16 *European Law Review* 359, at p. 360. See also *ibid.*, "Trial Delays in Italy" (1983) 8 *European Law Review* 146; *ibid.*, "Natural Justice in Italy" (1984) 9 *European Law Review* 290; *ibid.*, "Trial in absentia in Italy" (1985) 10 *European Law Review* 368; J. Andrews and A. Sherlock, "Trial within a reasonable time" (1988) 13 *European Law Review* 68; and V. Andrioli, "La Convenzione europea dei Diritti dell'Uomo e il processo giusto" (1964) 7–8 *Temi Romana, Rassegna di Giurisprudenza* 442.

[139] C. Warbrick, "The European Convention on Human Rights" (1992) 12 *Yearbook of European Law* 691, 742.

[140] *Survey of Activities 1959–90, European Court of Human Rights* (Strasbourg, 1991), at p. 48.

[141] Series A, No 164 (1990) 12 E.H.R.R. 210.

[142] *Survey of Activities, op.cit.*, note 140, at p. 49.

[143] See Bernardi and Palazzo, *op.cit.*, note 1, at pp. 196–7.

had occurred due to the length of time involved in the case. Mr. Bezicheri, a lawyer practising in Bologna, had been arrested in 1983 and had been accused of, *inter alia*, having been an accessory to a murder committed in 1982. It was alleged that in the course of his professional activities he had acted as an intermediary between the murderers and the instigator of the crime, who was in prison. He applied twice to the investigative judge for release, and his second application was dismissed after five and a half months of consideration.

3.   THE CRIMINAL LAW AND THE ECHR

This struggle between the ideals of the ECHR and the realities of Italian law has been most obvious in the arena of the criminal law. The ECHR has been exercising an influence on the *dottrina* in criminal law—and the existence of a substantial literature in the area bears out this assertion—and a measure of ECHR implementation through the work of the Italian parliament and the domestic courts inspired by scholarly writing cannot be ruled out. Before 1989, the field was dominated in Italy by the Code Rocco's heavy stress on crime control over freedom. Until its replacement in 1989, this code co-existed with a body of emergency legislation passed particularly in the 1970s and 1980s to tighten sanctions against terrorism[144] and to combat organised crime, a problem which still affects the country.[145] The spate of kidnaps that took place in the 1970s led to the introduction of legislation to increase the law enforcement capability of the authorities. For example, the police were given more power to place taps on telephones and to intercept mail. The pattern continued in the 1980s, and examples of emergency measures abound: Law 6. 2. 1980 n. 15 (the "Cossiga Law") introduced a range of measures which it was difficult to present as compatible with the ECHR, such as the extension of the time of acceptable pre-trial detention (repealed in 1985), an authorisation for the police to search premises when they had reasonable grounds for believing that a suspected terrorist was in hiding there and a power to detain for up to 48 hours for questioning before seeking authorisation from a magistrate.

Law 29.5.1982 n. 304 established a system of reduced sentences for those willing to co-operate with the authorities, the *pentiti* or "super-

---

[144] See M. Den Boer, "The Italian Police and European Police Co-operation" (Working Paper XIII, Working Paper Series *A System of European Co-operation after 1992*. University of Edinburgh (Department of Politics), 1993), p. 32.

[145] Legislation to combat Mafia crime has a long history in the country and the success of the authorities has had its ups and downs. See generally Den Boer, *ibid.*, pp. 37–41.

grasses" (turncoats), a system which led to numerous arrests in the early 1980s.[146] Furthermore, Law 17. 2. 1987 n. 29[147] re-introduced severe pre-trial procedures in order to help the authorities in the management of the "maxi-trials" of the late 1980s and early 1990s. Other legislation was strengthened in the fight against the Mafia, such as the preventive measures of Law 27. 12. 1956 n. 1423, reformed by Law 31. 4. 1965 n. 575 and Law 13. 9. 1982 n. 646. Unsurprisingly, many of these laws were challenged in Strasbourg, for example in the *Raimondo* case, as we shall see later.[148] This experience of emergency legislation was not unique to Italy, but clearly it had implications for civil liberties and for adherence to ECHR rules. Nonetheless, the ECHR made its presence felt. For an Italian scholar, two statutes passed at the height of the emergency show ECHR influence: Law 12. 8. 1982 n. 532, which set up the *"tribunale della libertà"* to examine the reasons for detention under the emergency regime, and Law 5. 8. 1988 n. 330, which placed limits on the grounds for detention and required the application of the notion of proportionality in pre-trial proceedings.[149]

It was however in the area of the mainstream criminal law that the conflict between the Italian and European models had by 1989 become most acute. Although it is difficult to speculate on the extent to which the Strasbourg delay cases prompted the reform of Italian law, there is no doubt that they made some contribution to Convention implementation through provoking scrutiny of some of the ills of the local legal culture.[150] *Brincat* v. *Italy*[151] supplies an example of this. After a client of the applicant, who was a lawyer and MP from Malta, had a serious car accident while in Italy, Mr. Brincat was asked by the insurance company to report on the circumstances of the accident, as a result of which both he and the client's wife went to see the car in a scrap yard. At one point, the owner of the yard saw the woman attempting to recover something from the fuel tank and alerted the police. The police discovered in her possession a banknote which had formed part

---

[146] See generally R. Clutterbuck, *Terrorism, Drugs and Crime in Europe after 1992* (London, 1990), at pp. 26–45.

[147] Also known as law *Mancino-Violante*.

[148] Series A, No. 281–A (1994) 18 E.H.R.R. 237. See text at note 180, below.

[149] See G. Vassalli, "Diritti dell'uomo e durata della custodia cautelare" (1989) 44 *Comunità Internazionale* 655, at pp. 658–659.

[150] M. Chiavario, "'Cultura italiana' del processo penale e convenzione europea dei diritti dell'uomo: frammenti di appunti e spunti per una 'microstoria'" (1990) *Rivista internazionale di diritti dell'uomo* 433, at p. 470.

[151] Series A, No. 249–A (1992) 18 E.H.R.R. 591.

of an abduction ransom. They were arrested on 5 December 1987, questioned and put at the disposal of the public prosecutor. Mr. Brincat was then transferred to Lagonegro, and his lawyer was informed that the case would be heard on 7 December. His detention (under the old Code of Criminal Procedure) was continued. On 14 December the (first) prosecutor declined jurisdiction and transferred the case to his counterpart in Paola. The second prosecutor received the file on 18 December, issued a warrant of arrest and on the following day the applicant was transferred. Mr. Brincat filed a complaint under Articles 5.3 and 5.4 of the ECHR on 19 December. Strasbourg found a breach of Article 5.3 concerning the lack of impartiality of a judge of the prosecutor to review the detention of the applicant as it was sufficient for a breach to occur that he may exercise judicial power at one stage and "may later intervene, in the subsequent proceedings, as a representative of the prosecuting authority."[152] The Italian government's argument that under the old Code the public prosecutor's office enjoyed the necessary guarantees of independence and impartiality was rejected by the European Court.

The strong "inquisitorial" traits of the old code, epitomised in this decision, ran counter to the ECHR. That Code conspired against the ECHR with its divided "investigation" and "trial" stages and with a prosecutor whose role appeared sometimes in conflict with the spirit of the Convention. Despite this, some of the "inquisitorial" characteristics of the old Code were able to meet the test of Article 6 of the ECHR in the eyes of the Court in some circumstances. *Padovani* v. *Italy*,[153] for example, shows an apparent disagreement between the Convention requirement for openness and for impartiality and the reality of the old Italian law, although the Court did not find a violation of the ECHR. *Padovani* raised the question of the impartiality of the magistrate in the "immediate criminal proceedings"[154] who had ordered the applicant's arrest, heard the case, adjudicated on the issues and in the end, issued the conviction. Although no breach was found, Judge De Meyer's concurring opinion interestingly reveals a degree of unease with the situation. He wrote that "[f]urther thought appears to be called for on this subject".[155] The question of the degree of objective impartiality involved in the successive exercise by the same magistrate of different functions in *Padovani* was perhaps a less clear-cut situation for the Court than was the vio-

---

[152] *Ibid.*, at para. 21.

[153] Judgment of the European Court of Human Rights, 26 February 1993.

[154] *Giudizio direttissimo.*

[155] *Op.cit.*, note 153, Judge De Meyer's dissenting opinion.

lation involved in the possibility of a successive exercise of the function of investigation and prosecution by the same prosecutor in *Brincat*.

Whatever the reason, the tide finally started to turn with the introduction of a new Code of Criminal Procedure in 1989,[156] which is based on the adversarial system and which grants equality of arms to the defence and the prosecution.[157] This new Code marks a very important change of direction. It relates in content and method to Articles 5 and 6 ECHR in particular, as it sets aside the traditionally inquisitorial tendencies of Italian criminal law and opts for an adversarial, Anglo-American approach to the criminal process.[158] In this sense, since its introduction, the Code has been playing a relevant part in facilitating the implementation of ECHR ideals in Italian law.[159] It allows, among other things, for the cross-examination of witnesses[160] and establishes a role for the prosecutor which is more in line with the Anglo-

---

[156] It came into force on 24 October 1989. For an overview of the changes brought about by the new code see: S. P. Freccero, "An Introduction to the New Italian Criminal Procedure" (1994) 21 *American Journal of Criminal Law* 345, at pp. 355–382.

[157] As the Reformation once required changes to the interior of church buildings to enable the celebration of a different style of service, so the change over to an adversarial system in Italian criminal law has also prompted the need for the refurbishment of existing court houses and the construction of new ones. Such initiatives to enable adversarial criminal trials to take place could be seen as a favourable domestic development conducive to further ECHR implementation in national law.

[158] E. Amodio and O. Dominioni (eds.), *Commentario del Nuovo Codice di Procedura Penale* (Milan, 1989), vol. I, p. XLIX.

[159] Council of Europe, *Information Bulletin on Legal Activities within the Council of Europe and in Member States* no. 31 (Strasbourg, 1991). Compare *Borgers* v. *Belgium* Series A, No (1993) 15 E.H.R.R. 92.

[160] Code of criminal procedure, Articles 496–498.

American requirements of the law and the case-law of the ECHR.[161]

The pursuit of reform to bring the legal system more into line with the requirements of the ECHR has undoubtedly been very slow. In general, the procedural exigencies of fairness required by Strasbourg have usually been viewed from Italy as an example of the influence of the common law percolating through their civilian style legal order by means of the ECHR[162] and it should be noted that that infiltration has not been universally welcome by the local legal culture. It is interesting to observe that the new Code and the change of legal culture it carries with it has been resisted by the judiciary, as many magistrates have been unwilling to see any imposition of limits on their ability to "seek the truth" in the "investigation" stage. The dominant legal culture saw the reform as having the potential to block the efforts of the authorities to counter terrorism and violent crime. Indeed, one of the criticisms levelled today against the new Code of Criminal Procedure is rooted precisely in this fear that its stress on due process may make it difficult to combat organised crime.

4. SOCIAL SECURITY CASES

Italy's acute difficulties with the ECHR have not been restricted to the criminal sphere or to the nation's willingness to contemplate draconian law in its prosecution of serious crime. In 1993, for example, the European Court adjudicated on various welfare assistance, pension and social insurance claims, and found that Article 6.1 of the ECHR had been breached due to the unacceptable delays involved in processing these applications by the

---

[161] See G. Neppi Modona, "Italian Criminal Justice against Political Corruption and the Mafia: the New Model for the Relations between Judicial and Political Power" (1994) 32 *Osgoode Hall Law Journal* 393, at p. 401. See also G. E. Longo, "La Jurisprudence la plus récente de la Cour de Cassation italienne en matière d'application de la Convention Européenne des Droits de l'Homme" in J. O'Reilly (ed.), *Human Rights and Constitutional Law: Essays in Honour of Brian Walsh* (Dublin, 1993), at pp. 85–91. The author claims (at p. 91) that the inspiration for the new code was derived from the ECHR, a view corroborated by the Council of Europe in its publication *Information Bulletin on Legal Activities within the Council of Europe and in Member States, op.cit.*, note 159. It points out (at p. 46) that the provisions of the new code take extensive account of the relevant Council of Europe Conventions. On the other hand, G. Modona and L. J. Fassler believe that the influence on the code is more transatlantic in flavour: see Modona, *ibid.*, and L. J. Fassler, "The Italian Penal Procedure Code: An Adversarial System of Criminal Procedure in Continental Europe" (1991) 29 *Columbia Journal of Transnational Law* 245, at p. 275.

[162] E. Amodio, "L'attivita del Consiglio d'Europa e il processo penale italiano" in M. Cappelletti and A. Pizzorusso (eds.), *L'influenza del Diritto Europea sul Dirittto Italiano* (Milan, 1982), at pp. 579 and 582.

national authorities. The delays involved ranged from four and a half years in *De Micheli* to 16 years and three months in *Billi*.[163] The crux of the problem was that the state funded pension system failed to provide equality of treatment and was plagued by inefficiencies.[164] No doubt, the existence of an increasingly aged population and one of the lowest birth-rates among the industrialised nations helped to explain in part the difficulties experienced by the system and its beneficiaries. The European case-law clearly reflects the depth of the crisis. It constitutes an ocean of "rubber-stamp" decisions decided in batches. Let us look at some of the cases. *Giancarlo Lombardo* v. *Italy*[165] concerned a pension claim by a former judge. He claimed pension payments out of his employment and said that the regulations were unfair against him. The Italian government, by pointing to the public law aspects involved in the state funded system, claimed that the applicant's case was not an issue of "civil rights and obligations" and therefore, that his application should be refused. The Court decided that the matter came within Article 6.1: in making the payments the Italian government was not using discretionary powers but was assuming the responsibilities of an employer, and because of this the relationship resembled that of a private employer under a contract. Once the obstacle posed by the distinction between public and private law as presented by the government lawyers was cleared, the Court looked into the lengthy delays, which involved more than eight years in this case. The authorities were found to be in violation of Article 6.1 of the ECHR.

Francesco Lombardo v. *Italy*[166] concerned a rather similar issue. The applicant was a former police officer who had become disabled and who applied for disability benefits. His application to Strasbourg arose out of the delay of eleven and a half years that it took the authorities to process his application. Again, the government insisted that this claim touched upon public law points and did not concern a civil right. The argument was equally unsuccessful before the European Court, and similarly, a violation of Article 6 of the ECHR was inevitably found due to the length of the pro-

---

[163] *Billi*; *De Michelli*; *Pizzetti*; *Sales*; and *Trevisan*. All five cases involved Italy and were decided on 26 February 1993.

[164] On the slow procedures of the Istituto Nazionale della Previdenza Sociale (INPS) and the reputed reluctance of Italian business to pay social security contributions, see "The artful dodgers" *The Economist*, 28 January–3 February 1995, vol. 334, no. 7899, p. 75.

[165] Judgment of the European Court of Human Rights, 26 November 1992.

[166] Series A, No 249–B (1996) 21 E.H.R.R. 188.

ceedings. In *Paccione* v. *Italy*,[167] to give a final example, a retired district medical officer filed a complaint about the assessment of his pension. There were various postponements of the hearing. The European Court found a breach of Article 6.1 of the ECHR arising out of the length of the proceedings but dismissed the applicant's claim for just satisfaction.

It should be noted that these cases are only three out of the barrage of Italian social security cases decided by the European Court, particularly in the early 1990s. Although it is in general difficult to see an immediate connection between the ECHR and law reform, Italian law in this area has very recently evolved in a highly significant manner. The deep reforms made in 1995 to tackle the chronic problems inherent in the entire Italian pension system have reportedly been so wide-ranging that they may make Strasbourg claims less necessary in future. Although the results will only be fully visible in years to come, it is hoped that the new system will effectively prevent the violation of the principles of equality and fairness enshrined in the ECHR.[168]

5. TRIALS *IN ABSENTIA*

Despite these reforms in the fields of criminal procedure and public administration, some areas of the Italian legal system remain resolutely out of step with the ECHR. An area in which Italian law may be open to criticisms rooted in the ECHR is that of trials *in absentia*.[169] Unfortunately, the Euro-

---

[167] Series A, No 315 (1995) 20 E.H.R.R. 396. See also *Terranova* v. *Italy*, Judgment of the European Court of Human Rights, 4 December 1995. The breach of Article 6.1 of the ECHR was due to the eight years and one month it took the judicial review of a treasury order requiring repayment of half of a sum the applicant had received as compensation for an invalidity that had occurred during discharge of his duties as a municipal employee.

[168] The new "capitalisation" system involves a radical departure from the system whose inefficiencies had led to so many Strasbourg applications. This radical overhaul of the system can be seen as a positive internal development which will reduce the frequency of claims to Strasbourg. The new system links pension payments to the contributions made by each retiree during his or her working life, and it encourages private sector participation in the retirement schemes. It is anticipated that the new system, starting on 1 January 1996, will have entirely replaced the old before the end of the first decade of the next century. The old system, in contrast, was entirely state run and was based on sharing among pensioners the contributions made by the existing workforce supplemented by tax revenue. See, for example, among the press reports generated by this debate: "Dini's gambit" *The Economist* 30 September–6 October 1995, vol. 336, no. 7934, p. 50; "Advantage Dini" *The Economist* 13 May–19 May 1995, vol. 335, no. 7914, p. 49; "Live now, live later" *The Economist* 4 March–10 March 1995, vol. 334, no. 7904, p. 41; N. d'Aquino, "A Country of Contradictions" in *Europe*, November 1995, no. 351, pp. 6–7.

[169] These are cases in which the accused is judged by default (*contumacia*) as he or she fails

pean Court of Human Rights has in a number of cases avoided dealing with the *in absentia* issue directly, and this has reduced the impact of the ECHR on municipal law. Let us examine a few examples. In *Colozza* v. *Italy*,[170] a Mr. Colozza was convicted *in absentia* to imprisonment of six years and fined for various offences. The authorities had failed to contact him at his last known address and because of this he was declared untraceable and treated as having absconded. When he was eventually found he contested the validity of the proceedings and applied to the Court of Appeal. His action was time-barred and the Court of Cassation later confirmed the decision to try him *in absentia*. The European Court found a breach of Article 6.1 of the ECHR. Nonetheless, somewhat disappointingly, the Court did not address whether a trial *in absentia* was in itself capable of violating the requirements of the ECHR, for "[i]t is not the Court's function to elaborate a general theory in this area"[171]. The Court limited its intervention to a finding of a violation as a result of the consequences the authorities had attached to the applicant's failure to notify his change of address, this being the factor which had led to the trial in his absence and which had therefore deprived him of his chance to participate in the case.

Other cases confirm this pattern. The fact that the same issue was successfully litigated again indicates the lack of domestic implementation. In *Brozicek* v. *Italy*[172], the applicant, a Czech-born German national, was charged with the offences of resisting the police, assault and wounding. The public prosecutor's office sent him a "judicial notification" of the accusation to Nuremberg written in the Italian language. The applicant was subsequently convicted *in absentia*. The European Court found a breach of Article 6.3(a) of the ECHR because an "accusation" has to be provided "in a language which [the suspect] understands", and Mr. Brozicek had informed the authorities of his lack of knowledge of Italian. The issue of how a trial *in absentia per se* conforms to the ECHR's requirements of fairness was not addressed, however. Therefore, a violation of Article 6.1 of the ECHR was found not because of the trial *in absentia* itself but because it was not established that Mr. Brozicek had intended to waive his right to participate. The consequence was that in the end, the applicant had not received a fair hearing. The Court observed that:

---

to appear in court (*contumace*).

[170] Series A, No. 89 (1985) 7 E.H.R.R. 516.

[171] *Ibid.*, at para. 29.

[172] Series A, No. 167 (1989) 12 E.H.R.R. 371.

the President of the Savona Regional Court did not seek to notify Mr. Brozicek in person of the summons to appear before his court. In accordance with Italian law, he ordered that it be lodged with the court registry, so that Mr. Brozicek was deemed to have been informed of each document relating to the proceedings and was judged *in absentia*.[173]

Equally, in *F.C.B.* v. *Italy*[174], Mr. F.C.B. was arrested in Switzerland and extradited to Italy where he was charged with armed robbery, murder and attempted murder committed in Bergamo in 1972. In 1980, the Brescia Assize Court of Appeal acquitted him and his co-defendants for lack of evidence. After his release, he moved to Germany, and gave his new address to one of the Italian consulates. In 1982 he was arrested in Brussels under a Dutch warrant which accused him of an abduction. In 1983, the Italian prosecutor was eventually successful in his appeal against the Italian acquittal and the Court of Cassation submitted the case to the Milan Assize Court of Appeal for a retrial. By this time, F.C.B. was in prison in the Netherlands. After tracing F.C.B.'s mother, the authorities served the process at her address and made this known to F.C.B.'s lawyer. Apparently there was poor communication between different departments: the trial proceeded *in absentia* despite the fact that the Italian authorities had helped their Dutch counterparts in securing the prosecution of the applicant in another case and therefore, it seemed difficult to justify the conclusion that the Italian authorities were unaware of F.C.B.'s whereabouts. The European Court found, unanimously, that a violation of Article 6.1 and 6.3(c) of the ECHR had occurred despite the presence of counsel during the trial. The Court applied the values of a fair trial that the ECHR supports and found that the Italian courts had not displayed necessary diligence in ensuring the applicant's (formal) knowledge of the trial. The court determined that the consequences attributed to F.C.B.'s conduct were "manifestly disproportionate" in view of the central place occupied by the right to a fair trial in a democratic society. At any rate, there was no indication that F.C.B. had intended to waive his right to appear in person.

There are similarities in the conduct of the Italian authorities in F.C.B.'s case and in the 1992 case of *T.* v. *Italy*,[175] with the question whether a trial by default was *per se* in breach of the ECHR being yet again side-stepped. T. was accused of raping his daughter and a judicial notification of the investigation and an invitation to provide an address in Italy was sent out to

---

[173] *Ibid.*, at para. 45.

[174] Series A, No. 208–B (1991) 14 E.H.R.R. 909.

[175] Judgment of the European Court of Human Rights, 12 October 1992.

him to an address overseas. Although he kept the Italian embassy in Saudi Arabia informed of his changes of address, he was nevertheless declared untraceable and a lawyer was appointed on his behalf. The applicant had been tried, convicted and an appeal refused by the time he was arrested at the Italian embassy in Copenhagen and repatriated to serve four years in prison. The European Court found a breach of the ECHR because an informal knowledge of the proceedings was judged not to imply a waiver of the right to participate. Italy has been repeatedly found in breach of the ECHR in this area but the Court has just as consistently left unanswered the substantive question as to the validity of the whole process. The change from the inquisitorial to the adversarial model in the new Code of Criminal Procedure has not entailed the elimination of trials *in absentia*, although a number of modifications have been introduced into the system.[176] The frequency with which the system of the trials *in absentia* has been challenged in Strasbourg suggests, at the very least, the need to keep it under review.

6. PREVENTIVE ADMINISTRATIVE ACTION

There is a final difficult area for Italian law when it comes to compliance with the ECHR: the abuses inherent in the system of preventive measures. The system currently in place is the product of a series of amendments and additions made to the framework first created by Law 27. 12. 1956 n. 1423.[177] The system was designed to authorise a variety of measures intended to prevent the committal of further offences, the hiding of evidence while criminal proceedings were under way and the prevention of the obstruction of an investigation. These measures have been frequently used in the prosecution of Mafia crime and they have not surprisingly been the focus of litigation in Strasbourg.[178] Although there are grounds to justify the use of preventive measures in a liberal democracy, the *dottrina* has questioned the domestic constitutionality as well as the lack of success of the present system.[179]

---

[176] L. Cresti, "Convenzione europea dei diritti dell'uomo e processo contumaciale italiano" in V. Grementieri (ed.), *L'Italia e la Convenzione Europea dei Diritti dell'Uomo* (Milan, 1989), p. 127.

[177] For a summary of its provisions in English, see *Guzzardi* v. *Italy* Series A, No. 39 (1980) 3 E.H.R.R. 333, at paras. 46–49.

[178] See Law 13. 9. 1982 n. 646, and the summary of Italian domestic law and case-law on the issue of preventive measures in *Raimondo* v. *Italy* Series A, No. 281–A (1994) 18 E.H.R.R. 237, at paras. 16–20.

[179] See the discussion on the abuses concerning "preventive measures" in G. Fiandaca and E. Musco, *Diritto penale, Parte generale* 2nd ed. (Bologna, 1989), at pp. 673–675.

Let us consider here one of the cases that reached Strasbourg. Preventive measures were ordered in the course of criminal proceedings against a Mr. Raimondo, who was suspected of belonging to a Mafia-type organisation. A district court ordered the seizure of 10 plots of land, six buildings and six vehicles all of which appeared to be at Mr. Raimondo's disposal. Later the district court revoked the seizure of property that belonged to third parties but at the same time it ordered the confiscation of some of the buildings and vehicles on the grounds that they had not been lawfully acquired. The court also placed the applicant under special supervision. Mr. Raimondo was later acquitted in the subsequent criminal proceedings against him. The European Court could not accept the delay in regularising the applicant's situation after his acquittal even though it declared itself "fully aware of the difficulties encountered by the Italian State in the fight against the Mafia." The delay in lifting the measures from the relevant registers once there was no reason for their continuation was found to be in breach of the applicant's ECHR rights.[180] The Court criticised the fact that it took the authorities seven months as regards some items of property and four years and eight months with regard to other items (real property) to lift the measures entered in the registry.

Unsurprisingly, the system of preventive measures has affected the rights of applicants in cases other than those involving the suspicion of the presence of organised crime. For example, in *Venditelli v. Italy*,[181] a Mr. Venditelli was fined and given a suspended sentence for infringing planning regulations in respect of works carried out in his flat in Rome. The flat was put under the preventive measure of sequestration so as to preserve the work as evidence in any subsequent trial. This sequestration was not however lifted after the Rome Court of Appeal ruled on 4 July 1990 that the prosecution was barred due to an amnesty. The attempt to obtain the lifting of the measure then became a lengthy process in which there was much shuttling around of the file between public offices, despite the fact that, as it was pointed out in a joint dissenting opinion in the European Court, "the applicant was locked out of his home by the public authorities, a situation which should have added some sense of urgency to the prosecuting and judicial authorities."[182] On these facts, the European Court found a breach of Article 1 of Protocol 1 but not of Article 6.1 of the ECHR. The warnings of the abuses such measures may facilitate, frequently pointed out by the *dottrina*,

---

[180] *Op.cit.*, note 178, at para. 36.

[181] Series A, No. 293 (1995) 19 E.H.R.R. 464.

[182] *Ibid.*, Joint dissenting opinion of Judges Walsh, Spielmann, Palm and Loizou, at para. 2.

rang true once again, and it would not be surprising if we were to see more cases in Strasbourg dealing with this issue in the near future. The state has not yet addressed the problems revealed by the *Venditelli* decision.

A system of preventive measures could be acceptable if it was "proportionate to the aim pursued" in the prosecution of crimes and if it was also particularly useful in the fight against criminal organisations with enormous financial power. If there is no proportionality or careful consideration of the circumstances of the case,[183] then such measures could become a parallel system of penalisation imposed outside the system of criminal law, without any of the protections and guarantees that the latter system provides. If this were to happen, it could amount to a *de facto* conviction without trial. ECHR implementation in this area should, therefore, take the form of helping the authorities to arrive at the right balance between the use of such measures in the prosecution of crime while at the same time respecting the high standards of protection of civil liberties which should be the hallmark of a liberal democracy. The case-law indicates that this balance has yet to be got right.

Conclusion

This chapter has touched upon many areas of the Italian legal system. To the question, does Italy need the ECHR, the answer is undoubtedly in the affirmative. The Convention has exercised its influence in a variety of areas. It has highlighted, for example, various weak points in Italian law which have been in need of urgent attention, such as the chronic delays in both the judicial and the administrative process—themselves a veiled form of arbitrariness—and the unacceptably slow speed of decision-making across the board. The ECHR, interacting with other factors, has provided a degree of inspiration for some of the changes in the legal culture which have taken place in Italy in the past few years. This study has also shown that although the ECHR had been "transplanted" into Italian law by way of incorporation, this has not been sufficient to achieve effective implementation.

Until very recently, the judiciary applied the principle *lex posterior* and declined to grant any self-executing character to the clauses of the ECHR. One difficulty for ECHR implementation in domestic law has therefore been

---

[183] The Catanzaro Court of Appeal, in its intervention in the case, commented on the "disconcertingly casual way in which the contested preventive measures concerning the person and the property of Mr. Raimondo had been adopted." See *Raimondo, op.cit.*, note 178 at para. 14.

its vulnerability due to this weak position in the domestic hierarchy of norms, a hurdle of relevance in a civil law jurisdiction. For a hierarchical system such as the Italian, the position of a statute in domestic law has to be first clarified and only then, can it be "applied" (deductively) to a situation. But to be "applied" in this way, rules must be self-executing or, alternatively, appropriate legislation must be passed. The Italian legal system has failed on both counts. The latest developments, however, indicate that although unconstitutionality cannot be based on the sole basis of a law being contrary to the ECHR, the domestic case-law has slowly moved away from the principle *lex posterior derogat priori*. The domestic case-law shows that the ECHR was applied according to domestic instincts (that is, ignoring the Strasbourg Convention and case-law) at first but that after some time, both practising lawyers and the bench gained more confidence and gradually started to overcome their reluctance to seek guidance from the ECHR. The result has been that, as we have seen, the judiciary now recognises that the ECHR can be granted a "special strength" in relation to posterior laws, as far as its use for the interpretation of national law is concerned, although it should again be noted that the ECHR does not yet enjoy constitutional rank. The different treatment given to the ECHR and EU law as regards their constitutional rank in Italian law constitutes an inconsistency as it could well be argued that both organisations meet the requirements of Article 11 of the Italian Constitution.

It is possible to speculate that the disappointment of the Italian applicants in their national administration of justice, which has led them to seek redress outside their state in large numbers, has indirectly advanced the cause for domestic reforms. Favourable internal developments, however, also seem to have helped to put the ECHR on the authorities' agenda, a situation which, in turn, has placed the issue of civil liberties in a better position to influence the evolution of municipal and case-law. Particularly now and in the immediate future, the ECHR may provide domestic law with the chance of achieving a better balance between freedom on the one hand and, on the other hand, the array of devices the state has deployed to combat terrorism, organised crime, drug-related crime, illegal immigration and so on. If so, the zenith of Convention protection in Italian domestic law (rather than before the European Court) may not yet have been attained.

9. THE RECONSTRUCTION OF HUMAN RIGHTS IN THE EUROPEAN LEGAL ORDER

Ingrid Persaud

Introduction

This chapter considers the protection of civil liberties in the context of the European Community (EC) or European Union (EU) as it is for some purposes. We look first at the various ways in which human rights are presently protected within the EC. This leads to consideration of one option for the future which has been widely canvassed: accession to the European Convention for the Protection of Human Rights and Fundamental Freedoms (ECHR). We examine the problems, real and perceived, that such accession would hold for the EC. As we shall see, there are institutional, political and jurisprudential dimensions to be considered. What emerges from our study is that unexpected areas of the Treaty of Rome exhibit signs of vulnerability to human rights scrutiny and that the recipients of the benefits of such rights, in so far as there would be recipients, would be unusual in that they would mostly be corporate entities. This suggests that the accession debate transcends issues of supremacy of EC law and raises deeper, philosophical concerns as to the nature of rights within a legal order such as the EC. The intention of the central sections of this chapter is to show, through the case law of the European Court of Justice, that the EC perception of rights is motivated by a functional approach, namely the desire to secure the aim of the single market. The EC is not concerned with the protection of the rights of the individual and indeed there are only two instances in which the language of rights has been deployed in defence of the individual. Instead human rights language has been invoked to ensure the adherence of member states to the single market in goods, services, persons and capital. This is the context in which, it is argued, the debate about incorporation should be viewed.

Although the primary aim of the EC has always been economic in nature, it is clear from the Treaty of Rome that other goals were also contemplated at the time. The preamble to the Treaty of Rome spoke of the "ever closer

C. A. Gearty (ed.), European Civil Liberties and the European Convention on Human Rights, 347–391.
© 1997 *Kluwer Law International. Printed in the Netherlands.*

union of the peoples of Europe". The EC was also to be viewed as "providing the basis for a broader and deeper community among peoples...and [as laying] the foundations for institutions which will give direction to a destiny henceforth shared". There is no mention of the protection of civil liberties or human rights in the original treaty, however. Indeed, any mention of the role of human rights in the EC had to wait until the Single European Act (SEA), an amendment to the Treaty of Rome signed in 1987. The preamble to the SEA stated that the member states are "[d]etermined to work together to promote democracy on the basis of the fundamental rights recognised in the constitutions and laws of the member states, in the European Convention on the Protection of Human Rights and Fundamental Freedoms and the European Social Charter, notably freedom, equality and social justice". Even if there is no formal accession to the ECHR, the continued sensitisation of the EC to human rights will mean that the actions of member states will be scrutinised more closely for consistency with human rights norms than has previously been the case and that individuals will continue to be given greater remedies against the state.[1] The same protection against failures on the part of EC institutions may not however be as forthcoming.

Part I: Historical Background to the EC

The aftermath of the second world war provided the impetus for the reconstruction of Europe, politically, economically, militarily and ideologically. The twin aims of the time were to set in place the rapid economic reconstruction of Europe and to thwart the threat of Soviet aggression. All of this was considered within the ideological framework of federalism. These aims were translated in their institutional context into the Council of Europe[2] which was intended to realise the goal of a federal Europe. Defence requirements were met by the establishment of NATO. Additionally, and in order to achieve economic reconstruction, France, Germany, Italy, the Netherlands, Belgium and Luxembourg formed the European Coal and Steel Community (ECSC) established by the Treaty of Paris in 1951. By 1957 the Treaty of Rome had been concluded, extending the ambit of these economic arrangements to a more general European Economic Community (EEC).

---

[1] *Francovitch* v. *Italian State* Cases 6 and 9/90 [1992] I.R.L.R 84; see also Article G(51) of the Treaty on European Union (Maastricht).

[2] The Council of Europe was set up in 1947 with the aim of "greater unity" within Europe as well as the facilitation of economic and social progress which was to be pursued through the organs of the Council: see generally Tomkins, Chapter 1.

Parallel arrangements known as the European Free Trade Area (EFTA)[3] were made for those countries which chose not to join the Communities, opting instead for more limited economic co-operation in the form of the elimination of customs duties and quota restrictions but with no common external tariff. There are now fifteen member states of the EC.

Not all the institutional arrangements have been successful from the point of view of their original aims. The Council of Europe, for example, has not succeeded in its grand political ambition to unite Europe. In contrast the EC treaties have gone from strength to strength. The EEC, EURATOM (dealing with nuclear energy) and the ECSC have merged their institutions so that they now share a Commission which acts as the executive body, a Council which functions as a legislature, an assembly (now known as the European Parliament) and a court, the ECJ which now has its attendant Court of First Instance (CFI). These institutions enjoy more power than any other international organisations. The ECJ has observed that the Communities collectively represent a "unique legal order in which States have limited their sovereign rights, albeit in limited fields, and the subjects of which comprise not only the Member States but also their nationals".[4] The European Free Trade Agreement has in contrast been somewhat overshadowed by the growth of the EC and indeed several members of EFTA are now members of the EC.[5] The EC and EFTA have also recently concluded the European Economic Area (EEA) agreement which seeks to extend to the EFTA states EC rules on the free movement of goods, services, capital and persons as well as competition[6].

Part II: The European Parliament and Human Rights

Although as we have already observed, human rights were not strictly within the competence of the Treaty of Rome, the European Parliament has a long tradition of highlighting human rights problems world-wide. As far back as 1977 the European Parliament together with the Council and the Commission issued a Joint Declaration[7] to the following effect:

---

[3] Established by Treaty in 1960.

[4] *Van Gend en Loos* Case 26/62 [1963] C.M.L.R. 105.

[5] Finland, Sweden and Austria.

[6] Agreement on the European Economic Area [1992] 1 C.M.L.R. 921. It applies to all EFTA countries except Switzerland.

[7] Adopted 5 April 1977.

1. The European Parliament, the Council and the Commission stress the
prime importance they attach to the protection of fundamental rights, as derived in particular from the constitutions of the Member States and the European Convention for the Protection of Human Rights and Fundamental Freedoms.

2. In the exercise of their powers and in pursuance of the aims of the European Communities they respect and will continue to respect these rights.

This Joint Declaration is partly a reflection of the need to compensate for
the omission of human rights from the Treaty of Rome. In its preamble, the
Declaration recognised the role of the Court of Justice in developing a
method of protecting human rights within the existing framework. The
Declaration may also be the embodiment of the unease felt by the institutions working within a treaty arrangement that does not mention human
rights while simultaneously linking the external policies of the Communities
with human rights[8]. Significantly, the Joint Declaration makes specific reference to the ECHR as a model for human rights protection within the EC.

Since the Joint Declaration there have been other, more ambitious, attempts to introduce human rights into the agenda of the EC. The SEA is important in this respect as is the 1989 European Parliament's Declaration of
Fundamental Rights and Freedoms[9] which sets out a catalogue of rights specific to the EC. The Parliament has been urging the Council, with the support of Spain in particular, to adopt this as the binding human rights code for
the EC. The 1989 Declaration draws inspiration from many sources: the
Single European Act; the case law of the ECJ; the constitutions of member
states; and the special responsibility of the European Parliament as the only
directly elected body of the EC to develop a model for European society[10].
The Declaration anticipates a widening gap in the protection of the rights of
citizens in an expanding EC which is inevitably expected to take on board
issues of justice and home affairs[11]. The document includes rights which are
to be found in most catalogues of this nature, such as Article 2 which states
that, "[e]veryone shall have the right to life, liberty and security of person"
and Article 19 which provides that "[e]veryone whose rights and freedoms
have been infringed shall have the right to bring an action in a court or tri-

---

[8] See generally Part IV, below, pp. 353–354.

[9] [EP] 12 April 1989, 1989, O.J., C120/51.

[10] Direct elections for the European Parliament have been held since 1979: see Article
138(1) of the Treaty of Rome.

[11] Maastricht adds new "pillars" of inter-governmental co-operation in the areas of justice
and home affairs; foreign policy and security matters; and economic and monetary union.

bunal specified by law" and further that "[e]veryone shall be entitled to have their case heard fairly, publicly and within a reasonable time limit by an independent and impartial court or tribunal established by law...".

There are also provisions on freedom of thought,[12] expression,[13] information,[14] privacy,[15] and assembly,[16] the right to choose an occupation[17] and to have an education,[18] and the protection of the family.[19] Further provisions also deal with collective social rights,[20] social welfare,[21] the ownership of property[22] and the death penalty.[23] More unusual provisions are also present such as Article 24 which state that "the preservation, protection and improvement of the quality of the environment" and "the protection of consumers and users against risks of damage to their health and safety and against unfair commercial transactions" are to be regarded as integral parts of Community policy, with the Community institutions being "required to adopt all the measures necessary for the attainment of these objectives". The underlying importance of the principle of legitimacy[24] is stressed in Article 17 which states that:

1. All public authority emanates from the people and must be exercised in accordance with the principles of the rule of law.

2. Every public authority must be directly elected or answerable to a directly elected parliament.

3. European citizens shall have the right to take part in the election of Members of the European Parliament by free, direct and secret universal suffrage.

4. European citizens shall have an equal right to vote and stand for election.

---

12   Declaration of the European Parliament of Fundamental Rights and Freedoms, Article 4.
13   *Ibid.*, Article 5.
14   *Ibid.*
15   *Ibid.*, Article 6.
16   *Ibid.*, Article 10.
17   *Ibid.*, Article 12.
18   *Ibid.*, Article 16.
19   *Ibid.*, Article 7.
20   *Ibid.*, Article 14.
21   *Ibid.*, Article 15.
22   *Ibid.*, Article 9.
23   *Ibid.*, Article 22.
24   For further discussion of the principle in the broader context of international law, see T. Franck, "The Emerging Right to Democratic Governance" (1992) 86 *American Journal of International Law* 47.

5. The above rights shall not be subject to restrictions except where such re-
    strictions are in conformity with the Treaties establishing the European Com-
    munities.

A cursory glance at the catalogue of rights in this Declaration shows that it
is not an attempt to provide comprehensive civil liberties protection. There
is, for example, no provision for the rights of suspects who are detained,
which in an increasingly federal structure, would be bound to assume
greater importance. There is also no mention of a system for the redress of
violations of the rights contained in the Declaration. It is further limited in
that it applies to nationals of member states only. The Declaration also covers rights different from those in the ECHR. It is considered that these are
more appropriate to the activities and competencies of the EC. Thus, the
right to pursue an occupation, to good working conditions, rights in respect
of social welfare and other collective rights are all absent from the ECHR
but appear in the Declaration.

Many of these rights are clearly of an aspiratory nature so it would seem
that the value of the Declaration lies in its symbolic significance rather than
in any potential it might have as another tier of scrutiny of EC activities. It
could also be argued that the Declaration does more harm than good. It
could be said to detract from the primary goal of EC accession to the ECHR,
and to contribute to the dilution of an effective human rights standard for the
EC in that it is yet another code to consider in the absence of a proper system under the ECHR. Later on in the chapter we consider what might be
included in an acceptable code designed specifically for the EC should that
prove to be an available and desirable route to be pursued.[25]

Part III: The Case Law of the European Court of Justice

The ECJ has also created legal concepts which allow EC law to penetrate
the domestic legal systems of member states in a manner which is far greater
than that enjoyed by international law. Through the doctrine of direct effect
the ECJ has made EC treaties, decisions and secondary legislation, such as
directives and regulations, directly enforceable by individuals in their national courts.[26] For example, if the right to move freely throughout the EC as

---

[25] See text at note 120, below.

[26] Regulations may be invoked against individuals and the State but directives may only be
invoked against the State or against emanations of the State (see further *Marshall* v.
Southampton Area Health Authority (152/84) [1986] E.C.R. 723). Treaty provisions may
also enjoy direct effect.

a worker is hampered, it is possible to seek redress in the national court, and unnecessary in such circumstances to take the case to the ECJ in Luxembourg. This is an additional aspect to the protection of human rights that should be borne in mind in what follows.

Part IV: External Relations and Human Rights

As we have already suggested, in addition to the work of the European Parliament in highlighting human rights, the EC Council has also raised the issue in its external relations with the rest of the world. In its development co-operation policy, the EC has linked financial and technical assistance to the protection of human rights. Acting on the Declarations already mentioned, as well as the preamble to the Single European Act, the EC has established its relations with Latin America, Africa and Asia on the basis of the human rights records of the various countries concerned.[27] The Lomé Convention which governs the EC's relations with certain African, Caribbean and Pacific countries makes specific mention of the need to protect human rights and democratic values. In Article 5 of the Lomé (iv) Convention it states that:

> Co-operation shall be directed towards development centred on man, the protagonist and beneficiary of development, which thus entails respect for and promotion of all human rights. Co-operations, operations shall be conceived in accordance with the positive approach, which respect for human rights is recognised as a basic factor of real development and where co-operation is conceived as a contribution to the promotion of these rights. In this context development policy and co-operation are closely linked with the respect for and enjoyment of fundamental human rights.

The Parties reiterate what they described as their deep attachment to human dignity and human rights, which are said to be the legitimate aspirations of individuals and peoples.

Even outside Lomé it has become EC practice vis-à-vis third countries to condemn publicly violations of human rights; to approach countries where there is concern about flagrant violations; and to take steps to encourage respect for human rights. Other co-operation agreements that are noteworthy for their linkage of aid to human rights include the Co-operation Agreement

---

[27] Commission Communication to the Council and Parliament on "Human Rights, Democracy and Development Co-operation Policy" SEC (91) 61 Final. Several Council meetings were also devoted to this matter such as the Dublin Council (June 1990) on human rights and good governance in Africa and the Rome Council meeting (December 1990) on the promotion of democracy and human rights in external relations.

with the parties to the General Treaty on Central American Economic Integration (1985) and the agreements with Chile, Argentina, and Mexico all of which were concluded during 1990. The EC Commission has stated that in considering issues of aid and trade the "internal developments in the societies of the developing countries occupy a prominent place among the factors to be considered."[28] Indeed, this is borne out by the fact that negotiations with ASEAN (Association of South-East Asian Nations) for a new co-operation agreement have been stalled because of Portugal's concern at Indonesia's record on human rights abuses in East Timor.

Within the Organisation on Security and Co-operation in Europe (OSCE), the EC has also taken the lead in establishing a human rights dimension to the process.[29] States may request further information and possible investigation of cases (even individual ones) that raise human rights issues. EC concern over human rights abuses in Romania, for example, was noted and a condemnatory statement to this effect was issued. In addition to the ECHR the Council has also referred in its external relations policies to the United Nations Charter, the Universal Declaration of Human Rights and the covenants on civil and political rights and economic, social and cultural rights.[30] The EC has also attempted to co-ordinate its policy on the recognition of the former Yugoslavia and the Baltic states by applying human rights criteria as laid down in the Declaration on Yugoslavia[31] and the Declaration on the Guidelines on the Recognition of New States in Eastern Europe and the Soviet Union.[32] This policy was applied by an Arbitration Commission which has become known as the Badinter Commission.[33] It is interesting to note that the EC did not follow the recommendations of the Badinter Commission consistently and in the cases of Bosnia-Herzegovina and Croatia,[34] for example, granted recognition even though this Commission was unconvinced that the ideals of democracy and human rights were adequately catered for.[35]

---

[28] Commission Communication to the Council and Parliament on "Human Rights, Democracy and Development Co-operation Policy", *op. cit.*, note 27.

[29] See further the Copenhagen meeting of the CSCE on 29 June 1990, 29 I.L.M. 1305 and the Moscow meeting of 3 October 1991, 30 I.L.M. 1670.

[30] See Commission Communication, *op. cit.*, note 27.

[31] European Political Co-operation, Press Release, 1 September 1991.

[32] European Political Co-operation, Press Release, 16 December 1991.

[33] After its chairman, Mr Badinter, the President of the *Conseil Constitutionel* of France.

[34] See (1992) 31 I.L.M.

[35] See further, R. Mullerson, "Law and Politics in the Recognition of New States" in *Inter-*

Part V: The Maastricht Treaty

The Maastricht Treaty, which creates a European Union,[36] is the most recent manifestation of the call for human rights to become part of the European Union legal order. The preamble to the Treaty recounts the member states' "attachment to the principles of liberty, democracy and [their] respect for human rights and fundamental freedoms and...the rule of law". The specific recognition of this attachment is in Article F which provides that, "[t]he Union shall respect fundamental rights as guaranteed by the European Convention for the Protection of Human Rights and Fundamental Freedoms signed in Rome on 4 November 1950 and as they result from the constitutional traditions common to the member states as general principles of Community law." The Maastricht Treaty provisions on justice and home affairs also contain references to other human rights standards. In Article K.2 the Treaty states that matters in this area, such as asylum and immigration, "...shall be dealt with in compliance with the European Convention for the Protection of Human Rights and Fundamental Freedoms...and the Convention relating to the Status of Refugees of 28 July 1951 and having regard to the protection afforded by member states to persons persecuted on political grounds". While these are the only direct references to human rights in the Maastricht Treaty some of the rights contained in the 1989 Declaration of Parliament have found their way into the Treaty. According to Article 8(a)(1) there is now, for example, a general right to freedom of movement within the Community for all EC citizens. Citizens of the Union are also entitled to benefit from the principle of democracy. By virtue of Article 8 citizens have the right to stand for and vote in local elections and elections for the European Parliament where they reside. The right of petition which is also in the Declaration finds expression in Maastricht in the form of the creation of a Parliamentary Ombudsman.[37]

The so-called Reflection Group, a high level group of experts preparing for the 1996 inter-governmental conference to review the Maastricht Treaty, is considering the introduction of a measure for censuring human rights violators[38]. It calls for a new treaty provision which would suspend or even expel member states which violate fundamental human rights or democratic principles. This would be part of a new Bill of Rights to strengthen EC le-

---

national Law, Rights and Politics (London, 1994), pp. 117–135.

[36] The Treaty on European Union entered into force on 1 November 1993.

[37] See Article 8d of the Treaty on European Union.

[38] See *Financial Times*, 5 September 1995, p. 2.

gitimacy. Other proposals include incorporating the European Social Charter; clauses on racism, xenophobia, the protection of minorities and the extension of the principle of equality between men and women.[39]

Part VI: Accession to the ECHR: The Balance of Advantage

1. POTENTIAL BENEFITS

The debate over EC accession to the ECHR stretches back some time.[40] At
present there appears to be little political will on the part of the EC or the
Council of Europe to move forward on the issue. The EC is coming to terms
with the new areas of co-operation under Maastricht and the ECHR institutions for their part are occupied with more pressing concerns, such as coping
with an increasingly heavy workload and advising on internal constitutional
changes. Yet there is symbolic value in accession. It would make clear to the
world that the EC was not just interested in the human rights records of the
less-economically developed countries to whom it gives assistance, but was
also concerned with its own human rights records. This would lend credibility to the external relations policies of the EC. Accession should also work
to ensure the uniform application and interpretation of the ECHR within the
EC so that cases like *Hoechst*[41] which we discuss below would not recur.
Having a human rights instrument as part of the EC legal order would create
legal certainty and would have a potentially conditioning effect on holders
of public power who would naturally be aware of this extra tier of review. In
other words the more human rights are part of the vocabulary and working
methods of the institutions, the more likely it is that we will see an increased
sensitisation to human rights issues.

The present system may actually leave applicants without a remedy for
alleged violations of human rights—something which would be remedied by
accession to the ECHR. In *Melchers*[42] the applicants attempted unsuccessfully to challenge before the ECJ the imposition of fines by the EC Commis-

---

[39] Note however that in a recent case the ECJ has ruled that women job quotas were unlawful in Germany when it found a state law on quotas to be a violation of the 1976 Equal
Treatment Directive: *Financial Times*, 18 October 1995.

[40] See further the report of the House of Lords Select Committee on the European Communities, *Human Rights Re-Examined*, HL 10.

[41] Joined cases 46/87 and 227/88, judgment of 21 September 1989. For further discussion
see text at note 105, below.

[42] Application No. 3258/87, Decision of 9 February 1990, not yet reported. For further discussion see text at note 102, below.

sion for breach of the competition rules on the grounds that the body had acted as both prosecutor and decision maker. They then tried to challenge, on the basis of the ECHR, the German government's implementation of this fine against them through the domestic legal system. The case was declared inadmissible; a member state could not be subject to the human rights machinery for faithful implementation of an EC decision since acts of the EC were not within the jurisdiction of the Court of Human Rights. Another gap in the protection of human rights is that while the secondary legislation of the EC may refer to the ECHR, the legislation may not be challenged for incompatibility with the Convention since the ECHR is not within the EC's competence. Thus the Directive on Cross Border Broadcasting[43] specifically mentions Article 10 of the ECHR, the right to freedom of expression, but despite this it cannot be challenged in Strasbourg. Similarly those concerned with immigration law in the EC can only look to the ECHR for reference rather than for a remedy. When border controls are lifted under the Schengen agreements[44] where will be a corresponding need to ensure that genuine refugees and asylum seekers are protected. However, the ECHR will not be in the forefront as a constraint on whatever agreement is finally put in place.

It could also be argued that accession goes to the very heart of the "democracy deficit" of the EC. The EC cannot be seen to be judging the human rights standards of member states while simultaneously enjoying an "immunity" from human rights scrutiny for its own activities. This is particularly relevant to Italy and Germany both of which continue to threaten to refuse to obey the primacy of Community law in respect of human rights "so long as", to quote from an Italian decision, "the Community does not have its own catalogue of fundamental rights".[45] These countries believe that their constitutions provide better guarantees of human rights than the EC treaties and are therefore reluctant to concede total competence to the EC in this area.

---

[43] 1989, O.J., L298/23.

[44] Denmark, Ireland and the United Kingdom are not parties to these agreements and Austria, Sweden and Finland currently enjoy observer status.

[45] *Frontini* v. *Ministero dello Finanze* [1974] 2 C.M.L.R. 386 at p. 372. See also *German Handelsgesellschaft* [1974] 2 C.M.L.R. 551. The compromise between the German Constitutional Court and the ECJ came in the *Solange II* judgment of 22 October 1986 in which the German court stated that it would not review the protection of human rights in the EC so long as the level of protection was adequate by German standards. For further discussion see Voss, above, Ch. 4. For the position as far as Italy is concerned, see Leonardi, above, Ch. 8.

2.   LEGAL AUTHORITY TO ACCEDE TO THE ECHR

The Maastricht Treaty does not elaborate on the legal basis that would allow the EC to accede to the ECHR or on how to overcome the problems of an international organisation being party to a human rights instrument to which only states are parties. Further only members of the Council of Europe are allowed to be a party to the ECHR and the EC of course is not a member. Even if these issues could be resolved, it is unclear what the legal basis would be for accession by the EC. The actual power might be derived from Article 235 of the Treaty of Rome which states that, "[i]f action by the Community should prove necessary to attain, in the course of the operation of the common market, one of the objectives of the Community and this Treaty has not provided the necessary powers, the Council shall, acting unanimously on a proposal from the Commission and after consulting the European Parliament, take the appropriate measures". Given this residual power to allow the EC to fulfil their mandate in the Maastricht Treaty, which is partly an amendment to the Treaty of Rome, coupled with the authority of the preamble to the Single European Act, an attempt could be made to accede to the ECHR. Fundamental rights have long been part of the language of the institutions—in particular the court, and therefore this horizontal policy of accession could be fulfilled through the use of Article 235. Additionally, since all acts of the Union must be in accordance with Article F, requiring respect for fundamental rights, the EC must therefore have the mandate to accede to the standard stated in that Article by virtue of the residual powers in Article 235.

There is however resistance in some quarters to the idea that the protection of human rights is now an object of the EC or of the European Union. While it might be arguable that human rights is an objective of the Treaty of Rome and of Maastricht it cannot be argued that it is an objective of the Coal and Steel Community. The rights of citizens of the proposed Union as set out in Article 8 of Maastricht are narrower political concerns and contain neither any mention of human rights nor any reference to Article F. Yet if human rights are not accepted as a clear objective of the member states, then Article 235 cannot be used. Given these difficulties it seems to be clear that the best route would be for a specific amendment of the Treaty of Rome, in accordance with Article 238.[46] This would allow an inter-governmental con-

---

[46]   Article 238 is as follows:

"The Community may conclude with a third State, a union of States or an international organisation agreements establishing an association involving reciprocal

ference to debate the issues fully, and would remove any legal ambiguities that might hinder accession. However, regardless of whether the EC accedes to the Convention under Article 235 or makes use of Article 238 there are a number of institutional, political and jurisprudential problems that would need to be addressed. It is to these we now turn.

3.   INSTITUTIONAL AND POLITICAL ISSUES

The Convention system in Strasbourg has of course its own machinery of a Commission, Court and Council of Ministers. Should the EC accede to the Convention, the issue of representation on these bodies would arise. There is the added complication that the member states to the EC are all also parties to the Convention. If they were to be represented in these bodies other parties to the Convention might consider that they were being given special status, in the form of effective "double representation". In the Council of Ministers the political ramifications of double representation would be particularly acute. The EC Commission has argued that representation in the Council of Ministers is not necessary "since a higher degree of protection is offered by a judgment of the Court (of human rights)".[47] However, since it is the Council of Ministers that would be charged with the responsibility of ensuring that judgments of the Court are properly implemented then it does seem important that all parties, including the EC, should be represented.

It would seem that there are at least four options available. The ECJ could decide to refer all cases involving a right under the Convention to the Court in Strasbourg. This would be a straight case of the ECJ giving up jurisdiction to deal with fundamental rights in so far as the matter was covered by the Convention. It is the solution that would probably be most favoured by the Strasbourg organs since it would preserve intact the integrity of the Court of Human Rights to pronounce on human rights violations and would allow the Court to develop its jurisprudence in a consistent manner. However, it is unlikely that the ECJ will accept such a situation since that Court considers itself the final arbiter on all issues of EC law, including issues of fundamental rights. This is in keeping with the doctrines of supremacy and

---

rights and obligations, common action and special procedures.

"These agreements shall be concluded by the Council, acting unanimously and after receiving the assent of the European Parliament which shall act by an absolute majority of its component members.

"Where such agreements call for amendments to this treaty, these amendments shall be first adopted in accordance with the procedure laid down in Article 236."

[47]   Commission Communication of November 1990.

direct effect that it has developed over many years. The ECJ would therefore be unlikely to be willing to have another court pronounce on matters within EC competence.

A second option would be the establishment of a new joint court. The recent experience of the conclusion of the European Economic Area Agreement (EEA)[48] between the EC and EFTA is however testimony to the reluctance of the ECJ to part with any jurisdiction—real or perceived. The draft EEA agreement envisaged the creation of economic integration between the EFTA and EEC and in this context it was agreed that there would be a joint court made up of judges from the EFTA countries and the ECJ. In accordance with the procedure in Article 228(1) of the Treaty of Rome, the Commission, Council or a member state may obtain an opinion of the ECJ as to whether an agreement negotiated by the EC but not yet concluded, is compatible with existing obligations under the Treaty. A negative ECJ decision may only be overridden by using the procedure for amending the Treaty. When the draft EEA agreement was put before the ECJ in accordance with Article 228(1) the court raised several objections and the agreement had to be re-drafted in the light of these.[49] The objections of the ECJ centred around its concern that its jurisdiction was being undermined in areas of EC competence. The ECJ objected, for example, to ECJ judges sitting on a joint court since this could create a conflict of loyalties. It also objected to the fact the ECJ rulings on interpretation were merely advisory and insisted that giving non-binding opinions would undermine the dignity of the ECJ. Most important of all, the ECJ believed that a joint court would hamper its freedom to develop EC law since the shape of future EC law would be influenced by the EEA Court.[50] Given this stance, the possibility of a joint court was abandoned. Instead an EFTA Court is being set up which will work informally with the ECJ.[51] The Community Court remains firmly in control of the interpretation and application of the EEA agreement. On the basis of this experience the second possible institutional court arrangement of a joint court made up of judges from the Strasbourg court and from the ECJ is unlikely to be greeted with enthusiasm, and is still less likely to receive ECJ approval.

---

[48] European Economic Area Agreement [1992] 1 C.M.L.R. 921.

[49] *Opinion 1/91*, [1992] 1 C.M.L.R. 245 and *Opinion 1/92* [1992] 2 C.M.L.R. 245.

[50] See further T. Hartley, "The European Court and the EEA" (1992) 41 *International and Comparative Law Quarterly* 841; H.G. Schermers, "Note on Opinion 1/91 and 1/92" (1992) 29 *Common Market Law Review* 991.

[51] The work of the Court began on 1 January 1994.

The third option is for the ECJ to retain total jurisdiction in all matters concerning fundamental rights—even where there is reference to the ECHR. The ECJ could decide for itself that it has the competence to pronounce on human rights violations based on the ECHR even though the issue appears to be outside the scope of existing EC law. This is entirely possible in a so-called "mixed agreement" where the parties to the treaty (in this instance the ECHR) are both the member states in their individual capacities and the EC is acting as a collective body. The Court of Human Rights might however take objection to such a dilution of its power and control over the ECHR.[52] A fourth option would be for the instigation of a procedure similar to the preliminary ruling mechanism under Article 177 of the Treaty of Rome. Under this procedure member states can request, and in some cases may be obliged, to seek a ruling of the ECJ on issues concerning the validity and interpretation of the Treaty of Rome. In the same way the ECJ could request rulings from the Court of Human Rights on questions involving the ECHR,[53] either at the request of the parties or the ECJ itself. There could be a time limit so that if there was no dissent from the Strasbourg court as to the ECJ's interpretation of a particular right within, for example, six months, then the ECJ could proceed. This would inevitably means a degree of subordination of the ECJ to Strasbourg as regards the interpretation and application of the ECHR but it might prove to be a workable compromise.[54]

Assuming that the issue of the representation of the EC is resolved, there are several other important institutional and procedural questions that remain to be resolved. It is a condition of admissibility of a claim under the ECHR that local remedies be exhausted. For the purpose of the EC as a party to the ECHR, when would this condition be fulfilled? One possibility is for the ECJ to be considered an internal court for the purposes of the Convention. Alternatively, this provision could be waived by respondent governments. There is the further question of who should be the proper defendant in a case where a member state of the EC, in execution of EC law, is alleged to have violated the Convention. This is the issue that arose in the *Melchers*[55] case. It could be left to the discretion of the Court of Human Rights to determine the proper parties to each action but there remains uncertainty. Also to be considered would be the sensitive question of whether

---

[52] Indeed in *Melchers* such a warning had already been sounded.

[53] The most prominent call for this particular route is by Judge Lenaerts of the Court of First Instance of the EC.

[54] This would also avoid instances like *Hoechst* (see note 41, above).

[55] See note 102, below.

member states of the EC could bring actions against each other in the field of application of EC law where there was an alleged violation of the Convention. In such a case use could be made of Article 62 of the Convention which precludes issues relating to "internal management" from its jurisdiction. Also relevant would be Article 219 of the Treaty of Rome which suggests that such disputes are within the sole competence of the ECJ.[56] As previously noted there is also the obvious problem that only parties to the Council of Europe (who are of course all states rather than international organisations) may presently be parties to the ECHR. To accommodate the EC, Article 66 of the ECHR would have to be amended.[57] Whatever institutional solution is achieved it is clear that accession would burden the already backlogged Court of Human Rights and would be likely to create delays and greater expense for individuals seeking redress.

Only two member states of the EC, Greece and Italy, have expressed themselves unreservedly in favour of the EC's accession to the ECHR. There are however compelling political reasons why the Community should accede. As already mentioned the Community is overtly linking financial assistance to human rights and this linkage would be more credible if the EC were also subject to some human rights assessment of its own activities. It could also be argued that accession goes to the very heart of the "democracy deficit" in the EC. The Community cannot be seen to be judging the human rights standards of member states or third states, while simultaneously enjoying a type of "immunity" from human rights scrutiny of its own activities.[58] On the other hand, many member states consider that the gap in the protection of fundamental rights is more a perceived than a real gap or that at any rate the gap (if it exists) is a marginal one. On this view, instead of accession the EC should concentrate on the development of general principles of EC law such as non-discrimination, legal certainty and proportionality and that this would be the best way further to safeguard rights. The accession by the EC would also affect member states that have negotiated reservations to the Convention or those that have not ratified certain protocols. Indeed, since Article F of the Maastricht Treaty does not mention the

---

[56] Article 219 states that, "Member States undertake not to submit a dispute concerning the interpretation or application of this Treaty to any method of settlement other than those provided for therein."

[57] Article 66 of the ECHR states that, "This Convention shall be open to the signature of the members of the Council of Europe...".

[58] See further above, note 45, for an example of the difficulties this creates for certain member states.

protocols specifically there is some doubt as to whether they are even included. Furthermore, the actual process of accession is likely to be long and cumbersome and it is argued that it should not be undertaken without some urgent rationale.

Part VII: The Implications of Accession for National Decisions on Incorporation

Three member states of the EC—the United Kingdom, Ireland and Denmark—have ratified but not incorporated the ECHR Convention into domestic law. Accession by the EC would seem to be a device to force the hand of these countries since they would then be required to incorporate the ECHR into domestic law in so far as it would be an obligation under EC law and would take immediate effect under the doctrine of supremacy. This notion of the incorporation of the ECHR by the "backdoor" of EC accession might be a misplaced concern since the "backdoor" is already being used.[59] An example is the *Heylens*[60] case where the ECJ specifically referred to Articles 6 and 13 of the ECHR in arriving at a decision concerning EC rules on mutual recognition of qualifications (rules to which all member states are bound).[61] Accession by the EC would only affect the legal systems of member states with regard to EC legal acts. It would not stray into areas outside EC competence. The fears of states that have not incorporated could also be calmed by an acknowledgment that many of the standards set in the Convention are already part of EC law through the affiliation of general principles of EC law. What would be new would be that citizens of the Union would be able to invoke the ECHR to achieve direct redress in relation to action taken by the EC.

---

[59] See H. G. Schermers, "Memorandum to the House of Lords Select Committee" in *Human Rights Re-Examined*, *op. cit.*, note 40, pp. 54–56.

[60] *UNECTEF* v. *Heylens* Case 222/86 [1987] E.C.R. 4097.

[61] The Court stated that,

> "Since free access to employment is a fundamental right which the Treaty confers individually on each worker in the Community, the existence of a remedy of a judicial nature against any decision of a national authority refusing the benefit of that right is essential to secure for the individual the effective protection for his right.... That requirement reflects a general principle of law which underlies the constitutional traditions common to the Member States and has been enshrined in Articles 6 and 13 of the European Convention for the Protection of Human Rights and Fundamental Freedoms."

Part VIII: The ECJ: Reconstructing Human Rights

Despite the lively debate about accession, there has been little discussion of exactly what impact on EC law such a change would have. Indeed, even the consequences of the ECJ's development of its own human rights jurisprudence have not been fully understood. In this regard the debate about human rights in the EC has taken place at too high a level of abstraction. When we turn to the detail, away from the high-blown rhetoric, it is clear that unexpected areas of EC competence such as competition, the provision of goods and services and agriculture are vulnerable to human rights scrutiny. In carrying out policies in these areas the EC or the member states might be in breach of the ECHR on, for example, the right to fair trial or freedom of expression. There are also potentially rather unusual recipients of these rights, including for example multinational enterprises. Furthermore, the human rights jurisprudence developed by the ECJ only incidentally concerns the protection of the fundamental rights of the individual. The Community Court offers little or no concrete assistance to individuals and has been concerned instead with advancing the "unique legal order" of *Van Gend en Loos*[62] and the completion of the single market. A *Celex* search revealed at least 66 cases raising a question of human rights. In only two of these cases, *Kent Kirk*[63] and *Wachauf*[64] did an individual actually receive a concrete benefit from the ECJ's stance on rights. Most interestingly, both of these cases concerned the incompatibility of *national legislation* with the provisions of the ECHR. They did not raise any question of the compatibility of *EC* legislation. The ECJ has always maintained that it will act on fundamental rights issues in the context of EC law only. It has been very cautious and consistent in demarcating jurisdiction between itself and member states. However an analysis of the case law of the ECJ suggests that it is really concerned with using human rights as a means with which to penetrate areas of member states' competence, areas which were previously their exclusive domain.

This pattern runs counter to the general view that the international law on human rights is in part an attempt to balance state and individual interests in a way which allows states to set their respective houses in order while being subject to external scrutiny. The ECJ appears on the contrary to be bent on usurping member states' power to rectify their own problems while simulta-

---

[62]   Case 26/62 [1963] E.C.R. 1.

[63]   Case 63/83 [1984] E.C.R. 2689.

[64]   *Wachauf* v. *Federal Republic of Germany* Case 5/88 [1989] E.C.R. 2609.

neously making itself and the acts of EC institutions immune to scrutiny by reference to human rights standards.

A second anxiety also emerges from careful consideration of the case-law. Many argue that the decisions of the ECJ on fundamental rights are inadequate, incoherent and sometimes plain wrong. For example, the substantive protection of rights offered and the margin of appreciation given to states differs markedly as between the ECJ and the Court of Human Rights. There is however a deeper concern about the very nature of the ECJ's interest in human rights. If we are to view human rights from a capitalist, single market stance then the case law of the ECJ is both adequate and coherent and developing in response to the needs of the EC. On this model, human rights in terms of individual protection do not and should not enjoy precedence over norms governing the free movement of goods, persons, services and capital. Through the eyes of a civil liberties lawyer, however, the gaps and mistakes seem glaring. Human rights norms are viewed by such lawyers as fundamental and as superior to other norms. Some are even *jus cogens*—such as the right to life and freedom from torture. It would never be possible, from a civil liberties stance, to equate freedom of expression with the free movement of goods. As we shall see, this is precisely what the ECJ has done in many of the cases considered below. The assessment made of the case law then depends largely on our view of rights, in particular whether they are a tool of economic power, or a reflection of standards of conduct in relation to the treatment of individuals. What is clear is that the ECJ has failed to develop a construction of rights which is grounded in the tenets of individual liberty. It has instead reconstructed these rights in terms of other requirements such as the supremacy of Community law and the completion of the single market in goods, services, capital and persons[65].

1. THE EARLY CASE LAW

The early case law of the ECJ[66] reveals that the notion of the protection of fundamental rights was not the initiative of the Court but was rather thrust upon it by some member states' demanding that if the ECJ were not to protect rights at least as well as their domestic constitutions did, then they re-

---

[65] See further, J. Coppel & A. O'Neill, "The European Court of Justice: Taking Rights Seriously?" (1994) 29 *Common Market Law Review* 669–692.

[66] For discussions of the development of the case-law, see R. Dallen, "An Overview of European Community Protection of Human Rights, with some special references to the UK" (1990) 27 *Common Market Law Review* 761–790; A. Clapham, "A Human Rights Policy for the European Community" [1990] *Yearbook of European Law* 309–366.

served the power to act where such rights were concerned. In other words these countries were asserting that there would be no supremacy of EC law on questions of fundamental rights if EC law did not provide adequate protection. In *Stork*[67] the ECJ was asked to consider whether an EC measure, imposed on the Ruhr coal-mining industry, which affected the applicant, violated Articles 2 and 12 of the German Basic Law governing the free development of the individual and occupational freedom respectively. The ECJ rejected jurisdiction stating that the EC institutions had only to act in accordance with EC law and did not need to be mindful of rules of internal law, such as constitutional guarantees.[68] The ECJ took a similar stance in *Ruhrkohlen-Verkaufsgesellschaft*[69] where the applicant had invoked Article 14 of the German Basic Law relating to the right to enjoyment of private property, when it again declined to examine the legality of action by a EC institution by reference to the constitution of a member state. Objections also came in *Sgarlata*[70] from some Italian citrus fruit growers as to the validity of an EC regulation regarding agriculture. The case was declared inadmissible on the grounds that the applicants were not "directly or individually concerned" within the meaning of Article 173,[71] the main provision for judicial review of Community actions. This happened in spite of the fact that their financial interests were affected by the price-fixing scheme and that the applicants invoked "basic principles governing all member countries". At no point did the ECJ consider that, even if they could not examine the compatibility of EC action with the constitutions of member states, it might still be possible

---

[67]   *Friedrich Stork & Co.* v. *High Authority of the European Coal and Steel Community* Case 1/58 [1959] E.C.R. 17.

[68]   The ECJ held that "...the High Authority is not empowered to examine a ground of complaint which maintains that, when it adopted its decision, it infringed principles of German constitutional law."

[69]   Cases 36,37, 38 & 40/59 [1960] E.C.R. 423. The ECJ held that "Community law, as it arises under the ECSC Treaty, does not contain any general principle, express or otherwise, guaranteeing the maintenance of vested rights". It is worth noting that Advocate General Lagrange considered that the Court would be bound to consider the issue of vested rights where appropriate in so far as it became an expression of a general principle of law.

[70]   *Marcello Sgarlata and Others* v. *Commission of the EEC* Case 40/64 [1965] E.C.R. 215.

[71]   The ECJ has imposed notoriously high standards on individuals claiming locus standi under Article 173—see further Greaves, "Locus Standi under Article 173 EEC when seeking Annulment of a Regulation" (1986) 11 *European Law Review* 119 and Rasmussen, "Why is Article 173 interpreted against Private Plaintiffs?" (1980) 5 *European Law Review* 1122.

to subject such action to scrutiny based on guarantees that were part of Community law through some generally deduced "general principles".

A slight shift in attitude is detectable in the case of *Stauder*.[72] The decision concerned the EC's butter mountain. Member states were authorised to dispose of surplus butter at a reduced rate to those in receipt of social assistance. One such beneficiary, a citizen of Ulm, felt his human dignity affronted by being forced to disclose that he was on social assistance in order to receive the butter. The ECJ was asked by way of a reference from the German courts to rule on the compatibility of this requirement with the general principles of EC law. The German courts also indicated that if the EC could not protect rights adequately they reserved the power to provide effective protection of fundamental rights themselves—even in areas of EC competence. Therefore, in the unexpected context of melting the butter mountain, the ECJ clashed head-on with a member state over the protection of fundamental rights. The matter was eventually resolved through a technicality with the ECJ deciding that the German text of the regulation was the cause of the difficulty (rather than the regulation itself) since it did not match other language versions of the regulation. It was therefore the fault of the member state and not the EC. However what was particularly interesting about the decision was that the ECJ used the opportunity to state "that, as interpreted, the provision at issue does not reveal any element jeopardising basic individual rights implicit in the general principles of Community law, which the court ensures shall be observed." This dicta represented a significant development on the earlier case law.

The next opportunity for the court to develop its ideas on human rights came in the case of *Internationale Handelsgesellschaft*,[73] a decision which once again concerned agriculture. Farming regulations of the EC provided for a system of "agricultural deposits". Several German firms challenged the validity of this system, stating that it violated German constitutional law[74] and that this also inevitably involved a violation of EC law since EC law encompassed German constitutional guarantees. The ECJ emphasised the autonomy of the EC legal order and rejected the introduction into EC law of

---

[72] *Erich Stauder* v. *City of Ulm, Sozialamt* Case 29/69 [1969] E.C.R. 419.

[73] *Internationale Handelsgesellschaft m.b.H.* v. *Einfuhr und Vorratstelle für Getreide und Futtermittel* Case 11/70 [1970] E.C.R. 1125.

[74] The company maintained that the loss of the deposit on the land was a violation of its basic rights and liberties and further that ratification of the Treaty of Rome had not overridden the German constitution's provisions in Article 24(1) which states that, "The Federation may by legislation transfer sovereign powers to intergovernmental institutions".

concepts of a wholly national character. The court emphasised that "...the validity of a Community instrument or its effects within a member-State [could not] be affected by allegations that it strikes at either the fundamental rights as formulated in that State's constitution or the principles of a national constitutional structure". The ECJ went on to declare that "[a]n examination should however be made as to whether some analogous guarantee, inherent in Community law, has not been infringed. For respect for fundamental rights has an integral part in the general principles of law of which the Court of Justice ensures respect. The protection of such rights, while inspired by the constitutional principles common to the Member States must be ensured within the framework of the Community's structure and objectives". Using its own definition of the content of the rights contested, the court then found that there had been no violation. It is this case which also marks a shift in the jurisdiction of member states in that the ECJ is stating that it will protect fundamental rights and that therefore this area is no longer within the exclusive competence of the member states. The German Constitutional Court did not, however, accept this position and cited as one of its reasons the fact that the EC "lacks in particular a codified catalogue of fundamental rights".[75]

While not making any attempt to instigate the creation of such a code, the ECJ was shifting its stance and ensuring that it would have greater opportunities to review acts (especially of member states), by reference to human rights. In the second *Nold*[76] case the Court specifically mentioned the ECHR as an additional source of reference for its development of EC-based "fundamental rights". Nold, a wholesaler, challenged the legality of a Commission decision requiring minimum purchases of coal the effect of which would have been to put him out of business. He relied on several grounds, including a breach of his fundamental rights concerning the right to property. His action was dismissed as groundless but the Court decision referred to a catalogue of rights which were described as an integral part of the EC system for the protection of individual liberty. The ECJ stated that:

> In safeguarding these rights, the court is bound to draw inspiration from constitutional traditions common to the Member States, and it cannot therefore uphold measures which are incompatible with fundamental rights recognised and protected by the constitutions of those states. Similarly, international treaties for the protection of human rights on which the Member States have collaborated or of which they are signatories can supply guidelines which should be followed within the framework of Community law.

---

[75] This is an argument that continues to be an issue, see further *Bundesverfassungsgericht*, Judgment of 12 October 1993 BvR 2134/92 and 2 BvR 2153/92, [1994] 1 C.M.L.R. 57.

[76] Case 4/73 [1974] E.C.R. 491.

It was to be some time before it became clear that the hopes raised by the second *Nold* case were not to be realised. The perfect opportunity to elaborate on an understanding of rights grounded in individual liberty towards which *Nold* was tentatively reaching, came in the *Van Duyn*[77] case. Ms. Van Duyn was a Dutch Scientologist who wished to take advantage of the free movement of workers within the EC territories and to work in the UK for the Church of Scientology. She was refused admission to the UK in accordance with its domestic law, the government arguing that a member state could derogate from the EC guarantee of freedom of movement for reasons of public policy, which in this case involved the fact that the UK considered the Church of Scientology to be an undesirable organisation (which it nevertheless allowed to operate within its borders). A reference was made to the ECJ in which the Court agreed that this was a permissible derogation. The Court allowed the UK a wide margin of appreciation even though there was a conflict between the government's action and Article 7 of the Treaty of Rome. Article 7 appeared unequivocally to stipulate that no discrimination on grounds of nationality was to be countenanced within the EC.[78] This decision allowed the UK effectively to discriminate between UK scientologists and Dutch scientologists. The loser in this was of course the individual. It was quite clear that the ECJ did not wish to upset the UK in this, its first preliminary reference to the court. The case also coincided with the referendum campaign to decide the UK's continued involvement in the EC. It was better to sacrifice Ms. Van Duyn than UK membership of the EC club.

This case also served as an opportunity for the court to advance the then tenuous concept of the direct effect of EC law, stating that Ms. Van Duyn could invoke the Treaty of Rome directly in proceedings before a national court. On the facts with which she was confronted, however, there was little to be gained for Ms Van Duyn in invoking the Treaty provision when the ECJ was prepared to sanction derogation of the right to non-discrimination and the freedom to pursue an occupation of one's choice on policy grounds that were transparently divorced from all notions of individual rights and liberties. The greater margin of appreciation given to states in *Van Duyn* was further illustrated by the case of *Rutili*.[79] Rutili was an Italian national born in France and living there. He was also married to a French national. His participation in certain political activities led the authorities to declare him a person "likely to disturb *ordre public*" and to ban him from living in certain

---

[77] *Yvonne Van Duyn* v. *Home Office* Case 41/74 [1974] E.C.R. 1337.
[78] See also Article 6 of the EC Treaty.
[79] *Roland Rutili* v. *Minister for the Interior* Case 36/75 [1975] E.C.R. 1219.

areas of France. Mr. Rutili challenged the authority of the French to limit his residence permit in this manner and the administrative tribunal made a reference to the ECJ.[80] The court recalled *Van Duyn* and the second *Nold* case to make it clear that the free movement of workers was a fundamental Community right that could be directly invoked and that the court could take account of general principles, the constitutions of member states and treaties in coming to a decision. It then expressly invoked the ECHR for the first time in the following way:

> Taken as a whole, these limitations placed on the powers of Member States in respect of control of aliens are specific manifestation of the more general principle, enshrined in Articles 8,9,10 and 11 of the Convention for the Protection of Human Rights and Fundamental Freedoms, signed in Rome on 4 November 1950 and ratified by all the Member States, and in Article 2 of the Protocol No 4 of the same Convention, signed in Strasbourg on 16 September 1963, which provide, in identical terms, that no restrictions in the interests of national security or public safety shall be placed on the rights secured by the above-quoted articles other than such as are necessary for the protection of those interests in a democratic society.

Rutili is important for the fact that the ECJ was there prepared to develop its jurisprudence by reference to the ECHR. Note however that it was invoking this strong language of individual rights in the context of a challenge to the *action of a member state*, not a challenge to an EC institution. Where member state action is concerned the ECJ now appears prepared, after *Rutili*, and only in the right circumstances (which did not exist in *Van Duyn*), to consider that fundamental rights pertain to the whole of the territory of a member state. Derogation from these fundamental rights is only possible by reference to public security, public health, or public policy as understood in the context of the ECHR. However, the ECJ also held that where the ban was not a total ban from the territory, but rather a partial restriction on movement within the member state, then the test of legitimacy was whether this ban would have been permissible in relation to a national of that state. In other words in Mr. Rutili's case, it was only necessary for the state to show that this action was non-discriminatory. The Court further considered that the Treaty of Rome could not be used to extend more favourable treatment to a foreign EC national than was enjoyed by a state's own nationals. This left it open to the French court, when applying the ruling, to exclude Rutili from areas of France if the same fate could lawfully be imposed upon a French national. The Court's view of non-discrimination is somewhat restrictive,

---

[80] The reference under Article 177 was to establish whether this was an acceptable limitation of the free movement of workers within the meaning of Article 48(3).

since in reality the use of derogations on the grounds listed above (as opposed to their theoretical availability) would usually be precisely in the context of discrimination against non-nationals.

It might be thought that the approach in *Rutili* in so far as it deals with total exclusion from a territory goes even further than the Court of Human Rights in terms of the protection of the individual, although ultimately the decisions of the two jurisdictions may not differ too greatly in practice. In the case of *Paramanathan* v. *Germany*,[81] Mr. Paramanathan was limited to living in certain areas of Germany while his request for political asylum was being considered. The Court of Human Rights decided that it should be left to the member state to determine the conditions to be fulfilled for a person's presence to be considered unlawful in a state. Greater discretion was given to the member state to determine how best to protect the fundamental rights within Article 2.1 of Protocol 4 of the ECHR.[82] This difference from *Rutili* might be explicable not necessarily as a result of the ECJ's greater protection of rights but rather on account of the fact that the two Courts had in mind different aims. The ECHR system is about laying down minimum standards while the ECJ is concerned to eliminate restrictions by member states which could thwart the goal of the free movement of workers in the single market.[83] Indeed, the concerns of the ECJ were made more explicit in the case of *Watson and Belmann*[84] concerning the free movement of workers, where it stated that it would consider, in the context of an alleged infringement of EC law, the extent to which this infringement might impact on the "economic rights" already protected by the Treaty of Rome. Bellmann, an Italian national living in Milan had provided lodgings for a British national. They were both found to be in breach of Italian law promulgated pursuant to certain EC directives in so far as Watson had not reported her presence in Italy to the relevant authorities and Belmann had not reported that he had a non-national living with him. They were both fined and an attempt was then made to deport Watson. The ECJ found the state's action to be in breach of the proportionality principle. The ECJ further expanded its sources of hu-

---

[81] Application Number 12068/86.

[82] Article 2.1 states that, "Everyone lawfully within the territory of a State shall, within that territory, have the right to liberty of movement and freedom to choose his residence".

[83] See also S. Hall, "The European Convention on Human Rights and Public Policy Exceptions to the Free Movement of Workers Under the EEC Treaty" (1991) 16 *European Law Review* 466–488.

[84] Case 118/75 [1976] E.C.R. 1185.

man rights in *Defrenne No. 2*[85] where it cited a convention of the International Labour Organisation. This case is particularly noteworthy as an instance where the ECJ allowed Article 119 of the Treaty of Rome, guaranteeing equal pay for equal work for men and women, to be invoked by an individual against a private party, Sabena Airlines.

2. THE ASSERTION OF A HUMAN RIGHTS JURISDICTION AGAINST MEMBER STATES

It was not until the *Hauer*[86] case that any in-depth analysis by the ECJ of an alleged violation of fundamental rights was undertaken, and once again a case concerning agriculture provided the opportunity. Hauer was refused permission to plant vines on the ground that this was contrary to an EC regulation designed to adjust wine-growing potential to market requirements. The construction of the regulation was referred to the ECJ. In making the reference the German court stated that if the prohibition included land appropriate for wine growing it might be incompatible with the German Basic Law guarantees of the right to property and the right to pursue trade and professional activities.[87] The ECJ took the opportunity to re-state its concern for the completion of the single market by declaring that "the introduction of special criteria for assessment stemming from the legislation or constitutional law of a particular Member State would, by damaging the substantive unity and efficacy of Community law, lead inevitably to the destruction of the unity of the Common Market and the jeopardising of the cohesion of the Community." The court went on to reiterate its stance that fundamental rights formed part of the EC legal order and, in doing so, it explicitly drew inspiration from the constitutional traditions of the member states and international treaties including the first protocol of the ECHR. The right to property was a right guaranteed in the EC legal order in accordance with the first protocol which the Court went on to observe also allowed limitations "necessary" for the protection of the "general interest". The ECJ then examined the national restrictions on property rights, the relationship between the measures provided for in the particular regulation and the aims pursued by the EC. It concluded that the regulation was justified "by the objectives of general interest pursued by the Community and [by reason of the fact that it did] not infringe the substance of the right to property in the form in

---

[85] *Gabrielle Defrenne* v. *Société Anonyme Belge Navigation Aerienne Sabena* Case 43/75 [1976] E.C.R. 455.

[86] *Liselotte Hauer* v. *Rheinland-Pfalz* Case 44/ 79 [1979] E.C.R. 3727.

[87] See Articles 12 and 14 of the German Basic Code.

which it is recognised and protected in the Community legal order". A similar conclusion was reached on the freedom to pursue trade or professional activities.

In its case-law, the ECJ has also commented on the distribution of power that it perceives should pertain in its relationship with member states in the context of fundamental rights. In *Cinétheque*,[88] for example, the court stated that, "although it is true that it is the duty of this court to ensure observation of fundamental rights in the field of Community law, it has no power to examine the compatibility with the European Convention of national legislation which concerns, as in this case, an area which falls within the jurisdiction of the national legislator."[89] Later in *Demirel*,[90] it had the opportunity to be even more explicit. *Demirel* concerned the right of a Turkish worker to bring his family into Germany. According to the ECJ the right to bring one's family into the EC was not covered by the Association Agreement between the EC and Turkey and therefore the alleged violation of Article 8 of the ECHR dealing with the right to family life was not within EC law. The court stated that it had "no power to examine the compatibility with the European Convention on Human Rights of national legislation lying outside the scope of Community law".[91] At first glance these two cases appear to be quite conciliatory on the part of the ECJ and even to be done in a spirit of "subsidiarity".[92] However it is suggested that the formula for competence conceived by the ECJ is effectively a restatement of the principle of supremacy of EC law in another guise. Whenever the EC acts in a particular area it is deemed to "occupy the field" of competence in that area. Even in areas where the EC has left action to the discretion of member states or areas where both the EC and the member states might have equal competence to

---

[88] *Cinétheque and others* v. *Fédération Nationale de Cinémas Français* Cases 60 and 61/84 [1985] E.C.R. 2605.

[89] *Ibid.*, at para. 25.

[90] *Demirel* v. *Stadt Schwabisch Gmund* Case 12/860 [1987] E.C.R. 3719.

[91] *Ibid.*, at para. 28.

[92] Article 3b of the Maastricht treaty states that

"...In areas which do not fall within its exclusive competence, the Community shall take action, in accordance with the principle of subsidiarity, only if and in so far as the objectives of the proposed action cannot be sufficiently achieved by the Member States and can therefore, by reason of the scale or effects of the proposed action, be better achieved by the Community."

For commentary on the possible content of this principle see Commission Communication to the Council and European Parliament, *The Principle of Subsidiarity* (EM 36) SEC (92) 1990 Final, 27 October 1992.

act, member states are obliged under Articles 5 and 8 of the Treaty of Rome not to act in a manner inconsistent with the aims of a single market. It is therefore unsafe to assume that because the EC has not explicitly acted in an area, it is within exclusive, national competence. It is for the Court to determine what is within EC and what is within member state competence, and it can do this on a case by case basis.

This notion that the Court is really protecting its own power and that it is not overly preoccupied with deferring to member states' sovereignty becomes clearer in the subsequent case law. In the *ERT* case,[93] for example, the Court stated that,

> [a]ccording to its jurisprudence...[see decisions in *Cinétheque* and *Demirel*] the Court cannot assess, from the point of view of the European Convention on Human Rights, national legislation which is not situated within the body of Community law. By contrast, as soon as any such legislation enters the field of application of Community law, the Court, as the sole arbiter in this matter, must provide the national court with all the elements of interpretation which are necessary in order to enable it to assess the compatibility of that legislation with the fundamental rights—as laid down in particular in the European Convention on Human Rights—the observance of which the Court ensures.

In neither *Cinétheque* nor *Demirel* was the Court dealing with legislation that implemented EC law. The divide between what constitutes an act of the EC, and what is of a purely national character, is however not always so clear. If a member state is implementing EC legislation would this then necessarily be an EC act over which the ECJ would have competence? What if the member state is acting as an agent for the EC—would this be enough in itself to constitute an EC act? The dividing line between an EC act and a national act is unclear and constantly blurred as member states realise the implications of the formulation of a single market.[94]

The extent to which the court is eager to condemn member states for failure to comply with the ECHR in an area involving a *Community act* is clear from the *Kent Kirk*[95] case. In this case, EC law had permitted member states to limit fishing in their coastal waters to local or traditional fishermen until 31 December 1982. On 25 January 1983 a further regulation was made by the Council continuing this special authorisation. By virtue of Article

---

[93] *Elleniki Radiophonia Tileorasi (ERT)* v. *Dimotiki Etairia Pliroforissis* Case 260/89 Unreported decision of 18 June 1991.

[94] The matter is made even more unclear with the entry into force of the Maastricht treaty, since, depending on the area in which it is acting, it is either the member states acting collectively, the EC acting or the European Union acting in any given situation.

[95] Case 63/83 [1984] E.C.R. 2689.

6(1) of this latter regulation, the derogation applied in the UK retroactively to 1 January 1983. Mr. Kent Kirk, master of a Danish fishing vessel, was charged with the offence of illegal fishing in the UK on 6 January 1983. The question of retroactivity, among other matters, was referred to the ECJ. The Court considered that, "[w]ithout embarking upon an examination of the general legality of the retroactivity of Article 6(1) of that regulation, it is sufficient to point out that such retroactivity may not, in any event, have the effect of validating *ex post facto* national measures of a penal nature which impose penalties for an act which, in fact, was not punishable at the time at which it was committed. That would be the case where at the time of the act entailing a criminal penalty, the national measure was invalid because it was incompatible with Community law." The Court continued:

> The principle that penal provisions may not have retroactive effect is one which is common to all the legal orders of the Member-States and is enshrined in Article 7 of the European Convention for the Protection of Human Rights and Fundamental Freedoms as a fundamental right; it takes its place among the general principles of law whose observance is ensured by the Court of Justice.

Consequently the retroactivity provided for in Article 6(1) of regulation 170/83 could not be regarded as validating *ex post facto* national measures which imposed criminal penalties, at the time of the conduct at issue, if those measures were not valid.

Kent Kirk establishes that the fundamental rights jurisprudence of the ECJ can be of direct help to an individual. It is also an example of the breadth of the fundamental rights issues that the Court is willing to contemplate—at least in instances involving member states' actions.

To similar effect is *Wachauf v. Federal Republic of Germany*.[96] In this case, the applicant was a tenant farmer, whose farm was devoted exclusively to dairy farming and who had therefore obtained a milk production quota. According to an EC regulation, this quota transferred on the sale, lease or inheritance of the land to the person who was taking over the farm until the surrender of the quota. Where the quota was surrendered to the state compensation fell due to the farmer. The German order which implemented this regulation stated that a tenant farmer could not surrender his quota and receive compensation without the consent of the landlord. Wachauf's landlord withdrew consent and he was deprived of his compensation. He claimed that his fundamental rights as protected by EC law had been breached since this

---

[96]   Case 5/88 [1989] E.C.R. 2609.

amounted to an "unconstitutional expropriation [of his property] without compensation". The ECJ held that:

> It must be observed that Community rules which, upon the expiry of the lease, had the effect of depriving the lessee, without compensation, of the fruits of his labour and of his investments in the tenanted holding would be incompatible with the requirements of the protection of fundamental rights in the Community legal order. Since those requirements are also binding on the Member States when they implement Community rules, the Member States must, a far as possible, apply those rules in accordance with those requirements.

Perhaps surprisingly in the light of this statement, the regulation was held to be valid. This was achieved by the Court shifting the blame entirely to the member state, claiming that it was not the EC measure but rather the German implementing instrument which was at fault in not providing compensation in accordance with fundamental rights' standards. The German authorities did re-assess their legislation and Mr Wachauf received compensation in due course.

Once again we see in *Wachauf* the ECJ showing itself not to be shy of reviewing directly the legislation of a member state for incompatibility with EC law and fundamental rights. In contrast, however, it appears unwilling to strike in the same way at the legality of EC legislation. In each instance we have examined so far, where there has been a challenge to EC action it has been eventually construed as a fault on the part of a member state and only when this has been established has the ECJ felt inclined to rely upon an analysis of rights. The *Wachauf* case was taken a step further by the ECJ in the *ERT* case referred to above when it observed that, "measures which are incompatible with respect for human rights which are recognised and guaranteed [in EC law] could not be admitted in the Community".

Johnston v. *Chief Constable of the Royal Ulster Constabulary*[97] threw up yet another situation in which the ECJ could have given effect to individual rights grounded in notions of individual liberties. On this occasion, however, it stopped short of such a ruling because it judged that the goal of the supremacy of EC law did not require such an intervention. Ms Johnston sued the RUC (the Northern Irish police force) for failure to renew her contract as a full time member of the RUC Reserve. She had been a member for six years when the chief constable decided that the contracts of women in the force would only be renewed in cases where the duties required of them could only be performed by women. This was based on the rule that women were not allowed to carry firearms. and could not therefore perform general

---

[97]   [1986] 3 C.M.L.R. 240.

police duties since these duties now required the carrying of firearms. Ms. Johnston was therefore employed on a part-time basis with the RUC Reserve with the attendant lower wage that this entailed. She took her claim to the local industrial tribunal, basing it on the Sex Discrimination (Northern Ireland) Order 1976 which had implemented the EC Equal Treatment Directive[98] in the Province. She challenged both the decision not to renew her contract and the RUC failure to provide her with a training in firearms. In his defence the chief constable produced a certificate from the relevant government minister, the Secretary of State for Northern Ireland, certified in accordance with Article 53 of the Sex Discrimination Order and stating that the refusal to offer Ms. Johnston full-time employment had been "done for the purpose of (a) safeguarding national security; and (b) protecting public safety and public order".

The ECJ considered that the directive in question, which contained elements of judicial control, "reflects a general principle of law which underlies the constitutional traditions common to the Member States. That principle is also laid down in Articles 6 and 13 of the European Convention.... As the European Parliament, Council and Commission recognised in their decisions, the principles on which that Convention is based must be taken into consideration in Community law." The Court went on to hold that the directive enjoyed vertical direct effect which meant that it could be used by Ms. Johnston, an individual, against the state or against any emanation of the state, such as (in this case) the RUC. However, her claim was frustrated by the fact that the Court then held that even though she could enjoy the direct benefit of EC legislation, the state could derogate from its responsibilities on the ground of public safety. Thus the Court only went as far as was necessary to ensure that the principle of direct effect of Community acts was a reality for the state to contend with and it then made this conclusion unassailable by grounding it in the language of human rights. What it failed to do was to use the language of rights to examine the extent to which the derogation in the directive complied with international safeguards as laid down in the ECHR to which the Court had earlier referred in the course of its judgment.

What emerges from this jurisprudence is that there are implications for all EC member states that have chosen to ratify the ECHR but particularly for those that have not incorporated it into their domestic law.[99] These latter states now have to apply ECHR principles to conform with EC law at least

---

[98] Council Directive 76/207 of 9 February 1976.

[99] See text at notes 59–61, above.

when legislating in areas within EC competence. It is clear, moreover, that the ECJ takes the view that economic rights, such as the free movement of workers, are to be protected on the same basis as, or at least are not inferior to, the more traditional civil liberties, such as the right to an effective judicial remedy. That both appear to be part of the same concept of fundamental rights is clear from *Heylens*, where a Belgian football trainer challenged the lack of a remedy against the French authorities for their refusal to recognise his qualifications. The ECJ held that the importance of the principle of free movement of workers required that refusal to facilitate this through recognition of qualifications must be subject to judicial remedies. It stated:

> Since free access to employment is a fundamental right which the Treaty confers individually on each worker in the Community, the existence of a remedy of a judicial nature against any decision of a national authority refusing the benefit of that right is essential to secure for the individual the effective protection for his right.... That requirement reflects a general principle of law which underlies the constitutional traditions common to the member states and has been enshrined in Articles 6 and 13 of the European Convention for the Protection of Human Rights and Fundamental Freedoms.

3.   THE APPLICATION OF THE ECHR TO COMMUNITY
     INSTITUTIONS AND COMMUNITY LAW

In *Confederation Française Démocratique du Travail (CFDT)* v. *European Communities*,[100] (or alternatively the member states jointly and severally), CFDT, a French workers' organisation made an application to the European Court of Human Rights citing the EC or alternatively its member states for alleged violation of Articles 11, 13 and 14. According to the CFDT the Council of the EC had failed to name them as one of the "representative organisations" from amongst whose nominees the representatives to a particular consultative committee of the EC would be chosen. CFDT, the second largest organisation of its kind in France, had been excluded—even though much smaller organisations had been selected. It was believed that the choice lay with the member state concerned, and this was the reason for citing the member states as well as the EC. An application was made to the ECJ to have the Council decision set aside but this was declared inadmissible since only a member state is entitled to bring an application to set aside a decision of the Council.[101]

The European Commission of Human Rights declared the case inadmissible *rationae personae* and *rationae materiae*. It stated that it,

---

[100] Application Number 8030/77, decision given on 10 July 1978.
[101] In this case the relevant article was Article 38 of the ECSC treaty.

> would like first to point out that the applicant is complaining of an act of an organ of the Communities, *i.e.* the Council of the European Communities, relating to the composition of another organ of the Communities, *i.e.* the Consultative Committee to the High Authority. This is an act whose effects concern the internal organisation of the European Communities who under Article 6 of the ECSC Treaty, Article 210 of the EEC Treaty and Article 184 of the EEC Treaty have their own legal personality and are represented by their own institutions, each acting within the ambit of their powers.

Therefore, in so far as the complaint reflected concerns relating to the internal competence of the EC, the Commission declined jurisdiction *rationae materiae*. Furthermore, the Commission declined *rationae personae* in that the EC was not a party to the ECHR. In contrast France is of course a party to the ECHR and the claim brought against the member state had therefore to be considered. It was decided that on the facts France could not be made individually responsible. The joint responsibility of the member states was not defined but it was believed that since it was really the Council of the EC acting, the member states could not be made responsible. At the time of the case France had not yet accepted the right of individual petition and the Commission also considered that the *other* member states were not exercising jurisdiction within the meaning of Article 1 of the ECHR, under which the "High Contracting Parties [undertake to] secure to everyone within their jurisdiction the rights and freedoms defined in [the substantive provisions of the ECHR]".

CFDT is in some respects quite a harsh decision in that the applicants were asking for review of a potential violation of their human rights within a system which had denied them any effective means of redress. Also, the notion of the collective responsibility of the member states should perhaps have been considered more seriously since within the Council the states should surely exercise their sovereign rights in a manner consistent with the international human rights obligations which they have willingly incurred. A more recent decision of the European Commission of Human Rights that does raise the possibility of supervision of EC acts by the ECHR mechanism is the case of *M & Co.* v. *Germany*[102] (referred to as the *Melchers* case above). The applicants were fined under EC law for breach of the competition rules in that there was a refusal on their part to sell goods ordered for the French market. The fine imposed by the EC Commission was challenged before the ECJ on the ground, *inter alia*, that the Commission had acted as both prosecutor and decision maker. The ECJ found that the Commission

---

[102] Application Number 13258/87, decision of 9 February 1990 (unreported).

was not a "tribunal" in the context of Article 6 of the ECHR[103] and that there were sufficient safeguards for due process in the relevant enforcement regulation.[104] The fine was eventually reduced but on different grounds unconnected with this issue. The German authorities then issued a writ against the applicant, Melchers, seeking to execute the judgment of the ECJ. Melchers mounted a challenge against the Federal Minister of Justice claiming that the writ had been wrongly issued as the ECJ had violated its fundamental rights as guaranteed under both Article 6 of the ECHR and Article 103(1) of the *Grundgesetz*. The Federal Constitutional Court threw the application out on the grounds that the fundamental rights guarantees referred to were already part of the jurisprudence of the ECJ and that therefore no separate examination relating to the protection of the applicant's rights could be undertaken before issuance of the writ of execution.

Melchers then filed an application against Germany with the European Commission of Human Rights. This was declared inadmissible. In keeping with *CFDT* the Commission declared the case inadmissible *rationae personae* as the ECJ was not a party to the ECHR and therefore its decisions could not be reviewed. It was also inadmissible *rationae materiae* since the contracting state had transferred its powers to a competent organ that respects human rights. Each writ did not therefore have to be examined for compliance with Article 6 of the ECHR. Interestingly, although the European Human Rights Commission held that it could not review the acts of the EC directly, it was nevertheless of the view that the contracting party remained ultimately responsible for acts in violation of the ECHR, and that this was regardless of whether or not the breach was a consequence of domestic law or of regulations entered into in compliance with international obligations. Furthermore, it continued, the transfer of such powers to a supranational body:

> does not necessarily exclude a State's responsibility under the Convention with regard to the exercise of the transferred powers. Otherwise the guarantees of the Convention could wantonly be limited or excluded and thus be deprived of their pre-emptory character.... Therefore the transfer of powers to an international organisation is not incompatible with the Convention provided that within that organisation fundamental rights will receive an equivalent protection.

The Commission also stated that it was satisfied that the:

---

[103] See *Musique Diffusion Française* v. *Commission* [1983] E.C.R. 1825.

[104] Regulation 17/62. The Court did not refer to the rather extensive case-law developed by the Strasbourg Court when coming to its conclusion.

legal system of the European Communities not only secures fundamental rights but also provides for control of their observance. It is true that the constituent treaties of the European Communities do not contain a catalogue of such rights. However, the Parliament, the Council and the Commission of the European Communities have stressed in a joint declaration of 5 April 1977 that they attach prime importance to the protection of fundamental rights, as derived in particular from the constitutions of Member States and the European Convention for the Protection of Human Rights and Fundamental Freedoms.... In addition the Court of Justice...has developed a case law according to which it is called upon to control Community acts on the basis of fundamental rights....

The Commission is cautioning member states that where they are *not* satisfied that there are these fundamental rights guarantees they reserve the right, notwithstanding *CFDT*, to review a contracting party's actions in pursuance of international obligations for incompatibility with the higher norms of human rights as represented in the ECHR. The jurisdiction of Strasbourg is re-enforced. Where the faith they have placed in the ECJ appears ill-founded, they indicate in *Melchers* that they will act.

Perhaps such action should already have occurred. It is clear, for example, that in the field of EC competition law, the actions of the authorities may be vulnerable on human rights grounds, at least as the jurisprudence of the European Court of Human Rights has developed. Even where the ECJ does recognise human rights, it does not necessarily do so in line with the Strasbourg case-law. Under regulation 17/62, for example, the Commission has quite wide enforcement powers for the investigation of alleged breaches of the competition rules. These include the right to enter premises and to take documentation. In the *Hoechst* case,[105] there was a challenge to the EC Commission's powers which alleged, *inter alia*, a violation of Article 8 of the ECHR (which deals with the right to privacy). The ECJ held that the protection of business premises was not covered by Article 8. However only a few months earlier the Strasbourg Court had indicated the possibility that business premises were covered by Article 8 in the *Chappell* case.[106] If there had been affiliation or at least closer co-operation between the Strasbourg and Luxembourg courts this would not have happened.

A more recent example of a potential discrepancy between the Strasbourg and Luxembourg courts is the case of *A* v. *E.C. Commission*[107] which concerned the employment by the Community of a person who was HIV

---

[105] See text at note 41, above.
[106] *Chappell* v. *United Kingdom* Series A, No. 152 (1989) 12 E.H.R.R. 1.
[107] [1994] 3 C.M.L.R. 242.

positive. After passing a competitive Community examination and being placed on a reserve list for administrators specialising in development co-operation in sub-tropical regions, the applicant submitted to a medical examination in which he directly informed the administering doctor that he was HIV positive. After the applicant had undergone additional tests, a letter was sent to him removing him from the reserve list on the ground that he was "physically unfit" for the post and that his unfitness was directly related to the nature of the post for which he had applied. Two unions, the Union Syndicale of Brussels and its equivalent in Luxembourg, intervened on his behalf and applied for an annulment of the decision removing him from the list. The several grounds relied upon including an allegation that the right to respect for private life had been infringed. The EC Court of First Instance ruled that in view of the applicant's medical condition, the declaration that he was physically unfit was a reasonable one. Since there had been no breach of an essential procedural requirement and that there was a probable link between the applicant's condition and his ability to perform the duties required, the application for annulment was dismissed. While there is no direct case law originating from the ECHR to assist us on this point, and no right of employment in the Convention, it is at least arguable that a human rights tribunal would have analysed the facts differently. They may have looked beyond procedural guarantees to the substantive question of the extent to which the use of knowledge that someone is HIV might be abusive of an individual's right to a private life. Evidence of such an analysis is however absent from the Court of First Instance.

4. THE CONFLICT CONTINUES

Another illustration of the difficulties that are fast emerging between the Strasbourg Court and the ECJ comes from the recent *Grogan* case.[108] The defendant, a students' organisation based in Ireland, published in student guides the names and addresses of clinics in the UK offering termination of pregnancy services. Judging this an infringement of the Republic's constitution, the Irish Supreme Court granted an injunction to restrain the activity. However it referred the matter to the ECJ in view of the students' claim that this national prohibition amounted to a restriction on the freedom to supply services as guaranteed by the Treaty of Rome.[109] The students also alleged an infringement of Article 10 of the ECHR, which protects freedom of ex-

---

[108] Judgment of the High Court [1990] 1 C.M.L.R. 689; The Irish Supreme Court decision is at [1990] 1 C.M.L.R. 689; the judgment of the ECJ is at [1991] 3 C.M.L.R. 689.

[109] See Article 59.

pression. The ECJ was asked whether the organised activity of terminating a pregnancy was a "service" within the meaning of the Treaty of Rome and secondly, whether in the absence of harmonised rules a member state could prohibit distribution of information about services lawfully available in another member state and furthermore, whether there was a right, in EC law, to distribute information about services lawfully available under conditions in one member state, to residents of another member state where such services were prohibited under its constitution. (The Irish court did not ask whether the constitutional rule protecting the unborn by a ban on abortion was itself incompatible with EC law).

Advocate General Van Gerven in his opinion[110] (which was of course not binding on the Court), considered that this organised activity of termination of pregnancies was a service. The Advocate General also considered that there might be an impediment to cross-border services and he therefore assessed whether the restriction could be justified in the light of Article 10(2) of the ECHR. He pointed out that the Strasbourg court had not yet had the opportunity to consider the compatibility of rules on abortion with the ECHR so in fact the issue was perhaps reaching the wrong forum first. As far as EC law was concerned the Court's task involved:

> balancing two fundamental rights, on the one hand the right to life as defined and declared to be applicable to unborn life by a Member State, and on the other freedom of expression, which is one of the general principles of Community law on the basis of the constitutional traditions of the Member States and the European treaties and international treaties and declarations on fundamental rights, in particular Article 10 [of the ECHR].

In terms of the potential restrictions to freedom of expression the Advocate General applied the principle of proportionality and considered that "the individual States must be allowed a fairly considerable margin of discretion". His findings therefore left open the possibility that a women who was restricted from travelling to obtain an abortion might argue that it contravened general principles of EC law.

The ECJ did not however concur with all of the Advocate General's findings.[111] It found that abortion was indeed a medical service within the

---

[110] Opinion of the Advocate General of 11 June 1991.

[111] For further discussion of the *Grogan* case and the many complex legal and political issues raised by it and by the issue of abortion in Ireland generally, see E. Spalin, "Abortion, Speech and the European Community" [1992] *Journal of Welfare and Family Law* 17–32; D. Rossa Phelan, "Right to Life of the Unborn v. Promotion of Trade in Services: The European Court of Justice and the Normative Shaping of the European Union" [1992] *Modern Law Review* 670–689; C. A. Gearty, "The Politics of Abortion" (1992) 19 *Jour-*

meaning of Article 60 of the Treaty of Rome. No exceptions were to be made for the special nature of abortion—it was simply a service. The Court then decided that the restriction on the provision of information was not an interference with the freedom to provide services because there was no economic interest on the part of the defendant in that the link between the clinics in the UK and the students' unions was too tenuous. Having found no restriction on the freedom to provide services, the ECJ did not then address the question of fundamental rights at all, holding merely that they had no jurisdiction "with regard to national legislation lying outside the scope of Community law". This is a remarkable judgment in so far as it takes a purely economic approach to a question of fundamental rights and is the example *par excellence* of the fact that the ECJ does not value human rights as part of individual liberties above other purely economic rights oriented towards completion of the single market. It avoids the very difficult questions on the *jus cogens* norm of the right to life by considering EC law in isolation as only the law applicable to an economic arrangement between states. It is a language that speaks of the supremacy of EC law rather than of human rights. Even if we accept that this case was not about the right to life but rather about freedom of expression then we should still consider whether the ECJ was correct in distinguishing between speech motivated by an economic as opposed to an non-economic interest.[112]

A recent case does however give us some hope that the current extent of the application of human rights might be increased. In the case of *Christos Konstantinidis* v. *Stadt Altensteig-Standesamt*[113] the ECJ was concerned with the scope of the right of establishment. The applicant was a Greek national living in Germany as a self-employed person. When he got married in Germany his name was entered in the register as "Christos Kons*tadi* nidis". He applied to have it changed to reflect the correct pronunciation and the Latin characters in his Greek passport. The authorities in transcribing his name under a standard procedure[114] made it "Hrestos Konstantinidis". The applicant lodged an appeal to the German courts who asked the ECJ whether, by requiring the use of the distorted transliteration of his name in his profes-

---

nal of Law and Society 441–454.

[112] The case has since been heard by the Strasbourg court which decided by fifteen votes to eight against Ireland—see *Open Door Counselling and Dublin Well Woman Centre* v. *Ireland* Series A, No. 246 (1992) 15 E.H.R.R. 244.

[113] [1993] 3 C.M.L.R. 401.

[114] Article 3 of the Convention on the Representation of Names and Surnames in Registers of Civil Status (1973).

sional life, the applicant had suffered discrimination on grounds of nationality as prohibited by Article 6 of the EC and an interference with his freedom of establishment under Article 52 EC. The ECJ held that it was contrary to Article 52 to require a Greek national to use, in pursuit of his profession, a transliteration of his name whereby its pronunciation was modified with the result of such distortion being that he was exposed to the risk of being confused with other persons in the market place.

In his opinion, the Advocate General Jacobs found that although there is no specific guarantee to the individual's right to their name, a broad reading of Article 8 together with the constitutional laws of member states is capable of producing a right of respect for an individual's dignity and integrity. Such a right would indeed be violated if one were compelled to abandon, modify or use another name. The Advocate General also suggested that a violation of fundamental rights *per se* could interfere with the free movement of persons, *i.e.* even where the authorities treatment was not discriminatory. He considered that "a Community national who goes to another member state as a worker or self-employed person...is...entitled to assume that wherever he earns his living in the European Community, he will be treated in accordance with a code of fundamental values, in particular, those laid down in the European Convention on Human Rights". Were the ECJ to follow this approach, the human rights provisions would have to be applied much more extensively and closer scrutiny of national law would have to take place since the absence of discrimination would no longer be the sole test.

5.   A CHANGE OF HEART POST-MAASTRICHT?

The Court of First Instance has recently agreed to more openness and democracy for EC institutions, in the important *Guardian* secrecy case.[115] While not going so far as to require the Community institutions to abide by the human rights standards it imposes on member states, the case shows a willingness to correct the perception of a democratic deficit in the EC. In this case a British journalist, John Carvel, requested access to several Council documents including minutes of the meetings of the social affairs, justice affairs and agricultural affairs Councils. Under legislation adopted pursuant to the Maastricht Treaty, the public may have access to Council documents under specific conditions and access may be denied on, for example, various grounds of public interest. Where such provisions do not apply, the Council nevertheless retains a discretion to refuse access to its documents in order to

---

[115]   Case T–194/94 *Carvel and Guardian Newspapers* v. *Council* 19 October 1995, reported in *Financial Times*, 24 October 1995.

protect the confidentiality of its proceedings. Mr. Carvel was given documents relating to the social affairs Council but not to the others because the Council claimed that they related directly to the deliberations of the Council and were not allowed under the rules of procedure. Repeated requests were met with a claim of confidentiality. Furthermore, the Council claimed that the documents relating to the social affairs Council should not have been sent to him for the same reasons and were sent only as a result of an administrative error. Mr. Carvel and the *Guardian* brought an action for annulment of the Council's decision.

The CFI only examined one of their submissions, namely that the Council had infringed the legal provisions relating to access to documents by expressing a blanket refusal to allow access to certain types of documents without balancing the interests of the parties before such a decision. The Court ruled that the relevant legislation made clear that in the exercise of its discretion the Council had to balance the interests of the public in gaining access to its documents against any interest of its own in maintaining confidentiality. Evidence provided by member states supported the conclusion that no proper balancing of interests had taken place in this case and the Court accordingly granted the annulment of the decision denying access to the documents. This push from the CFI to guarantee greater transparency in the decision making process of the EC is a welcome step in the process of narrowing the democracy deficit. Indeed, the Council of Ministers themselves realise that the *status quo* cannot be maintained for much longer and it has agreed a new draft code of conduct to pierce the veil of secrecy surrounding the law-making process.[116] The code aims to restrict the freedom of the Council to keep minutes secret and to add unpublished amendments to legislation.

Part IX: Solutions to the Human Rights Dilemma—Alternatives to Accession to the ECHR

The solution eventually adopted by the EC to fill the gap in human rights protection depends on the goal that is being sought. There are several (sometimes competing) ambitions which may be to the fore. If the concern is with the supremacy of EC law and the completion of a single market, then the solution may be different than if the main focus is the protection of the individual, as an individual, rather than as a factor in the productive process.

---

[116] *Financial Times*, 3 October 1995, p. 2.

It is clear from the analysis of the ECJ case law above that the concern from the Court's viewpoint is primarily with the fulfilment of the goal of a single market and if this can be done through the language of rights such language is deployed to achieve this end. In taking this approach, the ECJ is not putting the protection of the individual first. There are a spectrum of alternatives available. Concern for the proper functioning of a single market in which EC law reigns supreme dictates a minimalist stance in terms of the ECHR, and this would be a stance in which there could be no scrutiny of EC acts by the Strasbourg machinery. Human rights would then be safeguarded solely by the ECJ and there would be none of the institutional, political and jurisprudential difficulties already identified. At best this stance would mean the maintenance of the status quo with indirect review of EC acts by the ECJ, taking into account the ECHR, UN human rights instruments and general principles of law such as proportionality, legal certainty and equality. At the other end of the spectrum lies the possibility of embracing the ECHR fully and of making EC acts directly reviewable by the Strasbourg organs. This would necessarily involve the ECJ relinquishing competence in the area of fundamental rights of individuals and affiliating to the ECHR.

In between these two options there are a range of possible alternatives some of which we explore in greater detail below. There is the potential for shared jurisdiction between the Strasbourg and Luxembourg courts on the basis of the first EEA model that was proposed.[117] There is the possibility of informal consultation and information sharing by the two courts. The ECJ could even attempt to make its practice more consistent with that of the Strasbourg court without itself being directly reviewed by Strasbourg.[118] More ambitiously, the EC could adhere to the proposed catalogue of rights in the European Parliament's Declaration[119] or even create a new and binding EC-specific code. Alternatively, the EC could decide to concentrate only on certain rights that appear more relevant than others to the immediate activities of the EC, such as social rights. The route that is chosen is a function both of the criteria that are applied and of the view that is taken as to the role of law in civil liberties protection. A so-called "hard" law option, indicates the need for adherence to the ECHR. This would entail being bound by an established set of rights with an appropriate enforcement machinery for meting out sanctions in the event of non-compliance with the terms of the

---

[117] See above Part VI, 3.

[118] This could be done either through some co-operation procedure or by means of Article 177-type references.

[119] See generally Part II, above.

Convention. The "soft" law option suggests in contrast that law need not be in a legally binding form for it to be effective. Law is then seen as a process of achieving the protection of rights through the pro-active work of the ECJ and the perception within the EC of the need to protect individuals. Given the current concern of the ECJ with the goals of supremacy and the completion of the single market, it is unlikely that the ECJ could be trusted with the task of securing individual rights outside that very particular context.

There is the further argument that if the EC wish to have a code of "civil liberties" in the context of present EC activity then such a code should not be akin to the 1989 Declaration of the European Parliament but rather should contain provisions on the following subjects:

(a) privacy and data protection;
(b) insurance law;
(c) access to employment and education;
(d) protection of the property rights of non-nationals;
(e) policing and extradition arrangements;
(f) the effect of harmonisation on the differing legal status of minorities;
(g) the impact of new technologies on human rights, *e.g.* biotechnology, environmental protection.[120]

The Declaration only deals with privacy, data protection and access to employment and education from this list. The rights covered here accurately reflect traditional EC activity, but do not really reflect an understanding of the expanding competencies of the EC and EU with the corresponding need to provide adequate protection from a civil liberties rather than from a purely economic viewpoint.

On the whole member states do not appear to be impressed with the Declaration. Another suggestion has been that any catalogue of rights created specially for the EC should attempt to be consistent with other models within Europe, and should therefore have the rights contained in the ECHR but perhaps not those in the additional protocols that have not been ratified by all member states. Another but contrasting goal underpinning certain suggestions for change is that the EC should go beyond and aspire to a higher standard than the ECHR. On this basis, it is argued that it should take on the "third generation" rights such as the right to a clean and safe environment, food, development and education, and should frame its catalogue of rights in a manner which does not restrict the development of further

---

[120] For a general survey of the potential of human rights jurisprudence, see P. Sieghart, *The Lawful Rights of Mankind* (Oxford, 1986).

rights through other sources of EC law, such as general principles or citizens' rights. It would seem fair to say that in its current form the Declaration is not a serious alternative to accession from the point of view of civil liberties protection. Yet in the absence of accession it remains a powerful symbol reflecting the need for democratisation as well as human rights protection in the EC.

In his evidence to the House of Lords Select Committee, Professor Bob Hepple suggested another alternative to affiliation to the ECHR.[121] He drew attention to what he considered were the advantages of accession to the Council of Europe's European Social Charter (ESC). This document concentrates on social rights and raises interesting questions as to the relationship of the ESC with the EC's own Social Charter.[122] Affiliation would be on the basis of the Single European Act, the Social Charter of 1989 and the Maastricht Treaty's Social Protocol which aims to continue and extend the work of the Social Charter.[123] Indeed, the EC's Social Charter states that it draws inspiration from the Conventions of the International Labour Organisation and from the European Social Charter of the Council of Europe. Even the ECJ has cited the ESC as a source of the general principles of EC law.[124] A further advantage of this approach is that the ESC is also closer to the goals of the EC as reflected in the parliament's 1989 Declaration. It contains, for example, rights pertinent to the free movement of labour such as the right to organise; to bargain collectively and other rights aimed at the protection of the family. Apart from its general appropriateness, the ESC would be less complex to apply than the ECHR since it lacks the tiers of enforcement of the Convention. There is no right of individual petition. It is also not within the jurisdiction of the European Court of Human Rights or the Commission on Human Rights. The ESC works on the basis of a system of biannual national reports to a Committee of Independent Experts who examine the reports and make recommendations. These recommendations are transmitted to the governmental committee and the parliamentary committee of the Council of Europe which also make comments. These are all

---

[121] B. Hepple, "European Social Dialogue—Alibi or Opportunity" *Institute of Employment Rights* (London, 1993). For the House of Lords report, see note 40, above.

[122] Community Charter of the Fundamental Social Rights of Workers, 9 December 1989, *Social Europe* 1/90, pp. 46–50.

[123] Maastricht Protocol on Social Policy and the Agreement on Social Policy Concluded Between the Member States of the European Community with the Exception of the United Kingdom of Great Britain and Northern Ireland, included in N. Foster, *Blackstone's EC Legislation*, 6th ed. (London 1995), p. 125.

[124] See *Blaizot* v. *Belgian State* Case 24/86 [1988] E.C.R 379.

fed through to the Council of Ministers which has the power on the basis of such reports to issue binding recommendations to the High Contracting Parties.

One could argue however that given that the EC has its own Social Charter (albeit a non-binding "solemn declaration"), affiliation to the ESC would be a duplication of protection. There are however some important differences remaining. The ESC offers protection to *everyone* within the territory of the contracting state while the Social Charter is expressly for the benefit of those who qualify as "workers" within the meaning of the case law of the ECJ.[125] The Social Charter has also not proved an unqualified success in that it was agreed by only eleven member states (the UK not being included) and was specifically formulated as a non-binding declaration. No EC legislation in the field of social policy has therefore yet been based on the Social Charter and it is doubtful whether it can ever be the basis of social policy legislation for the EC, either from a practical or a legal viewpoint. The ESC also offers greater protection in the scope of substantive rights protected in terms of greater health protection, social and medical assistance and protection of the rights of migrant workers. It would, moreover, be easy to accommodate the ESC within the Maastricht process since the social protocol does not prejudice the accession by the Union to any other international instruments. Perhaps affiliation to the ESC should be seen not in the context of an alternative to the ECHR but rather as something that ought to be considered in any event in order to provide improved protection for labour in the EC.

Conclusion

The ever-widening gap in the protection of human rights in the EC is to some extent attributable to the tension between rights as grounded in notions of individual liberties and alternatively as flowing from a free trade perspective on the world. If we were to conclude that the ECJ is concerned only with the latter model then we might be driven to the view that it is neither the most appropriate nor the most successful forum for the protection of human rights. As we have seen, the ECJ has consistently used the language of rights to pre-empt national autonomy and as a means of extending EC power into areas traditionally the preserve of the nation state. In contrast,

---

[125] For the meaning of a worker in the EC context, see *Levin* Case 53/81 [1982] E.C.R. 1035; *Lawie-Blum* v. *Land Baden-Wurttemberg* [1986] E.C.R. 2121; *Steyman* [1988] E.C.R. 6159; *Battray* [1989] E.C.R. 1621.

where rights might have been utilised to challenge the integrity of EC measures the ECJ has been less active—although it may be that the *Guardian* case presages a new approach. Given the current situation and the mandate of the Maastricht treaty, it is worth contemplating the implications of a more activist stance on the part of the EC. This would inevitably raise the question of the implications of an unambiguous human rights approach on the ECJ's power to act. A more rights-oriented stance on the part of the ECJ would not necessarily eliminate its overriding free market concerns. The question would then become one of whether the balance of advantage lay with EC accession to the ECHR or with some other action. While the Strasbourg organs of the ECHR certainly have a greater claim to an understanding of rights based on a model of individual liberties, neither that Court nor that Commission would claim to be a perfect tribunal that always achieves the right result.[126]

Yet what is the "right" or most appropriate result when applying human rights standards to the EC? The judicial enforcement of rights by multinational enterprises might actually be destructive of appropriate state and EC action. A most striking example is the area of competition. Should notions of human rights, with the complex procedural rules to be found in Article 6 of the ECHR for example, be applied to make what is already a difficult task well nigh impossible? Corporate entities could invoke the language of rights to circumvent the competition rules and thereby to re-enforce the uneven playing field that Articles 85 and 86 of the Treaty of Rome were designed to attempt to eliminate. It is perhaps not useful for the EC to adopt rights language when defending the competition rules against powerful business interests. There may certainly be room for considering the application of the human rights model to improving the Commission's enforcement procedure[127] but beyond that the net benefit is doubtful and the potential drawbacks difficult to quantify at present: so much would depend on the defensive litigation that would inevitably follow incorporation. Until the EC makes a clear decision as to its form and role in Europe it will continue to be vulnerable to human rights scrutiny and yet be unable to forge a clear alternative understanding of the application of rights within this new and fast-developing legal order.

---

[126] See generally Tomkins, Chapter 1.
[127] See Regulation 17/62 O.J., (1959–62), 87.

TABLE OF CASES

EUROPEAN CASES

I *European Commission, Committee of Ministers and Court of Human Rights*

TABLE OF CASES

TABLE OF CASES

TABLE OF CASES

TABLE OF CASES

II *European Community Commission, Court of First Instance and Court of Justice*

DOMESTIC CASES

FRANCE

TABLE OF CASES

TABLE OF CASES

TABLE OF CASES

TABLE OF CASES

TABLE OF CASES

TABLE OF CASES

TABLE OF CASES

TABLE OF CASES

INDEX

INDEX

INDEX

INDEX

International Studies in Human Rights

1. B. G. Ramcharan (ed.): *International Law and Fact-finding in the Field of Human Rights*. 1982   ISBN 90-247-3042-2

2. B. G. Ramcharan: *Humanitarian Good Offices in International Law*. The Good Offices of the United Nations Secretary-General in the Field of Human Rights. 1983
                                         ISBN 90-247-2805-3

3. B. G. Ramcharan (ed.): *The Right to Life in International Law*. 1985
                                         ISBN 90-247-3074-0

4. P. Alston and K. Tomaševski (eds.): *The Right to Food*. 1984   ISBN 90-247-3087-2

5. A. Bloed and P. van Dijk (eds.): *Essays on Human Rights in the Helsinki Process*. 1985
                                         ISBN 90-247-3211-5

6. K. Törnudd: *Finland and the International Norms of Human Rights*. 1986
                                         ISBN 90-247-3257-3

7. H. Thoolen and B. Verstappen: *Human Rights Missions*. A Study of the Fact-finding Practice of Non-governmental Organizations. 1986   ISBN 90-247-3364-2

8. H. Hannum: *The Right to Leave and Return in International Law and Practice*. 1987
                                         ISBN 90-247-3445-2

9. J. H. Burgers and H. Danelius: *The United Nations Convention against Torture*. A Handbook on the Convention against Torture and Other Cruel, Inhuman or Degrading Treatment or Punishment. 1988   ISBN 90-247-3609-9

10. D. A. Martin (ed.): *The New Asylum Seekers: Refugee Law in the 1980s*. The Ninth Sokol Colloquium on International Law. 1988   ISBN 90-247-3730-3

11. C. M. Quiroga: *The Battle of Human Rights*. Gross, Systematic Violations and the Inter-American System. 1988   ISBN 90-247-3687-0

12. L. A. Rehof and C. Gulmann (eds.): *Human Rights in Domestic Law and Development Assistance Policies of the Nordic Countries*. 1989   ISBN 90-247-3743-5

13. B. G. Ramcharan: *The Concept and Present Status of International Protection of Human Rights*. Forty Years After the Universal Declaration. 1989
                                         ISBN 90-247-3759-1

14. A. D. Byre and B. Y. Byfield (eds.): *International Human Rights Law in the Commonwealth Caribbean*. 1991   ISBN 90-247-3785-0

15. N. Lerner: *Groups Rights and Discrimination in International Law*. 1991
                                         ISBN 0-7923-0853-0

16. S. Shetreet (ed.): *Free Speech and National Security*. 1991   ISBN 0-7923-1030-6

17. G. Gilbert: *Aspects of Extradition Law*. 1991   ISBN 0-7923-1162-0

18. P.E. Veerman: *The Rights of the Child and the Changing Image of Childhood*. 1991
                                         ISBN 0-7923-1250-3

19. M. Delmas-Marty (ed.): *The European Convention for the Protection of Human Rights*. International Protection versus National Restrictions. 1991   ISBN 0-7923-1283-X

International Studies in Human Rights

20. A. Bloed and P. van Dijk (eds.): *The Human Dimension of the Helsinki Process*. The Vienna Follow-up Meeting and its Aftermath. 1991   ISBN 0-7923-1337-2

21. L.S. Sunga: *Individual Responsibility in International Law for Serious Human Rights Violations*. 1992   ISBN 0-7923-1453-0

22. S. Frankowski and D. Shelton (eds.): *Preventive Detention*. A Comparative and International Law Perspective. 1992   ISBN 0-7923-1465-4

23. M. Freeman and P. Veerman (eds.): *The Ideologies of Children's Rights*. 1992   ISBN 0-7923-1800-5

24. S. Stavros: *The Guarantees for Accused Persons Under Article 6 of the European Convention on Human Rights*. An Analysis of the Application of the Convention and a Comparison with Other Instruments. 1993   ISBN 0-7923-1897-8

25. A. Rosas and J. Helgesen (eds.): *The Strength of Diversity*. Human Rights and Pluralist Democracy. 1992   ISBN 0-7923-1987-7

26. K. Waaldijk and A. Clapham (eds.): *Homosexuality: A European Community Issue*. Essays on Lesbian and Gay Rights in European Law and Policy. 1993   ISBN 0-7923-2038-7; Pb: 0-7923-2240-1

27. Y.K. Tyagi: *The Law and Practice of the UN Human Rights Committee*. 1993   ISBN 0-7923-2040-9

28. H.Ch. Yourow: *The Margin of Appreciation Doctrine in the Dynamics of European Human Rights Jurisprudence*. 1996   ISBN 0-7923-3338-1

29. L.A. Rehof: *Guide to the* Travaux Préparatoires *of the United Nations Convention on the Elimination of All Forms of Discrimination against Women*. 1993   ISBN 0-7923-2222-3

30. A. Bloed, L. Leicht, M. Novak and A. Rosas (eds.): *Monitoring Human Rights in Europe*. Comparing International Procedures and Mechanisms. 1993   ISBN 0-7923-2383-1

31. A. Harding and J. Hatchard (eds.): *Preventive Detention and Security Law*. A Comparative Survey. 1993   ISBN 0-7923-2432-3

32. Y. Beigbeder: *International Monitoring of Plebiscites, Referenda and National Elections*. Self-determination and Transition to Democracy. 1994 ISBN 0-7923-2563-X

33. T.D. Jones: *Human Rights: Group Defamation, the First Amendment and the Law of Nations*. 1997   ISBN 90-411-0265-5

34. D.M. Beatty (ed.): *Human Rights and Judicial Review*. A Comparative Perspective. 1994   ISBN 0-7923-2968-6

35. G. Van Bueren, *The International Law on the Rights of the Child*. 1995   ISBN 0-7923-2687-3

36. T. Zwart: *The Admissibility of Human Rights Petitions*. The Case Law of the European Commission of Human Rights and the Human Rights Committee. 1994   ISBN 0-7923-3146-X; Pb: 0-7923-3147-8

37. H. Lambert: *Seeking Asylum*. Comparative Law and Practice in Selected European Countries. 1995   ISBN 0-7923-3152-4

International Studies in Human Rights

This series is designed to shed light on current legal and political aspects of process and organization in the field of human rights.

MARTINUS NIJHOFF PUBLISHERS – THE HAGUE / BOSTON / LONDON